CASH BEFORE YOU CRASH

CASH BEFORE YOU CRASH

Protect Your Profit and Cash-flow to Speed Up Your Growth

Fourth Edition

A.K. Guha • N.H. Atthreya

Viva Books

New Delhi | Mumbai | Chennai | Kolkata | Bengaluru | Hyderabad | Kochi | Guwahati

Publisher's note

Every possible effort has been made to ensure that the information contained in this book is accurate at the time of going to press, and the publisher and author cannot accept responsibility for any errors or omissions, however caused. No responsibility for loss or damage occasioned to any person acting, or refraining from action, as a result of the material in this publication can be accepted by the editor, the publisher or the author.

Every effort has been made to trace the owners of copyright material used in this book. The author and the publisher will be grateful for any omission brought to their notice for acknowledgement in the future editions of the book.

First Published 2002
Second Edition 2004
Third Edition 2006
Fourth Edition 2012, Reprinted 2014

Viva Books Private Limited

- 4737/23, Ansari Road, Daryaganj, New Delhi 110 002
  Tel. 42242200, 23258325, 23283121, Email: vivadelhi@vivagroupindia.net
- 76, Service Industries, Shirvane, Sector 1, Nerul, Navi Mumbai 400 706
  Tel. 27721273, 27721274, Email: vivamumbai@vivagroupindia.net
- Megh Towers, Old No. 307, New No. 165, Poonamallee High Road, Maduravoyal
  Chennai - 600 095 E-mail: vivachennai@vivagroupindia.net, Tel. 23780991, 23780992
- B-103, Jindal Towers, 21/1A/3 Darga Road, Kolkata 700 017
  Tel. 22816713, Email: vivakolkata@vivagroupindia.net
- 7, GF, Sovereign Park Aptts., 56-58, K. R. Road, Basavanagudi, Bengaluru 560 004
  Tel. 26607409, Email: vivabangalore@vivagroupindia.net
- 101-102, Moghal Marc Apartments, 3-4-637 to 641, Narayanguda, Hyderabad 500 029
  Tel. 27564481, Email: vivahyderabad@vivagroupindia.net
- First Floor, Beevi Towers, SRM Road, Kaloor, Kochi 682 018
  Tel. 0484-2403055, 2403056, Email: vivakochi@vivagroupindia.net
- 232, GNB Road, Beside UCO Bank, Silpukhuri, Guwahati 781 003
  Tel. 0361-2666386, Email: vivaguwahati@vivagroupindia.net

www.vivagroupindia.com

ISBN: 978-81-309-2151-8

Published by Vinod Vasishtha for Viva Books Private Limited, 4737/23 Ansari Road, Daryaganj, New Delhi 110 002.

Printed and bound by Raj Press, R-3 Inderpuri, New Delhi 110 012.

M0200/M0230

This book is dedicated to my late parent Sushil Kumar Guha, and Monikuntala Guha, who taught me to stand, talk and walk on my feet and complete the journey of life.

Ajoy K. Guha

HAPPY READING

Many names suggested by our many readers over the years and we thank them:

Collect Money and Close Sales

Art & Science of Credit & Collection Management

Systematic Approach to Collection Management

Close Sales without Losing Customer

Perfect Selling

"The Science and Art of Collection" ....with smaller secondary title:' Making a Sell is Only the Beginning'

"More Important than Profit"

"Profit is Nothing without Cash"

"Profit is Good, Cash is Better"

Art & Science of Collecting Money & Closing Sales

Collect Dues & Over Dues Close Sales without Losing Customer

Collect Money on Time & Complete All Sales – Protect Your Profit, Cash-Flow, Liquidity & Speed Up Your Growth

How to Collect Dues & Overdues on Time & Complete All Sales – Without Losing Customer

Complete Selling

Protect Your Profit, Cash-Flow, Liquidity & Speed Up Your Growth

Art and Science of Credit & Collection – The missing chapter in our business books

Profit is Good, Cash is Better – How to Collect Well and Ensure Real Profits

Below the Bottom Line – The Fine Art of Collecting Payments

Dear Mr Doe,

"What do you do with your beard when you go to bed at night?" a little girl asked her grandfather. "Do you put it on top of the covers, under the covers, or in your nightshirt pocket?"

Grandpa had never thought about his beard at night, so he couldn't answer the little girl's question. But when he went to bed that night, he tried putting his beard on top of the covers, under the covers, and in his night-shirt pocket. But no way seemed right.

All night long, Grandpa tumbled and tossed. He lay on his back, he lay in his side, and he lay on his stomach. He couldn't get comfortable with that beard. He couldn't go to sleep.

You see, the little girl's question had made him beard-conscious. I wonder what question I could ask you to make you cheque-conscious?

Your account is long past due, you know.

Sincerely,

L. E. Frailey
—*Handbook of Business Letters*

PRINCIPLES OF SALES RECEIVABLES MANAGEMENT

1. A sale is complete only when the last paisa is collected on agreed time. (That includes sales-tax concession forms, bank guarantees, tax-deducted-at-source certificate etc.)
2. Money due from customers: if you don't ask for it, you don't get it.
3. You should be able to collect your money and retain the customer too. And that is not difficult.
4. Debtor – the older it gets the more difficult it is to collect money and we have less energy to follow-up for its recovery.
5. Don't over-commit. Deliver what you promised – which means delivering every clause in the acknowledged order.
6. In an organization, collecting money is everybody's business. Let all work be client-centred.
7. Get rid of the dead-beat customers. In this era of paper-thin margin, you can't build a healthy organisation on sick, weak and indifferent customers.
8. Focus on customer complaints and sundry debtors.
9. Delight the customers. Consistently give excellent service and become their weakness. Make him need you. Interest him to do business with you always. Interest and fear of losing you will keep you together.
10. Compete on benefits, advantages, features, service, value proposition, price, discount, market share, uniqueness, technology, innovation etc.; but don't compete on credit. Chances are that it may make your business very weak.

Five Main Reasons Why Customers Don't Pay

Reasons	Percentage of customers	Percentage of overdue amount
1. Inefficiency in our office	70%	65% to 75 %
2. Inefficiency in customer's office	30% (reasons 2–4)	10% to 15%
3. Customers facing fund problem		2% to 5%
4. Customers purposely delay our payment		2% to 10%
5. Complaints (It could be genuine or it could be a ploy)		5% to 10%

Collection is the last activity in a transaction, and therefore there are no shortcuts.

Read *Cash Before You Crash* … or … Crash or Crash. Doing business will be more enjoyable after you read this book.

Sundry Debtors
HOSPITAL
For Commercial Diagnosis
When SELLING, don't give CREDIT to
WEAK, SICK & INDIFFERENT
Customers.....
Chances are, you will be occupying
the next bed......very soon.

Contents

Foreword

Embarking on the job of writing an introduction to this book, let me at the outset, unequivocally recommend "Cash Before You Crash" to anyone who wishes to learn how to collect money from customers. But then, a book like this, sort of recommends itself, having now gone into its 4th edition.

I do confess that this is the first time I am trying my hand at writing a foreword. I am doing so, at the request of my friend Ajoy Guha, who surprisingly has more confidence in my critique than I myself have. Having said this bit, I must add that, in the slim chance that you the reader, is actually venturing to read this Foreword, your risks are not quite as great as in being treated by a doctor who is yet to kill his first patient. My empirical research shows that only 2.5% (?) of the readers of a book do read the foreword, while the rest gets on with the heart of the matter - the book itself. Notwithstanding this obviously disappointing conclusion, I am going to do my best to introduce the book "Cash Before You Crash" to you, because of my conviction that collection of receivables is an underestimated and less written-about topic in our country, also because I respect the authors' feel and knowledge of this complex subject, and lastly because I recognize and salute the readers' honest intent to learn the "best practices" of Collection.

We acknowledge that Working Capital Management and Cash Cycles are vital for any company, and we all become more acutely conscious of this in times of crises. That "Cash is King", is common knowledge, but we rediscover this old adage about liquidity, only when competitive pressures or market shrinkage start impacting financial results.

Time and again, we have seen companies which are unable to pay their suppliers or even employees' salaries, coming up with surprisingly good profit numbers on paper, and this means rank-bad management of working capital. This is why many wise managers focus on Free Cash Flows or Cash Profits, rather than conventional profit numbers. For the layman, there are three major components of working capital, Inventories, Receivables and Other Current Assets. Among these, I find that things mostly go wrong in Receivables, perhaps because here one has to engage largely with the uncertainties of external competitive environment. Given this context, the authors' excellent effort to demystify the nuances of Collection deserves high accolades.

Very early in my career, when I was working for a well-known engineering and construction company, I was having trouble in collecting the last 10% of the value of a project (better known as Retention Money) from a large public sector organization, so much so that I was quite clueless and despondent about my job. Under pressure to collect the receivables, and feeling intensely accountable, the situation completely overshadowed all other joyous and beautiful aspects of my life, at that time. I had no access to systematic processes of collection back then, and had to toil for 6 months on nurturing relationships as well as on the "never ending" list of customer complaints, to finally close the account. Different firms operate in diverse business environments, and can face myriad such challenges in collection, each of which needing a customized approach. The scale and age of the out-standings, payment cycles, instances of bad debts, etc., all differ from industry to industry, but there is no running away from the reality of this basic issue.

Selling to a customer is fashionable, and therefore, very popular with authors over the world, but collection is considered drab, mundane and utterly unglamorous! But without a strong execution of this activity called collection, no "Sale" is really complete, and no profit is realised. Reading the book second time round, it was like a refresher to me, with a lot of fresh thoughts and ideas popping up through the pages, besides reinforcing time-tested tools and techniques. How could we categorize this book - a text book, a resource book, a book on business management, or a manual? Thinking through, one can safely state that this is an amalgam of all these, a virtual one-stop source of knowledge on that very neglected element of every business transaction cycle, - "Collection of Customer Receivables." It covers the theoretical and behavioural aspects of the job, and goes beyond, to provide in-depth practical hands–on advice in every little aspect of the broader topic.

In India, the art and science of collecting money, has its own peculiarities. Our culture has many idiosyncrasies around parting with cash, which perhaps make the job even more, shall we say, exciting in our country. In "Cash Before You Crash", the authors have interwoven their rich professional experiences in the especial context of an Indian business milieu to provide us with a strong synthesis of wit and practical insights from the marketplace. For instance, in India, if you don't ask for your money, you'll hardly ever get paid.

Besides, as Indians we have our own confusions when it comes to separating business and personal goodwill. Our attitude is very often tilted strongly against hurting the feelings of our business associates. As a result, not wanting to risk our relationships, we sometimes do not know how to press for our dues from clients. As a counterpoint to this dilemma, I'd like to reiterate what Ajoy says, "In India, you are rewarded for good sales. But there is no appreciation for collection. The attitude towards money has to change. Our culture is strongly against hurting anybody's feelings, ... You have to collect your payments and also keep your client. (In fact) collection can be seen as an opportunity to take the customer relationship further!" That's a fine balancing act, and also happens to be the core message of this book.

Sumit Banerjee
Vice Chairman – Reliance Cement

Preface to the Fourth Edition

Until Third Edition this book was titled "Cash Before You Crash" and I am overwhelmed by the response it got. Book review appeared in all the Leading newspapers in the country.

This book was primarily meant for my colleagues in SALES and the Salesmen who face new challenges everyday in the market. Although I firmly believe in a business "Collecting money is everybody's business" but at the end of the day "a sale is complete only when the money comes in" – the reward for organization's hard work. Without good cash-flow Growth is impossible.

Chapters are further fine tuned with more day-to-day incidents in the world of selling. Chapter on Legal action is updated with new judgments on Cheque bouncing cases.

This book is devoted to all my Gurus who have helped me to enhance business knowledge through their various management books.

Sincere thanks to my many readers who have sent the various Cartoons on the subject incorporated at relevant chapters.

Lastly, we thank Mr Sumit Banerjee for writing an apt forward for this fourth edition.

A.K. Guha
N.H. Atthreya

Preface I

This book is the outcome of an appeal by my co-author, Professor N.H. Atthreya. In one of his public workshops, he said, "There are hundreds of books on sales management but probably not even a dozen on credit management. More significantly, not a single book has been written yet in the Indian context. This can preferably be written by a practitioner, yes, by one of you."

This appeal I heard five years back. Since then I researched on it both in the field and library. I also implemented many a possibilities Dr Atthreya suggested, in the companies I worked. As I went on, I developed the needed systems.

This book is based on the key concepts presented at the workshop I referred to. I therefore, requested Dr Atthreya to be my co-author, and I am glad he agreed.

To show what systematic credit and receivables management can do in our context, the book begins with three case histories.

In the rest of the book, we outline in fair detail the principles and practices, the theories and systems that I successfully adopted.

I gratefully acknowledge my debt, to the many writers on this subject who enriched my knowledge on credit management.

I am most thankful to P.S. Deodhar, President, Aplab Group of companies, for writing a valuable foreword to this book.

A.K. Guha
N.H. Atthreya

Preface II

Many receive the call. Few answer it.

A.K. Guha belongs to that rare few. For years, I have been appealing to executives participating in my workshops on credit and receivables management to attempt a book on the subject. Only one in the person of Mr. Guha accepted the challenge.

Like a good professional, he did not merely do a good job of credit and receivables management but decided to share his vast knowledge and practical wisdom. Let us hope to have more such professionals.

I believe executive-scholars are the need of the day. They can write with conviction and in terms of current reality. They have first class experience, and enjoy high credibility.

This book is the product of the painstaking work of Mr Guha. Full marks should go to him. 'You initiated me in this game. True, I did some home work. To say you continue to support me, I request you to be my joint-author, if not the co-author'. In response to this request, I find my place here as a joint author.

One phenomenon I face in my workshops is the stand taken by some: You don't know the conditions in our industry. Nothing more can be done than what we are doing.

I tell them: You are doing the very best you can. Is 'good' good enough for your situation? If the answer is no, we should explore more and more possibilities.

One of my clients who saw a point in this challenge went about the job a little more systematically and got unusual results. I requested the concerned executives to contribute a case history or two. Dr V.V.R. Sastry of Greaves Foseco kindly responded with a few case histories and synthesized their experience for our readers.

My invitation to you, reader, is to write your own experiences and send to us. When the next edition comes, it can be included. Or, there can be a supplementary book on case histories of credit and receivables management.

N.H. Atthreya

Preface III

We are indebted to our readers who appreciated our efforts and motivated us to update and expand this book. Credit is due to many unknown faces whom we met in our in-house and public workshops. They were instrumental in crafting and giving shape to the subject by their numerous queries they faced in credit and collection management.

Going by the suggestions, we have been receiving from our professional friends and friendly readers, we have reorganised the materials. Wherever necessary we updated the text and data and reviewed the original in the light of recent developments on the subject and related areas.

The first edition proved to be popular with corporates as well as universities and colleges around the country. We hope the second edition too will meet their expectations.

We consider it a privilege to have the co-operation of all in keeping the text most up-to-date and welcome their valuable suggestions for any improvement in the treatment and presentation of the subject.

A.K. Guha
N.H. Atthreya

Acknowledgements

This book has become possible because of the generous and resourceful support of many who gave us liberally of their time and talent. We are grateful to all of them and in particular to the following:

P.S. Deodhar for his valuable foreword and overall support; Professor T.S. Venkoba Rao, Siddharth Roy, Mohini Shroff for their deft editing and support at the critical stages; A.K. Sen, R. Satyagopal and L.N. Godbole for perusing the text and offering valuable comments and suggestions; and Uday M. Chithale for his help in the chapter on statutory requirements.

We are thankful to Rajiv Kamat for extending his help in the preparation of the chapter on legal action; C.S. Sapre, S.V. Athawale, G.R. Kunder and S.K. Bopardikar for assisting us in collecting numerous data and for constructing the various checklists. We are indebted to P. Nambiar for offering valuable comments and suggestions for improving the manuscript.

Special thanks to D.E. Bhagwat and M. Santosh for processing the manuscript; Br. Blaise Thadathil SSP for his warm and resourceful support; and Darrel D'Souza for his cheerful and alert assistance. Last but not the least thanks to Manoj, Robin and Pathikrith Mukherjee for their insightful cartoons and to many unstated at home, abroad and at work, who gave us space and support.

A.K. Guha
N.H. Atthreya

They only taught us to sell like hell. I find now it is hell if we sell without cash.
IIM

Preamble

by N.H. Atthreya

**WHO SAID
CREDIT RECEIVABLES MANAGEMENT
IS EASY?**

Is managing receivables,
collecting the credit dues
a problem or an opportunity?

Many think it is a problem.
They have good reasons to think so.

It is difficult
in any part of the world.
It is also the more so in our country
because of certain peculiar conditions,
some avoidable
and some not so avoidable.

Firstly, everybody does it
and we give credit against our will.

Secondly, creditors do not care
to give in time.
They show difiant annoyance,
if reminded.

Thirdly, many in business overtrade
and they often have
much less than they owe.

They choose to live and thrive
on the "tolerance" of the creditors.

Fourthly, government buyers seem to take
a sadistic delight
in making suppliers of goods dance.

Fifthly, laws of contract are there
but they are purposes inoperative,
for all practical purposes.

Law administration is
on the side of the law evader.

Sixthly, transporters and banks
tend to collide with the debtor.

Seventhly, corporations seem to believe
that the number game is more important,
than the hard-core reality,
that paper profit is economic performance
and they hug the illusion
that credit sale is complete sale.

Eighthly, creditors do not care to ask in time.
They fear that they will lose business
if they ask for what is due to them.

Under these circumstances
it becomes all the more necessary
to practice the science and art
of collecting one's dues and collecting in time.
It calls for strategy and system,
it calls for will and skill.
When a challenge is handled in one way,
it is a problem. When handled (or managed)

in another way,
it is an opportunity.

What is the other way?

My author and I describe in detail
the systematic way they have evolved and applied
and got commendable results.
They have also given some convincing cases
to prove their point.

I know atleast of a dozen organizations
who have seen the opportunity side
of this situation.
What they do is based
on a few philosophic principles and strategies.

Let me briefly outline them in simple language.
The task is to get our money
in our pocket
in agreed time.

A sale can be considered
complete
only
when the last rupee due
is in our hands.

Gross sale
is not business.
Net sale
is.

Go therefore for
net cash
not
gross volume.

Realize the high cost
of overdue accounts.

An estimate from
a leading accounting firm
indicates the following;

Past Due Status (Paise on the Rupee)	Likely Recovery (Percentage)
30 days	97
90 days	90
120 days	80
6 months	67
1 year	45
2 years	23
3 years	12

Add to this
the inflationary factors,
the loss of interest,
the lost use of the money,
the reduced monetary value of money,
and most importantly the impact on cash-flow
and potential opportunities;
and you see how substantially
your business can be hit
by the slow recovery of accounts receivable,
not to speak of the no recovery of your dues.
It truly seems a cash or crash proposition.
Know and take care
of factors that
facilitate collection
and that debilitate collection.

Use flexible strategies
for different types of debtors.

Finally
remember
to get thrill out of
collection management
you need

a bill
a will
a skill
(and at times)
a kill.

Anybody
in the organization
can make collection difficult.
So
it has to be everybody's responsibility.

Educate therefore
everybody
in the elements of
business economics in
the game of collection.

WHAT EXPERTS SAY

This book should prove indispensable for anybody engaged in the business of selling anything, no matter what the size or type of the organisation.

Besides authoritative commentary, it provides the reader with invaluable guidance in a manual format, making the book user-friendly and of practical utility.

Uday M. Chitale
Senior Partner, M.P. Chitale and Co.
Chartered Accountant

Credit management involves co-ordinated organizational efforts in the same manner as product development and production control. The book deals comprehensively with the systems and procedures in credit management function.

Prof. T.S. Venkoba Rao
M.I.E., F.I.I.E.

Expertly written. I was very happy to go through it. The checklists, formats, and design are excellent.

L.N. Godbole,
M. Com., LLM, Ph.D., FCS

WHAT THEY SAY ABOUT THE BOOK

This book is the most comprehensive and I am sure it would act as a ready reckoner to all the industries, trade and business. My congratulations to Mr. Guha for the excellent work accomplished.

"Cash Before You Crash" will make a useful item to possess, in fact, a must for every modern office.

—Rakesh Gandhi, Director, Mira Inform Pvt. Ltd., Graydon, Netherland BV.

All in all a book whose ideas are useful and implementable, is meant for anybody who is in business; professionals and self-employed, entrepreneurs, retail businessmen, small businesses and also corporate managers and management students.

—Business India, July 8-21, 2002; also appeared in Business India Book Club Best Seller

After 28 years in the business, spread over 12 industries, having started his career as an accountant assistant and working his way up the corporate to Vice-president and setting up his own consultancy, Guha probably knows what he is talking about.

—Times of India, 26 January, 2003

At the outset and on the basis of a cursory glance, it seems that your book is very useful, containing almost all issues relating to credit management and have been thoughtfully laid down.

—Robin Banerjee, Head of Commercial (Exports), Hindustan Lever Limited

We at Motorola were very impressed with this Book.

—George Lewis, Motorola, Bangalore

Legal cases can be made effective for collecting outstandings says 'Cash Before You Crash"

—The Hindu, Chennai

A book that will help you to avoid a cash crisis and provide a way out of most collection problems. It serves as a ready reference to management, sales, commercial and collection personnel.

—Ahmedabad Management Association

"Cash Before You Crash"—a book must reading for all employees (especially people in sales) of business organisations which indulge in credit sales.

—Rajesh Mukne, National Credit Manager,
Tech Pacific India Ltd.

WHAT THEY SAY ABOUT OUR WORKSHOP

Overall the seminar on 'Cash Before You Crash' at Ahmedabad Management Association really remained quite interesting and effective. Particularly the examples cited based on the practical experience were worth remembering.

—HN Basopia, Assistant Manager, Accounts, Reliance Industries Ltd.

I would like to thank you for providing such beautiful insights for collection overdues which has really changed my perceptions I was carrying with me, especially on the side of relationships with customers and also your Pareto Principle even knowing this I haven't thought in those directions. I would like to thank you for sharing your knowledge and experience with us in such a simple manner.

—Piyush Patni, Director, Safeworld Systems Pvt. Ltd.

This workshop was interesting, informative and enlightening.

—Tata Honeywell

Practical Solutions.

—SK Bhatia, Director, Tulshidas Khimji

I would like to take this opportunity to once again express our gratitude and appreciation for the very informative and useful learning sessions you conducted for us at the Ratnagiri Conference.

—KJ Deshpande, Director, Dopkin Inks Pvt. Ltd.

The facilitator's domain knowledge was impressive for its depth and the way he illustrated practical problems was enlightening.

—Thermax

Workshop was informative and well-illustrated—collecting money without losing customers.

—Asian Paints

The practical knowledge and experience of the facilitator was amongst the best things.

—Faiz Siddique, Manager, Credit and Collection, UPS Jetair

The course was practical and useful.

—S D'Costa, KRYFS Laminations Pvt. Ltd.

This was a knowledgeable programme to attend.

—Mohan Sharma, HRM Executive, Clairant (India) Ltd.

I have attended your seminar on collection and credit management and it was really wonderful. I have started implementing some of your suggestions and they are really fruitful. Thank you very much for the same.

—Mani VGS, Excel Industries Ltd., Executive Marketing–Agri Business

We are very happy to recommend Mr Guha's workshop on 'Credit and Collection Management', 'Cash Reduction Strategies', 'Negotiating in Purchase and Sales'. Our participants found them practical, useful and implementable.

—KK Nair, Director, Ahmedabad Management Association

We are grateful to you for an effective training programme on 'CREDIT CONTROL'. I can see everyone charged-up after the event.
Thanks for your suggestion on next training mooted on 'customer care'. We'll get back to you in 2 weeks' time.

—R. Vanamali, Managing Director, Endress + Hauser

It was pleasure to attend your seminar and it will definitely help me in future. Thank you for your sincere guidance.

—Kshitij M Joshi, Godrej & Boyce

PURCHASE NEGOTIATION: The feedback of Graduate Engineers induction was just excellent. They appreciated your six-day programme which changed their mindset too.

—Sharad S Shah ESSAR STEELS

It was really great by attending the seminar on Commercial Sales Negotiation. Can it be possible for you if you can send the all slides of the presentation on negotiation skills?

—Quamar Ahmad, Godrej Industries Ltd.

I take this opportunity in thanking your good selves for providing a nice and valuable inputs in the past two days session of Cash before You Crash. I am sure that it was a great interactive session and also I hope you would have also enjoyed addressing us.

—S.Manjunath, Manager Operations – Bangalore

It was a very nice and interesting seminar on Commercial Negotiation Skills and I could get a lot of inputs from the same for doing my marketing in the field of training. Your handouts and notes are also very much worthy. I would love to attend more of your such programs in future. May I request you in case if you could send me a small write-up on global negotiations.

—Vasant Prabhu – Consultant and Trainer

It was indeed a great experience for me to spend those two days. This mail can be the common platform for all the participants and of course the Boss (Mr. Guha) to interact with each other as frequently as possible.

—Ravindra M. Keni, Business Manager -Channel Mgmt.
ION EXCHANGE (INDIA) LTD.

Great Ideas

—Sanjay Kulkarni, Themax Ltd

All your valuable inputs during the two day training sessions was very interesting and if implemented would be a very value adding activity for the organisation.

—Ambalal J. Solanki, Lubi Group of Industries.

Seminar on "AFTER SALES SERVICE" was excellent and an eye opener for our future improvements in the company. We will ensure that we will implement it effectively.

—P. Ramkrishnan, TVS, Regional Service Manager(west).

It was also my pleasure meeting you at the workshop of After-Sales-Service and having personal interaction. I really regained a lot from this seminar after completion of MBA (Marketing & Finance) in may 2003.

—Anish Kr. Agarwal, Marketing Manager, Remsons Industries Ltd

It was indeed nice to meet and interact with you. In fact, your passion for training is amazing. I hope to hear more from you in future.

—Dhananjay Behera, Chief Manager (PR & HRD), Tata Refractories Limited, Orissa

I have been attending several of your two day courses during the last one & half year.

1. Dealer's Management.
2. Cash before you Crash.
3. Presentation Skills & Sales Presentation.
These are extraordinary. I'm trying my best to effectively use every inch of the above two courses in my regular work. They are "extremely informative", very much effective in Sales & Marketing. And everybody in Sales & Marketing must attend the above courses".
The added advantage "Little extra to make the courses glorious" is the interaction between the participants. This is excellent. Every participant learns something new from each other.

—Debnath Datta - General Manager (Mkt), M/S Indu Corporation - The sole distributor of Tata Steel

Firstly Thank you for the Training imparted to our employees on "Time Management" on 4th June 2005. As per our discussion with regard to the feedback for the same. Our employees found it quite informative and it enabled them to think on the different aspects that affect/contribute to our Time Management.

—Hazel, Executive –HR, Bestretch Elastomers International Limited

I read with great interest your "Cash Before You Crash" and has become very handy and an asset to me.

—S Vasudevan, DURA Chemical Corpn Ltd.,

All my fellow Managers, including myself, enjoyed the Seminar on 'Costs Reduction Strategies' immensely.

—Asoka Verma - Jayaswal Neco Limited, Nagpur

It is suggested that all senior people must attend this programme as fulltime participants. At HO all VPs Have attended and report is very good.

—Director - Jayaswal Neco Limited, Nagpur

Thanks for your pleasant lecture on strategies for cost reduction at Hotel City Residency, Durgapur on 19-20/05/2006.

—Anil Kumar Chaturvedi - Asst. Manager (Purchase) Corporate Ispat Alloys Limited

ONE

The Challenge

Focus: Customer Relationship Management – The Need of the Hour; But, Who Is Your Customer?

'Relationship is a gradual process. It does not mean taking the customer for lunch or dinner. It also does not mean calling and talking to him frequently. Relationship happens by making commitments, keeping commitments and practising commitments.'

TURN MISTAKES OR LOSSES INTO OPPORTUNITIES

When you study your overdue, statistics says 70% of the customers whose amounts are overdue do not pay because your system and procedures did not deliver as per the understanding in the order. I am talking about 'overdue debtors'.

Therefore, I often suggest to business executives, CEOs, managing directors, owners of small and middle-scale industries that they should put more focus on their day-to-day customer complaints and sundry debtors. If they ask:

1. Why is my customer complaining?
2. Why is my customer not paying?

This will give you a good insight into your organisation's systems and procedures that need correction and those which need improvement.

On the other hand, out of the balance 30%, about 2% to 5% customers are indifferent. They may or may not have an intention to pay. They think credit is not allowed, it has to be taken away. They assume suppliers are their interest-free bankers. It is a fact,

Do you calculate how much interest per day is being lost to your banker?

The longer the average debt remains outstanding the more you are financing your customers by paying interest in your bank for their borrowings.

Bank interest dampens everyone's hard work. Interest corrodes the organization.

if ultimately they really do not pay, it hurts the business badly. We shall deal with them appropriately in relevant chapters.

ERA OF CUSTOMERISING

Today survival and growth are directly related to how you are serving your customers. Business is all about customer satisfaction. Business executives should constantly seek answers:

A. In case of external customers:

   1. How can I get new customers every day?
   2. How can I keep my present customer for ever?
   3. What efforts are required to get back the lost customers?

B. In case of internal customers, they must enquire:

   1. The employees – how are they treated? And, how do they treat our external customers?
   2. Who are the colleagues and what is their team spirit?
   3. Are employees from other departments treated as if they are customers?

Although customerising is the need of the hour, we shall only deal with external customers in this book. Well, this book does say that if you do not care about external customers your business is likely to suffer. It will suffer more because they will not pay for the goods they have purchased because whatever they have received is not as per their order. The objective of this book is to help you to collect your money on time and complete the sale, without losing the customer.

Customer means business. Customer means profit. Customer means cash flow. Customer means growth.

It is an established fact that an order received to supply goods is the outcome of the creativity, hard work, and concerted effort of a company's sales force because:

- All customers are different
- Customers want to get the best out of every deal
- Customers are being approached by numerous competitors

Under these circumstances the sales force has to make that extra effort and clinch the order with the interplay of their:

- Experience
- Preparation and presentation
- Intelligence and presence of mind
- Knowledge of the product and its market

All these elements have to be interplayed and applied in a manner that customers are convinced that the company is offering them the best value for their money.

CATEGORISING A CUSTOMER

At one time, the customers were classified into the following groups:

Star	Usually in high-growth markets, and requiring lots of investment, but promising big returns
Cash Cows	Operations which generate large positive cash flows
Question marks	Operations which require quite a bit of cash but whose future is uncertain
Dogs	Business investments with poor prospects and in which the company has a weak market position.

Even now, words like 'cash cow' are very commonly used to describe a credit-worthy customer. Today we have our own perceptions about classifying the customers' business. In line with our perceptions, the customers are then categorised as A, B, C, or (if required) D types. We need to keep constant vigil on the health of customers' business, and if needed, the category should be changed. This helps in deriving easy procedure for controlling the sales transactions with each customer. This will also help in having a clear understanding with the customers, the dealings will be healthy, it will not lead to any dispute and there will not be an overdue situation.

Understand the decision makers and the power players at customer's office

Develop and maintain relationship with the right people; relationship goes miles.

1. The Buying Process Initiator

2. The Buying Process Approver
3. The Buying Process Influencer
4. The Buying Process Decider
5. The Buyer
6. The User

In the projects you will have to find out who's who:

1. *Decider*: Authorises and initiates project and agrees to the terms of reference.
2. *Approver*: The approver is the person who has the final say in whether the purchase will go through
3. *Recommender*: Wants change and needs to be convinced it is an integral part of the business. Projects always have friends and enemies. Ensure this person is on your side!
4. *User*: Beneficiary; Implements, and influences Recommender
5. *Gatekeeper*: Experts who are listened to by Decider and secretaries/personal assistants who can limit or extend access to Decider/Recommender
6. *Stakeholders*: Can be outside the project entirely (e.g. legal, moral and ethical third parties)

Don't over-commit; deliver what is promised

Besides delivery of goods, make sure that you have adhered to all the clauses of an order. The journey from customer satisfaction to customer loyalty is a story about you and me. Because you are a customer, and I am a customer as well. When buying, you and I both expect value for money.

(a) Solution to our problem
(b) Benefits, advantages and features
(c) Basic service standards
(d) Product reliability
(e) Useable products which do not break and are not damaged on receipt
(f) Product with a life span as promised
(g) Installation and maintenance
(h) Fast, efficient service

The customer must feel good that he has dealt with your company. For creating customer loyalty and relationship you need to create trust and work on it continuously to maintain it.

AN ORDER OR A CONTRACT IS NOT A POLITICAL PROMISE

Having received the order after such hard work, it becomes the responsibility of the logistics department to see that the order is executed to the satisfaction of the customer, i.e. comply with all the clauses of the order as agreed.

Logistics, commercial, sales administration, distribution or credit control, different companies call their order processing departments by different names, depending on the responsibilities and the duties they are entrusted with. Now, it will be the duty of this department to take all those steps necessary to complete an order in all respects.

A sale is only complete by receiving the money in time, at minimum cost. By doing this, it will be able to keep the business profitable, facilitate cash in-flow, higher turnover resulting in higher growth.

To achieve this, a logistics department will have to coordinate its functions of sales forecast, production planning, inventory management, procurement, physical distribution, credit control and order processing. It will have to work in close coordination with marketing, customer care, after-sale-service, production etc. To achieve optimum results, it will have to keep a close vigil on all its activities.

Today, extending quality service to a customer is of utmost importance. Modern technology is at our disposal. The rise in use of computers has come to our rescue, and we can now think of extending excellent and timely service to our customers. This is the era of information technology. Enterprise resource planning, electronic data interchange and supply chain are the latest management buzzwords. The trend is how to extend more and improved service to customers. In the course of our discussion, we will see how information technology and computers are helping a business to extend more and improved service and that too at much lower cost. The latest mantra is 'to do more with less'.

Business is Satisfying Customers & Making Money

More Customers you satisfy, more money you make

PROFITABLE
GROWTH

But then, since we are moving from selling to service, it is now no more important what you have sold, it is the manner in which you have handled the pre-transaction activities, activities at the point of transaction – and most importantly, the post-transaction activities or after-sales service. This will determine your business and how far it will be able to grow.

It is against such a background, this book on credit, collection, commercial aspects, and cash flow has evolved. Now, it is outdated to say 'chasing the money'. Today, the concept is to help your customers to pay your money in time.

CUSTOMER-ORIENTED FOLLOW-UP

Firstly, we need to find out whether goods are properly received by your customers at the expected time. After few days, inquire whether the supplied good is in perfectly good condition, and if it is ok, you can now find out if he has received the invoice correctly. Call again much before due date, inquire about the goods and then remind him on payment that is falling due. Tell him that you are expecting the payment when due; help your customer much in advance to provide for your payment. If you are a company which is concerned about its customers, if you believe that one selling is not the end of the road, the goods that you have sold or the services that you have rendered are in the right perspective and matches the customer's expectation, then you can expect your money on time. This is all about persistent follow-up.

Secondly, today reputed firms are realising that recovering money by serving legal notices and filing suit are time-consuming procedures and sometimes ineffective. I know many financing companies even get involved in customers' business, with their expertise they even help their customers to restructure the business in managing their cash flow. They realised that until their customer gets his money or makes money in business, they do not stand a chance of loan recovery. Also, we have come across many cases where the financing companies have found buyers for the sellers to transact profitably. After the deal the financing companies recovered their loan from the sellers. And sometimes finance firms themselves have purchased merchandise in repayment of their loan, and thereafter sold these merchandise at a profit.

Although we have been either involved or have come across many recovery cases, handled very tactfully and successfully, we are not in a position to name these companies on their request. In India, be it debtors or recovery problem, cash crisis is discussed within the four walls of the top executives' cabin.

How do you tackle those situations where a customer who does not bother paying you, customers who never pay before at least three visits are made, customers whose cash flow is dependent on delaying your payment, customers who have a genuine fund problem or those customers who have a complaint against the goods you have just supplied? Again, with some customers, it is possible that your invoice and supporting documents are not in order.

This book has dealt with all these problems and gives you practical solutions, so that you are able to recover your money and also carry on your trade with these customers. This is a complete book in the Indian context on how to allow credit, collecting the money on time, commercial aspects of a sales transaction, and enhancing your cash flow.

A special section is devoted to consumer credit and collection system for cellular and basic telephones, paging, factoring, instalment and hire purchase, leasing, housing finance, radio trunking service and credit card companies. Every idea introduced in this book has been tried out. You will also find them useful, easy to understand and follow them. Properly controlled collection of accounts should not be difficult, and if successfully operated, it can even be made enjoyable.

Besides, this book answers the question raised by management guru, Peter F. Drucker in his book *Financial Management in High Turbulent Times*. His observations were:

- Risks exist in your business which may cause your company to suffer, or in the worst cases, to disappear
- Some risks are covered through insurance, as for example, fire and theft
- There are more risks that you must identify and prepare a plan against

He asks us to reflect on some of the more important risks:

1. (a) Assume that the most important customer of the company stops buying from you. Where would the profits of your company be once you deduct the net commercial margin provided by this customer?
   (b) What action plan could you put in place to reduce this risk?

2. (a) Could your company withstand a large increase in unpaid bills and insolvent customers?
   (b) How would this affect your profitability and liquidity?
   (c) With what weapons would you react?

3. (a) Do you know how much working capital, that is to say liquid resources, your company requires to survive a deep crisis of 90 days? Develop various scenarios of events.
   (b) How much can accounts receivables contribute?

4. (a) Are your operational procedures from order to customer invoice, quick?
   (b) How many days does it take to process and invoice an order?
   (c) Is your information system focused towards expediting the process and minimising administrative errors?

5. (a) What is the REAL collection time from customers?
   (b) Are your customers financing customers who contribute little or nothing to your profitability?
   (c) What decision could you take to reduce the average collection time without reducing the profitable volume of your business?

6. (a) What is the percentage of outstanding receivables over your sales?
   (b) How has it changed in the last few years?
   (c) How long do you take to collect debts?
   (d) What changes in the collection system must you introduce to shorten the period of outstanding receivables?

7. (a) What is the percentage your company has of bad debts over sales?
   (b) Do you know what information was missing, or not taken into account, when you decided to sell to an insolvent customer?

8. (a) On what concrete and operative must you base your decision to sell to customers?
   (b) How can the computer help you?
9. (a) Will your management team commit to objectives on current asset ratios?
   (b) When analysing the balance sheet, do you take and follow corrective actions?
10. (a) Are you satisfied with the level of information you get from accounting?
    (b) Do you know the cost of poor quality of receivables?

PRACTISING CREDIT AND COLLECTION MANAGEMENT

Allowing credit and then collections generally should be regarded as a challenge between the debtor and the collector. The creditor should be determined to see that his profits are preserved, and that the debtor pays, and pays promptly. I remember a friend telling me, 'In today's world, money is the sixth sense of a man, without which there is no use of other five senses, and everybody knows what blood is to a human being, cash is to a business.'

In India, credit management is still far from being recognised as the essential business philosophy it is. Even today many companies usually rely on a member of the accounting staff to monitor credit sales and organise cash collections. Often credit control is not regarded a prime responsibility, and all too often credit work is filled in only when time permits or when a cash crisis occurs.

The key to successful credit functioning in any company is primarily the calibre not only of the individual chosen to head the operation, but also the various department heads and regional heads performing the credit control functions. They should spread this culture down the line because collecting money is everybody's business.

The transition period from order acceptance to credit sale, and to realisation of money in time, has to be handled efficiently. Therefore, the requirements of credit staff are different from that of an accountant's staff and a separation of work means that the credit work is done by specialists whose time and energy are not diluted by accounts work.

What we are approaching is a revolution in modern business which cannot be dealt with by methods which may have served well enough in the past. And thus, the basic challenge which everyone must be prepared to meet first is the 'resistance to change' they will find in their own organisation.

We need to move over to electronic data interchange, supply chain management, enterprise resource planning to achieve optimum customer satisfaction. If we are to cope successfully with the marketing conditions of tomorrow, we must begin to make a habit of change today. We should realise that the revolution will be permanent, and that it will seriously damage, if not destroy, the organisations which fail to readjust themselves to the new conditions. Likewise, in today's liberalised economy, if management does not control credit and the accounts receivable, debtors will control the future of the company.

Who is a customer? One who pays on time . . . a mutual respect

Deliver what is promised, do customer-oriented follow-up, make sure the customer has received what he expected. *Remember, collection is an opportunity to take the relationship further. In fact, this could be a last opportunity for many to correct the situation, in case if you have not delivered what you have promised.*

Overdue debtors – How much money are you losing per day?

If you still do not receive your money, do calculate how much interest per day your company is loosing on overdue debtors, i.e. on bad customers, on bad business, on bad quality sales. I would like you to draw out your facts and figures chart:

Total debtors	Not due	Due Overdue	Interest lost on overdue accounts till date	Interest being lost per day on overdue account
Account 1 Account 2 Account 3				

Note: We intend to make our point only by considering the bank interest. However, if you add the associated costs to the above, the situation will be alarming.

First they eat away your profit. Then they start eating into your investment. In this era of wafer-thin margin, how many sales transactions must you have made just to earn a little profit? And if this is being eaten away by slow payers, you must do something about it.

Another way of looking at overdue debtors: Say, you make ten sales to make a meagre profit of rupees one lakh, and you will need one bad customer to eat away the complete profit. Show this facts-and-figures chart to your bad customers. Tell them to change. If they still don't change, then change them. You are not their banker.

Every member of your staff works to satisfy a customer. Their reward is in that payment and when that doesn't come, it dampens everyone's hard work.

Get rid of the dead-beat customers

Usually 2% to 3% of your total customers are bad customers. However, if the overdue customers are more than 3%, then you are not selecting your customer properly. If your selection procedure is good, then you are not working hard enough to collect your money. When dealing with difficult customers just remember *Turnover is vanity; profit is sanity; and cash is fact.*

Today what we need is quality sales. The customer should pay, and pay on time. Sometimes you may have to take bold decisions. Do your part 'pucca', and then train your customer to pay on time. If he does not improve, fire him. In this era of wafer-thin margin you cannot run your business like a trust. Get rid of the dead-beat customers. *Don't do business with people who have no commercial sense. Customer Relationship Management has to be practised with customers who mutually respect the understanding called 'purchase order'.*

Make a difference

Credit is a tool to increase sales and not a toy to play with. Understand your credit-giving power. Not all companies can allow the same amount and period of credit. Just because competition is giving more credit does not mean you should follow the same tactic. Make a difference – if you be part of the crowd, you will get lost in the crowd.

There are many other competitive prompts such as benefits, advantages, features, price, delivery, quality, service or something new the competition is yet not offering. If you use credit as competitive tool, your cash flow could be weak, it could be disaster for your company. All multi-nationals and blue-chip companies started small and grew. Ask them, 'What made you so big and strong?'

THREE SUCCESS STORIES

Let us discuss three collection case histories—two of manufacturing companies and one of a trading company. These are cases where the methods suggested in this book have been tried.

There are three stages in each. Stage I is the original position. Stage II shows the results of focused attention. Stage III shows the results that became possible because of organised knowledge and practical ideas obtained by participating in Dr. Atthreya's workshop on the subject. All this is preceded by the highlights of the case.

Case I: An Organised Collection Effort

Highlights

- Sales went up by Rs 50,00,000 (7.5%)
- Interest came down by Rs 42,00,000 (35%)
- Collection costs came down by Rs 32,000 (55%)
- Bad debts came down by 100%

- Discount allowed reduced from Rs 48,00,000 to Rs 22,00,000 (54%)
- Profit went up from Rs 56,00,000 to Rs 97,00,000 or (73%)

The Setting

Nature of business: Manufacturing and marketing
Products: Wide variety of engineering items
Sold to: 50% directly to government departments. Rest through dealers, OEMs, traders, and commission agents
Number of customers: About 1200

STAGE I

There was no stated credit policy.

About 20% was planned to be received in advance which did not happen.

Budgeted collection days: 75 days

Current debtors: 96 days (in amount Rs 175,00,000)

A credit controller was appointed, to improve cash flow and meet a budget as given in Table 1.1:

Table 1.1

(Figures in lakhs)

Sales forecasted (30% more then last year)	660.00	660.00
Cost of goods sold (55%)	363.00	
Gross margin	297.00	
Administrative expenses	50.00	
Collection costs	0.58	
Bad-debt losses	20.00	
Discount allowed	48.00	118.58
Operating income	178.42	
Interest on debt	122.00	122.00
Forecasted Profit Before Tax (PBT)	56.42	56.42
Debtors in days	75	

STAGE II

Six months after focused attention was given, I got the following results

Table 1.2

(Figures in lakhs)

Sales achieved	400.00	400.00
Cost of goods sold (55%)	220.00	
Gross margin	180.00	
Administrative expenses	60.00	
Collection costs	0.06	
Bad-debt losses	0.00	
Discount allowed	10.00	76.06
Operating income	109.94	
Interest on debt	48.00	48.00
Forecasted PBT	61.94	61.94
Debtors in amount	196.00	
Debtors in days	89	

STAGE III

Six months thereafter, it was found that focused application pays. Informed and skilled application pays even more. The results are shown in Table 1.3.

Table 1.3

		(Figures in lakhs)
Sales achieved	710.00	710.00
Cost of goods sold (55%)	390.50	
Gross margin	319.50	
Administrative expenses	120.00	
Collection costs	0.26	
Bad-debt losses	0.00	
Discount allowed	22.00	142.26
Operating income	177.24	
Interest on debt	80.00	80.00
Forecasted PBT	97.24	97.24
Debtors in amount	155.00	
Debtors in days	80	

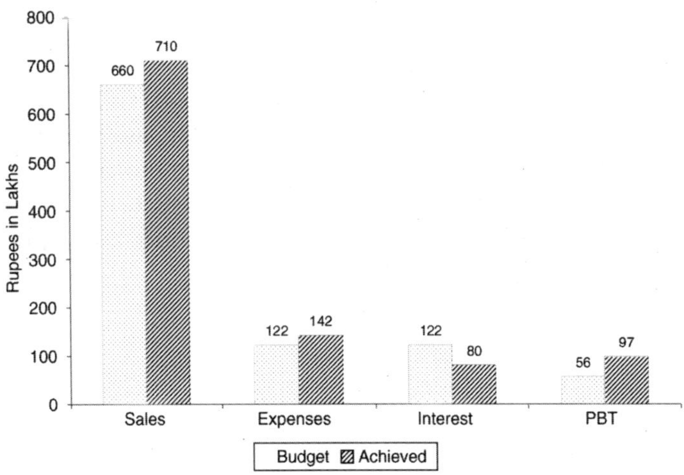

(a)

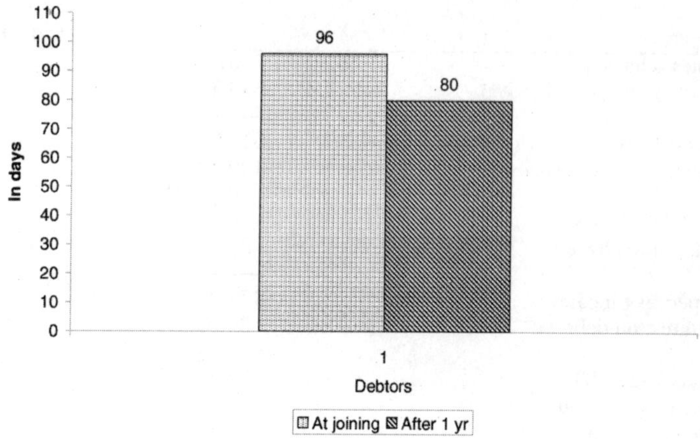

(b)

Fig. 1.1 Case I: Highlights

Case II : Cash-flow Slow-down

Highlights

* Sale up by 12% or Rs 400 lakhs.
* Large accounts started operating within agreed limits.
* Buying power of the company went up by 15%.
* Bad-debt losses came down from 6 lakhs to 1 lakh.
* Funds were available for starting new business and other investments.

The Setting

Nature of business: Trading
Location: Middle East
Products: Food stuff, refrigerated items, transportation services
Number of customers: 800
Sold to: Supermarkets, shop keepers and hotels

STAGE I

Debtors: 80 days
Status: 50% of large accounts were overdue

The actual budget position is given in Table 1.4

Table 1.4: Budget (Receivable Investment)

(Figures in lakhs)

	Jan	Feb	March	April	May	June
Receivables (debtors)	1050	1585	1579	1474	1621	1267
Receivables (from annual maintenance contract)	250	0	0	0	0	0
Credit sales	610	600	550	650	450	450
New AMC	60	0	0	0	0	0
Total receivables	1970	2185	2129	2124	2071	1717
Collection (Sales)	380	575	625	450	700	475
Collection (AMC)	0	25	25	50	100	25
Gross receivables	1590	1585	1479	1624	1271	1217
Less: Bad debt	5	6	5	3	4	4
Net receivables	1585	1579	1474	1621	1267	1213
Average age (days)	78	79	80	75	84	81

STAGE II

12 months after informed, focussed, systematic attentions were given the achieved (Receivable Investment) figures are

Table 1.5: Achieved Budget

(Figures in lakhs)

	Jan	Feb	March	April	May	June
Receivables (debtors)	1050	1615	1589	1438	1517	1167
Receivables (from annual maintenance contract)	250	0	0	0	0	0
Credit sales	610	600	550	680	600	650
New AMC	60	0	0	0	0	0
Total receivables	1970	2215	2139	2118	2117	1817
Collection (Sales)	355	575	600	550	900	700
Collection (AMC)	0	50	100	50	50	25
Gross receivables	1615	1590	1439	1518	1167	1092
Less: Bad debt	0	1	1	1	0	0
Net receivables	1615	1589	1438	1517	1167	1092
Average age (days)	79	79	78	67	58	50

Case II: Highlights

(a) Budget—Credit Sales

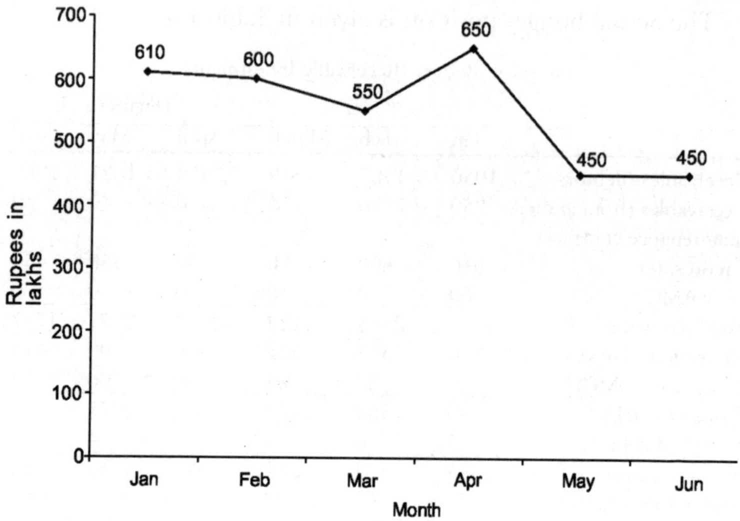

(b) Achieved—Credit Sales

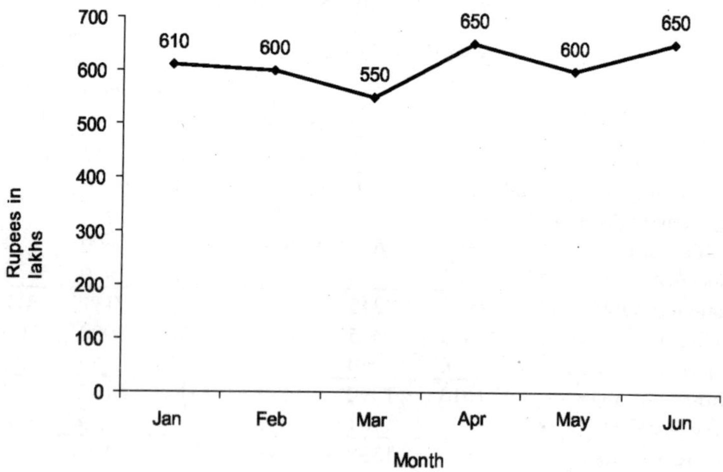

Fig. 1.2 Case II: Credit Sales

(a) Budget—Collections (Sales + AMC)

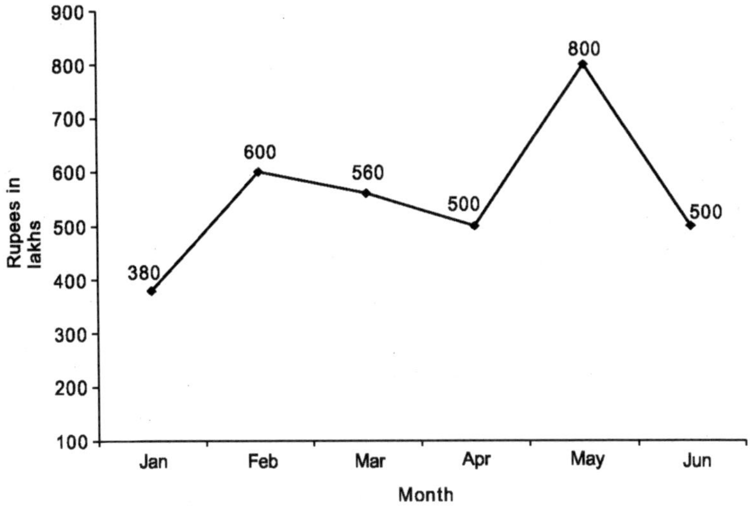

(b) Achieved—Collections

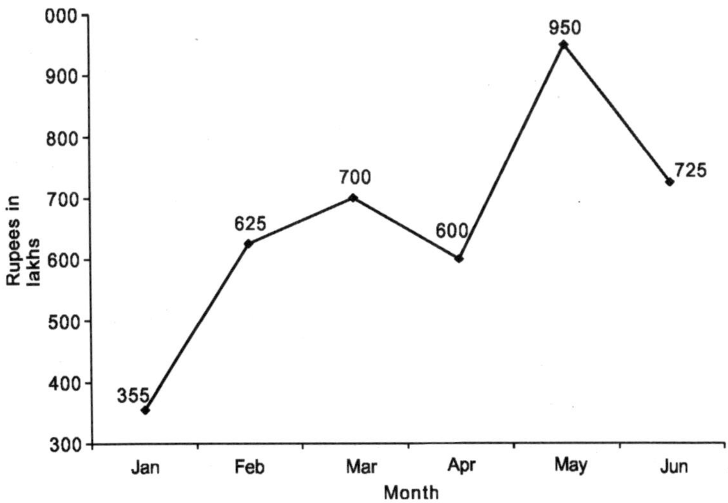

Fig. 1.3 Case II: Collections (Sales and AMC)

(a) Bad Debt Provision

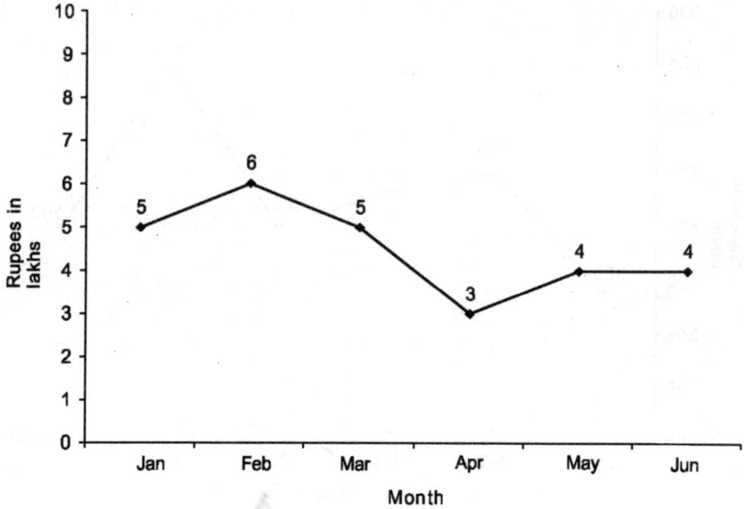

(b) Bad Debt Expenses

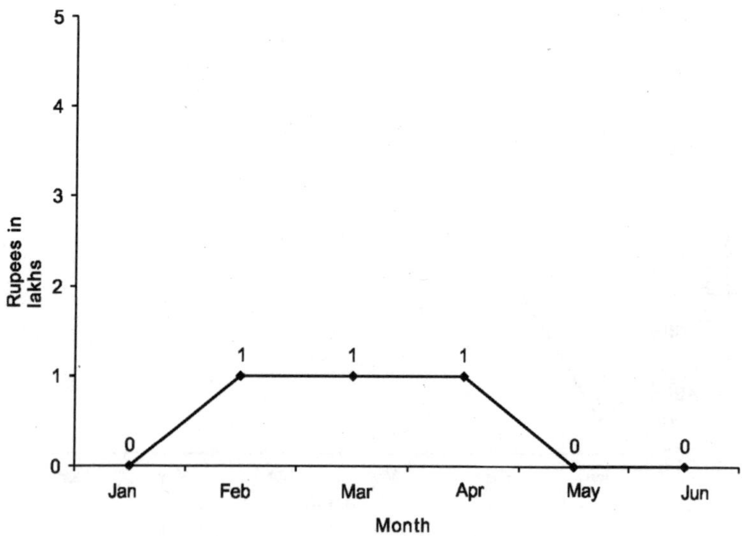

Fig. 1.4 Case II: Bad Debts

(a) Budget Debtors in Days

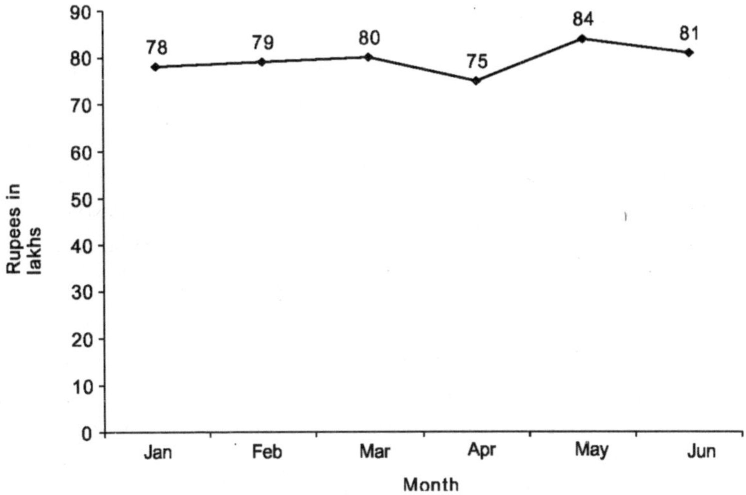

(b) Achieved Debtors in Days

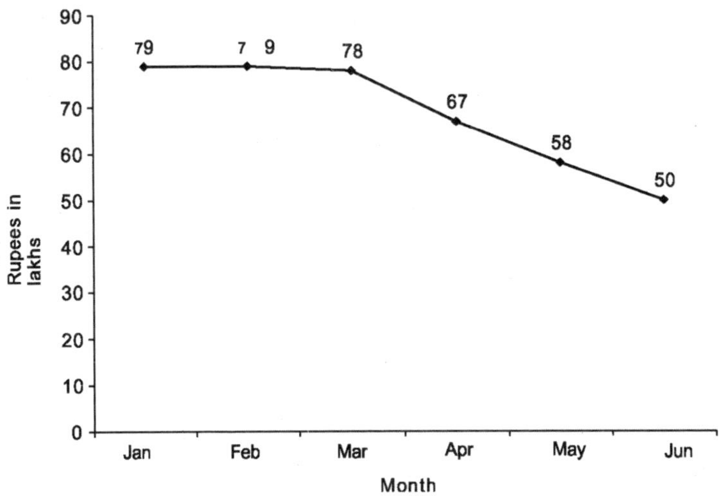

Fig. 1.5 Case II: Debtors in Days

Case III : An Overdue Situation

Highlights

* Over 6-months debtors brought down from 62 to 17	
* Over 10 years dues collected from goverment parties over	10 lakhs
* Over 5 years	30 lakhs
* Over 3 years	80 lakhs
* Over 1 year	90 lakhs
* Liquidated damages recovered: over	18 lakhs
* Sales up by 27%	
* Interest cost down by 25%	
* Bad debts did not take place	
* Bank guarantees held up were reduced to the tune of Rs 30 lac	
* Since cash flow was good, better buying terms could be negotiated.	

Setting

Nature of business: Manufacturing and marketing
Products: Power transmission equipment
Sold to: Wholesalers, dealers, traders, OEMs and few government parties
Number of customers: 1650

STAGE I

Debtors 142 days and 880 lacs with the following breakup

Below 3 months	– 60 days	– Rs 372 lakhs
3 to 6 months	– 20 days	– Rs 124 lakhs
Over 6 months	– 62 days	– Rs 384 lakhs

STAGE II

One year after focussed and informed action, debtors in days fell from 142 days to 82 days, in amount, from 880 lac to 645 lac

Below 3 months	– 56 days	– Rs 440 lac
3 to 6 months	– 9 days	– Rs 71 lac
Over 6 months	– 17 days	– Rs 134 lac

Debtors

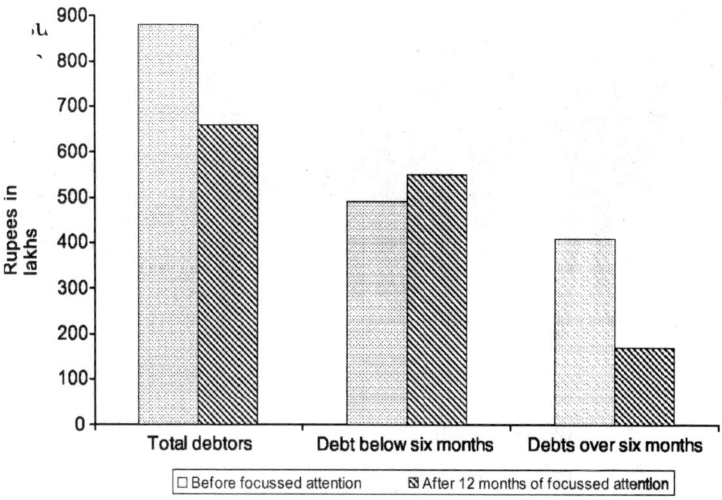

Fig. 1.6 Case III: Debtors

In our organization, collecting money is every bodies business

TWO

Credit and Collection Management— The Name of the Game

Trade credit is widely used in the business world for both selling products and buying materials. Credit sales is a marketing tool to strengthen the company's competitive position in the market, facilitating growth of its business. When credit is extended, the money is often realised but it also may not. Some customers may take a very long time to pay and some may finally not pay at all. At times, it may become very difficult for the business to come out of this debt trap.

Credit control can be rightly defined as a service to sales. It takes all those steps necessary to see that all sales transactions are complete in time, at optimum cost.

The business can face a situation where the financial capacity is over stretched due to over trading as it will not be able to pay the suppliers. It then faces a cash-flow problem. Dun and Bradstreet listed that one of the reasons for business failure is over trading. Secondly, in such a situation the profits of the business are also eroded. In due course of time, the business will not be able to break even. It's more than time, effort and money. When payment doesn't come the funds are tied up in Capital, and face rising debt, added interest cost, borrowing difficulties, loosing edge to competition, and growth suffers.

The fact is that prompt payment can only be expected if an effective strategy is worked out and continuously applied. This strategy is normally even more important than controlling

Frederick Adler

wastage, avoiding idle time, having efficient layouts of factory equipment, and all the other factors that have a bearing on ultimate profit.

A company can have the finest product, the lowest possible level of wastage, a superb sales record and the most dedicated work force of all time, but if it does not get paid in time, it will die.

The transition period from order acceptance to credit sale to realisation of money in time has to be handled efficiently. It calls for a professional job from the Credit Manager. He must perform all those functions necessary to complete a sales transaction. A sale is complete only when the money comes in. And profit is realised only after money is received.

CASH CYCLE

It is always said that in business more the risk one takes, the more sales one gets, resulting in better profits. If we study the working capital cycle (fig. 2.1) a business takes risk while turning the stocks into sale on credit.

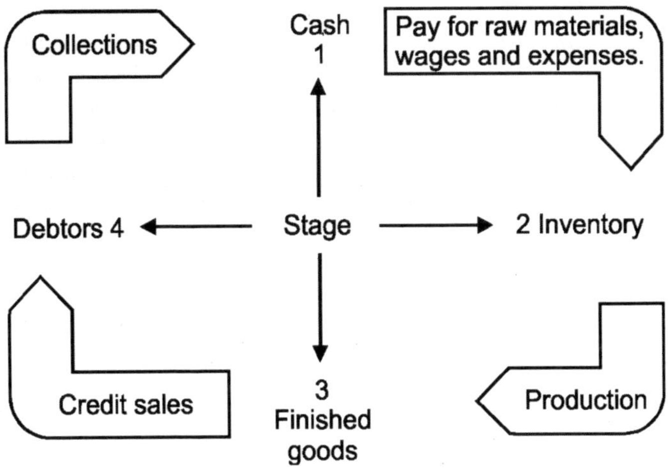

Fig. 2.1 Cash Operating Cycle

The whole concept of mass production economy in modern business depends on continuous selling activity and necessitates credit sales. Thus a substantial amount of cash gets tied up in accounts receivables/debtors. The success of a business depends on how fast this money is collected to meet all commitments and how smooth is the cash flow.

Cash, Payment-on-time & Business Growth

Eminent Consultant and advisor Mr. Ram Charan in his book "What the CEO wants you to know" a book that simplifies the complexities of business in a simple language, in the Chapter "Every Business is the Same Inside "states" *Money making in business has three basic parts: 'cash generation, return on assets (a combination of margin and velocity), and growth'*.

In another paragraph he says '*Cash gives you the ability to stay in business. It is a company's oxygen supply. Lack of cash, decreasing cash, or consumption of cash spells trouble, even if the other elements of money making – such as profit margin and asset velocity – looks good.*'

Another practical book "Essence of Good Management" by Kwang Ro Kim a visionary who built LG India from scratch to a $ 2-billion organization in one decade flat has brought out in a diagrammatic flow-chart clearly the concept of "Payment in Time and Growth":

If the payment is received in time then it amounts to good cash flow and you will be able to pay in time to Transporters, Vendor for better component/raw material/products, Service Franchise and others.

You can also make on time investment in Service Infrastructure, R&D, Production Engineering and Quality Control Infrastructure.

He also says that Good payment leads to Good Quality and on the other hand Poor Payment leads to Poor Quality and Poor Performance.

A poor payment (poor collection) the organization is likely to lose Price and Quality advantage in the market affecting future growth.

Working Capital

In the business, working capital represents current assets, these assets usually are converted into cash within the next 12 months. This would include cash, accounts receivable, inventories and marketable securities.

A firm's current liabilities are the debts that must be paid during the next year.

One succefful businessman said!!

Money is the sixth sense – without which there is no use of the other five senses.

The difference between current assets and short-term debt is defined as net working capital. This reflects an important measure of firm's liquidity. Net working capital is the excess cash, receivables, and inventory, held by the firm above the level of short-term obligations.

Relationship between Income and Funds

Firms cannot pay bills with income, they will need cash or fund.

Cash or funds may be generated by income and by other means. It is liquidity matter, while income is profit matter. For example, by selling on credit, income is generated and not cash. It is after the credit period is over, and if you are paid for the sale, that the cash is generated.

Important Elements of Working Capital

Let us discuss three important elements of working capital.

(a) *Cash*: Normally this means the amount of money available from the company bank account and with cashier.
(b) *Inventory*: includes raw materials, materials-in-process, finished goods and items bought in for sale.
(c) *Accounts receivable*: The money owed to the company by its customers (debtors).

It is important to recognise the distinction between the three forms of working capital because they must be balanced. In other words, the amount held in cash must be sufficient to pay the wages, taxes, and other payments such as telephone bill, electricity charges, provident-fund, bonus, etc. In short it should be able to meet all day-to-day expenses.

At the same time, the business must also have enough Inventory of one kind or another to meet the orders received. The only way to again convert this inventory into cash is by selling them and receiving the money. Thus, amount of working capital tied up in receivable is also very crucial.

This balancing act is not easy and only too often neglected. This negligence can arise because of an unawareness that both inventory and receivables form part of working capital. Both are thus allowed to grow large, while the businessman is only concerning himself with the cash.

It must also be recognised that the true working capital available is not just cash, inventory, and debtors. From these must be subtracted the amount owed to the creditors.

The Lead Time Calculation

While keeping control of the cash cycle it is essential to know the likely time that will elapse between spending money and getting it back.

For example:

Average time the raw materials are held in inventory	30 days
Time taken to manufacture the goods	40 days
Time the finished goods are in store before delivery	5 days
Time before customer pays	70 days
Total	145 days

One is supposed to take advantage of credit period being received from creditors. This calculation (based on averages and best estimates) indicates that wages and other running costs must be met for 145 days before any money can be expected to come in. If, in addition, suppliers have to be paid within, say 45 days, then they will have to be satisfied 145 – 45 = 100 days before the customer pays up.

Such calculations help to determine how much cash the company will need to finance its operations. In addition, having worked out the lead-time, the cost of the time that it takes for customers to pay is more easily seen. This is a factor very frequently overlooked in the business. If, for example, the business is paying 2% above base rate to borrow money, then that is the cost of the outstanding customer debt. In effect, the business is borrowing at a price and lending the money, or some of it, to a customer for nothing.

It is capital that is locked in inventory, and debtors need to be liquidated faster and faster for the business to grow.

ADVANTAGES OF CREDIT TRADING

To the Supplier

- Increases sales
- Increases liquidity / cash flow

- Increases profits
- Increases productivity
- Increases purchasing power
- Promotes growth

To the Customer

- Spreads financial load
- Makes possible advance shopping
- Increases purchasing power
- Makes better quality goods available

CREDIT, LIQUIDITY AND PROFIT

Among the current assets debtors hold the key to liquidity. To meet regular commitments such as wages, salaries, rent, rates and factory expenses, raw-materials components, leasing, installment and interest charges—a business depends on timely cash-inflow. If cash inflow is sluggish, then we have a cash-flow problem which will result in declining purchasing power, slowing down of quantum of production (with the result that orders are not executed in time), lower sale and lower profit; and the business incur liability for liquidated damages, and even cancellation of orders. The reputation and goodwill of the company will be seriously damaged. At a time like this, other avenues of raising cash such as loan from banks, financial institutions, etc. have to be sought, thus incurring interest costs. Therefore, it is important that debtors are turned into cash with ease and speed. It is against this background credit management has gained considerable importance in modern business.

A company takes a policy decision on the credit period that it is going to allow. This decision will evolve from factors like what the competitors are offering, the volume of order expected, the nature of product being sold, government policies in acquiring raw-material, and expected return on investment. If debtors are not getting turned into quick cash as planned, then this could either be terms being too long, because of an overdue situation. At this point, it is interesting to examine the declining value of overdue accounts (Table 2.1). This table takes into account only bank interest, not inflation.

Table 2.1

Current debtors due are worth	100%
30 days overdue debts are worth	98%
90 days overdue debts are worth	94%
180 days overdue debts are worth	88%
One year overdue debts are worth	76%
Three years overdue debts are worth	28%
Hence any sundry debtors over 3 years are worth nil	
(Discounted at bank rate of 24% interest per annum)	

Majority of the debts over one year old can be considered as bad debts. What is more likely is that s ıch overdues are in dispute and may have to be written off. Iı other words these amounts are never going to be realised leading to decline in profits. Or who knows, it may even amount to accumulating losses to the company.

COST OF CREDIT

Cost of Credit can be defined as expenses incurred during credit period—interest, litigation expenses, bad debts, other cost such as staff salaries, equipment, stationery, credit information, conveyance. These costs are readily ascertainable and those companies that are selling on credit terms should consider these as a part of the total administration cost built into price structure. For delayed settlement, a company should charge interest and conversely, it should give discount for ash-on-delivery or for settlement before the payment is due.

Opportunity Cost of Funds

When a firm frees or ties up its funds, it gains or loses an investment opportunity This is the correct cost of funds tied up in receivables. If the firm only considers the debt costs, it fails to recognise the impact on the firm of increasing or decreasing total debt. To avoid this shortcoming, the analyst should also use the opportunity cost of funds while making receivables decisions and not merely the interest rate on borrowings.

CREDIT SALES: GIVING POWER or Financing Receivables

First ....in the start

........A Part of CAPITAL contributed by Owners (& Shareholders)

Then

.......Retained Profits in the Business
.......Credit provided by the Suppliers/Vendors (Creditors)
.......Security Deposit – If it is received only for Growth & not to manage the day-to-day Cash-flow
.......Bank Support for Growth only
.......Various Reserves
.......Collection from Sundry Debtors
this can be termed as POWER.

And when the Company is Doing Badly

.......Company start relying on Financing activities,
.......Bank's support for meeting day-to-day cash-flow
.......Collection from Sundry Debtors
this is termed as WEAKNESS...the company is headed for trouble.

COST OF SERVICING ACCOUNTS RECEIVABLES

As with all operations, the willingness to allow credit sales involves certain costs. With respect to receivables, we can identify four major costs to the firm:

1. *Financing the receivables*: Carrying accounts receivable ties up a portion of the firm's financial resources. These resources must be financed from one of three sources:
   (a) Retained profits in the business.
   (b) Debt provided by the creditors.
   (c) Capital contributed by the owners.
   (d) Security deposits.
   By using these funds the firm incurs further costs.
2. *Administrative expenses*: To keep records on credit sales and payments, the firm accepts additional expenses. For example, it may hire a receivables bookkeeper, provide an adding machine and supplies, and allocate office space for a working area and files. In addition, most firms conduct investigations of potential credit customers to determine their creditworthiness. These and other expenses, such as telephone charges and postage, constitute the administrative costs of maintaining receivables.

3. *Collection costs*: When an individual or company does not pay its bills on time, the firm must take additional steps to increase the chances for eventual payment. Such actions require the firm to incur collection costs. Money will initially be spent to prepare and mail reminders that the payment is overdue. If these are not successful, the firm may hire personnel or collection agencies to visit the delinquent customer and demand payment.
4. *Bad-debts losses*: After making serious efforts to collect on overdue accounts, the firm may be forced to give up. If a customer declares bankruptcy, no payment may be forthcoming. If the customer leaves the city or state, it may be too costly to trace him and demand payment. In these cases, the firm is forced to accept a bad-debt loss on the account. Most firms expect to incur some bad-debt losses in the normal course of business. High-risk customers may be the major source of these losses, but occasionally a sound firm unexpectedly runs into liquidity problems and eventually enters bankruptcy. These losses are properly viewed as a cost of administering a credit policy. A decision to appoint a credit controller can be justified if the bank interest (or cost of opportunity) is going to reduce lower than his salary and perquisites, through reduction in the level of debtors and consequent reduction in bank borrowings (or loss of opportunity).

The Role of Credit Control Department

Credit control is all about the credit control department, making its customers cheque conscious and making them feel uncomfortable until they have paid.

In India the following functions are generally performed by credit control department:

1. Assessing the credit standing of both existing and new customers.
2. Selection of the appropriate payment terms, which will not only determine the required rate of cash-flow but also the volume of permissible sales, individually considering the risk involved and potential profit expected by the company.

3. Controlling of the debtors ledger (A/c receivables).
4. Collection from debtors at the agreed time ensuring that trade will continue with these customers.
5. Collection of sales tax concessional forms.
6. Monitoring and collection of bank guarantees/earnest money deposit or security deposit.
7. Raising and settlement of marine insurance claims.
8. Collecting TDS certificates.

CREDIT POLICY

The basis of Credit Policy should satisfy at least two criterion.

1. What is the acceptable level of receivables for the company? The influence of competition, the nature of product, steady or seasonal market, company's marketing strategy and above all the working capital availability and its requirement will decide the acceptable level of receivables.
2. Who will decide the terms of payment and credit limits? Both are different aspects of risk control and should be decided separately. The sales manager feels that it is interference with his customers, if the credit manager without consulting him decides the terms and credit period or takes all those steps necessary to collect money. The best situation is to hold regular meeting between sales and credit and decide the terms of credit period of each customer. The sales manager will advise the credit manager of a new prospect who he hopes will take a certain volume of goods. The credit manager's job is to check the financial condition of the prospect and try to set a credit limit which will be on the basis of expected sales and terms of sales. In case the credit limit is not sufficient, then shortening of the terms could be a solution. Thus a close relation should exist between sales and credit; however, the final decision should lie with the credit manager, as the sales manager may likely be get carried away by the temptation of making more sales. If needed, the credit manager should stop sale to a non-credit worthy customer.

The credit policy starts off by examining your collection policy for possible causes of poor collections. Frequently, the lack of clear-cut collection policy is at the bottom of the firm's collecting inefficiency.

Collection policy should set up specific rules and important matters as the following should be given due weightage:

- How should a credit be given
- When to give credit
- To whom credit should be granted
- Profit of credit trading
- Cost of giving credit
- Dangers of credit trading

Here is How one Paper Company States its Credit Policies

1. There can be no fixed rules governing the granting of credit and enforcement of collections, yet certain general principles must be observed with reasonable exception in unusual circumstances.
2. The objective of credit policy is to assist legitimate business on a mutually sound basis, but to avoid assuming the position of a financial institution in an undue effort to promote sales, with its resulting abnormal credit losses, increased collection costs and excessive investment in accounts receivable.
3. In order to promote uniform practices, this credit policy is outlined for the guidance of all company divisions.
4. Within the credit policy, it should be possible to determine what amount of credit will minimize capital invested in accounts receivable, keep losses from uncollectible accounts to an acceptable minimum, and at the same time maximise sales.
5. Since favorable consideration creditwise is given to customer who has the ability to profitably operate his business, the converse is true, and, with customers who are unable to make profit, caution should be exercised in the granting of credit.
6. Our credit department is lenient, yet liberally firm with the thought in mind that the majority of our customers are honest. No set rules apply to all customers; each individual case must be treated separately.

Until last year the mountains looked beautiful ... now they keep reminding me of our company's cash-flow.

Business Plan

Before setting a credit policy, management should once again go through its business plan such as—goals, risks, organization, financial, exit options, etc.

A credit manager should find out the effectiveness of the plan, by asking himself the following questions:

- Is the business making the progress that it projected for itself?
- Has there been a noticeable loss of direction and/or momentum?
- Is the trade wondering whether the company is less competitive or less service-oriented than it should be?
- Is the company borrowing more money than the strong level of sales indicates is appropriate to pay the company's monthly bills?
- What about company's budget? Is there good financial control over company expenditure?

The answers to these questions will be enormously helpful to any management who is looking to compare key areas in a company's progress. If the answer to one or more of these questions is ambiguous to the extent then it will leave a doubt that there are problems that might be difficult to recognise.

Types of Growth

The next consideration before setting up a credit policy should be to study the type of growth the company is venturing into:

Is it Steady growth? Is it Sporadic growth? or is the growth of the company volatile?

Whatever may be the growth, the management should try to be at its best and most responsive, so that whatever the future may hold, it should be able to escape the growth traps.

Many companies, with whom we interacted, started a credit department only after it faced serious debtors problem. This is not a correct method. Credit policy, credit department and credit procedures should start with the first credit being allowed, irrespective of whether it is a small-scale company or medium or big corporate. The marketing head, the financial head, the credit manager/head together should be the initiators of the credit policy of the company.

"Our Company Credit Policy – Ha!"

Types of Credit Policy

Now the management should be ready to decide what type of credit policy they would like to adopt. The size of a company is irrelevant and a written credit policy is a must for any business whose sales programme includes selling on credit terms. No company can expect to collect for sales within a time frame appropriate for specific company or business if the company lacks a credit policy or if it does not fit its requirements. The question of whether credit decisions will be made by an experienced professional, a less experienced professional, or an entrepreneur, has obvious relevance as it relates to the quality of the results. The absence of a credit policy can lead to credit decisions that are inappropriate for a company, whose standard for acceptable credit accounts should be based on a primary criterion of good liquidity.

The three credit policies are *restrictive, moderate*, and *liberal*. Each type of policy involves a different mix of ingredients, different business philosophy, different goals, and different financial needs. A company can have a combination of all three policies. This may be acceptable, but, the test of a credit policy is not how many guidelines you use from how many separate and different sources; the test is whether it does a good job for a specific company. If it meets the criteria, then it is a good policy.

Credit Procedures and Credit Policy

Do not confuse credit policy with credit procedures.

Credit policy is the basis or criteria for determining which types of credit accounts offer a manufacturer or distributor, (reseller) the mix of financial and business strengths that are compatible with the company's philosophy. Other factors might enter into a decision to accept or reject a prospective customer for a credit line—a distributor already in the applicant's sales and service area, or a questionable reputation among trade members. A credit policy should tell a credit manager what he or she, and his or her assistants are expected to achieve, not how they should go about doing it.

Credit procedures on the other hand are an adult version of show-and-tell. They show you the tools (forms, letters, and reports) that are necessary to do a job, and they tell you the proper sequence for using the forms and letters needed to gather and evaluate information from applicants' banks and suppliers. These tools are some of the departments' internal guidelines for doing the total job of credit management – and doing it well.

Good credit procedures eliminate immediately many of the elements associated with a non-routine, hapazard approach to decision making, that lead to costly mistakes. Extra risk is the price your company pays when there are no step-by-step procedures to build a case for or against the granting of an applicant's request for a credit line. Good credit procedures involve a conscious effort to repeat successful and sequential procedures so that the person who makes credit decisions is immediately aware when any step in the process is missing or incomplete. Procedures should interface comfortably with your credit policy and should result in a contribution to the goals as stated in the credit policy.

Assessing Credit Policy

From time to time, a company should also review its credit policy and find out whether it is strict or lenient. This can be concluded by studying the

- value of orders rejected as compared to net credit sales.
- monthly collection of overdues as compared to accounts due on beginning of every month.
- amount of bad debts to credit sales

Study can be done on percentage basis. The opinion on the outcome will differ from company to company. It will depend upon the nature of business and the amount it has decided to finance accounts receivable.

Exception To Credit Policy

One Time Buyer/New Customer – Compelling Reasons for being flexible

1. Salesman confirming 5 Cs of Credit (Character, capacity, capital, conditions and collateral).
2. Relationship with buyer. (Company's or Salesman's)
3. The customer's payment history – (market-report)

4. Profit margin on the product in questions – (tight margin be more careful.)
5. Status of the product – slow moving or fast moving
6. Status of Sales Goal or Year-end target to be achieved by Salesman, provided Salesman takes absolute responsibility for collection (during year-end only).
7. Customer's cooperation in Deferred Payment. Only profit is lost if not paid. (practiced by good TO & good profit company)
8. Mean versus ends – should the customer really want the goods, it may be possible to make the sale if the customer agrees to pay the outstanding invoices along with current one.

CREDIT MANUAL PREPARATION

A well-organised company will always lay down its procedure for work in the form of a manual. A manual speaks about the company's professional approach to its investment in debtors by a profit-conscious management.

All sales ledger, credit and collection procedures should be reviewed periodically in any business and a checklist compiled of important features. This checklist can be used for developing the credit manual, as well as for management information purposes. In preparing a manual, gaps detected in procedures can be usefully filled. Once prepared, the credit manual is useful for:

(a) Day-to-day reference to resolve problems and improve documents.
(b) Training new staff starting and integrating them more rapidly.
(c) Giving to auditors, to reduce the time that staff are tied up.
(d) Reviews of procedures by senior management.

Suggested Contents of a Credit Manual

A credit manual should ideally cover following:

1. Credit objectives and policy
   (a) A clear statement by top management

   (b) Responsibilities of departments, e.g. sales, production, logistics, customer care etc. for aspects of credit policy.
   (c) Industry standards and competitors' practices.

2. Credit organization
   (a) Organization chart, showing reporting lines
   (b) Job descriptions of credit personnel.
   (c) Qualifications/background for each job.
   (d) Training system, in-company and external.
   (e) Performance appraisals and salary reviews.

3. Debtors' budgets and plans
   (a) Process and timetables for long-term plans, annual budgets, and interim forecasts.
   (b) Information required from sales and others.

Monthly Reporting

1. Monthly reporting procedures
   (a) Forms and instructions for debtors.
   (b) Forms and instructions for credit department expense.
2. Credit checking procedures, including:
   (a) Credit information sources to be used.
   (b) Calculating and using credit limits and risk categories.
   (c) Range of possible payment terms.
   (d) Securities and guarantees for risky accounts.
   (e) Credit insurance procedures (if available and for export)
   (f) Procedures for handling problem orders.
   (g) Stop-shipment policy and procedures.

3. Invoicing procedures
   (a) The control points
   (b) The checklists for invoicing to government department, wholesalers, retailers, major accounts customers etc.
   (c) Supporting documents.
   (d) Manner in which these bills to be submitted.

4. Collection procedure, including:
   (a) Responsibilities for classes of accounts.
   (b) Timetable for standard procedures.
   (c) Treatment of special accounts.
   (d) Rules for using third parties, collection agencies, and solicitors.
   (e) Insolvency and write-off procedures.
   (f) Handling of disputes, debit notes and credit notes.

5. Appendix of forms and reports, including samples of:
   (a) Application for credit facilities.
   (b) Letter sent to new accounts.
   (c) Order confirmation.
   (d) Invoices and credit notes.
   (e) Conditions of sale.
   (f) Statement of account.
   (g) Collection letters / alternative wordings.
   (h) Aged debt analysis.
   (i) All computer analyses, reports and copy screen displays.
   (j) Department logs, reports and forms.
   (k) Corporate forms with clear instructions.
   (l) Budget forecast forms.

All documents should have simple explanations and examples. The credit manager should ensure that the manual is kept updated with changes as they happen. The best way to ensure this as being done is to have the manual in daily use.

ILLUSTRATION – I

The sales manager of firm 'X' felt that if the credit policy is liberalised from one month to two months, he will be able to achieve 30% more than last year sale. This assumption was based on market survey demand analysis and experience. His firm's policy was to achieve 25% return on investment. The sales manager, the finance manager and credit manager together tried to work out the effect of the above liberal policy and to find out whether the same will be profitable. The logical steps were put down on paper in the following manner:

	Present Policy	Projected Policy
Credit period	1 month credit	2 months credit
Credit sales	10,00,000	13,00,000 (30% increase)
Expected return on investment	25%	
Sales price per unit	Rs 10	
Average unit cost	Rs 8	
Average variable cost	Rs 6	
Debtors turnover ratio	12	6
At new level of sales the total cost and unit sales will be :		
Present sales × Average cost =	10,00,000	×0.8 = 8,00,000
Additional sales × Marginal cost =	3,00,000	×0.6 = 1,80,000
	13,00,000	9,80,000

The average cost per unit at new level of sales (1,30,000 units sold at Rs 10 per unit) is

$$\frac{9,80,000}{1,30,000} = \text{Rs } 7.54 \text{ per unit}$$

Profitablity of additional sales

$$= 10 - 6 \text{ or } 4 \times 30000 \text{ units}$$
$$= \text{Rs } 1,20,000$$

Present average investment in receivables

$$= \frac{\text{Annual sales}}{\text{A/R Ratio}} \times \frac{\text{Average cost per unit}}{\text{Selling price per unit}}$$

$$= \frac{10,00,000}{12} \times 0.8 = \text{Rs } 66,667$$

Average investment in receivable after change in credit policy

$$= \frac{13,00,000}{6} \times 0.75 = \text{Rs } 1,62,500$$

Additional investment in A/c receivables

$$= \text{Rs } 1,62,500 - \text{Rs } 66,667 = \text{Rs } 95,833$$

Required rate of return on additional sales

$$= 25\% \text{ on } 95,833 = 23,958$$

Profitability of additional sale, i.e. Rs 1,20,000 is much higher than the required rate of return on additional investment, i.e. Rs 23,958.

ILLUSTRATION – II

To work out the cost-benefit analysis of progressively strict credit and collection policy programmes. Firm A decides to spend more (may be by allowing discount) in each programme. (Although we have assumed that sale will remain same in all the programmes but in practice if one is able to collect the money in spite of his firm's policy being strict, then the sale should show an upward trend.)

		Present Programme (Rs)	Programme X (Rs)	Programme Y (Rs)
Annual collection expenditure		Rs 60,000	Rs 85,000	Rs 1,15,000
Average collection period		3 months	2 months	1 month
Percentage of bad debt		6%	3%	1%
Present sale	Rs 10,00,000	Assumed that these figures will not change with change in collection effort		
Present unit price	Rs 10			
Present average cost per unit	Rs 8			
Annual sales		10,00,000	10,00,000	10,00,000
Turn over of A/R		4	6	12
Average A/R		2,50,000	1,66,667	83,333
Average investment (at average cost)in A/R		2,00,000	1,33,334	66,666
Reduced investment in A/R			66,666	1,33,334
Required return on reduced investment (25%)			16,667	33,334
Bad debt losses (% of sales)		60,000	30,000	10,000
Cost of bad debt losses (average cost)		48,000	24,000	8,000
Reduction in cost of bad debt losses from present cost			24,000	40,000
Required return on reduced investment plus reduction in cost of bad debt losses			40,667	73,334
Additional collection expenditure from present expenditure			25,000	55,000

THREE

The Winning Team—Collecting Money is Everybody's Business

In many Indian companies, there is no specific person designated as credit manager or credit controller. It usually falls on a member of the accounting staff to monitor credit sales and to organise cash collections. Credit control is not regarded as his principal responsibility, and all too often credit work is filled in when time permits or when a cash crisis occurs. Many of the companies who do employ a full-time credit manager regard him as a debt collector of relatively low status in the hierarchy. This status of the credit manager can only be improved by a more enlightened top management, recognising the potential contribution a professional credit manager can give. The credit department should be an independent unit with fundamental grasp of both finance and marketing. Thus, in the hierarchy of management, the credit manager should be equated with sales manager and finance manager and he should report to managing director/sales director/finance director.

RELATION WITH OTHER DEPARTMENTS

The credit/sales relation should be positive. The credit manager who bombards the marketing department with a stream of procedures, controls and blacklists, will be regarded as a negative figure whose purpose is to restrict sales, impose limits, demand money and stop deliveries. Such actions are accepted and

A long collection period may mean you're profitable on paper — while you are sinking fast.

— Joseph T. Straub

recognised only if there exists a climate of understanding and confidence between sales and credit. Written communication, preceded by a face to face chat or a phone call, will surely help in creating such an atmosphere.

Periodic meetings between credit manager and marketing manager should include the following points on their agenda.

(a) Minutes of the last month's meeting—review of action taken
(b) Last month's collection results and debtor figures.
(c) Discussion on problem accounts.
(d) Review of payments held up for various reasons.
(e) Proposed blacklist.
(f) Changes in distribution network.
(g) Marketing prospects.
(h) Cash discounts.
(i) Problems in controlling consignment stock.
(j) Should we charge interest on overdue accounts?
(k) Next month's joint meeting with sales, service and production department.
(l) Programme of customer visits.

The credit manager should keep top management informed of important decisions, for example, taking legal action or stopping supplies of a certain customer. The credit manager must transmit promptly both ordinary reports, and special reports when appropriate. He must see that his superiors have all the information needed to evaluate his personal effectiveness.

His reports should ensure that top management knows in broad outline the problems encountered in collection of money, ways they are handled and the results accomplished.

As discussed earlier, the credit manager's position in a hierarchy of the company should be on par with sales manager and finance manager reporting to the operation directors. Although he performs mainly sales activities, it is very important to have a close relation with Finance. Most of the activities of finance department evolve around collection of money by the credit manager.

The credit manager is also expected to maintain the co-ordination of sales and finance. He has to strike a balance between utmost sale and utmost collection. He will have to make mutual effort between these two departments to overcome their natural conflict of interest in credit policy. Credit terms are significant factors in obtaining orders. Length of credit period, size and nature of discounts, relative liberality in granting credit —all can be instrumental in persuading prospects or potential customers.

The credit manager is responsible for keeping control over credit policy and its implementation. The sales executives may be more interested in obtaining orders than in collecting amounts due, resulting in a tendency to grant credit to customers who are not creditworthy. The sales department, wanting to increase sales favours liberalising credit policies, where as the credit department, wanting to control credit losses, favours tightening them. Thus, creating a close coordination to strike the correct balance between these inclinations will serve the best interest of the whole company.

The credit management function, which will become even more important to the health of the business as growth continues, must be kept at the centre of activity. Ideally the organizational structure should allow for the following:

- The credit manager will have sufficient status to influence sales planning, i.e. he will be a member of management team.
- In this age of Enterprise Resource Planning (ERP), Electronic Data Interchange(EDI) and Supply Chain Management(SCM) – procurement, order processing, pricing, production planning, invoicing, physical distribution, inventory management, credit control and collection could all be centered in one area.
- Sales policy shall be subject to and influenced by considerations of credit control.
- There should be a close link between the sales manager and the credit manager both for the setting of policy and also to ensure that day-to-day activities include the effective collection of money. Credit manager needs to be in a position in using the opportunity for a sales man to ask for the payment on his next call.

In case of a slow paying customer, a word with the purchasing head can work wonders.

There was a time when the credit department, or the sales department, relied on the accounts department to bill customers, handle all the relevant documents like Hundi, Letter of Credit, IDBI documentation. etc. With the development of country wide management information systems, although these are still handled by the billing department, the credit manager is made responsible for sales accounting. The order processing, despatch & billing departments are brought under his direct control.

The credit manager should maintain good relations with service department on a day-to-day basis. Any complaints could result in payments being held up if not attended properly, and the customer taking his trade to the competitors. In companies manufacturing technical products requiring installation and repair services, caution and close contact of the sales, credit control and service department are essential. Availability of service, such as technical advice on the installation of a new product, is a powerful selling argument. In a decentralised organizational structure, bridging a gap between credit control department and service department is very important from the customer's point of view and these relations should be of a continuous nature to serve a customer better and collect the money in time.

Since the credit manager is in a position where he gets to analyse all the service complaints—deficiency in the products, deficiency in the packing methods, he can be an extension of quality control department, market research department and contribute with valid feedback from the market.

Finally, his relation with the production department is also very important. If the materials are not manufactured as per specifications, if the goods are not delivered within the delivery date instructed by the customer, if the spares are inadequate in quantity or quality, if the test certificate is not provided, if the manuals are not provided or they are not informative, the customers will take their trade elsewhere. Thus, the credit manager has to be an extension of production department also.

HIRING A CREDIT MANAGER

A credit manager is certainly not an accountant, nor is he a great salesman. He must be a blend of both. He must be the one staff member sitting and coordinating between sales, marketing, finance, production, purchase, after-sales-service and customer care departments. He can be in the midst of operating a supply chain management or commercial department.

The credit manager should have an accounting or a financial background, good knowledge and experience with data-processed reports (and what it takes to process them), and a personality that allows him or her to interface effectively with all levels of company personnel and customers. The credit manager must have the experience, knowledge, and ability to make good, timely credit decisions, to know when (and how firmly) to press a delinquent account for payment, to recognise and implement within-department changes before the need impacts the department's performance, to use experience as the base to make perceptive credit decision that will allow the company to avoid inaccurate cash forecast or negotiating borrowings. The benefits, both short- and long-term, are enormous.

Before the qualification of the individual candidates can be considered, questions must be asked regarding the company or business.

(a) What is the current size of the company, including the figure for annual sales?
(b) What is the total number of the company's active accounts?
(c) What is the average monthly total of receivables balances?
(d) Of the average aging (days of sales) of receivables accounts?
(e) What is the company's plan for growth?
(f) Is growth projected as something that will be accomplished slowly, at a moderate rate of speed, or rapidly?
(g) What is the anticipated rate of annual growth?

Perhaps the most important consideration relevant to the requirements of the company and the qualifications of the respective candidates is the current size of the company and the projected rate of annual growth. A company that is already doing annual credit sales in crores of rupees cannot afford to hire a person who is not an experienced and capable professional. If that same company is on fast track—one calculated to show growth of at least 20 or 25 per cent per year—add 'aggressive, innovative, and a strong capacity for work and for personal growth' to the basic requisite of 'an experienced, capable professional.'

The Credit Controller Should be of a Special Brand

1. The man
   - (a) Tough and determined
   - (b) Polite and courteous
2. His goal
   - (a) Maximum profitable sales
   - (b) Steady turnover of accounts receivable
   - (c) Proper bad debt ratio or no bad debt
3. His knowledge
   - (a) Principles and practice of marketing
   - (b) Credit and collection management
   - (c) Principles of accounting
   - (d) Statement analysis
   - (e) Fundamental economics
   - (f) Market trends
   - (g) Business problems and needs
   - (h) Sources of information
   - (i) Legal formalities or experience in litigation
   - (j) Knowledge of acts and rules
     - (i) Sale of Goods Act,1930,
     - (ii) The Indian Contract Act, 1872,
     - (iii) The Arbitration Act,1932,
     - (iv) The Partnership Act,1932,
     - (v) The Negotiable Instruments Act, 1881,
     - (vi) The Companies Act, 1956,
     - (vii) The Central Sales Tax Act, 1956,
     - (viii) The Sales Tax Act and Rules,
     - (ix) Excise Duty and Octroi Duty Rules,
     - (x) Procedure of settling Marine insurance claims
4. Special qualities
   - (a) Knack of getting money from unwilling customers
   - (b) Art of writing good follow-up and reminder letters
   - (c) Motivating his collection staff
   - (d) Dealing firmly with weak customers

He must be thorough with his company's policies, associates, product mix, procedures adopted, etc.

HELPING A CREDIT MANAGER SETTLE IN

A checklist will help him to understand the company better and to decide on a appropriate Credit and Collection Policy, if not already in place. This can be as given in Table 3.1.

Table 3.1: Credit and Collection Policies Check List

Credit approval
Is a written application required with every credit request?
Do you have a standard form for credit application?
Is it completed personally by the applicant?
Is it reviewed for completeness?
Are all information verified for accuracy and timeliness?
Are applicants checked out with credit reference/bureau?
Does your evaluation consider residential (premises) stability?
Does your evaluation consider bank balances?
Does your evaluation consider other assets?

Invoices
What is the procedure for invoicing?
Are invoices prepared promptly?
Who is authorised to sign the bills?
What is the procedure of checking before signing?
Is invoice preparation always accurate?
Are payment terms clearly stated?
Are customer's special instructions followed carefully?
Who is handling Government Bill documentation?

Collection
What is the procedure for collection & deposit in bank?
How far the sales personnel are involved in collection?
Are salesmen made responsible if any of their customer does not pay?

Terms of sale
Do you offer a cash discount?
Do you use a late payment penalty?
Is the time limit / date for payment clearly stated?
Are goods sold under warranty/guarantee?
Are goods replaced in case of guarantee?

Factors that influence the choice of terms
What competitors are offering?
Working capital available to finance the debtor?
Higher risk - shorter terms?
Kind of product being sold?
The size of the order?

Transport
Are all goods despatched through bank approved transporters?
Who is in charge for despatch?

Excise
Responsible person? Excise Rates? Classification of item proper? Tariff list filed?
Are the duty rate & packaging rules applicable checked?

Packing
Packing details?
Responsible person?

Insurance
Are goods-in-transit covered?
In case of shortage/damage who lodges the claim?
On date how many claims are pending for settlement?
Who are our underwriters?

Installation, erection and commissioning
Is installation within our preview?
Do we have a separate team to handle installation?
Do they submit a installation report?
Otherwise what is the procedure for after-sales follow-up?
Is there a standard form for after-sales follow-up?
Who controls the after-sales follow-up report?

Annual maintenance contract (AMC)
Do we undertake AMC?
What is the procedure for controlling AMC?
Who is responsible for controlling AMC?
What is the basis of charging AMC fees?
Does it include spare replacement?

Distribution
What are our channels of distribution?
How many wholesalers, dealers/OEM and other customers do we have?

Pricing
What is the basis of our pricing?
Is bank interest considered while pricing?

Bank guarantee (BG)
What is the procedure for following up BG?
Are all BG renewed in time?
Do we write to bank for cancellation of BG's if the job is completed before due date?

Sales tax forms
What is the procedure for following up:
(i) "C" forms
(ii) Other forms
Any standard sequence of follow-up of letters?

Budgets
Budget (Receivable investment) already drawn?
Any department budget (expense) already drawn?
Any department target already drawn?

Statements
Are monthly statements submitted to all open accounts?
Total number of accounts we have in our debtors' ledger?
Are statements prompt and accurate?
Is age analysis taken out on a monthly basis?

Contingent liability
Any court case?

Other
Statements are taken out monthly/fortnightly/weekly?
Presently, what is the Debtors Turnover Ratio in Days?

Proof of identification (monthly analysis)
Do we
- determine our average collection period on a regular basis?
- compare our current collection period with industry averages?
- compare our current collection period with our previous experience?
- compare our collection period with your payment terms?

Why customers don't pay
Financial crisis?
Dissatisfaction?
Inefficiency in their office procedure?
Purposeful delay?
Inefficiency in our office procedure to follow-up?
What is the procedure for handling complaints?

Follow-up
Is an ABC analysis done on overdue accounts?
Do we have a systematic procedure for follow-up on slow accounts?
Is there a standard sequence of follow-up of letters?
Is the tone of these letters progressively stronger?
Do we use the telephone to contact delinquent accounts?
Is our telephone technique effective?
Do we have a late-payment penalty?

Do we put delinquent accounts on cash-on-delivery basis?
List of provision for bad/doubtful debts.

Aggressive collection
Is there administrative, system development (internal) and procedural (external) control in the department?
Is our staff-force enough?
Are they firm, determined, polite & courteous?
Do they work in groups?
Do our staff-force have the following characteristics?

- somebody good in documentation
- somebody good in negotiation
- somebody good in following up shamelessly.
- somebody good in ground support.
- somebody good in talking over telephone.
- somebody good in supervising ledger accounts (on computer).

Advertisement
How much do we spend on advertisement?
What is the basis for fixing the budget?

Stock
What is the stock turnover in days?
(stocks + work-in-progress/cost of sales)/365
Any consignment (sale) stock?

Export
Who is responsible for export documentation?
What are our terms for export?

External resources
Do we have a working relationship with a collection agency?
Are accounts turned over automatically after a specific time period?
Do we refer the most serious delinquencies to an attorney?
Who approves a case for litigation?
Who are our attorneys?
How many cases are under litigation?

Plans
Do we have any long/short plan?
If yes, then:

- Where are we?
- Where do we want to go?
- How do we get there?
- When will it be done?
- Who will do it?
- How much will it cost?

Answers to all the questions in Table 3.1 will help him to have a good grip of the company he newly joined.

Take a hard look at the procedures you currently use to process new accounts, to assign credit limits, to monitor accounts receivable, to control credit limits, and to follow up on in-house and third-party collection efforts. If a review of your current procedures indicates that you need to reorganise them, now is the time to begin.

Begin with a simple physical layout which includes the amount of space that will be alloted to the credit department based upon the number of people who currently occupy or will occupy the space.

The next step should be an evaluation of the present system for processing data. If it isn't a computerised system, incorporate into the thinking and planning the question of how soon an appropriate system can and should be installed.

ORGANISATION OF CREDIT CONTROL DEPARTMENT

In India the credit manager is faced with the task of creating a credit department from an existing sales ledger organization. Although in our opinion a good credit control is totally dependent on good accounts receivable system and a credit manager should be in control of the ledger, it is not necessary to separate debtor accounting from the accounts and shift to credit control department. A credit manager is supposed to know about bad debt, discount, price difference, goods returned and ensure timely accounting of such entries in respective debtor's account. In other words, he should know the status of each bill in any customers account. He must ensure that the timing of statements and the ledger should be available when required. In case of backlog, he should be able to determine the priorities.

Duties and Responsibilities of Credit Manager

1. Credit rating of both existing and new customers
2. Monitoring of debtors and debtor follow-up
3. Collection of debts
4. Monitoring of sales follow-up
5. Developing and maintaining customer relation
6. Monitoring and controlling the sales accounting

7. Liaison with bank and trade association.
8. Close interaction with sales manager, finance manager and service department.
9. Review of credit and collection policy.
10. Supporting the staff to enable them give their best through proper direction and guidance.

The credit manager's major responsibilities in setting up a department will be to:

- Define the role and duties of each credit & collection staff.
- Monitoring their activities giving proper direction and guidance.
- Motivating the staff to bring out their best and utilising their individual strengths in various/respective functions.
- Strengthening the team spirit & interaction other departments.

The credit manager's staff-force should be enough and must include the following:

(a) somebody good in documentation
(b) somebody good in negotiation
(c) somebody good in collection (shameless and determined to collect)
(d) somebody good in ground support (paper work and account reconciliation)
(e) somebody good in talking fluently and persuasively over telephone (preferably a lady)
(f) somebody good in supervising ledger accounts (0n computer)
(g) everyone should be good at letter drafting
(h) somebody having good exposure to legal formalities

The requirements of a good credit clerk are different from that of a good accounts clerk. A credit clerk is expected to talk fluently and persuasively over the telephone, carry out skilled correspondence and above all a good sense of detecting problems and making judgments. Credit work requires a higher level of skill and intelligence, thus it is not correct to combine the accounting and credit work. The size of the credit department will depend upon the number of active customers and volume of business.

While dealing with customer complaints, the credit manager should be in a position to control billing dept, despatch department and service so as to ensure a better customer service. A credit control department is an extension of customers grievances and should be in a position to ask the concerned departments to attend to the same on priority basis.

In Table 3.2 the allocation of work in a credit control is described:

Table 3.2: Infrastructure of Credit Control Department

Credit Manager

Computer supervisor	Key accounts supervisor	Non-key accounts supervisor	Support supervisor
Support master file, Co-ordination with accounts department and typist pools.	Dealers Public sector A-grade OEM customers	B and C grade customers	Co-ordination with despatch, billing, after-sales service, production, quality control, order processing dept. etc.

Functions of a Credit and Collection Department

The routine work of credit control department can be summarised as below:

Daily and Weekly Work

1. Staff visit to debtors.
2. Amount collected by staff/ received directly. Updating debtors position.
3. List of debtors exceeding credit limit.
4. Reminders sent to various overdue parties.
5. Action plan OEM / Government parties.
6. Sales follow-up.
7. Any court cases.
8. If any Cheque is dishonoured then start the follow-up.
9. Complaint attended and balance status.
10. Support to regions/branches

11. Follow-up with dealers.
12. Find out—number of challans pending for billing.
13. Complaints status.
14. Transit insurance claim status.

Monthly

1. Debtors statement (A/R)
2. Age analysis (current, over 6 months) and (overdue accounts)
3. Total collection (breakup staff-wise, current and over 6 months)
4. Budget
5. Court cases
6. Pending sales follow-up.
7. Pending complaint to be attended.
8. Statement of account being posted to parties.
9. Bank guarantee status.
10. Sales tax forms status
11. Transit insurance claim status.
12. Monthly report.

Yearly

1. Confirmation of balance.
2. Provision for bad and doubtful debt.
3. Bad debt to be written off.
4. Contingent liability (pending court cases)
5. Details for annual report.

Over Head Budget

Like any other department, a credit control department's expenses budget is drawn and monitored on a monthly basis. The budget should include expenses such as interest charged for credit period allowed, cost of maintaining accounts (computerized accounts), probable bad-debts (% over sales). salary, rent, electricity, cost of investigating credit worthiness of customers, and legal expenses.

Case Study: A reputed engineering company's regional credit controller describes his recovery work as follows:

It can be seen from Fig. 3.3 that as soon as the invoices are received from Head Office, for all the invoices, we send reply card intimation-cum-reminder to the customer as well as to the bank. We get good response for this reply card type reminders (sample enclosed). Thus, as a first step, all the invoices irrespective of the amount, payment terms, customers get reminded by us immediately.

Post Cards

1. First post card – from KVT Ltd to bank and customer

POST CARD

Your Order No.
Our Inv. No. Dt. For Rs.

Dear sir,
Against our above invoice, an amount of Rs. ____________ is still outstanding as per our records.

________ month(s) are over now, but we have still not received this payment

We appreciate, you might have some genuine problems to clear our payment. But, please keep us informed about the same.

We therefore request you to return us the enclosed reply card duly filled to enable us to know the status of our bill. Please co-operate by replying us immediately.

The second post card to be enclosed with first post card for bank to reply only.

POST CARD

From: Customer
Inv. No. Dt. For Rs.

1. Customer has retired the documents. Payment vide cheq./DD no.________ dt. _____ for Rs. ______ sent to KVT Ltd, Bombay on _________ .
2. Already intimated the customer on , but no response yet.
3. As your customer has not responded inspite of reminders, documents have been returned to KVT Ltd., Bombay on
4. This bank has not received the above referred documents.
5. Any other remarks:

Follow-up

Further, follow-up is done under the following groupings: (TARB)

* Invoices of value > 75K - Top priority - 'T' group
* Invoices of value < 75K - under Active follow-up - 'A' group
* Invoices of value < 75K - under Routine follow-up - 'R' group
* Balance payments follow-up - 'B' group

Group 'T'

As soon as the invoices are received from head office, details of Rs 75000 invoices are noted down separately and immediate follow-up actions initiated. Follow-up is done by means of personal visits or phone-calls depending on payment terms, customer relations.

For outstation cases, as most of our payment terms are like 'payment in 30 days', 'after acceptance', etc., we cannot get the payment in hand by just making one or two personal visits. Personal visits are made only for very important cases.

After the personal visits, phone-calls, letters confirm the same.

Group 'A'

The invoice master register is scanned through by me everyday. I make my own judgment and decide which are the invoices that need telephonic or personal follow-up. Those invoices are transferred from Invoice Master file to 'Active follow-up' files and vigorous follow-up is done till the payment is received.

Once the payment is received, the invoice copy and its correspondence are transferred back to the invoice master file, thus the 'active follow-up' files contain only the outstanding invoices.

Group 'R'

The rest of the less than Rs 75000 invoices, for which I decide that no active follow-up is required (for various reasons like good customer who always takes prompt action, invoices of small value less than Rs 20,000 or so with payment terms 'through bank or in 30 days', etc.) get covered under this routine follow up group. For all these invoices, only written reminders are sent at the end of every month.

Note: Whenever our sales engineers go on tour, details of these payments are also given to them for personal follow-up.

Even after 1 to 1.5 months, if some of these payments may not realised, I may decide to transfer such cases to group 'A'. From then on these payments are chased vigorously till settled.

Group 'B'

This is further divided into two groups viz.,

1. Balance payments of current financial year: Routine written reminders, fortnightly phone calls (if local).
2. Old balance payments: All these cases in general will be of problematic or disputed types which are reviewed, and necessary reminders are sent to customer or head office to progress and sort out. This exercise is also done fortnightly.

The balance payments require a lot of follow-up as the amount involved being small, they get low priority. We have therefore allotted some period in each month to follow them up. As we do not receive much of invoices or despatched documents from head office in the first 2 or 3 days of a month, the cases are reviewed and progressed further.

Note: These balance payments also get followed-up personally when the sales engineers go on tour.

Branch Offices' Role in Payment Follow-up

The details of out standing payments are sent to our branch offices periodically for necessary follow-up by means of personal visits, phone calls and feedback recorded by us. As far as our SBD office is concerned, as all the invoices and other inputs are sent directly from head office, we do not provide them any outstanding list unless and otherwise asked for.

Sales/Service Engineers' Role in Payment Follow-up

All the engineers, before going to meet the customers, check with us if any payment follow-up work to be done. As the information is readily available in our Invoice Master Register, we give them the details immediately for necessary follow-up.

List of Files and Folders Maintained

1. Invoice number file
2. Payment receipt memo file
3. C/D forms file
4. General correspondence with head office and branches.
5. Monthly/yearly payment reports file
6. Important customers o.s. statement file
7. Stock diversion details
8. Engineers tour follow-up payment details
9. Bills/DNs to be raised by HO against diversions, forwarding etc.
10. Reminder internal memo/telexes for follow-up with HO/ branch offices
11. Target vs achievement analysis file
12. B.G. file (not maintained properly—to be improved).
13. Local invoices under active follow-up
14. Outstation invoices under active follow-up.

As soon as the mail papers pertaining to recovery are received by us by mail, we sort out the same and put into the following folders

AG — Papers for action (according to individuals)
PF — Papers for filing

IF — Invoices for filing
IR — Invoices for register entry
IO — Invoices for O/A updation
DB — Despatch documents received at Bangalore office
PT — Papers for typing

If we feel that the sales engineers may not be able to do the follow-up effectively for various reasons like more time required for sorting out the case or lot of running around to be done between purchase/stores/user accounts, or if amount is very huge, we go along with the sales/service engineers and follow up ourselves. (Thus, the auto conveyance is cut down)

For outstation visits, we give the sales engineer an exhaustive list of all outstanding payments (old/new, full/balance, bank/direct, etc.) pertaining to the place of visit. On his return, we get the feedback from him and further follow up is done by us.

Our payment follow-up activities are not strictly based on ABC analysis as expected by head office. As per head office comments, A class (>11 lac) must be personally followed-up/visited immediately, B class (30K to 1 lac) also must be (apart from written reminders) visited personally and then C class needs to be vigorously chased by means of letters or phones. To do this kind of a follow-up, we need additional manpower and also our expenditure will go up considerably as outstation cases also need to be covered.

As we do not have sufficient staff in recovery, we can follow-up only as per our 'TARB' basis.

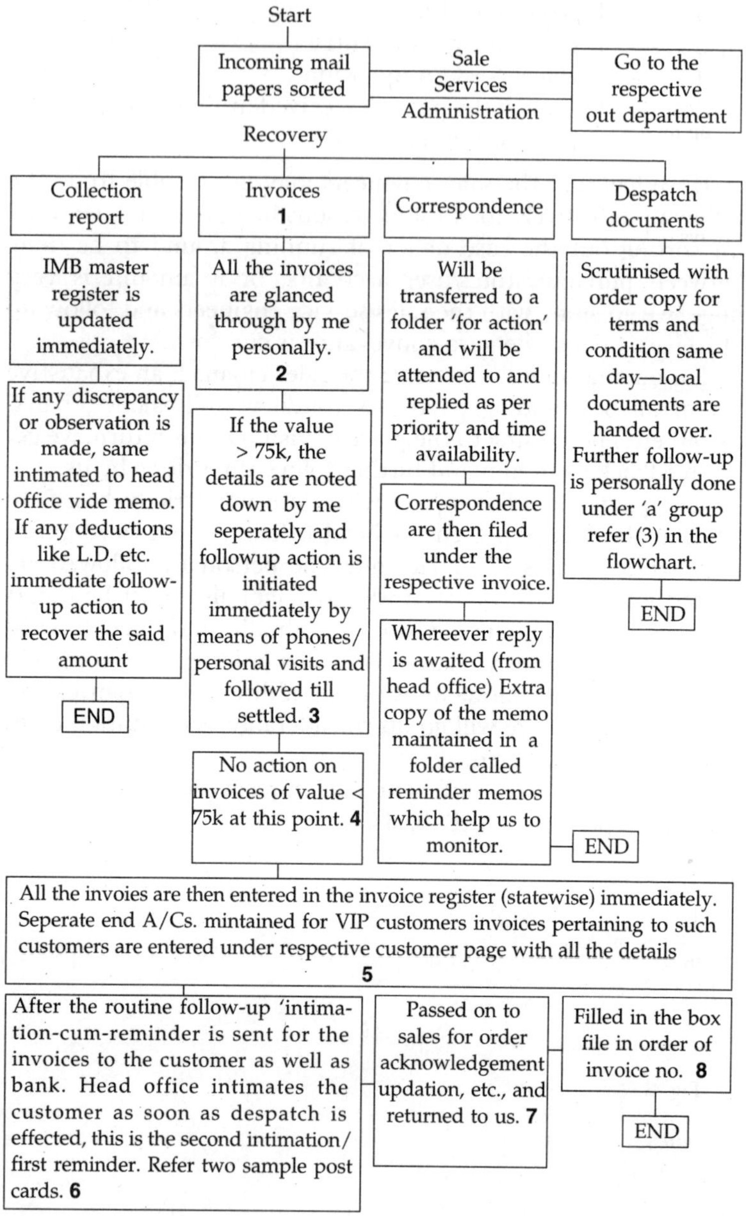

Fig. 3.1 Work Flow Part I: Recovery Section Procedures—Inputs and Action

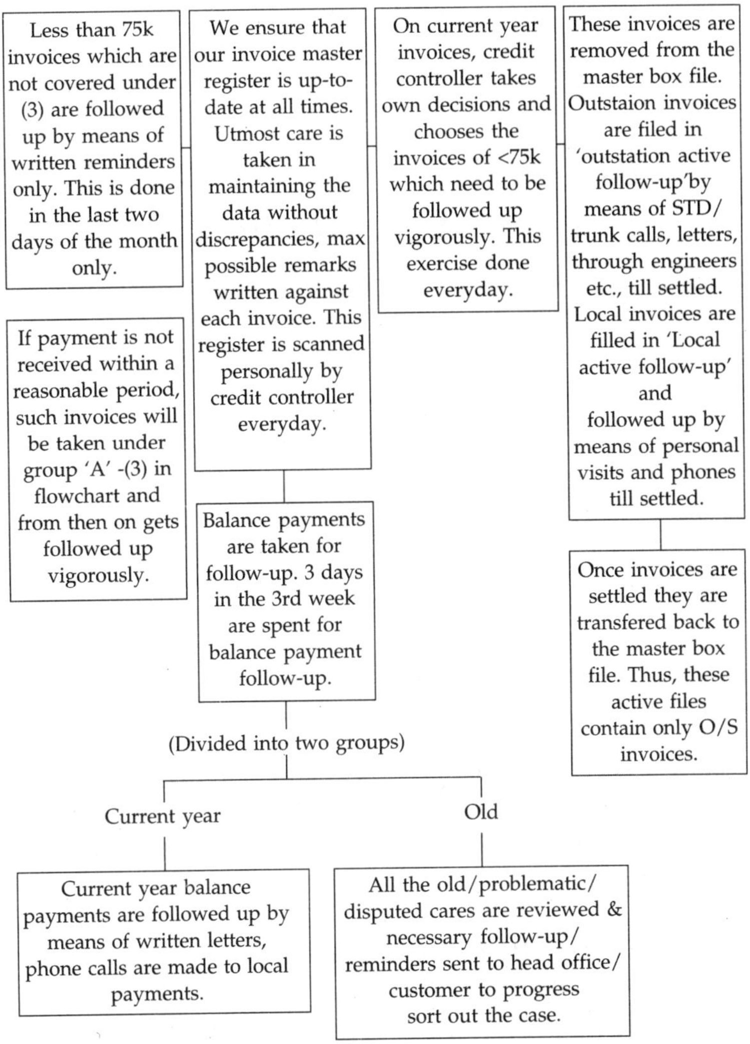

Fig. 3.2 Work Flow Part II: Out Invoice Master Register and Action

Courtesy: Geetha Ravishankar, Manager, Recovery Aplab Ltd, Southern Region.

FOUR

Our Money in Our Pocket at the Agreed Time— Terms of Payment

An agreement to sell on terms is a contract. It is the duty of the buyer to live up to the terms of the contract. Most business credit is based on terms offered by the competition. Sometimes, the terms of payment can be tricky. There could be a trap for the unwary. It is therefore necessary that the terms are clearly spelt out at the beginning of the relationship.

Terms of payment and methods of billing are very important in the efficient management of the accounts receivable. Thus, knowledge of payment terms is very important from the business point of view. One should understand its impact on cash flow and how advantageously it could be put to use on day-to-day basis.

OBJECTIVES AND ESTABLISHMENT OF TERMS OF PAYMENT

This is something to which serious thought needs to be given. Usually the factors which influence the choice of terms are :

1. What competitors are offering and position of competitors coming up.
2. Working capital available to finance the debtors
3. Extent of risk—If the risk is higher, then the term should be shorter.

"The indifferent customer"

I have already favoured you with a purchase order . . . you also want me to pay for the goods?
. . . that too on time?

4. Kind of product being sold
5. Market demand for the product
6. Size of the order and its breakeven point or revenue from its sale
7. Government regulation, if any
8. Goodwill in the market or sellers market profile
9. Tax allowances
10. Cost of the good to be sold
11. Consumer's attitude

Some of the points mentioned are inter-related. For example, a company which has a reputation for selling quality product, enjoys good demand, tends to charge shorter terms than their competitors. If the size of the order is distinctively high, one may be offered better terms.

A term offered is the interplay of all these factors.

Selection of the appropriate payment terms (to offer to your customers) is a vital step in establishing the supplier–customer relationship because this, together with the credit limit decision, will determine not only the resulting rate of cash-flow, but also the volume of sales permissible.

Payment terms should help us to accomplish the following objectives:

- Credit risk should be kept minimum
- Turnover should go up
- Should improve cash flow
- Profits in aggregate should substantially increase as a result of the extra sales due to improved cash-flow.

All these can be achieved only if the payments are received at the agreed time.

One may not be able to do much with government departments but then these orders are most secured and the payments are usually in two parts. Say 90% or 95% (whatever it may be) we may surely get at the agreed time (i.e. against proof of despatch or through bank or after a stipulated period) provided all the conditions of the order are complied with. Along with the amount one must claim 100% of the tax and duty (sales tax, excise duty) since the same is paid by us in advance into government treasury.

CREDIT TERMS

Credit terms are related to:

- Periods or time
- Delivery
- Cash discount
- Interest charges on overdue payments
- Other conditions, like advance, bank guarantee etc.

Time-based Credit vs Cash Discounts

Time-based credit terms are most commonly offered, say 30 days net or 60 days net. In many cases, it is unavoidable since it has become a practice by both small and big business to offer time based terms.

However, a decision to give half-monthly terms in return for, say 1 per cent cash discount may double or at least boost the sales figure within the same period. Table 4.1 is an example where company X is doing business on 30 days credit and company Y allows 1% cash discount to the customers if they pay within 15 days. It is further assumed that all the customers of company Y take advantage of this cash discount. As a result the cash-flow is far better in company Y thus resulting in higher profits as compared to company X .

Payment Related to Delivery

This may be used either because the credit risk is unacceptable or because the size of the order is so small that it does not justify the expenses of maintaining a credit account.

Cash with Order

No work is commenced until payment arrives.

Cash before Shipment/Despatch

Production of goods may commence on receipt and acknowledging of an order, but goods are despatched only after payment is received.

This term is not recommended where goods are being produced to customer specification since non-payment will

Table 4.1

		Company X			Company Y		
		30 Days net			1% Discount if paid within 15 days		
Month	Sale week	Sale per week 30 Days net	Cash payment	Balance	Sale per week	Cash payment	Balance
1	1	1250		1250	2500		2500
	2	1250		2500	2500		5000
	3	1250		3750	2500		7500
	4	1250		5000	2500		10000
					Payment due	5000	5000
2	5	1250		6150	2500		7500
	6	1250		7500	2500		10000
					Payment due	5000	5000
	7	1250		8750	2500		7500
	8	1250		10000	2500		10000
		Payment due	5000	5000	Payment due	5000	5000
3	9	1250		6250	2500		7500
	10	1250		7500	2500		10000
					Payment due	5000	5000
	11	1250		8750	2500		7500
	12	1250		10000	2500		10000
		Payment due	5000	5000	Payment due	5000	5000
Sale in 3 months (Rs)		15000			30000		
Cash flow (Rs)		10000			25000		
Net profit @ 5% (Rs)		750			1500		
Less 1% Disc (Rs)		Nil			300		
Net Profit (Rs)		750			1200		

leave unsalable goods. Cheques should be cleared before goods are produced. One may also call the term as payment against order acceptance.

Load over Load

Payment of this delivery has to be received before next delivery is made. Normally used in trades involving a regular weekly or monthly delivery.

Letter of Credit (LC)

Letter of credit terms are occasionally used for domestic business. It is commonly used in export business. The buyer instructs his bank to open a L/C in favour of the supplier for the value of the order and payment is made by the bank on receipt of the suppliers' invoice and/or signed delivery note and/or consignee copy of the transport receipt duly endorsed. It is merely a way of securing payment by a bank guarantee.

Cash Discount

Cash discount is another term of settlement which includes the granting of cash discount in return for payment within agreed period . This is a very common term widely offered even outside India. A discount is a reward for prompt payment and it must, therefore, be related to the period of time gained by the supplier on his cash flow. It is a way of motivating the customer to settle his account within a stipulated period (much earlier than agreed during order acceptance) for a small reward.

For example let us assume that 90 days credit (from end of month of invoicing) will be taken if no discount is offered. It is decided to offer 2.5% for payment by the end of first month of invoicing.

The true annual cost is calculated as below:

Amount of time gained i.e. 90 days less 30 days = 60 days, divided into 365 to produce the annual rate, multiplied by the rate of discount.

$$\text{Thus} \quad \frac{365}{90 - 30} \times 2.5 = 15\% \text{ (approximately)}$$

Unless the borrowing cost of the supplier exceed 15% p.a. the above would represent an uneconomic rate. In case the borrowing cost is say 22%, then this leads to an interest saving of 7% on the amount of collection. Discounts can be valuable if used selectively. A reduction of the period also reduced the risk and the use of discounts to increase sales volume on high-risk accounts is recommended.

When our discount terms are agreed, they must be capable of being used. To offer a discount for payment in 7 or even 10 days is presuming no delays in delivery or postal transit. In practice such short terms are almost unworkable without the use of a personal delivery or courier service.

Interest Charges

The practice of charging interest on overdue accounts appears to be on the increase. Very high interest rates, coupled with frequent liquidity problem caused many companies resort to interest charging so as to speed up collections.

Four main points have to be considered.

1. Interest on overdue payments may only be charged if it is specifically permitted in the company's condition of sale.
2. The effect on the business must be considered. If competitors are not charging interest, there is a real danger that some business will be lost. A decision to go it alone in a very competitive market could be very harmful.
3. The rate of interest to be charged should be reasonable and between 1% to 2% higher than banks minimum lending rates.
4. If the customer refuses to pay interest and supplier is not prepared to go to extreme lengths to enforce payment, there is no point in charging interest. However, it is observed that ultimately the strength of the supplier in the market will determine the approach.
5. A serious attempt to charge and recover interest may damage supplier's goodwill in the market. The best way to implement this is by reserving the right to charge interest from time to time at the discretion of the credit manager.

Advance

These days it has become common practice to ask for advance along with the order. Again it will depend on the nature of the product against which you can ask for advance. Any product whose production starts after receiving an order or above value is high, has an implied condition that a certain amount should accompany the confirmed order.

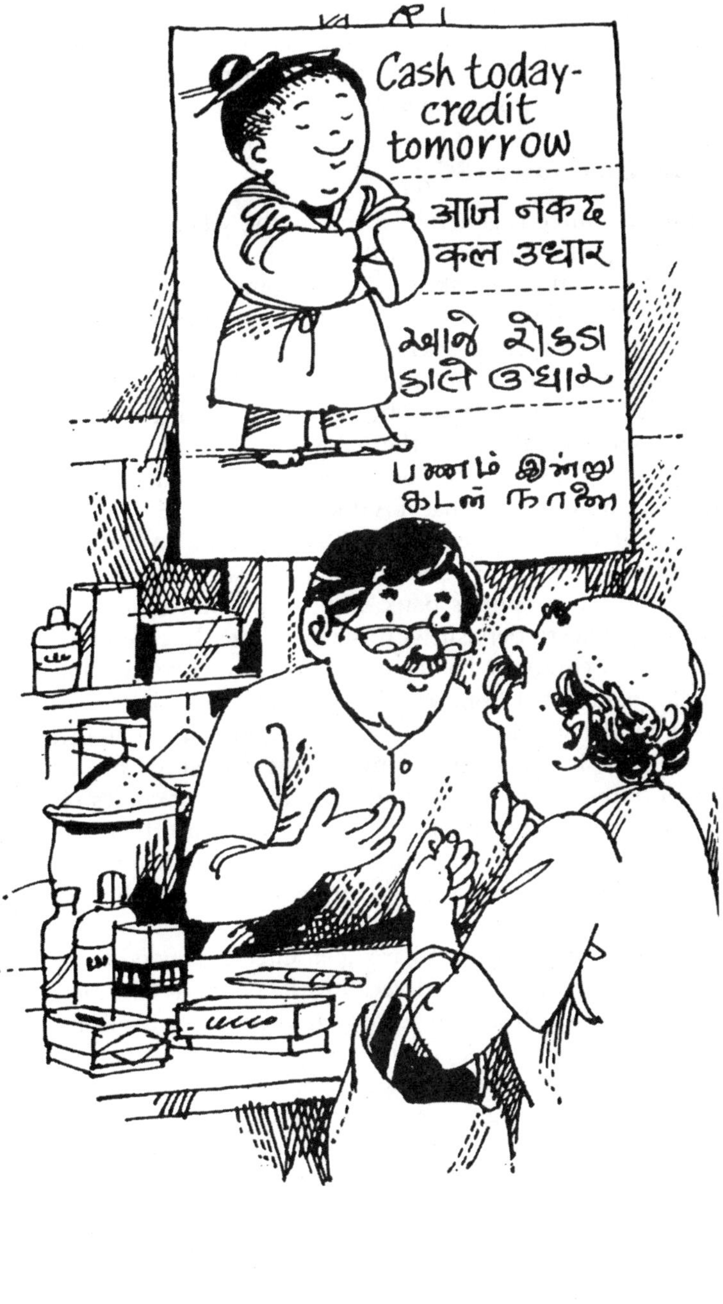
Cash today-
credit
tomorrow
आज नकद
कल उधार
આજે રોકડા
કાલે ઉધાર

Further, all defaulters (black-listed), slow payers, new customers (whose credit standing is still suspect) and above all those customers (where goods are made to their specifications) should pay 40% to 50% as advance along with confirmed order, or the company should cover up at least the direct expenses of such products through advance.

Bank Guarantee (BG)

Bank guarantee is generally given by the seller to the customer towards performance, security deposit and bid. Just as your company want to be risk free, the customer also would like to be on the safer side. There are various types of BGs such as Advance Guarantee, Performance Guarantee, Security Bond etc.

Legally, a bank guarantee is covered by Indian Contract Act, Sec. 126. A Contract of guarantee is a contract to perform the promise or discharge the liability of a third person in case of his default. A supplies goods worth Rs 1 lakh to B, and A's Banker promises to B that if A does not satisfy all the conditions of the order, then the bank will compensate to the extent of amount agreed. The common practice is that a guarantee is given by the supplier's bank. A bank guarantee is prefered to keeping security deposit with the customer. In case of Security Deposit, a company has to pay hard cash while in the case of bank guarantee a nominal charge will have to be paid to the bank by the supplier to issue (and if needed to renew) the BG. A supplier is expected to provide the guarantee on a stamp paper of prescribed denomination in number of copies required by the bank. The bank will stamp and put their reference number on it. Bank will retain 2 copies and return the balance copies, including thc original copy, which the supplier sends to his customer.

A word of caution: A bank guarantee is as good as cash for the customer. Apart from describing the purchase contract, there is one point which says that the guarantee can be revoked by the customer without giving any reason and the bank will have no choice but to pay. In one instance, a well-known company (when it learnt its customer may resort to such a revoke) made an attempt to get a stay order from the Bombay High court before their bank could pay. The case was moved in the court within 24 hours, but the court overruled the stay order application. Hence, one should know the customer's trading habit before agreeing to give bank guarantee.

Indemnity Bond

Section 124 of the Contract Act defines a contract of indemnity as a contract between two persons only. One party promises to save the other party from loss caused to him by the conduct of the promisor himself or by any other person. One of the goverment departments deducted 40% of the bill amount for breaching one provision of sales tax rules. The maximum penalty called for as per sales tax rules equals to 40% of the bill amount and hence the amount was deducted by the government department with the assumption that the same have to be paid to the ultimate authority, i.e. sales tax. The fact is that the penalty amount was to be levied by the sales tax authority after assessment of their books which may not take place at least before a year. It would have been absurd to wait for their assessment. Under the circumstances, to get this balance of 40% the company indemnified the government department saying, 'in case you are penalised by the sales tax authority at the time of assessment for our fault we will bear the amount of penalty' and the amount was thus released.

Indemnity bonds are used, only in special cases and executed on a stamp paper. (Refer Indian Stamp Act 1922 rate applicable for respective states). Its' contents are often prescribed by the person/department who is demanding the same.

Security Deposit/Earnest Money Deposit (EMD)

Security Deposit or EMD is covered by Sale of Goods Act.It is another common custom in India to form an agreement for sale by paying earnest money. If a seller breaks the contract, the buyer will retain the amount and likewise if the contract is fulfilled the amount is returned or adjusted by crediting against the price payable. Thus earnest money serves as security against fulfillment of contract. For example, a dealer deposits Rs 1,00,000 as earnest money, being 50% of the value of goods purchased, with an agreement to pay the balance amount before taking delivery. In case he fails to pay then, the seller is within his right to forfeit the amount of EMD.

Other Terms of Payment

(a) All defaulters should pay against proforma invoice.

(b) In case of industrial products or engineering companies, installation/commissioning must be carried out only after full payment is received or in stages say 50% against confirmed order, 40% against delivery or LR/RR (proof of despatch) and balance 10% after commissioning.

(c) For obvious reasons if the goods need to be transported in consignees name, the seller must receive the payment in advance against proforma invoice.

Some Important Inco-terms

These are also known as shipping/delivery/insurance terms.

Readers to note that the treatments in incoterm are practised differently in national and international level. In international level the practice of 'Incoterm 2000' is formulated by International Chamber of Commerce, France, and there are only 13 incoterms for import and export.

Inco-terms are contract terms agreed upon by both buyer and seller, which decide at what point of transaction the title of the goods passes from seller to buyer. Between seller and buyer the responsibilities like—who should arrange for transit insurance?,who should pay for freight?, whether the buyer must collect the goods from seller's works or is it the seller's responsibility to deliver the goods at buyer's place of business, or at an agreed place, and so on—should be clearly specified.

The credit manager must not only understand how they work but how to make the most appropriate choice. The principal terms are as follows:

(a) *Cash:* Synonymous with a cheque, certified bankers' cheque, demand draft, money order.

(b) *Cash before delivery (CBD):* No sooner the goods are scheduled to be ready for delivery, a proforma invoice is to be sent asking the customer to pay, so that the goods can be delivered as decided.

(c) *Cash with order:* In the true sense, this is the safest method of trading. But then, this term can be used with one time order or order from an unknown customer. If receiving cash means hard currency then one must adhere to

Income Tax Act - Section 40A (3) which reads as below: *Disallowance of expenditure incurred in business or profession in respect of which payment in a sum exceeding Rs 20,000 is made otherwise than by a crossed cheque drawn on a bank or by a crossed bank draft*. In layman's language, any payment above Rs 20,000 should be received in cheque only and not in hard currency.

(d) *Cash on delivery:* From practical point of view a cash on delivery term is workable in any of the following manners:

(i) Customer collects the goods from your factory against payment.

(ii) Goods are sent by Value Payable Post. Payment is collected by the postman on delivery.

(iii) Goods are delivered at customer's godown by transporter. Payment for transportation expenses are collected on delivery. Transporter should be asked to collect demand draft (or bankers' cheque). A cheque could be risky, it may be dishonoured.

(iv) Goods transported on as 'Self Basis' and documents are forwarded through bank. The customer can take delivery of the goods after making the payment to bank. Most likely transporters and carriers will usually not handle goods if payment has to be obtained from the consignee at the time of delivery.

If you have not received your payment, then the goods must be transported on 'Self Basis' and not in the name of the customer. If it is in the name of the customer, the ownership of the goods may not get transferred to him, but the customer gets the legal right to clear the goods. Further, he may or may not pay for the goods in his possession.

Suppose the goods are not cleared from the transporter because he no longer needs them, in such case, the seller will have to seek the customer's co-operation in advising the transporter to rebook the goods.

(e) *Ex-works (.......named place):* The price will include packing for despatch. The buyer must arrange for collection from the seller's premises and all carriage and insurance costs to his own premises. Ownership and risk pass from the seller when the buyer is notified that the goods are at his disposal. From a credit viewpoint , these are the best contract terms. So long as the buyers or his Representatives sign for the goods, there can be no problem about proof of delivery. No delivery period is involved so the credit period is clear-cut.

(f) *FOB (Free on Board):*

The principal obligations of the seller are :

(i) To place on board transport the specified goods
(ii) To pay all handling and transport charges
(iii) To cover all expenses incurred up to that point.
(iv) To notify the buyer to enable him to arrange insurance
(v) To bear any costs such as octroi charges, etc.

The principal obligations of the buyer are:

(i) To advise the seller in good time which transport is to be used
(ii) To ensure such transport plys in the same route
(iii) To bear any cost and charges from taking delivery to his premises and to pay for the goods as per agreed terms.
(iv) To provide substitute transport

Other points to note are:

(i) Buyer must arrange and pay for freight and insurance
(ii) Ownership of goods passes when goods are booked/ boarded for despatch

(g) *C.I.F. (Cost, Insurance, Freight (... named palce):* A CIF contract does not really relate to the sale of goods but a sale of documents relating to the goods. Delivery of transport documents is equivalent to delivery of the goods.

The principal obligations of the seller are:

(i) To book the goods for transportation
(ii) To pay the freight up to specified destination
(iii) To arrange appropriate insurance

(iv) To render these documents to the buyer so he may obtain delivery or recovery for the loss of the goods if the terms so provide.

The principal obligations of the buyer are:

(i) To bear all risks after goods have been handed over to the transporter

(ii) Take up the documents , if in order, and pay according to the contract terms

(iii) Pay even before arrival, receipt or examination of goods

(iv) Take delivery and bear the costs of unloading

(v) Bear the cost of demurrage

(h) *C&F (cost and freight) (... named place):* As for C and F, the arrangement of the insurance is an obligation of the buyer. Quotations may be FAS, FOB, CIF according to the extras to the base price, as under:

Ex-works cost
Packing } **FAS (Free Alongside Ship)**
Forwarding to loading port
Loading into hold of the ship } **FOB**
Insurance } **CIF**
Sea freight to port of destination

FOB price relates to the port of loading
CIF minus insurance is CF price

Clearing charges at the port of unloading (landing) and custom duty are added to CIF when the delivery is ex-Jetty. Loading charge is added to the ex-jetty price when the delivery is FOR (free on railways) in landing port.

(i) *FOR (free on railway) (... named place):* Freight to be paid by the supplier up to the booking station or destination station as the case may be. In case of FOR booking station, to avoid risk of damage or loss en-route, it may be of advantage to include the element of transit insurance by the seller in the FOR term as the supplier will be held responsible until the goods arrive in good condition at destination. It is advantageous to place all contracts on FOR destination term since the cost of delivery to the railways and for obtaining the relevant receipt are usually borne by the seller.

(j) Franco or door to door: This gives the seller the responsibility for all costs 'door to door'.

(k) Landed cost: According to convention, sea freight, excise duty, insurance, port and handling charges are debited to the cost of stores. Marine insurance covers the risk of losses during the voyage and not ship shade and shore. Landed cost of shipped stores is, therefore, inclusive of all these charges. Inland freight is collected under a separate head.

OTHER COMMERCIAL POINTS

Supplier's Performance

It will be advantageous for a credit manager to understand the various systems and records maintained by various government departments and large customers, where he is a supplier.

The Customer's Point of View

The various records maintained and the systems followed by them are described below:

(a) Registration of Suppliers

Intending suppliers apply for registration of their names. Registration is made after due check on their manufacturing, executive and financial capacities. The acceptance of standard conditions of contracts should be a condition precedent to registration. After proper scrutiny, a common list of registered and regular suppliers are maintained. The list is reviewed constantly and periodically and made up-to-date, keeping record of their performance.

(b) Performance Register

This register shows the contract placed with each supplier indicating also the performance against individual order. The performance should relate to

(i) Deliveries made in time.

(ii) Supplies delayed for reasons beyond supplier's control

(iii) Supplies delayed unreasonably.

(iv) L.D. imposed (liquidated damages)

(v) Stores supplied to specification.

(vi) Stores accepted under deviation

(vii) Heavy rejection in supplies offered.

The following terms are generally in use with regard to government department supplies.

(c) Indent

It generates the purchase operation and constitutes pre-purchase procedure. Indent is placed sufficiently in advance and according to time table.

(d) Tender

Tender is an offer for a sum for which a contractor will execute a work or make a supply. Printed forms are often used for the purpose of obtaining offers in reply to invitation of tenders. A tender is an offer which may or may not be accepted.

(e) Earnest Money

Tender documents, inter alia, do state the amount of earnest money to accompany each tender. Earnest money is a fixed sum which may be 2% of the estimated value. Contractors who have to make fixed earnest money deposit may do so in cash with the cashier or in any of the following forms, pledged in the name of the Accounts Officer: deposit receipt, pay order, demand draft or guarantee bond of the nationalised bank of India or treasury or Reserve Bank challan. (Bank undertake full responsibility to indemnify the buyer in case of default).

Government securities (stock certificate, bearer bond, promissory note, etc.) are not accepted.

Earnest money is refunded to unsuccessful tenderers. In case of successful tenderer, earnest money, free of interest, may constitute the security deposit. In the event of the tenderer receiving the contract and failing to furnish the required security within the stipulated period, he may still supply the goods. However, the payment against such supply is made only after security deposit money is recovered.

(f) Security Deposit

It is taken for the fulfillment of the contract. While earnest money cannot be a substitute for indemnity bond, security deposit may be, in the form of cash deposit or bank guarantee. If the contractor agrees for a deduction of a part of his payment against running bills to build up his security deposit, this may be say ... 5% of the tendered value. There may not be any need to ask for security deposit from a supplier already registered for a store. Earnest money deposit and security deposit for fulfillment of a contract may be waived by competent authority, should the circumstance so warrant. Pricing of tender papers, earnest money and security deposit are inhibitions to eliminate superfluous tenderers, indemnity bond or security deposit is no match to balance the loss for non-delivery by the contractor. The security deposit should be refunded by the paying authority within 30 days of receipt of no-demand-certificate. This NDC is issued by consignee or end user, on the fulfillment of the contract.

(g) Customs Duty

A government raises revenues by levying taxes on goods. The taxes are in the form of custom duties or excise duties.

Custom duties are levied upon the goods which enter into or pass out of a country. That is, the custom duties are the duties which are levied upon imports and exports. Such duties may also be termed as import duties or export duties. The subject of custom duties can also be studied from any standard textbook.

(h) Excise Duty

Unlike custom duties which are levied on goods when they enter or leave the country, excise duties are levied on goods which are manufactured or produced within the country itself. Excise duties are usually levied at the point of manufacture though there are several instances in which they are levied at the point of sale rather than at the point of manufacture. Like customs duties, excise duties can either be 'ad-valorem' or 'specific'.

(i) Sales Tax and Income Tax Certificate

Tender is invited inclusive of sales tax or other local taxes. Central sales tax is charged by Union Government and local sales tax by State Government, the rate of which varies from state to state. Sales tax is realised by the seller. Inter state sales are liable to be taxed under the CS Tax Act. The claims on sales tax, etc. are admitted only if the charge is legally leviable. Tenders should be accompanied by valid income-tax clearance certificate.

(j) Force Majeure

Offers are often subject to force majeure clause by which it is meant, caused beyond reasonable control, such as, war, invasion, civil disobedience, government orders or restrictions, strikes, lock-outs, fire, earthquake, flood, accident. A strong force majeure clause is essential in a contract to protect the supplier from buyer against such contigencies. The seller should accept orders subject to force majeure clause.

(k) Rate Contract

It is a contract under which during the period of its currency, the contractor engages to supply materials, on demand, irrespective of quantity at fixed unit rates or prices within a given period of the receipt of such demand.(eg. DGS & D rate contract)

(l) Liquidated Damages

It means an agreed sum of money is payable by a party responsible for breach of contract to the second party for ascertained damages arising from the non-fulfilment of the contract.

In most sales contracts, the time for and date of delivery are considered as the essence of the contracts. If a contractor fails to supply the material at the time and rate as stipulated in the order, then the purchaser, under the provisions of the standard conditions of the contract shall have the right to recover liquidated damages. The express consent of the supplier to such provision should be obtained so that it constitutes a proper pre-estimate of damages in case of delay in supplies. The levy of LD may vary from customer to customer. The levy is usually charged on the amount before taxes and duties.

Alternatively, the purchaser shall have the option to purchase same quantity of the same material or its nearest substitute from elsewhere, or even cancel the order at the 'risk' and on account of the contractor, and the contractor shall be liable to pay for any loss, thus sustained by the purchaser. The indentor (or user) may be consulted to ascertain, if any loss has occurred for the failure of the contract or to deliver material in time.

Comparatively small delays may sometimes be condoned with a warning and in the case of habitual defaulters, the buyer may consider removal of their names from the approved list of the contractors for a specified period or indefinitely. If fresh tender is called for risk purchase item, the defaulting firm should also be given chance to quote.

The date of delivery is the date on which delivery is actually effected.

(m) Inspection

The order will specify the place of inspection, whether at seller's premises before despatch of goods or after the goods have been received at buyer's premises.

The function of inspection in stores receiving section is to determine what it is and what it does. The operation consists of comparing a product with accepted specification and/or other recognised standards. Such inspection is only for screening products that conform to specification from those which do not conform.

(n) Warranty

A supplier is also expected to give an implied undertaking that certain fact regarding the subject matter of a sale contract is presently true or will be true. The usual practice is to have it printed on organization's letter heads. A 'warranty' is different from 'guarantee' which implies the promise of performance.

By knowing the buyer's or customers point of view discussed here, a seller will be able to make the transactions more smoothly.

FIVE

Will They Pay?
They Will, If ...

'In touching money we touch the keystone of character.'
—John Ruskin

CREDIT RATINGS: KNOW YOUR POTENTIAL CUSTOMERS

Failure of debtors to pay in reasonable time can explain a need for increased working capital. Close checks should be maintained on bad and doubtful debts and an index maintained showing the performance of debtors in terms of debts in relation to average daily sales. It must be appreciated, however, that it may be dangerous to press debtors too much or the company may lose goodwill. Thus a safe measure is in assessing whether the potential customer is financially sound and will pay in time. Thus a company must do risk analysis and categorises its customers as A, B, C or D class and set credit limits appropriately.

Setting credit limit means: firstly, maximum amount a customer will be allowed to buy on credit and secondly, period or days the customer will be allowed to settle this amount in full.

However, an ABC analysis of customers does not mean that an A-class customer enjoys more amount than a B-class customer and likewise does not mean that a B-class customer enjoys more than that of C-class. To be more specific a B-class customer may enjoy better sales amount compared to A-class customer but certainly at a very short term of payment or against hypothecated security or Bank Guarantee.

He keeps on changing his hats . . .
Will he pay the amount . . .?
Will he pay on time ??
Will he . . . ???
Won't he ?

GDOC Categorization

Customers may be categorized into following:

(a) Government department and semi-government organization.
(b) Dealer (includes distributor, wholesaler, retailer and selling agents).
(c) OEM, other manufacturer and end user.
(d) Consumers or actual users of the goods or services.

Government Department and Semi-government Organization

These type of customers are always considered as A-class customers. If you have complied with all the formalities in the order, then your money will surely come, except when such department runs out of funds and this could be a temporary problem. If one is not able to comply with all the conditions of the order, then precaution should be taken to avoid such point, at the stage of submitting quotation or tender, especially while acknowledging the order. Besides government departments provisionally accept the tender with a firm delivery date. The final order comes only after acceptance of changes in design, technical specification, etc. The stages between submission of drawing and approval of design may prolong for a considerable period. The credit manager should get involved from the very first stage and if he feels that it will be difficult to deliver the goods before the stipulated date, he should make all efforts to get the delivery date amended; otherwise, when the department ultimately makes the payment, it may carry a big cut towards liquidated damages for delayed delivery.

Dealers or Traders

These include distributors, wholesalers, retailers and dealers and they may fall into any category A, B or C class depending upon their financial status, market goodwill, paying habit, etc. Dealers are mostly selected by calling the interested parties through advertisement or recommended by trade or if they personally approach the company.

Through whichever mode they show their interest in becoming dealer, they should be selected keeping the following points in mind:

(i) The ability and the willingness of the dealer to handle the product.
(ii) Credit and market standing of the potential dealer.
(iii) Knowledge about the product characteristics and its market.
(iv) Ability to maintain sufficient stocks of the product.
(v) Capacity to secure (improve) business.
(vi) Ability to cover the territory or areas over which goods have to be sold.
(vii) Other products dealt with by the dealer—whether they are allied products or competitive ones.
(viii) Ability to arrange for repair and maintenance of the products, if need be.
(ix) Willingness to co-operate with the manufacturer in maintaining price.
(x) Willingness to share advertising cost.
(xi) Willingness to adhere to principal's payment terms.
(xii) Willingness to keep deposit of a certain sum.
(xiii) Are they credit worthy.

OEM and Other Manufacturers

Many companies ask the potential customers to fill up a contract form or questionnaire. After studying the form/questionnaire, the credit manager will try to understand the financial capacity, the character, the market standing of the customer. He will immediately write to the referees (provided by the potential customer) asking about the nature of their dealing, the credit enjoyed, the paying habit and the period for which they are transacting with the potential customer. These information become the basis for the credit manager to decide the credit amount to be allowed, period of credit, the terms of payment and the mode of payment that has to be agreed upon with his potential customer.

One of the international companies requests its potential dealers and big customers to fill up this type of form:

Form 5.1

Credit Control Questionnaire (Dealer)

1. Name of the Company/Firm:
2. Location of Business/Telephone/Telex:
3. Commercial Registration No: Permanent I-Tax No:
4. C.S.Tax No: Local S.Tax No:
5. Name & Address of Two Major Partners/Owner(s)/Directors:

Sl. No.	Names	Address	Specimen Signature
1.	____________	____________	
	____________	____________	
	____________	____________	____________
2.	____________	____________	
	____________	____________	
	____________	____________	____________

6. Location of Stores(s)/Telephone/Telex:
7. Authorised Person(s) to be Contacted at Stores(to accept delivery)
   1.
   2.
8. Authorised Person(s) Responsible for Placing Purchase Order:

1.	Designation:	S.Sign.:
2.	Designation:	S.Sign.:
3.	Designation:	S.Sign.:

9. Authorised Cheques Signatories: (Single or Jointly)

Sl. No.	Names	Designation	Specimen Signature
1.	____________	____________	____________
2.	____________	____________	____________
3.	____________	____________	____________

10. Names & Address of Bank(s) Account No.
    1.
    2.
    3.
11. Trade Reference(s)—(Names & Address)
    1.
    2.
    3.

12. State Briefly—Equity Distribution (composition) :-
    Capital:
    (i) Paid up Rs (ii) Loan Capital Rs
    Working Rs ________________
    Total Rs ________________

13. Trading Fields—Major Products BRANDS Handled:
    1.
    2.
    3.
    4.
    5.

14. Trading Methods:
    Distribution via Wholesale

Direct to Retail	:	%
Direct Indent	:	%
Sales Contract	:	%
Indent Contract	:	%
Mail Order	:	%
Others	:	%

15. Sales Turnover:
    Last Year in Rs:
    Current Year Till Date in Rs:

16. No. of Staff :
    No. of Sales Staff :
    Salesmen Remuneration Basis :

17. Sales Potential of Product(s)— Quantity Amount
    1.
    2.
    3.
    4.
    5.

18. Trade Terms Allowed by You (Yes/No)
    Cash Discounts :
    Volume Discounts :
    Promotional Discounts :
    Other Terms :

19. Working Margins Normally Achieved:

	Actual	Example
Gross Margin	%	20%
(state if calculated on Cost of Sales)		
Overheads	%	10%
Promotional Expenses	%	1%
Commission Paid	%	2%
Other Outgoings	%	1%
Net Margin	%	6%

20. Financial:
    Total Asset - Fixed: Rs Current: Rs
    Total Liabilities - Long Term: Rs Current: Rs
    Average Stock Held Per Month : Rs
    Average Debtor Per Month : Rs
21. Payment Terms (Mode of Payment):
22. Credit Limit Required:
    Period : Days
    Amount : Rs
23. Source of Funds: (Please Tick)
    1. Sales Collection _____ 2. Bank Overdraft _____ 3. Bank Reserve _____
    4. Bank Cash Credit _____ 5. Others (please state) _____
24. We the undersigned, undertake to pay singly/jointly any DEBT due to the K.V.T. India Limited on DUE DATE.
    1. ______________________ Signature 2. ______________________
    Designation (With Company's Seal)
    1. ______________________ Witness 2. ______________________
25. Sales Engineer's/Officer's Recommendation for Discount:
    Signature: ____________
26. Divisional Product Manager's Approval:
    (with reference to product knowledge
    reputation, experience, ability etc.) Signature: ____________
27. Credit Controller's Approval—Signature
    (after verification of financial, trade & bank references)
28. (i) MODE OF PAYMENT:
    (ii) Any Security Deposit/Bank Guarantee/Advance:

29.

Amount	Period	Discount %	Computer Code

General Manager's Approval – Signature ________________

Unrealistic credit can mean unending problems.

Approving a credit limit and credit period of a customer is a very tricky affair. In spite of his balance sheet analysis, trade references or bank reference, it will be very difficult to understand the potential customer's paying habit. A detailed discussion is given in the last part of this chapter.

ABCD Categorization

Categorizing customers into A, B, C, or D grade will differ in policy from company to company. Further, this has to be reviewed periodically and if there is a change in the paying habit, then the category of such customers has to be changed accordingly.

A power transmission manufacturing company categorizes its customers in the following lines.

A Grade: The buying policy of many consumers is to purchase the goods from manufacturers and they should be retained. Consumers whose yearly requirement orders are received and offtake is high, plus payments are received in time fall into A grade. They enjoy credit facilities.

B Grade: Consumers who do not put yearly order will yet fall into B-grade if their offtake is high and payments are received in time. They enjoy credit facilities.

C Grade: Consumers whose offtake is medium or low, collect material promptly and make payments in time, fall into C grade. They may enjoy credit facilities.

D Grade: Consumers who habitually delay or postpone and those who are avoiding making payments are D grade. They may not enjoy credit facilities.

Periodically the parties (consumers) accounts are reviewed by the concerned CM/Sales manager and the grades are changed (updated) on the basis of their performance in the last period.

However Dr Atthreya suggests to categorize the customers as follows:

- All those customers who settle account before time are A-Class customers
- Those who pay in time are B-Class
- Those who pay on reminding are C-Class

Grading of a customer, setting up the credit limit in monetary term and credit period of a new customer is generally set after evaluating him in one, two or more of the following ways:

(a) By asking for trade reference and bank reference and checking them.
(b) Salesman report
(c) Trade journal and competitor's opinion
(d) D.G.S & D. Registration
(e) CRISIL
(f) Credit visits

If required indepth information can be gathered by:

(a) Customers balance sheet analysis
(b) Checking with company registry
(c) Press reports
(d) Ledger history
(e) Other 3 "C"s of credit

CREDIT PROCEDURE

The following is a step-by-step method for how obtaining credit information from an applicant, evaluating the information, and assigning the credit line or approving a first order:

1. A request for credit account is received from a salesman or directly from a customer.
2. Credit department acknowledges the request.
3. Sends the credit applicant a credit control questionnaire and includes a self-addressed, stamped envelope, and also asks for:
   (a) current audited balance sheet.
   (b) contact credit references (from data on the credit control questionnaire) by telephone or letter. One must be to the applicants banker and other/s to trade reference.
4. Information gathered from the applicants' references (suppliers and bankers) to be entered on the computer in credit control questionnaire form.

5. Information is consolidated and refined. The rupees total or requested credit line is compared in line with the experience of the supplier, banker, and balance sheet. If the supplier and banker experience continues to be good and is at or above the high credit amount you are being asked to carry, then the account should qualify for the requested credit line. If the accumulated data indicates slow-pay account with trade payments becoming increasingly slower, this could be sliding into serious trouble. This account should not be sold on credit terms.
6. The customer should be sent a letter stating that you have approved a credit line for the requested amount or a lower amount. If the amount is lower than the amount that was requested, your explanation should not reflect unfavourably on the new customer. Cite the fact that your company is a grantor of minimum credit amounts until you have accumulated more experience with the company. Mention that you feel sure that the customer company is equally prudent in its approach to credit matters; express your appreciation for the opportunity to be of service, and close with the statement that you are available to help if there is ever a problem.

Documents and Guarantees

Trade and Bank Reference

It is a traditional method of credit checking. This is not so reliable because it is often found that the referees do not give a bad report in most of the cases as the company will quote only those suppliers with whom the dealings are good.

To open a new account the request is to be made to the credit department through various sources. The salesman may make his request to the credit department in the following (form) manner:

The stress on 'Terms and Condition'

The saying goes: In business, when you are selling goods for money, one hand does not believe the other hand.

Form 5.2

Before an Order is Received

To: Credit Dept. Date:
From: Salesman

1a. ADVICE OF NEW CUSTOMER

The following firm is interested to place/has placed an inquiry/order with us:

Trade & bank references obtained:

1.
2.
3.

Likely monthly level of purchases Rs..........
Existing suppliers :
Reputation :

Payment terms sought (if different from net x days):

Other information :

Signature

The next letter (form) is sent by a potential customer. Usually this readymade form is carried by a travelling salesman.

Form 5.3

Attention: Credit Department

I / We request you to open a credit account in the name of :

I / We give below the names and addresses of referees of whom the customary enquiries may be made.

I / We note that the payment terms are net x days from date of the invoice and agree to pay in accordance with these terms.

Expected maximum amount of credit required:

Rs.........total/month (delete whichever is not appropriate)

Signature....................... Designation.....................

Banker's name & address:

Trade referees:

1. Name Address:

2. Name Address:

N.B. Referees should be able to speak for credit figures comparable with that indicated above.

Form 5.4

Reply from Credit Department to Customer

Dear Sir,

We thank you for your recent order, number _____________ of

value Rs._______________

To avoid any unnecessary delay, this order is being processed immediately on our standard terms of ....

So that we can handle future orders on credit terms we ask you to complete the attached form and return it to us along with a copy of your current / latest balance sheet.

Our Conditions of Sale are printed on the reverse of this letter. Would you please note that all cheques should be made payable to ____________ and sent to the following address:

____

____

Thank you for your co-operation.

Yours faithfully,

If the request is recommended by your own salesman then the report format should also include:

1. The character and competence of the management of the potential customer.
2. The level of activity and the general impression obtained from factory and office.
3. The names of other suppliers for useful contacts
4. Details of major customers of the client (it is very important to know on whom he depends, the character of his clients)
5. The anticipated level of business

The credit manager must check up all these references letter and a letter for such purpose could be as below:

Form 5.5

Request for Trade Reference: (Confidential)

Dear Sir,

Messrs. XYZ & Company of Bombay wish to open an account with us and have given us your name as a reference. We should be grateful if you would supply us with whatever information you can about the firm's general standing.

To save your time, we enclose a ready-to-reply form.

Also, we enclose a stamped, self-addressed envelope and shall be only too glad to render you a similar service should the need arise. It is hardly necessary to add that any information you supply will be treated in strict confidence.

Thanking you,

Yours faithfully,

Form 5.6

Ready-to-reply Reference Form

1. How long have you known this firm? ....months / .... years / Many years

2. How much credit do you normally allow? Rs...................

3. What are your payment terms? Pro-forma/ Monthly/ ....days

4. Are payments generally made to your satisfaction? To terms / Up to one month late / More than 1 month late / Very slow / irregular

5. In your opinion, are they likely to be reliable for credit upto Rs...........

6. Any other relevant information will be appreciated :

The above information is given in strict confidence and without responsibility on my / our part.

Date............. Signed:.................

Bank references are more reliable than trade references but not satisfactory procedures for granting credit because again the bank will prefer to safeguard his client's interest. The credit manager should check the bank reference.

Next letter is to your own banker and a reply is generally received as below.

Form 5.7

Request for Bank Reference: (Confidential)

To,
The Branch Manager,
International Bank ,
Fort Branch.

Dear Sir,

We have received an order for Rs........ from Messrs. XYZ & Company, address .... or Messrs XYZ & Company, address.......wishes to open an account with us. They ask for credit and have given the Bank of Baroda, Dadar Branch as a reference.

Would you be good enough to make enquiries and let us know whether the reputation and financial standing of this firm justify a credit of the above amount. or.... justify a credit of Rs...........

Thanking you,

Yours sincerely,

Form 5.8

Reply from Bank

From : International Bank,
Fort Branch

PRIVATE & CONFIDENTIAL

To : M/s. Williams India Ltd.,
Bombay

Your inquiry of 14.3.92 Ref......

Please note that the enclosed information is communicated to you in the strictest confidence for your private use only and is not to be imparted to others.

It is given without responsibility or guarantee on the part of this Bank or any of its officers.

For International Bank,

Manager
Fort Branch.
Encl: a/a

Encl: 1

Another Reply from Bank

M/s. Tulsidas Radios:

We are informed:

"The above Party is a Partnership Firm, retailers in Electronic & Electrical goods, banking with us since 1978 and presently enjoying cash credit facility. The partners are reported to be honest and straight forward, with moderate means, having satisfactory dealings."

Encl: 2

Another Reply from Bank

M/s. Samson Enterprises

We are informed:

A/c. Partnership concern.

Name of partners: 1) James Samson
2) Frederick Samson

Maintaining normal Current account with us since 1984 not enjoying credit facilities with us.

Encl: 3

Another Reply from Bank

M/s. Shivdas Exporters

We are informed:

"Constitution: Partnership.
Partners: Mr. Jain Shivdas
Mr. Binani Shivdas

Nature of Account: Cash Credit

Business/Company Established/Incorporated on 17/10/97

Means of Proprietor: Moderate to Fair.

Experience as to their dealings: Satisfactory . They are enjoying credit facility with us.

Encl: 4

Another Reply from Bank

M/s. Zakaria Traders

We are informed:

"Constitution: Partnership

Name of the partners: Smt. Khaleda Zakaria
Miss Aniza Zakaria

Cash Credit allowed since last seven months.

Encl: 5

Another Reply from Bank

M/s. Ibrahim Electronics

We are informed:

"Constitution: Partnership.

Proprietor: Mr. Abdullah Karim
Mr. Ismail Karim

Nature of Account: Current

Banking since: 4/12 Year: 1984

Business/Company Established/Incorporated on: 4/12/1984

Nature of business activity: Electronic shop

Experience as to their dealings: Satisfactory

Encl: 6

Another Reply from Bank

M/s. Premlal Traders

We are informed:

"The subject of your inquiry is a partnership firm.

Partners: Mr. Vasant Premlal
Mr. Ganesh Premlal

Sales/Service of typewriters, televisions, fans and steel/aluminium furnitures etc. Partners are respectable persons. The firm maintains account with our Thane Branch since 22.2.83 and their dealings with us are good. They are enjoying O/D against FDR.

With experience, one will know how to interpret such information. Bank reference is usually requested at the same time as trade reference. The approach to the client's bank should be made through one's own banker.

Trade and Competitor's Opinion

With so many trade associations, it is an easy source of inquiry information. The credit manager may get information from trade association, if he is a member. Where possible interchange of information should be developed with other firms in the industry, who may or may not be direct competitors. The real value lies in providing an early warning system about bad payers, in safeguarding each other against potential bad debts and in helping one another on matters of fact, such as change in the finance director, change in invoice passing procedures, change in financial status etc.

DGS & D Registration

The credit manager must also find out whether the prospective customer is registered with DGS&D. All firms dealing in stores purchased by DGS&D, whether they are in India or abroad, are eligible for registration.

The bonafides of the supplier including the equipment, plant and machinery, technical capacity and funds position are verified partly through enquiries on the spot by the DGS&D officers. The vendors are also rated on the basis of delivery, quality, price and reliability. Thus, registration with DGS&D raises the firms' standing in business not only with Government departments but also with foreign firms and establishments.

CRISIL

Credit party information can be also obtained from CRISIL or Credit Information and Services of India Limited. The credit ratings are based on the current information, provided to CRISIL by the borrowing company or obtained by CRISIL from sources it considers reliable. In determining ratings, CRISIL will analyse various aspects like business efficiency, financial efficiency, management's efficiency concerning the borrowing company.

CRISIL is shortly starting information services for the corporate sector. Such services will help the credit manager to assess the credit worthiness of a prospective customer.

CRISIL advertisement appeared in *The Times of India* describes the points they consider while evaluating a company:

Answer all these questions before investing or just look at a CRISIL rating:

- What is the company's business?
- What are the key success factors in the industry?
- What is the industry growth rate?
- Who are the players in the industry?
- What is the government's policy towards the industry?
- Is there cyclicality? Seasonality?
- Is the industry import intensive?
- What is the degree of competition in the industry?
- Is it vulnerable to imports?
- What is the rate of technological change?
- Is there an international competitive advantage?
- What are the entry barriers?
- What is the company's product?
- What is its market position?
- What factors determine success in the marketplace?
- Who is the industry leader?
- What is the market size?
- What is the company's market share?
- What is the pricing policy?
- How is the product positioned?
- What are the industry credit norms?
- How efficient are collection systems?
- What is the customer's bargaining power?
- What is the degree of customer loyalty?
- Is there a diversified customer base?
- What are the prospects in the marketplace?
- What is the company's cost structure?
- What is the industry cost structure?
- Who is the technological leader?
- How important is R & D?
- What is the minimum economic size?
- Is the company technologically competitive?
- What are the key raw materials?
- What is the supplier's negotiating power?
- What is the demand-supply scenario for raw materials?

- How important is vertical integration?
- Do material prices fluctuate widely?
- What are industrial relations like?
- How powerful are the unions?
- Is there a history of labour strife?
- Is the company overmanned?
- What is the age of facilities?
- What is the safety record?
- What is the level of overheads?
- What is the capacity utilisation?
- What are the inventory management policies?
- How capital intensive is the industry?
- What are the effluent treatment facilities?
- Who owns the company?
- Who runs the company?
- What is the promoter's track record?
- What is the management's attitude towards risk?
- How are group companies performing?
- What are the intra-group transactions?
- Are there planning and control systems?
- What is the attitude towards shareholders?
- What is the tax policy?
- Is succession decided?
- What is the attitude towards debt?
- What are the management's goals, philosophy and strategies?
- Is the management responsive to environmental change?
- What is the past financial performance?
- What is the existing financial position?
- Is the profitability steady?
- What are the performance trends?
- Is the ploughback adequate?
- Are accounting policies changed?
- Are disclosure standards fair?
- What is the interest coverage?
- What is the capital structure?

Old proverb: Prevention is better than cure.

Someone has to pay for extended credit periods.

Don't let it be you.

Choose your customer carefully.

Get rid of dead-beat customers!

Bad debt needs to be paid for—by you!

- Are treasury operations tight?
- What is the liquidity position?
- What is the company's financial flexibility?
- What is the dividend policy?
- How good is Forex management?
- What is the return on capital? On sales?
- Is the capital structure right?
- Can finance costs be reduced?
- Does the share price fluctuate?
- What is the long term earnings potential?
- Can the company be taken over?
- How are inventories valued?
- What is the basis of revenue recognition?
- Are expenses being capitalised?

Note: With one credit rating agency's questionnaire we are only trying to emphasize that, how important it is to refer to Credit Agency's Report.
Courtesy: With permission of CRISIL

Credit Visit

All the sources of information discussed so far should be explored. Since to rely on one or two sources alone carries the risk that it may be out of date or misinformation, decision based on such information alone may damage credit manager's reputation.

Very often time is too short and a decision has to be made within a day. If the amount involved is well within the rating, this can often be sufficient to approve the order but if the volume of business is quite high, then credit manager should exercise care in taking decision.

The credit manager should not make his final decision until he has visited the prospective buyer. A joint visit with the sales manager is a good idea because the buyer is at once made aware of the sales/credit relationship. During this visit the credit manager tries to get a reply to the following questions.

- Company organization and family tree?
- Are the directors or managers experienced people?
- Who has the decision making or purchasing power?

- What is their purchasing policy?
- Do they have properly thought out marketing and production plans?
- What is the attitude of the staff to the management?
- Respectful and co-operative or fearful and downtrodden?
- Is the organization's product well established and in demand?
- Are the plant and equipment in good condition?
- Who are the principal customers?
- Does the accounting system operate efficiently?
- Is information up-to-date and immediately available?
- What is their opinion about our company?

In short, the purpose of credit visit is to enable the credit manager develop a fair credit decision.

Sometimes, the credit decision may not be favourable and in such cases the alternative arrangement would be asking for security deposit or bank guarantee. In India it is most common to ask for security deposit for an amount equal to risk involved. This arrangement is mutually beneficial especially in case of a dealer.

In depth assessing is needed when the size of the credit decision demands fuller investigation.

Balance Sheet

The most important source of detailed information is the annual balance sheet.

Balance sheet is a statement of the company's affairs. However, if the accounts were examined, the day they were completed, this would usually be at least four to six months after the financial year; and during this time the company's financial position may have drastically changed because it is just as easy for a profitable company to become insolvent as an unprofitable one. Further while studying the balance sheet, opinion should not be formed based on one year figures. One must study the trend with at least three year figures. If possible, cash-flow should be studied for several months. One should always be aware of distortions caused by inter-company transactions.

Above all, company's performance should be related to the industry in which it operates. (Inter company performances are regularly published in different trade magazines).

In India, there are still companies who resent being asked for their accounts and who refuse on the grounds of privacy or without giving any reason. On the other hand, some companies respond positively. They even allow to see management accounts made up to previous month end. Whenever accounts are produced for examination, it is essential that confidence is respected and such accounts should be kept in safe custody and they should not pass through many hands.

There are many ways of reading a balance sheet, depending on the view point of the reader. The credit manager tries to assess the 'ability to pay in time' of the prospect in the context of a long-term relationship through ratio analysis. There are four principal aspects of a company's financial standing on which a credit manager should concentrate.

1. Solvency
2. Asset Management
3. Profitability
4. Capital Strength

Solvency

Solvency means the ability of a company to meet its current debts i.e. those due within one year of balance sheet date, from its current assets (those capable of being turned into cash within one year). The obvious first test of solvency is to compare one with the other. This is known as the current ratio.

Solvency ratio/s should help the credit manager to get answers to three basic questions about customer's firm:

- Is there enough cash, or expected cash, to meet the needs of the firm for a given period of time?
- Is there enough cash, or expected cash, to cope with the unexpected events?
- Is there enough cash, or expected cash, to take advantage of unforeseen opportunities?

$$\frac{\text{Current Assets}}{\text{Current Liabilities}}$$

The traditional good ratio is 2:1 as is seen in example below:

ABC & Co. Ltd.

(Rs in lakh)

Current Assets	
Stocks	Rs 500
Debtors	Rs 620
Cash	Rs 50
Total current assets	Rs 1170
Less: Current Liabilities	
Creditors	Rs 380
Taxation	Rs 200
Net Current Assets	Rs 590

The main danger in relying on this ratio as the key to solvency is the inclusion of stocks. A high-stock figure may include slow moving or obsolete items that may never be sold. To overcome this problem, another ratio is calculated—the quick ratio or 'acid test'. By removing stock from the above formula, the quick ratio concentrates on the really liquid assets, where values are fairly certain. It helps to answer the question, "If all sales revenues should disappear, could the business meet its current obligations with the readily convertible 'quick funds on hand?"

$$\frac{\text{Current Assets Less Stocks}}{\text{Current Liabilities}}$$

A 1:1 ratio used to be regarded as a necessary sign of liquidity but many companies have proved capable of surviving on far thinner ratios than this. It is advisable to review the situation quarterly.

Asset Management

(i) Debtors Ratio
(ii) Stock Turn Over

Debtors ratio: The quality of debtors as a current asset should also be checked. Providing that the turnover figures are available, the collection period can be calculated to give an idea of the rate of cash-flow.

$$\text{Collection Period in Days} = \frac{\text{Debtors} \times 365}{\text{Sales}}$$

If receivables are being turned over only three or four times a year (90–120 days) compared to an industry average of say 65–70 days, this points to a lack of credit control. The actual ratios are less important than the trend over a period of years. If this can be compared with the average for the industry, the analysis becomes more valuable and meaningful.

Stock turnover ratio: Stock is a critical area for businesses. It can account for more than half of many small manufacturing and retailing firm's total asset investment and for most firms outside the service segment. It can account for half the current assets. Also, stock is very sensitive to changes in business activity within the overall economy. The industry, or the individual firms stock is also costly to carry and is a risky asset if you are in a business that is exposed to frequent obsolescence or style changes.

$$\text{Stock Turn Over} = \frac{\text{Cost of Goods Sold}}{\text{Stock}}$$

Cost of goods sold is the expense item which includes the purchase price of the stock in a retail business or total cost of goods for sale in manufacturing firm (raw materials, labour and overhead). Stock is reflected in value terms on the balance sheet.

Stock turnover, as a ratio, shows how fast your stock or merchandise is moving, i.e. how productively this asset is being employed.

Stock management can be evaluated on the basis of number of times the stock is turned over during a period, or by how many days stock the firm maintains at a given point of time. The approach is same with raw- materials, work in progress and finished goods.

Profitability

A business is always started with the intention of making profit and if it is not making profit it will ultimately cease trading. In business a company cannot stand still except for very short periods and the credit analyst must look out for signs of healthy growth or of decline. As in all ratios, trends are all important and will make sense if put into right context. If company has falling profit record over a five years period when most companies in that industry were increasing their profits, there is evidently something wrong.

The credit manager should seek reply to these basic questions:

- Is the company making enough money?
- Is the owner's return satisfactory and whether it is as per industry standard?

The most commonly used measure of profitability is:

$$\frac{\text{Profit}}{\text{Net Assets}}$$

which can be calculated from the following ratio also

$$\frac{\text{Profit}}{\text{Sales}} \times \frac{\text{Sales}}{\text{Net Assets}} = \frac{\text{Profit}}{\text{Net Assets}}$$

These terms do not make balance sheet interpretation any easier but the underlying concept is the real value of the company—expressed either as a source of funds (capital employed) or as the use of those funds (net assets). How effectively the assets are being employed is measured by comparing the profit to net assets. It will be meaningless if profit ratios are not compared from year to year within the industry in question.

Capital Strength

This third aspect of a company's finances are concerned with the ratio of risk capital (equity) to loan capital or debt to net worth. Many of the companies being formed will have a very high debt ratio—also known as being highly geared. Loan from directors frequently appear in the accounts of these companies, far outweighing the equity capital. Under the circumstances the credit manager must pose a number of questions before making a major credit decision.

- Why do the owners not risk more of their own money?
- Are the loans secured on the company's assets?

- Is there a danger to a highly geared company to run into liquidity crisis. Trade creditors then may be receiving fraction of their debts after the holders of secured loans have obtained their full share.

The ratio of debts to equity shows how much debt a firm has relative to its net worth or equity. To a credit manager, this ratio is an indication of a company's ability to withstand adversity and meet its short and long term debts obligations ; lower the debt ratio the better (should not be more than 2:1 or 3:1 in exceptional cases). It will depend on the product he sales and how long he is in business.

$$\text{Debt Ratio} = \frac{\text{Total Liabilities}}{\text{Total Owner Equity}}$$

$$= \frac{\text{Current Liabilities} + \text{Long Term Debit}}{\text{Share Capital} + \text{Preference Shares} + \text{Retained Earnings}}$$

Other than the above key ratios the cerdit manager may study the net profit to net sales, and net sales to working capital, to understand how efficiently the business is running. There are others but detailed balance sheet analysis could be very time consuming and a credit manager has to strike a balance between the need for quick decision and the desirability of a detailed analysis. Further, a ratio analysis does not provide answers. It can be an indication and will guide the credit manager to find out the strengths and weaknesses of the potential customers.

In other words, the credit manager should try to seek evidence of historical trends to three main questions:

- Does the prospect seem capable of paying for the goods or the services the company wishes to supply?
- Does the prospect likely to continue in business long enough to justify whatever costs have to be incurred in making a supply e.g. tooling, distribution or marketing?
- In the event of a crisis, are the unsecured creditors reasonably well placed?

Registrar of Companies

This office has to be approached for a specific purpose, for example, if the prospect refuses to discuss its annual accounts or the annual accounts pertaining to 3 or 4 years old. Another reason for approaching the company registry could be that one of these days your company may decide to recover the amount through litigation and file winding up petition.

Table 5.1: Balance Sheet and Profit and Loss—General

Name of Company			
Sources & application of funds	Year ended	Year ended	Year ended
Item no.			
Net assets employed			
1 Fixed assets			
2 Investments			
	____	____	____
	____	____	____
3 Stock & work-in-progress			
4 Debtors			
5 Other			
	____	____	____
6 Total current assets			
	____	____	____
7 Creditors			
8 Bank overdraft			
9 Other			
	____	____	____
10 Total current liabilities			
	____	____	____
11 Net current assets			
	____	____	____
12 Net assets			
	____	____	____
Sources of finance			
13 Issued capital			
14 Reserves			
	____	____	____
15 Total shareholders' fund			
16 Loan capital			
17 Other			
	____	____	____
18 Total capital employed			
	____	____	____

Profit and loss account

19 Sales	____	____	____
20 Purchases	____	____	____
21 Trading profit	____	____	____
22 Interest paid	____	____	____
23 Profit before tax	____	____	____
24 Profit after tax	____	____	____
25 Profit retained in the business	____	____	____

Table 5.2: Balance Sheet Analysis—General

Name of Company

Key ratio	Method of calculation*	Year ended	Year ended	Year ended
Current	6/10			
Quick	(6–3) /10			
Coverage of current debt	10 as % of 12			
Profit on sales	23 as % of 19			
Assets turnover	19/12			
Return on capital employed	23 as % 0f 18			
Collection period in days	(4/19) /365			
Stock turnover in days	(3/20) /365 or (3/19) /365			
Working capital turnover	19/11			
Debt ratio	16 as % of 15			

–NOTES

1 Liquidity is good/bad ; improving/steady/worsening.

2 Profitability is improving/steady/worsening.

3 Use of assets are vigorous/slow ; improving/steady/worsening.

4 Debt ratio is rising/steady/dropping.

–

* The numbers in this column refer to the item numbers eg.1. Current ratio is equal to item 6 / item 10

Table 5.3: Balance Sheet and Profit and Loss Summary—An Example

Name of Company	Case Study		
Sources and application of funds	Year ended	Year ended	Year ended
Item no.			
Net assets employed			
1 Fixed assets	2507	3360	3407
2 Investments	67	83	128
	2674	3443	3535
3 Stock & work-in-progress	4555	6320	7802
4 Debtors	1817	4594	3661
5 Other	44	76	66
6 Total current assets	6416	10990	11529
7 Creditors	4340	7078	7527
8 Bank overdraft	729	2189	3013
9 Other	1915	1293	1253
10 Total current liabilities	6984	10560	11793
11 Net current assets	(568)	430	(264)
12 Net assets	2006	3873	3271
Sources of finance			
13 Issued capital	204	205	205
14 Reserves	1272	2209	1343
15 Total shareholders' fund	1476	2414	1548
16 Loan capital	530	1459	1723
17 Other	–	–	–
18 Total capital employed	2006	3873	3271
Profit and loss account			
19 Sales	13657	16466	21610
20 Purchases	–	–	–
21 Trading profit	(71)	1224	407
22 Interest paid	448	658	1239
23 Profit before tax	(519)	336	(832)
24 Profit after tax	(451)	307	(758)
25 Profit retained in the business	–	–	–

Figures in brackets indicate that the figures have a negative sign.

Table 5.4: Balance Sheet Analysis—An Example

Name of Company		Case Study		
Key ratio	Method of calculation*	Year ended	Year ended	Year ended
Current	6/10	0.9:1	1:1	1:1
Quick	(6 -3) /10	0.3:1	0.4:1	0.3:1
Coverage of current debt	12/10	0.3	0.4	0.3
Profit on sales	23 as % of 19	(3.8)	2.0	(3.9)
Assets turnover	19/12	6.8	4.3	6.6
Return on capital employed	23 as % of 18	(25.9)	8.7	(25.4)
Collection period in days	(4/19) /365	48	102	62
Stock turnover in days	(3/20) /365			
or (3/19) /365	122	140	132	
Working capital turnover	19/11	–	38.3	–
Debt ratio	16 as % of 15	36	60	111

NOTES

1 Liquidity is good/bad ; improving/steady/worsening.
2 Profitability is improving/steady/worsening.
3 Use of assets are vigorous/slow ; improving/steady/worsening.
4 Debt ratio is rising/steady/dropping.

* The numbers in this column refer to the item numbers eg. current ratio is equal to item 6 / item 10

Figures in brackets indicate that the figures have a negative sign.

Press Reports

Daily reading of Financial Journals (e.g. *Financial Express* or *Economic Times*) is very essential not only to obtain the latest news and report of the customers but also to keep abreast of trends and problems in the industry.

Most industries have a trade journal, weekly or monthly, that carries useful information not of sufficient news value to reach the national press. After being read, all news items and articles of interest should be cut and filed on a customers status file along with other information.

Ledger History

It is studied to understand/ review the change (if any) in the buying habit and payment habit of existing customer and to categorise them accordingly.

The Other Three 'C's of Credit

The traditional three 'C's of Credit—Character, Capital and Capacity—are well known. However, in today's environment, many Americans believe that there are three more 'C's of credit and risk analysis that cannot be overlooked: Competition, Costs and Cash-flow.

In fact these days, it might be even more important to know and understand the customer from Competitive, Cost and Cash-flow standpoints than it is to assess Character and Capacity. With respect to character the customer doesn't really have to be a nice guy to pay promptly and be a good credit risk. And as for capacity, it can be drain on cash-flow if it is not fully and properly utilised.

Right product in the right market place also does not say much, because competition can sometimes put a customer out of business.

Cutting cost has become a prime focus of corporate America. The new corporate buzzword is 'doing more with less.' Cost is important because a company that does not minimize cost through quality control measures will be weakened and ultimately may not survive.

Cash flow is a pure measure of a firm's wherewithal and viability. Cash flow sources of net income, depreciation, and deferred income taxes must be able to support capital spending, dividends, and changes in the working capital. Otherwise, cash will be depleted and debt must be taken on. Without a strong cash flow, a company's growth can be blunted, and without growth, the company could die.

Checklist to check on three 'C's can be:

For Competitive Prompts

- Are they competitive with respect to price?
- What are the competition's terms?
- Is service is a factor?
- How important is quality in the market place?
- Does technology come into play?
- Nature of competition?
- Can they survive a major price war?

For Cost Prompts

- Are they doing more with less?
- Have cost been reduced or increased?
- Any cost reduction programmes in place?
- Any quality control measurements utilised?
- How well contained are cost?

For Cash-Flow Prompts

- Can cash flow sources support the business?
- What the quality of earnings?
- How strong is borrowing wherewithal?
- Are there any hidden cost associated with cash flow?
- What are the industry standard for earnings and cash flow?

Cash-Flow Statement

A basic part of every business operation is cash-flow. Since the most important and the most frequently used source of funds for loan repayment comes from the businesss' normal operations, it is vital that primary consideration be given to cash-flow in any credit appraisal. For purposes of financial analysis, cash- flow is considered to be the net income for a period, after adding back items deducted as expenses but that currently do not involve the use of cash funds. Likewise, items that are not a current source of funds may be deducted from the net income figure.

Cash-flow is one of the most difficult and complicated areas to forecast because many intermixed forces can affect the outcome of business operation. A firm's ability to meet its short-term obligations is important to both the credit analyst and the firm's management.

A cash-flow forecast is a planned procedure for estimating cash receipt and disbursement over a specified time period, usually on a monthly basis to one year. Since cash is usually budgeted on a monthly basis, management has time to arrange for necessary financing; in turn, the credit analyst can be alerted to situations that may create difficulties in meeting obligations. Although the cash forecast is ased primarily on historical data, it also must consider many other factors, including projected expenditures for new plant and equipment, expansion in future sales volume, and the effect of economic conditions on collections and selling terms.

The credit analysts' goal is to predict loan repayment, which is directly correlated with future cash flows. The installment loan officer must know the loan seeking firms' plans and market estimates before earnings and cash flows can be accurately predicted. In making such predictions, he or she evaluates historical information, forming opinions as to the competency and consistency of the forms' management and evaluating the degree of asset protection. As a general rule, a small business term loan is paid out of earnings rather than out of liquidation of inventory and receivables, as in consumer credit transactions. Therefore, anticipated earnings, along with the other elements of cash-flow, should exceed repayment requirements by a reasonable amount.

It is generally believed that the information presented in a statement of cash flow, should help assess the following:

- A firm's ability to generate positive future net cash flow.
- A firm's ability to meet its obligations and to pay dividends, and its need for external financing.
- The effects of a firm's financial position of both its cash and non-cash investing and financing during the reporting period.
- The reasons for differences between the net income and associated cash receipts and payments.

After credit ratings procedure is complete, the credit manager sends his comments to sales manager and the sample format of the comments could be as under:

Form 5.9

Credit Referral Note

To: The Sales Manager/Salesman — From: Credit Department

Division/Branch — Date:

Ref:

Sub:

Enquiry/Order No.__________ dated __________ Value __________

Existing Buyer

1. Order can be accepted ☐
2. Order can be shipped/ transported ☐
3. Please refer again before despatch ☐
4. Order cannot be accepted/despatched because customer is overdue and/or over limit. ☐

New Prospects

1. Information obtained details attached ☐
2. Credit account may be accepted ☐
3. Payment terms to be established ☐
4. No information available yet ☐
5. Initial order may be supplied up to on payment terms of ☐
6. Risk category is ☐
7. Temporary credit limit is ☐
8. Any other comment __________________
____

The customer code must be applied for in the normal manner.

Lastly, it needs to be noted that there can never be an exact, scientific method to guarantee the identification of business failures. All the above techniques are tools in the hands of credit manager to determine priorities and to set off an alarm in case of danger.

TIME REQUIRED FOR ASSESSING CREDIT WORTHINESS

No business can delay the delivery of a prospect because his credit worthiness is still to be assessed. Service to the customer is very important; otherwise the business may run the risk of cancellation of order. In case the customer requires the goods immediately and if he is asked to wait, very likely he may take his trade elsewhere. In such cases, the company policy should be to persuade the customer for an advance (fully or partly) and execute the order in the interest of good customer relations.

Most customers applying for credit facilities are fully aware that it does take a little time to open accounts with reputable business house.

The average time taken for the processing of the acceptance of a credit amount should not normally exceed 15 days, but quicker processing should be undertaken should delivery be more urgently required.

In case of large companies if the credit manager is satisfied with his ratio analysis and also if the information gathered from various sources is in favour of a potential customer, then the next step will be to look into his liquidity, i.e. how much credit he has requested and whether the dent in his liquidity will leave a safe margin. On the basis of this the grade, credit amount to be allowed and for what period (meeting competitor's terms) will be decided.

However, where the requests are for small credit amounts, they may be in thousand. Their financial statements may not be available. Moreover, to perform credit analysis will be a time consuming and costly task.

Such accounts can be best handled with a credit policy that strives for a good balance between Cash At Risk and First Year Profit.

Example:

A firm sells products with a 25 per cent profit margin. The credit manager has to decide on an application for credit of Rs 5000 only. The potential customer is expected to buy every month @ Rs 5,000 i.e. annually Rs 60,000 if credit is approved. On the basis of this information the credit manager calculates the first-year profit and cash at risk as follows:

First-year Profit		Cash at Risk	
Sales	60,000	Credit limit requested	5000
Cost of sales (75%)	45,000	Less profit (25% margin)	1250
First year profit	Rs 15,000	Cash at risk	Rs 3750

In the above example, the first year profit greatly exceeds the cash at risk and therefore the credit manager allows the credit.

Credit should not be allowed on one time order, unless the above criteria is satisfied. In many companies the policy is not to extend any credit in the first few months/years.

WHICH ACCOUNT IS CREDIT-WORTHY?

The question is one that might draw a variety of answers, answers shaded in varying degrees of caution, depending upon the parameters established by individual companies. Some companies use more liberal guidelines than others in arriving at an answer, e.g. your company might routinely extend credit terms to accounts whose traditional payment pattern is to pay several days after due date. This might not be compatible with the cash-flow requirements of companies who don't feel they can afford to carry customers for those additional days. Your credit department will screen credit applicants on the basis of a more liberal set of criteria than those companies that do not carry accounts (or as many accounts) that pay consistently several past terms.

The following guidelines should help you get the information and ask the questions that will enable you to recognise whether an account is or is not 'creditworthy'.

A creditworthy account should offer the following:

1. Good supplier experience and strong bank experience data, e.g. Does the company or business use a bank for augmenting cash flow? Does it use the credit line each month? Occasionally? Seldom? Not at all?
2. Balance sheet (for two or three years) that indicates good profits and steady growth.
3. A business plan that is committed to a pattern of steady rather than sporadic or accelerated growth.
4. A business history that is long enough to have established a favourable trend (or a favourable indicator, if the business is less than two years old).
5. In the case of a sole proprietorship or partnership, their reputation and experience in the business they are in. Are they dependent on one or two staff members whose skills

compensate the gaps in the owner's experience / skills. Are these employees in service for months or years?

6. Is the corporation, antecedent data relating to the experience and reputation of top management (CEO, COO, MD, Finance Officer, Marketing Head, etc).
7. If a corporation, has it made a public offering? Is it positioning itself for one? If there has been a public offering, how has the stock been received? Is it up from the initial offer price? Down from that price?
8. Is management adhering to the sound principles of business or is it pushing to book sales (doubling every quarter, etc.) at the expense of receivables that will not turn rapidly enough to make the necessary contribution to cash flow?
9. No account (unless top-rated) should be approved for the release of an order or the assigning of a credit line, unless enough quality experience data has been received and evaluated.
10. Are there weak credit controls within the customers' company? This can jeopardise cash flow and the customers' payment capability.
11. After evaluating the prospective customer, does it fit the guidelines of your company for an acceptable credit risk?
12. If it fits the guidelines, you have a new credit customer. If it does not fit the guidelines, try to work with the customer on terms other than straight credit. Conditions within the company may change for the better, which might then enable your company to gradually phase into a relationship of low-rupees credit sales.

The effective use of good screening procedures will save time and money of your company. It is irrelevant to the subject of credit worthy accounts whether your company is a manufacturer and distributes its own products, or your company is reseller of other companies product, or whether your company is in a service industry. If your company sells its products or services on credit terms, the company's credit account should represent the most comprehensive compilation of data and analysis. If you do not have much experience in evaluating accounts (or prospective accounts), guidelines are crucial in avoiding costly judgmental error. There must be a set of procedures and guidelines for determining what is and what is not acceptable credit risk.

Agency for Information on Credit & Status Report and Collection from International Parties

MIRA INFORM is a leading business information company with almost 20 years experience closely working with Graydon Netherland, BV which is a subsidiary of Graydon Holdings NV – a group of companies owned by Europe's leading credit insurance firms: NCM, Hennes, Coface. This credit reporting group is the most influential in Europe, with a turn over of over US $ 100,000,000 and has over 130 offices. MIRA can provide you cost-effective and freshly prepared credit reports for any part of the world. These are accepted as important decision making tools. MIRA can access +50 million fresh reports online for your offices. MIRA has been acknowledged by most of the users as a time-tested credit information providers. MIRA's services are recognized by Company Law Board, Registrar of Companies, Ministry of Commerce, Government of India, several nationalized and private banks, financial institutions and Barrie Union members – world over. For further details contact MIRA on Telephone numbers 91-2228081714, 28079467; Fax 91-22-28074108, 28079691; Cell No. 9821163446, 9892278558.

Credit Information Bureau (India) Limited (CIBIL)

This portion is reproduced from the web-site. You are requested surf the website of CIBIL for detailed information.
Email: info@cibil.com

Until now lenders found it difficult to gauge the credit history of individuals, partnership firms, private companies, etc. Credit was often granted to persons who had defaulted in the past, and sometimes individuals with good credit history were denied credit – all due to lack of information. Now we have CIBIL, a credit information bureau to provide credit grantors with latest information, fast and latest.

CIBIL – India's first credit information bureau – is a repository of information, which contains the credit history of commercial and consumer borrowers. CIBIL provides this information to its members in the form of credit information reports.

CIBIL is a composite credit bureau, which caters to both commercial and consumer segments. The Consumer Credit Bureau covers credit availed by individuals while the Commercial Credit Bureau covers credit availed by non-individuals such as partnership firms, proprietary concerns, private and public limited companies, etc. Banks, financial institutions, state financial corporations, non-banking financial companies, housing finance companies and credit card companies are members of CIBIL.

For credit grantors to gain a complete picture of the payment history of a credit applicant, they must be able to gain access to the applicant's complete credit record that may be spread over different institutions. CIBIL collects commercial and consumer credit-related data and collates such data to create and distribute credit reports to members.

A Credit Information Report (CIR) is a factual record of a borrower's credit payment history compiled from information received from different credit grantors. Its purpose is to help credit grantors make informed lending decisions – quickly and objectively.

THE BENEFITS OF A CREDIT BUREAU

Credit bureaus facilitate increased lending opportunities for credit grantors while allowing easier access to credit for borrowers. The existence of credit bureaus in developed countries has facilitated increased market penetration of credit (to more than 66% as a percentage of GDP as compared to 3% for India) while keeping non-performing loans in check (approximately 1% of outstanding credit).

Operating Efficiencies

Credit/Portfolio/Quality

The use of CIRs accessed from a credit bureau will enable credit grantors' loan officers to accurately evaluate borrower risk by making comprehensive credit histories available to decision makers. The CIRs will facilitate an objective and transparent assessment of credit applications. Concurrent borrowers and serial defaulters will be identified and minimized early in the approval process – consequently reducing associated recovery and write-off costs. Similarly, premium borrowers will be identified and serviced faster. Ultimately, CIRs will enable Members to judiciously mix relationship-based lending and information-based lending. CIRs will serve as the first level of due diligence in the appraisal of a credit application.

Speed and Cost

The use of CIRs will make processing loan applications easier, faster and cheaper by sometimes eliminating the need to additionally research and verify borrower details. The average loan in India is sanctioned in 2–3 days. A credit grantor using CIRs will be able to significantly reduce this turn-round time and thus have a competitive edge in the marketplace.

Credit Grantors

The use of CIRs will enable loan officers to make objective and informed credit decisions quickly, competitively and cost-effectively. The use of CIRs will enable them to increase their lending volumes and improve the quality of their credit portfolios while reducing their delinquencies and loan processing costs. This will translate into improved profit margins.

Borrowers

The widespread use of credit data will provide consumers with fast and easy access to the lending resources they need while reducing operating and risk costs for credit grantors. These reduced costs will be passed on to an extent to consumers with demonstrated credit performance in the form of lower interest rates. This easy availability of reasonably priced credit will provide borrowers with the means to a higher standard of living.

It is beyond the scope of this book to discuss all of CIBIL activities; however we would like to highlight the following:

- Creditworthy borrowers will benefit from CICRA by way of faster processing, competitive rates and lower processing charges.

- Credit grantors will benefit by way of lower NPAs, higher credit off-take and better risk management.
- The best way to improve your credit score is to pay your dues on or before the due date and never borrow beyond your means.

CREDIT INFORMATION COMPANIES (REGULATION) ACT (CICRA)

Now we have an act for collection, sharing and regulated dissemination of credit information. This bill was passed by the parliament in May 2005 and thus, the Credit Information Companies (Regulation) Act was enacted.

We cannot reproduce the complete text of the Act; however we would like to list the highlights:

- CICRA empowers credit information companies to collate credit information reports on borrowers.
- This Credit Information Report (CIR) is a factual credit payment histories, compiled from information received from different credit grantors.

Credit grantors obtain and use such reports to take well-informed lending decisions.

SIX

Qualifying the Understanding— Order Acceptance and Control

The credit limit is a maximum amount to be allowed for a specified period. This amount serves as a guideline to account performance. This may be also called credit line. It fixes maximum risk believed to be acceptable and the limit needed to accommodate sale volume. The judgment of credit manager in deciding credit lines should develop with experience and not under the arguments or pressures from the sales department.

It is a good principle to tell customers of their credit limits. This avoids subsequent misunderstanding, if order acceptance is delayed because of a limit problem. Whether the limit is maximum figure or a reflection of customer's need should be clearly stated. Reason for refusal should be notified to the customer by credit department by way of discussion and explanation.

RISK CATEGORY

Every customer is placed in a risk category according to the kind of credit limit established. Risk categories can then be used to determine the degree of order entry control and overdue follow-up.

Example of a basic risk category structure with A, B, C and D categories are as follows:

Keep a close vigil on your customers' business activities . . . how is their business doing? Are they paying other creditors on time?

Table 6.1: ABC Analysis—Riskwise Ratings

Risk Category	Type of Customer	Order Referral	Purpose of Credit Limits/Reviews
A	Government and public bodies, hospitals, schools, and large, strong public companies	None	To indicate a change in payment or buying behavior
B	All others	Over Rs. X	
C	Customers of doubtful standing and/or persistent bad payment behavior	All orders	To detect maximum balance allowable
D	Parties blacklisted	All orders	No credit, trade with advance, LC, BG or S. deposit.

Category A: The Blue Chip Group: Should be reserved for customers with zero or extremely low credit risk. This will include central and local government bodies, hospitals, universities, nationalised undertakings and national or international companies of highest standing. Since inclusion in this top category means no form of order entry control, it is essential that a regular check is made on the fortunes of admitted companies. The credit limits on category A customers will be a guideline that the payments are going to arrive within say one month of due date. No order referral is necessary since this category customers can increase their purchases without giving rise to significant credit risk.

Category B: Having covered buyers at both end of the risk scale we are left with the middle range, the B category. This is where the majority of customers will be grouped. Credit limits in this category will be guidelines, as in category A, but a measure of order entry control is necessary because these companies are not of the highest standing and sometimes unexpected purchases from them could cross the credit limit. In such cases, it makes sense to try and relate the referral level to the credit limit. Referral is necessary above a particular value of order. Find out if any reference has talked about the buyer in monetary terms much higher than the credit limit fixed. However this could be an exceptional case.

Category C: This is at the other end of the referral scale. This category includes buyers whose payment behavior demands strict control whether or not their credit limit is a problem. Order referral will be 100 percent for category C customers.

Category D (Customers/Dealers/Wholesalers): Order referral is not necessary. They are very commonly asked to keep a prescribed amount with company towards security deposit irrespective of their sales turnover. Sale is on Cash-on-delivery basis or against proforma. No credit is allowed. The individual cases may be reviewed from time to time with regard to their financial status, buying habits, etc. No order referral is necessary.

Credit limits in periods and amount should be evaluated and reviewed from time to time. Also customers should be moved from category to category according to changes in their risk status or as a result of significant changes in payment performances. It is vital that credit status information files are kept up-to-date.

With existing customers the credit manager is expected to gather his knowledge from ledger account, studying their paying habits and categorizing them accordingly.

Having set the credit limit in monetary term and period, the next important step will be to acknowledge, process and control the orders. The credit vetting needs to be put to practice.

It is a good practice to check all techno-commercial points of each order, otherwise it is very likely the payment could be held up for various reasons. Refer chapter on *First Things First – Tools for the Job*.

ORDER (ORAL AND WRITTEN CONTRACTS)

It would be very difficult to point a finger at a business transaction in today's business world that does not have its roots in a contract—written or oral. Whether two firms or two individuals do or do not come together for a formal signing of contract documents, a real or an implied contract usually has its roots in the standards of a company's products, in the claims the manufacturer makes for them, in the standard of performance for an industry, or in some other yardstick or combination of guideline levels of quality and / or service. Contract can be oral or written, real or implied. An improperly or inadequately written contract can cost your company a tidy some if the sleeves of your deal begin to unravel.

Basic Requirements for a Contract

A document must meet four basic requirements before it qualifies as a contract. An endless array of other material might be a part of a contract, but these are the essentials:

- Something of value must change hands, i.e. buyer will receive goods and pay money and the seller shall receive money for the goods supplied.
- The contracting parties must be mentally competent.
- The subject matter must meet the legal requirements for a contract.
- There must be an offer and an acceptance.

No amount of extraneous legal jargon will give a document contract status if what is purported to be a contract does not meet the basic four point criteria. A contract must offer a promise to do something or not to do something, or agree on the part of the promisor, to make something happen. All these 'something' must be between two or more people, entities etc.

Other important points of a written contract could be:

- *Terms intent:* These must not be vague. Both parties must want a contract.
- *Delivery:* Promise to fulfil, deliver or perform within a time frame.
- *Damages:* Where the terms of a contract are broken.
- *Legal:* Ordering by a court of a contract to be performed.
- *Arbitration (optional):* A step for settling dispute outside the court before taking the final plunge of legal action.
- *Repudiate:* Where one party breaches a contract.
- *Rescission:* Where fraud or misrepresentation causes a contract to end.
- *Puff:* Vague points of a contract, not a term, may not be important.

- *Condition:* A fundamental term of the contract; any breach of this will void the contract.
- *Warranty:* Breach of this may allow damages but will not void the contract.

Oral Contracts

Oral contracts are legal. However, in all but the most simple, concise, and straight forward transaction or deal, you should not use them. In case of legal dispute, unless impartial witnesses can recall the exact language of the oral contract, it can become a courtroom slugging match with the word of one man or woman attempting to prevail against the word of the other. If more than two people are part of the oral contract, more version will come out in the court.

Written Contract

Have a written contract. It will overcome all the hassles of oral contract. However, do not take chances and assume that you understand or are correctly interpreting the subtleties and the combinations of legal language.

Any person who handles credit and account receivable (an owner, a neophyte, or a well-schooled professional), and does not consult his or her company's attorney when a contract or a provision of a contract is unclear, is putting the company or business at unreasonable risk. It is unwise to assume that you know enough regarding applicable law(s) to make a competent judgement regarding the position of your company under the terms of the contract, unless you are an attorney or a trained paralegal.

Contract and Cash Traps

Cash traps among contractors frequently result from taking on bad business in the first place, or worse, not fully understanding the requirements of the job they have bid on and won.

Tender proposals, and invitations for bids issued by large organization, Government departments, and other organisation and institutions require great deal of attention to detail. In many cases, contract clauses are incorporated by reference only.

The unseasoned, or overly eager contractor faces eight potential errors in bidding and providing contract services that will result in cash traps downline.

1. Failing to read closely all the clauses, parts, conditions of the solicitation.
2. Unrealistic optimism in determining your company's ability to perform task and in the process assume risk. One must critically approach each solicitation:

   Answer these questions honestly:
   (a) Is our staff competent to handle the job?
   (b) If necessary, is additional labor readily available?
   (c) Are my facilities, quality control standards and procedures in place and adequate?
   (d) Can I meet all delivery schedules?
   (e) Can I be budgeted tightly and stay on target?
3. Bidding on unreliable purchase descriptions or specifications. Purchase descriptions and specifications may contain ambiguous, confusing, out dated or misleading information.
4. Bidding on estimations instead of actual cost data.
5. Bidding under time pressure. It is a very common practice to start preparing for the bid during the last hours on the pretext that the price to quote, may get licked or prices are awaited from the vendors. Why other preparations cannot be done much in advance.
6. Contracting for beyond the state-of-art product/s. Occasionally, corporations or government departments seek creative and exploratory procurements that are negotiated with performance specifications. End product to such products may include prototypes, tests, and evaluation models. Firms eager to conduct creative and exploratory type projects must have highly capable, technically-oriented staff who can carefully analyse solicitations to determine if projects are feasible.
7. Accepting an unrealistic time frame to complete, deliver or perform. Having not performed in time, most of the companies end up paying heavy penalty in the form of liquidated damages or price difference.

8. Hesitancy to take remedial action when a problem crops up.
9. Failing to determine the break-even point of the unit. It is very important to understand at what point of time during the course of the transaction the company will make profit and how much. Very likely due to competition your company may have to incur expenses towards freight, octroi, door delivery, demonstration, training, packing and forwarding, and during inspection at company's premises or by sending a prototypes or sample for testing.
10. Other important points that are overlooked are terms of payment, mode of payment, delivery or inco terms (delivery or shipping terms), after all this you may have to allow further discount to match the competition.

ORDER REFERRAL

After orders are checked, the next step will be order referral. An order acceptance is sent to the customer only after order referral is made by the credit department.

Procedure to follow with A, B and C type customers before accepting their orders may be as follows:

The procedure for OEM orders and acceptance and control is clearly described in Fig. 6.1.

Stage I: Customer's order entered on an order entry form including allocated computer code No. (without this it will be rejected automatically). Details of the order are fed into the computer and the risk category is ascertained. Category A status allows the order to move straight to Stage III, while B & C proceed to Stage II.

Stage II: There is no need for an order referral level in a computer system. All orders are added to the total value of previously accepted orders not yet shipped. Further exclude that part of the new order (or of existing order) which is not scheduled for delivery for further month. The total is added to the payment due from the customer on date. The grand total is then compared to the credit limit. If the account has crossed his credit limits than further despatches are not made to the customer until payments are received.

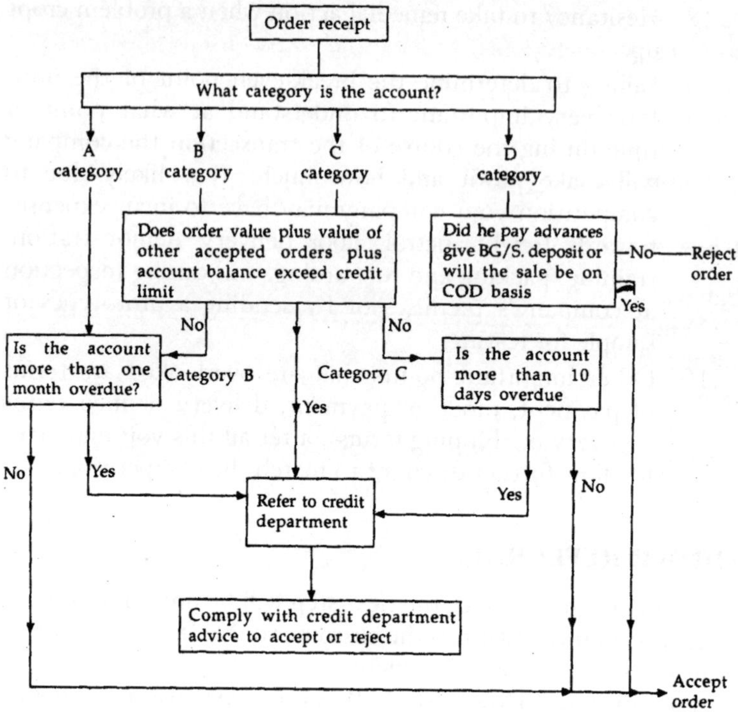

Fig. 6.1

Stage III: For categories A & B, a check is made whether the account is more than one month overdue. For category C the account should not be over 10 days, otherwise, it will lead to stage IV.

Stage IV: The final decision is made by the credit manager and not computer—to accept or reject depending on whether goods are made to customer's specification or off-the-shelf products.

The basic approach should be to use limits & categories in a positive manner. It is better to play safe and always reject orders which cross the limit but then on some occasions, the credit manager may have to find ways of accepting marginal orders, especially when the company's sale is down. With C category customer tackling the limit problem may include switching to a shorter credit period and even offering a cash discount wherever justifiable.

D category customer can buy only on COD basis or against advance payment only. Intimation of the total value may be sent by means of a pro-forma invoice. Allowing cash discount for advance payment may be justificated.

At this point, it will be worthwhile to discuss what maximum discount a trade should allow:

Cost of Discount (An example)

Say we are borrowing at 18% from bank.

What is the maximum cash discount we should allow. Suppose we induce those customers who are enjoying 90 days credit, to pay within 30 days for a cash discount of 2.5%. If the customers take advantage of this cash discount and pay within 30 days, the company will gain 60 days. One would like to know whether such a proposal was profitable for the business. Let's examine:

Amount of time gained, i.e. 90 days less 30 days = 60 days, divided into 365 to produce the annual rate, multiplied by the rate of discount. Thus

1. $\frac{365}{90-30} \times 2.5 = 15\%$ approximately

2. $\frac{365}{90-30} \times 3.0 = 18\%$ approximately

Maximum cash discount we can allow is 3%.

PUBLIC SECTOR CUSTOMER

We have already discussed the technical aspects of accepting order from government departments and semi-government enterprises. To repeat once again one must get involved at the stage named provisional order. All the stages before executing these orders should be studied. For example, before getting final order, there would be stages like submitting design, approval of designs, approval of sample, approval of right design, test, specification approval. A credit manager is expected to follow up and see that time is not wasted in any of these stages. For any reason if there is inordinate delay then the credit manager must write to the respective authority explaining the situation and asking for more time or atleast make an attempt to make the government department know the situation and why the delivery will be delayed.

Before an order is accepted, the credit manager must make sure all the conditions laid down by the public sector companies are acceptable, especially where the payment terms say 90% or 95%, is against proof of despatch and balance after acceptance of material.

Where the payment terms are say 95% and 5% or 90% and 10%, many companies prefer to forgo the balance amount as they find that they may not be able to fulfill the last few conditions of the order. This is dangerous as eventually the government department will recover the full 90% or 95% amount paid if full compliance is not made with the conditions of the order. A order file is closed by the public sector's paying authority after the balance payments are made. Till then all earlier payments to the suppliers are treated as advance. This is discussed in more detail when we talk about recovery.

THE DEALER

Controlling the dealer needs a different kind of treatment. Every company that decides to have dealers network also has to decide the ratio between dealers' order and direct consumers' order booking. In case the dealers decide to stop trade suddenly or if they protest for better terms, the company's business should not get hampered. It will be a policy decision for a company as to what ratio they will prefer. In two companies known to the authors, the dealer/consumer ratio was 45:55 & 30:70 respectively. Both the companies preferred to be on the safer side as against dealers.

A dealer's, trader's or selling agent's performance is evaluated after considering the points in Form 6.1.

Form 6.1

Performance Evaluation and ABC Analysis of Dealers

Please tick in the relevant column	Excellent	Good	Fair	Poor
1. Did he achieve his last target?				
2. Did he achieve his last turnover?				
3. Knowledge of product features				
4. Product market				
5. How much new business did he secure in the new year?				
6. How much orders he was able to transfer from our competitors?				
7. Did he cover up the territory allocated?				
8. Is repair and maintenance rendered by him satisfactory?				
9. Did he maintain the price structure?				
10. What is his present credit worthiness?				
11. Market standing—present status				
12. What was the stock turnover?				
13. Payment habits				
14. Did he share advertisement cost?				

HIGH CREDIT OR EXTENDED CREDIT

A high credit request substantially that is above the normal level usually involves special marketing or production consideration. This would be also an opportunity to make significant increase in sales and profit. The credit manager must take care to investigate thoroughly, looking all the while for a way of justifying the additional credit.

- He should determine the reason for the extra credit
- Is the customer most likely to be awarded a special contract?
- Is the customer to build up stock hoping for a upturn in the market?
- What type of product he is dealing with?
- His past payment record? Did he pay on time?

In case of the third situation the credit manager must request for some kind of security such as bank guarantee, security deposit. If the risk appears too high, payment may be secured by letter of credit, back-to-back credit or a transferable credit arrangement. The high credit or extended credit should be offered only after all the relevant member of the firm has approved.

Lastly, another measure of control is the decision to suspend deliveries as a means of extracting payment and reducing the risk of a bad debt. This cannot be taken lightly in any company. Proposing customers to be blacklisted can be a sensitive area and it could easily develop into a friction between sales manager and credit manager. It will be much better to alert the sales manager to this situation so he can intervene. A telephone call from sales manager to the customer can sometimes accelerate the payment. Credit manager must take a note of such habits. In case the credit manager's own company is facing working capital shortage, then it becomes all the more important for him to know the paying habits of customers and control the despatch in a manner which will fetch the company 95% to 98% at agreed time leaving nothing to chance.

CONSTANT MONITORING OF CREDIT ACCOUNTS

Monitoring is the credit professional's synonym for watching and the importance of that activity is not to be taken lightly. Every account, regardless of how strong it might seem to be when your company offers a credit line, has the potential to become a problem, i.e. some companies may go from prompt payment to slow payment. Even this statement does not exclude reputed companies. Therefore, monitoring the company's account receivable on an ongoing basis is one of the most effective ways to identify problems in their earliest stages. The following will help you to touch the important bases:

1. Monitoring the current payment habits of your customer against what they did three, six, or twelve months ago.
2. Compare how the customer is currently handling payments to other suppliers versus yours.
3. Refer current accounts receivable aging statement and compare it with the one that is three months old.
4. Is there a change in the pattern of payments in the last three or six months? Should the change be categorised as minor, progressively more noticeable, or major?

5. Is there a noticeable change in the number of past-due days in one, a few, or several accounts?
6. Have you made it a priority to find out the problems or reasons for the slowing of payments?
7. Are you working with these customers to reduce the average number of days from the invoice date until past-due invoices are paid ?
8. Are you comfortable with the safety of these past-due accounts?
9. If you are concerned regarding the safety (all or certain accounts), what are you doing to eliminate your company's risks.

ACCOUNTS RECEIVABLE—GOOD QUALITY AND POOR QUALITY

What are the differences between a receivable of good quality and one of poor quality? The following offers a comparison.

Good Quality Accounts

1. Pays within the terms of sale or not more than 10 days past the due date.
2. Never attempts to take a discount when one has not been earned.
3. Has a good reputation for prompt payment among all current and past suppliers.
4. Has access to high-rupee level of bank support. Also, the bank reports that repayment of loan funds to bank has been as agreed.
5. Does not use ploys, such as a missing invoice (and relevant documents for supporting), one of the signatories is not available, you have not adjusted credit note, quality and quantity discrepancy etc. to delay the payment.
6. Is a consistently dependable contributor to the monthly cash-flow figure. Payments are assured.
7. Regular and big orders
8. Agrees to be our referral
9. Technically and commercially sound in dealings.

10. Transparency in creating contacts
11. Gives good feedback and market information.
12. Takes active part in new product development and market development.
13. Consideration for our product and quality.
14. Always tries to be part of solution.
15. Contributes by making suggestions for improvement from time to time.

Poor Quality Accounts

If it does not meet the above mentioned fifteen criteria. Plus:

1. Never pays until several reminders are sent.
2. Is in business, but not growing.
3. Suffers from consistently inadequate cash-flow.
4. Operates under weak budget and financial controls.
5. Produces a good product (or product line), but not an effective marketeer.

Business is Satisfying Customers & Making Money

More Customers you satisfy, more money you make

P₹OFITABLE
GROWTH

SEVEN

The Game of Debit and Credit—Now with Computers

Let us talk about a typical business transaction and the way it actually gets completed.

Mr Prasad, who is an electrical goods manufacturer writes to ZZZ Ltd, for quote for certain items.

↓

ZZZ Ltd, sends their offer to Mr Prasad on COD basis. In case Mr Prasad would like to avail of credit facilities then he should provide the bank and trade references.

↓

Mr Prasad would like to avail of the credit facilities and hence he seeks permission of a regular supplier to provide his name as reference to ZZZ Ltd.

↓

Mr Prasad forwards the name and address of the reference and also his banker's name to ZZZ Ltd. Along with these he also sends his first order.

↓

Information about money is almost as valuable as the money itself.

Walter B. Wriston

Statistics are no substitute for judgement.

Henry Clay

And may we add action?

ZZZ Ltd, receives favourable reply from the references and decides upon the amount and credit period to be allowed to Mr Prasad and informs him accordingly along with acceptance of his order.

↓

ZZZ Ltd supplies the goods and also encloses a copy of the invoice.

↓

Mr Prasad finds that there are two pieces short in the consignment and informs ZZZ Ltd of the same.

↓

Mr Prasad receives an apology letter by post and along with it he also receives the credit note towards adjustment of those two pieces short received.

↓

While checking the bill, Mr Prasad also detects that ZZZ Ltd has undercharged him by an X amount, thus informs ZZZ Ltd, requesting for a debit note for the same. Since 15 days credit period which was allowed to him was over, he also sends his cheque for invoice amount less credit note plus amount short charged.

↓

ZZZ Ltd was too glad to send the debit note and thanks Mr Prasad for paying the amount in advance.

↓

The first transaction between ZZZ Ltd and Mr Prasad rightly comes to an end.

It is not very common that both the debit note and the credit note get adjusted in the same invoice itself, and usually they are adjusted in the subsequent invoices. It is also very likely that such mistakes of short supplies and calculation errors happen a number of times, and keeping a track record of each transaction becomes very essential. Moreover, all payment terms may not be 100 % on COD basis. It could in parts. This and all other similar complications of a credit department require technological support. Let us take a look at certain key areas and then go into programing tips for the different functions.

DEBTOR ACCOUNTING

A good credit control is very dependent upon an up-to-date and efficient ledger system and if the credit manager is not in control, his own operation can be endangered by basic problems such as the timing of statements, the availability of ledger and the determining of priorities in backlog situations. The computer helps the credit manager to be in charge and yet have time for extra responsibilities.

Fundamental Requisites of Good Debtor's Accounting

1. The system should provide an accurate record of each step in the collection process until final disposition is made in the case of each account.
2. It should automatically bring accounts to notice at the proper time.
3. It should avoid unnecessary duplication of records and effort.
4. It should provide for classifying or segregating the accounts into three categories: current, past due and suspense or legal (customer's credit suspended or account turned over to a solicitor or collection agency for collections).
5. It should be arranged so that cash received is posted daily to the collection records before it goes to the general book-keepers in order that these records will be kept up-to-date daily.
6. It should have provisions for safeguarding the records from loss and destruction.

RECEIVABLE LEDGER

The basic purpose of a receivable ledger is to record the company's credit sales to, and payments from, customers, and on any adjusting entries in such a manner that each individual transaction can be traced and verified from date of despatch to receipt of payment.

The receivable ledger is balanced every month in the following manner:

Balance at last month-end

Plus	:	Net invoiced sales this month and debit notes raised this month
Less	:	Cash received and credit notes raised this month
Plus/Minus	:	Sundry adjustments (journal vouchers)
Equals to	:	New balance

Brought-forward method involves a continuous ledger to which new items are added each month. For the purpose of statement, it is normal to carry forward the total owing from the previous month and to show individually only the new month's transactions.

The drawback of this system is the need for constant manual reconciliation of the previous balance. However, through a computer it is possible to keep the ledger history bill-wise, i.e. total number of bills pending and the total amount of which equals to ledger balance, can both be maintained simultaneously.

Essential inputs in receivable ledger are invoices, receipts, debit notes, credit notes, contra items and journal items. It should be ensured that they are given the correct customer account or code number and that their reference numbers are easily identifiable and distinctive. This means taking care that all departments responsible for raising such documents have an up-to-date list of account number, names and addresses. The allocation of series of invoice numbers to different divisions or branches must be planned to avoid the possibility of the same numbers being used twice. A simple way to ensure this is by prefixing alpha or numerical code to invoice numbers.

Apart from entering the invoices in the ledger, they should be sent out to customers with proper supporting material at the earliest. Otherwise, the customer may use this as an excuse and delay settlement.

The credit manager should take keen interest in designing invoice and its layout. Customer order numbers, name, address, terms of payment, invoice number, date and account numbers must be easily identified. Credit notes should always carry a clear reference to the original invoice and/or customers debit note.

Customer's payments are received in the form of cheques, bank transfers, direct debits, postal orders or currency notes. Responsibility for listing, totaling and banking lies with the accounts staff, but the way each day's receipts are posted to the receivable ledger should be dictated by the credit manager. Speed and ease of identification are the key points. The faster it is posted in the receivable ledger the better it is, otherwise the order processing is being held up and decisions are delayed.

Another responsibility of the accounts staff is to inform the credit manager immediately of any dishonoured cheques—taking care to distinguish between those which are returned by the bank marked 'refer to drawer' and those which are merely marked 'please re-present'.

If possible, payments should be reconciled within 24 hours of receipt. Correct allocation of cash is very important and strict controls should operate to prevent an accumulation of un-reconciled payments. This demands discipline in the ledger clerk's job and the credit manager must not tolerate cash remaining allocated beyond say one month after receipt. On-account payments often cannot be avoided and indeed are sometimes the only way of maintaining satisfactory cash flow. On the other hand, sometimes receipts of on-account payment in place of the full amount requested should sound a warning bell. It is almost invariably a sign of cash shortage and must be followed up immediately.

THE CUSTOMER MASTER FILES

Control of this should rest with credit manager and involve the following precautions:

1. Input of new or amended information to be exercised only by the credit department.

Form 7.1

The Customer Master File

CUSTOMER MASTER LIST

1. Code No. __________ 2. Alpha Code __________
3. Name __________
4. Address __________
5. Phone No/s. __________ Contact Person (Name & Desig.)
6. Commercial Regn. No. __________
7. Godown Address __________ Phone No. __________
8. Sales Tax Regn. No. __________
9. Central Sales Tax Regn. No. __________
10. Banker's Name & Address __________
11. Sales Budget / Target __________
12. Mode of Payment __________
    (Cash/ Direct/ Through Bank/ Bills Of Exchange/ L.c. Etc.)
13. Trade Reference (Remarks) __________
14. Bank Reference (Remarks) __________
15. Class (Abc Analysis) __________
16. Salesman __________
17. Credit Limit Amount __________
18. Credit Period __________
19. Product Code __________
    (Which Are The Products They Usually Buy)
20. Dealer/Distributor/Stockists/Oem End User __________
21. Security Deposit (If Any) Rs. __________

2. Issue of account numbers to be in the hands of only the credit department.

Other departments will need access to the file for shipping address, invoicing address, account numbers, etc. but only credit department should be allowed to approve any alteration or addition to the file.

In manual system, this data is usually kept on a card index file which, because it is needed by different users, has to be reproduced several times, with great risk of error and lack of control. If it can be put on the computer tape or disk storage, these problems virtually disappear since complete tabulations—either in card form or as a print out—can be provided to all the users simultaneously and control over additions and amendments are easily centralized.

A comprehensive up-to-date name and address file is an essential basis for operating the receivables ledger by computer.

STATEMENT OF ACCOUNTS

Many, if not all, trading companies send periodic statements to their customers, usually monthly. The purpose is to draw attention to unpaid items and to induce payments.

The two key features of statements are timing and clarity. Statements should be ready for dispatch within as few days as possible after the monthend. On a manual system where they have to be typed or photocopied, long delays are difficult to avoid.

The clarity of statements demands considerable thought and planning if the end result is to help the customer identify unpaid items and reduce queries to a minimum. Here too computers play a big role.

Table 7.1 and 7.2 below are examples of computer statements having most of the features and headings normally required.

The following points may also be noted:

1. Usually the statement is 'open-item'—only un-cleared items are shown. But in case the payments are received on account in that case ledger system (showing all debits and all credits) will be appropriate.
2. Each type of transaction is clearly identified by an abbreviation rather than a code.
3. Some use one value column, with 'CR' to denote credit items. This saves valuable space. And some prefer to show debit, credit, unadjusted debit (unallocated) advance and balance in separate column.
4. There is a running balance
5. Many companies put customer's order number against each item.
6. An age analysis of the balance is given.

Table 7.1: Balance Forward Statement

Ford Cars Limited,
J.B. Road
Bombay-400025

Statement of Account

To: Date: 28-2-93
AKG & Company
Bombay

Date	Type	Description	Ref.	Debit	Credit	Balance
		Brought forward				0.00
23/12/92	1Adj	Opening balance	A679	1098.83		1098.83
21/01/93	Inv	R'vate Vintage Car	84001	575.00		1673.83
31/01/93	Pay	Cheque	84001		575.00	1098.83
Current	30 days	60 days	90 days			
0.00	0.00	1098.83	0.00	Amount due:		1098.83

Table 7.2: Open Item Statement

International Automobiles Limited,
365 Wardha Street,
Bombay-400035

Statement of Account

To : Date: 31-1-94
XYZ & Company,
Bombay

Date	Type	Description	Ref.	Debit	Credit/Outstanding
01/12/92	1Adj	Opening balance	A578	6114.00	6114.00
30/11/93	1Adj	Opening balance	A501	4000.18	4000.18
31/01/94	Inv.	Car sales	84002	11500.00	11500.00
Current	30 days	60 days	Over 90 days		
11500.00	0.00	4000.18	6114.00		Amount due: 21614.18

We shall be closed on February 20 and 23.

7. It is generally desirable to show on the statement all items up to the end of calendar month. Many companies produce a statement with a tear-off portion on the right, headed 'Remittance Advice.' It is hoped that customers will return this with their cheque, thus assisting in cash reconciliation. In practice the percentage of customers who use this slip is very small and there is a case for using this part of the statement to give more information e.g. customer's order number and due date for payment.

AGE ANALYSIS

For any credit operation, unless the live accounts are below, say 100, a properly designed age analysis of the receivable ledger is vital. Generally produced monthly, this will provide information on the age of each customer's account, the total balance compared to the credit limit and the amount of cash required to keep it within terms. We have discussed this in chapter one. Table 7.3 shows a typical analysis.

This is a summary statement of each customer. Another aged analysis statement is drawn prior to this, consisting of aged value of each bill in every customer's account.

Points to Note

(a) Payment terms, credit limit, risk category and area office (location) are all clearly visible.

(b) Unreconciled cash (unadjusted credit) and advance are not aged but shown in separate columns.

(c) Customers who have exceeded their limit are highlighted by an asterisk. A better way of identifying over-limit accounts, especially in a large organization, is to have a separate tabulation. If different product groups are involved, the analysis can be programmed on the computer to print in the required sequence, similarly if analysis under regional / branch offices are desired. It can be so programmed. Another useful sequence is to have an analysis by risk category. How a computer can help will be discussed in the last part of this chapter.

(d) Age analysis can be from the date of bills or due date-wise (credit period)

Table 7.3: KVA & Ltd. Age Analysis of Debtors

Code customer	Balance	Upto 30 days	Over 30 days	Over 60 days	Over 90 days	Unassigned payment	T.O.	Credit limit	Date of last act.	Terms of payment
1001 Lds Ltd. Tambe Estate Sion, Bombay-33	21614.18	11500.00	0.00	6114.00	4000.19	0.00	10000.00	10000.00	28.2.93	Th.Bank
2001 Cdf and Co. Trading Est., Colaba, Bombay	1040.49	0.00	0.00	0.00	1040.49	287.50	–250.00	2000.00	30.3.93	30 days
3001 Jay and Joy Ltd., Veer Bazar, Calcutta.	1098.83	0.00	0.00	1098.83	0.00	0.00	500.00	1000.00	31.1.93	60 days hundi
4001 R & D (I) Ltd., R & D House, R & D Road, Assam	14225.00	14225.00	0.00	0.00	0.00	0.00	21500.00	15000.00	23.2.93	L/C at sight
Totals percentage	37978.50	25725.00 67.7%	0.00 0.0%	7212.83 19.00%	5040.67 13.3%	287.50	31750.00			

CREDIT NOTES (CUSTOMER'S DEBIT NOTES)

Most manufacturing companies have the credit note problem and this is usually given low priority amongst the routine procedures of the receivables ledger/credit department. The credit manager must not ignore the problem but establish controls.

A debit note from a customer is a claim for credit made on a supplier arising for one of the three principal reasons.

1. Goods or services not received (either wholly or in part)
2. Goods or services believed to be incorrectly priced or invoiced.
3. Goods returned

Issue of credit notes is proof of customer liability. This depends upon action by the other departments production, engineering, quality control, sales, despatch, invoicing – none of whom is ever particularly interested in spending time on these queries. More often than not, the onus will be on the credit manager to activate people outside his control. Proper records of all credit notes must be kept within the department. Sales department should be asked to send all customers debit notes to the person in charge of these files and internal instruction given to forward them to credit department.

If the value of debit notes warrants it, a copy of such incoming debit note should be sent to the appropriate person/department with a request for clearance. This must be followed up regularly. If the complaint/claim is not accepted, a letter of explanation must be written to the customer. Similarly the issue of part credit should also be covered by a letter.

The credit manager should highlight periodically different aspects in his report to management.

1. The effect on cash-flow. Calculate how many days' sales are accounted.
2. The impact on profits resulting from the need to carry provisions against credit notes.
3. The detrimental effect of uncleared credit notes on customer relations.

FILING

A well organised filing system though never in the limelight, is nonetheless essential for an efficient credit operation. It is only when filing gets out of hand that its importance is recognised. Certain developments, by their nature can only be filed one way, i.e. correspondence and status files (alphabetically) and invoices (numerically). Other papers, such as remittance advices, need a little thought. Many companies keep all the remittance advices for one month together in date sequence. This may be satisfactory until something is taken out. A much better system is to file the advices by customer. Big customers will have individual files and others will merely run alphabetically.

As per income tax rules, a record has to be preserved for nine years and that makes control on filing still more important.

AID TO PROGRAMMERS

The following dataflow chart, flow chart, menu features will help the programmers to develop a software on bills receivable, order processing and billing and transport routing, to effectively control the computer operations.

Accounts Receivables (Module)

A computer application on receivables should have the following features:

1. Daily cash receipt online.
2. Daily cash received on individual open items as contrasted with a balance forward technique.
3. Cash received based on user-specified criteria (oldest invoice, specific matching, and suspense (unapplied cash)
4. Cash received on a partial invoice basis.
5. Enter adjustments to open items such as payments, invoices, credits, and unapplied cash.
6. Preclude deletion of customer master accounts for customers with non-zero balances.
7. Handle payments for which customer master accounts have not been established (suspense accounts with specific identification of remittances).

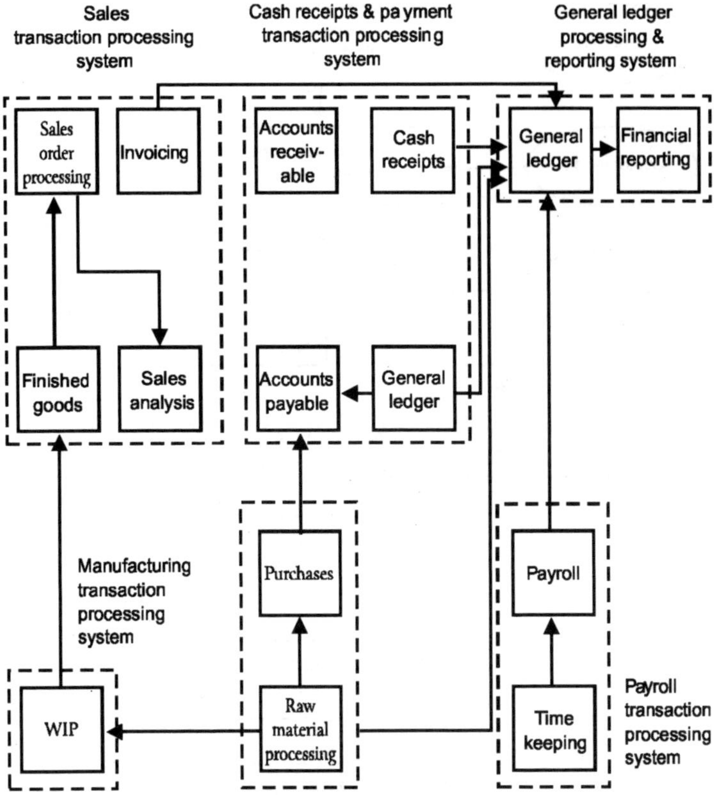

Fig. 7.1 Processing-integration-control

8. Capacity to override, with exception reporting, masterfile control information such as shipping instructions, billing addresses, discounts and so on.
9. Verify all semi-permanent data (customer name, customer number etc.) prior to transaction processing.
10. Facilitate customer balance reporting (accounts receivable balances) for the following levels of detail:
    — Summary totals by customer (balance forward, purchases, payments, adjustments, ending balance): optional capabilities include year to date transaction information, balance forward, purchases, payments, adjustments, ending balance) and comparable information for the previous year.

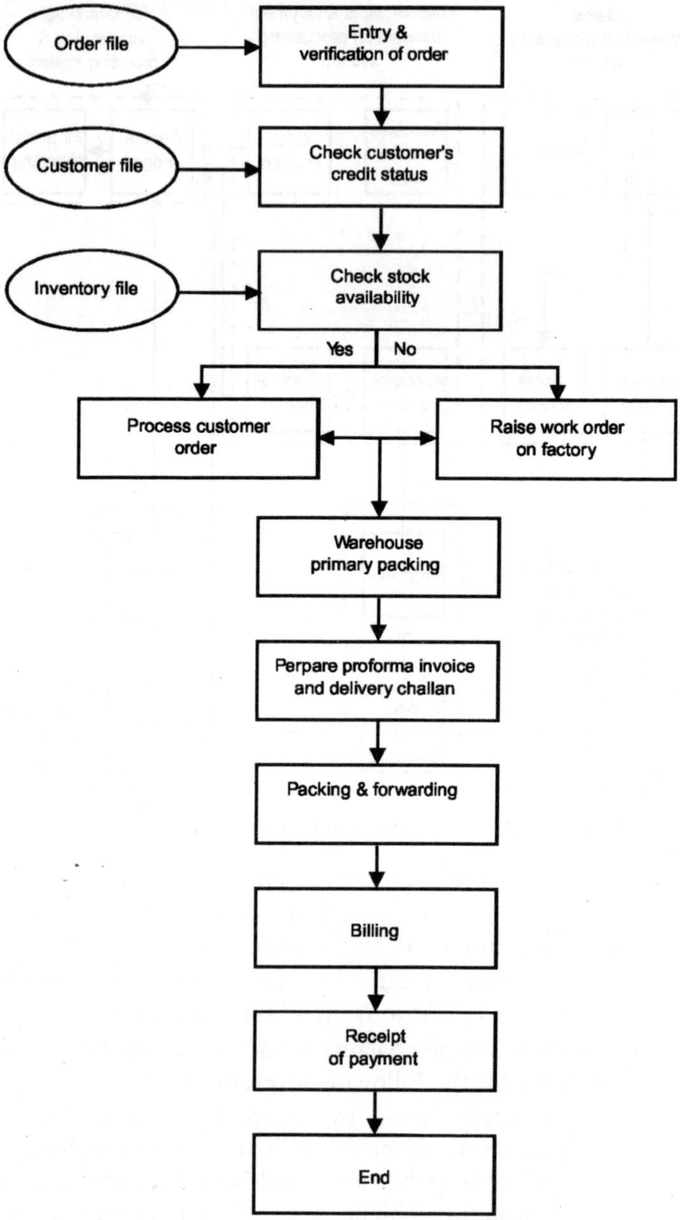

Fig. 7.2 Credit Control–Data Flow

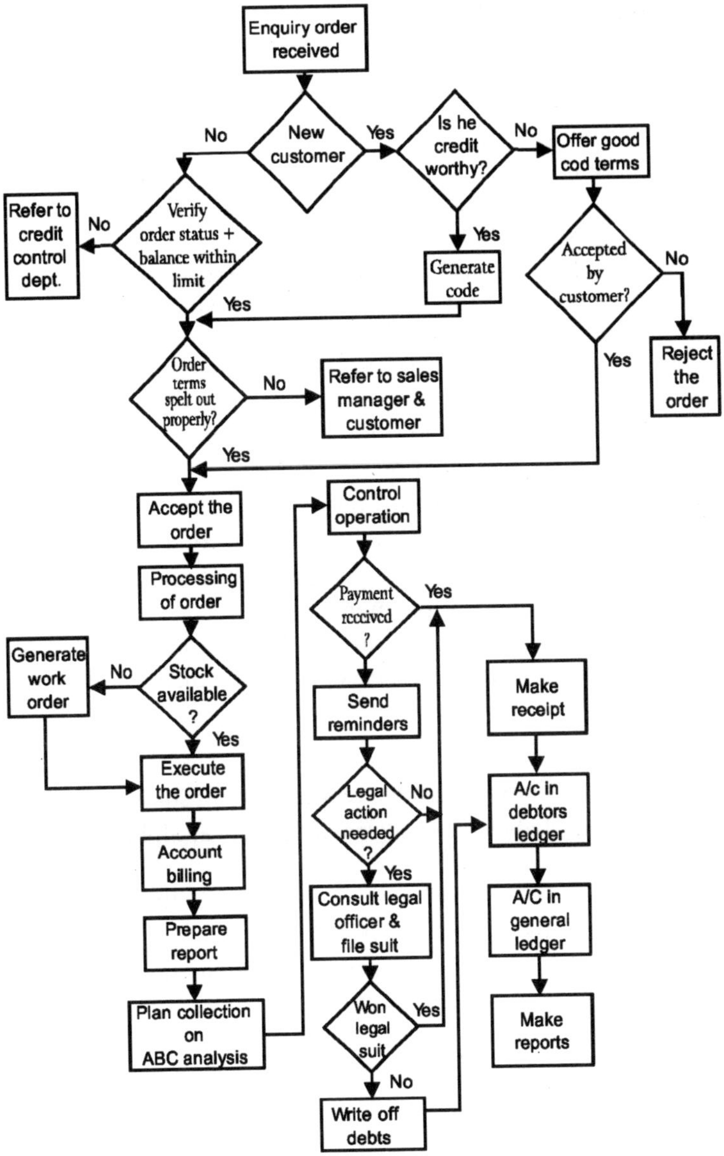

Fig. 7.3 Credit Control Dept–Work Flowchart

   — Summary totals for all customers (balance forward, purchases, payments, adjustments, ending balance): in addition, the system should provide prior year comparable information.

11. Accommodate 'x' customers in total and 'y' active customers
12. Provide flexible billing facility. Interface with Order Processing Module
13. Capacity to add automatic interest charges for user specified accounts and accounts for which user-specified criteria are met within the current month.
14. Interface directly with the general ledger system for sales, cash receipts, freight, sales tax, discounts, returns, credits, interest charges, and other adjustments.
15. Support X or 13 period fiscal year.
16. Accommodate discount terms based on:
    — Cumulative rupees purchases in total
    — Cumulative rupees purchases for a specific product
    — Timeliness of payment
17. Maintain customer masterfile information, which, as a minimum would include as per format mentioned above.

Reports

1. Aged accounts receivable reports (details/summary/aging).
2. Mailing Labels (user defined sequence, alpha, numeric, selective).
3. Invoices with account details and user-defined messages.
4. Statements at predefined intervals.
5. Statements with dunning messages (bases on user-defined criteria)—Letter reminders in sequence.
6. Registers (cash, sales, debit note, credit note and adjustments, etc.) detailing monthly transactions and that provide all posting references and other information.
7. Batch balancing and control information (detail listings, control, totals, etc.)
8. Customer lists based on user-defined criteria (alpha, numeric, industry dependent, selective).
9. Sales tax reports, concessional forms (collected, due etc.).

10. Daily business reports (gross sales, discounts, net sales, cash receipts, beginning accounts receivable balance and ending accounts receivable balance).
11. Sales analysis reports (by salesman, customer, territory).
12. Exception reports (credit limits, unusual volume, days outstanding, adjustments, etc.)
13. Cash receipts forecast (by day, specific period, etc.)
14. Customer's (A/R) Ledger. Compilation of customer history.
15. Order status – salesmen, product, division, branch, area-wise.
16. Order status – customer-wise (exception reporting-unusual volume, credit limits, over due bills).
17. Challans not billed.
18. Challans for gifts, samples, evaluation, demonstration purpose (or no charge bills)
19. ABC analysis (collection planning based on part to principle).

Sales–Order Processing (Module)

Sales order processing captures and processes customer orders and produces invoices for customers and date needed for sales analysis and inventory control. It must also keep track of the status of customer orders until goods are delivered. Computer based sales order processing systems provide a fast, accurate and efficient method of recording and screening customer orders and sales transactions. They also provide inventory control system with information on accepted order so they can be filled as quickly as possible. In that event, consider automating some or all of the following modules:

- Order entry (including credit authorization)
- Sales analysis
- Inventory management
- Transport management

Order Entry (Module)

An automated order entry system should minimize the amount of clerical effort to process orders, check the credit status of customers, and provide comprehensive management reports.

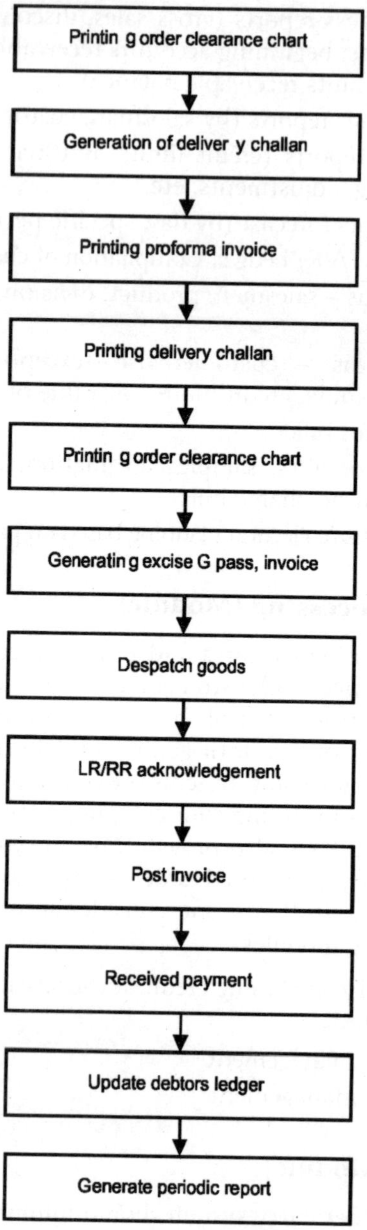

Fig. 7.4 Order Processing & Billing–Data Flow

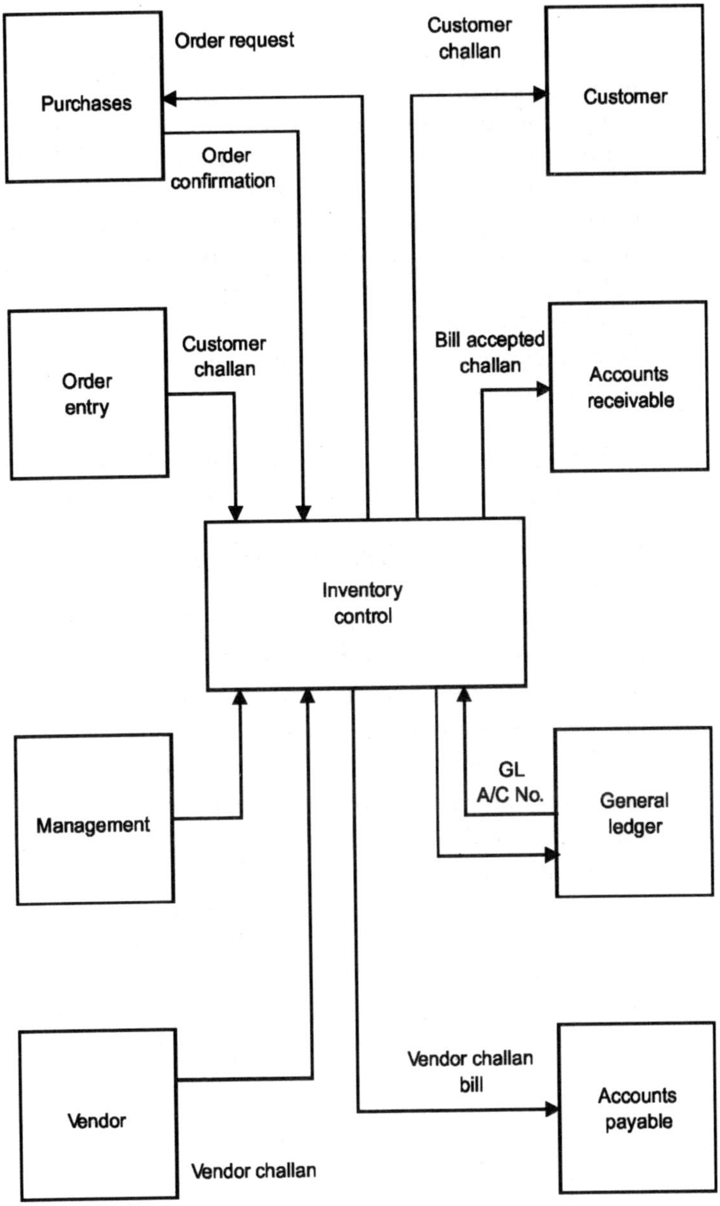

Fig. 7.5 Inventory Control System Data Flow

Features

1. Enter complete order information including customer number, salesman number, ship to address, special freight considerations, inventory item data, government contract number, whether the item is for resale, whether the item is renegotiable, and so on.
2. Check, as applicable, whether valid tax/duty exemption certificates are on file. Whether road permit is applicable.
3. Calculate unit price during order entry by using a quantity discountable and a product list price.
4. Verify a customer's credit status during order entry on a line item basis.
5. Enter changes on-line to the customer master-file, including information regarding the addition of new customers, deletion of former customers, and changes to existing customers.
6. Reject user attempts to delete customers with balances of any type.
7. On-line editing for all data elements for each customer line item and customer information.
8. Apply credit check to customer balances.
9. Process standard contract orders.
10. Validate transporting information including :
    Transport date; Transportation type; Carrier;
    Carrier return date; LR/RR number; date; Truck no.
11. Enter line item data including:

Item number;	Unit of measure;	Item description;
Terms;	Quantity;	Freight class;
Price;	Customer product ID;	

12. Handle up to z items per sales order and be able to handle multiple transportation per order.
13. Invoice each transportation or lorry receipt separately.
14. Capacity to handle up to x different quantity price breaks.
15. Schedule orders and project an order completion date. If appropriate, the order entry system should interface with the purchasing system.
16. Process standing and blanket orders.

17. Support x customers in total and x number of active customers.
18. Support x number of orders at any one time.
19. Allow for cyclical billing via a user-designated code.
20. Facilitate multiple billings to a given customer within a billing cycle.
21. Apply automatic interest or late charges to customer billing and account balances.
22. Interface directly with other modules, including inventory control, accounts receivable, general ledger, and sales analysis.
23. Provide open-item accounts receivable reports.
24. Perform automated housekeeping functions at period end, such as zeroing of month to date totals, accumulating balance forward amounts, and calculating interest and other charges.
25. Support a 13-period fiscal year.
26. Process new customers and corresponding orders during the current cycle.
27. Calculate interest charges from payment due date.
28. Apply excise duty, sales tax, freight terms, and miscellaneous charges.
29. Calculate most advantageous transporting date based upon transit time to customer location.
30. Accommodate discount terms for cash and end of month payments.
31. Produce dunning letters.
32. Prepare invoices.
33. Inquiry capability for customer data by searching customer number or customer name.
34. Maintain an open item invoice file containing, at a minimum, the following:

Invoice number;	Customer Code;	Invoice amount;
Invoice date;	Invoice type;	Reference data;
Contract data;	Freight arrangements;	Tax and Duty;
Product data;	Division;	Area.

35. Maintain data in the customer master file. Refer exhibit number VII-1.

36. Maintain an open order file containing, at a minimum, the following items:

Order number;	Transport status;	Amount;
Customer number;	Order type;	Order date;
Order responsibility;	Reference data;	
Cross reference;	Invoice	

37. Perform complete editing and validation of data before system updating, including interface updates (general ledger, inventory).

Reports

1. Daily orders by customer and inventory item.
2. Order confirmations and back-order notices with the capability of entering user-defined messages.
3. Back order reports by customer and item.
4. Order backlog report with the following information:

Customer number;	Customer name;	Transaction date;
Ship to location;	Total units;	Order amount.

5. Masterfile change report with before and after information.
6. Masterfile contents with control totals for number of customers and hash totals
7. Customer lists based upon user-specified criteria (alphabetical for all customer number selected lists, etc.)
8. Outstanding bills and orders (by date, number, customer, etc.)
9. Hard copy and inquiry regarding status of customer orders.
10. Credit memos.
11. Invoice registers for invoices prepared during the current processing.
12. Order register for orders processed.

Sales Analysis

The purpose of the sales analysis system is to provide timely summaries of historical data, to facilitate market analyses and to produce commission statements.

Features

1. Maintain sales data by:
   Catalog number; Quantity;
   Charge to customer/account; Salesman;
   Territory; Product code;
   Sales price.
2. Provide transaction entry and editing in an on-line interactive mode.
3. Reject only those entries containing errors.
4. Maintain a suspense account for entries with validation errors.
5. Identify all errors for a given transaction for which an error condition has been detected.
6. Support x customers in total with x customers active at any time.
7. Support x salesmen in total with x salesmen active at any time.
8. Support x inventory items in total with x items active at any time.
9. Automatic end of period housekeeping, such as zeroing monthly figures and accumulating year to date amounts.
10. Support 13-period fiscal year.
11. Perform trend analysis on sales summaries.
12. Accommodate primary and secondary salesmen.
13. Accommodate "house accounts" when salesman is not applicable.
14. Accommodate present manual account number sequences.
15. Calculate both current period and year to date information, as well as comparable prior period data.
16. Accommodate the prior period adjustments and update the prior period data.
17. Provide comparison of actual data to budgeted data and provide variance analyses.
18. Produce trend reports based on prior period, current period, and budget data, and use such reports as turnaround documents.

19. Facilitate flexible or variable budgeting using rates, standards, or projected figures.
20. Maintain as a minimum, the following sales masterfile informations:

    Product identification; Product category;
    Product description; Product unit of measure;
    Weight; Current cost per unit; Preceding cost per unit;
21. Maintain, as a minimum, the following sales masterfile information:

    Customer number; Salesman code;
    Product identification; Product category;
    Prior year sales, amount; Current year sales, amount;
    Prior year sales, units; Current year sales, unit;
    Prior year sales, weights; Current year sales, weights;
    Commission data; Margin.
22. Maintain, as a minimum, the following customer masterfile information:

    Customer name; Customer number;
    Bill to address; Ship to address;
    Salesman; Balance data.
23. Maintain salesman masterfile information.
24. Perform all edit tasks prior to any file updates.

Reports

1. Product masterfile listing, including analyses and / or forecasts for various categories.
2. Sales masterfile listing.
3. Product category sales analysis and forecast.
4. Salesman sales analyses (by salesman, customer, and territory).
5. Customer sales analyses (by customer type, territory, salesman, alphabetical).
6. Item sales analysis report (by category).
7. Detailed sales report.
8. Daily sales recap (by territory, salesman, customer, item) with comparison analysis.
9. Product analysis by salesman.
10. Salesman commission statements.

11. Market analysis by industry type, geographic territory, product line, type of customer, and sales history totals.

Inventory Management (Module)

The objectives of the automated inventory management system consist of:

- Avoiding stock-outs while at the same time minimizing inventory levels.
- Maintaining information on inventory items, including quantities on hand and on order.
- Preparing challans.

Features

1. Provide transaction entry and editing in an on-line interactive mode.
2. Reject only those entries containing errors.
3. Maintain a suspense account for entries with validation errors.
4. Identify all errors for a given transaction for which an error condition has been detected.
5. Permit transaction entry for a subsequent period prior to closing the current period.
6. Accommodate on-line maintenance to the inventory management system.
7. Process "issues" and returns transactions including:
   Quantity; Part number;
   General ledger account; Issuing responsibility.
   Number
8. Process adjustments to inventory quantity on hand and unit price.
9. Process transfers between inventory locations (catalog number, quantity, transfer from transfer to, document number and/or material request number authorizing the transfer.)
10. Automatic interface from order entry system, including part number, quantity, charge to customer, account number, and sales price.

11. Process receipts of inventory, including item number, quantity, account number, vendor, and purchase order number.
12. Support in-transit inventories.
13. Accommodate user-defined inventory locations such as company, division, warehouse, stock location, and material type.
14. Calculate prices by item number based on user-defined pricing methods.
15. System-generated reordering capability based on reorder levels.
16. Automatic interface to the user-defined general ledger accounts.
17. Maintain detailed transaction files to facilitate detailed listings of inventory transactions, including activity from other systems.
18. Reassign and compute "ABC"codes based on annualized and season usage, cost, margin, and sales.
19. Compute and maintain actual cost history for inventory items based on all transactions processed by the system.
20. Process quantity adjustments based on physical counts.
21. Calculate order points and economic order quantities (EOQs).
22. Automatic interface with accounts receivable, order entry and credit authorization systems.
23. System-granted purchase orders based on user-defined criteria (inventory quantity on hand plus on order is less than min/max or reorder point, positive MRP net requirements, etc.).
24. Prepare and process cancellation notices for on-order quantities.
25. Permit discretionary 'overbuy' of inventory items.
26. Automatic generation of challan lists.
27. Accommodate up to x digits for stock numbers.
28. Accommodate inactive and active part numbers and change status.
29. Accommodate two lead times (from supplier to dock and dock to stock).

30. Automatic conversion from one unit of measure to another.
31. Track inventory shrinkage.
32. Automatic rejection and notification for transactions that would cause a negative inventory quantity.
33. Process partial-case shipments.
34. Provide physical inventory aids, including input screens, forms, and the like.
35. Track committed but not shipped items.
36. Automatic rejection and notification for deletion of masterfile items regarding nonzero balances.
37. Automatic housekeeping for end of period processing, including zeroing current period balances and accumulating year to date figures.
38. Limit checks and notification for transactions above limits and inventory quantity limits.
39. Automatic update of prior period balances for prior period adjustments.
40. Accommodate bulk price updates.
41. Maintain an inventory masterfile with, as a minimum, the following information:

Warehouse;	Inventory location;	ABC Code;
Actual cost information;	Order rules;	Freight code;
Standard cost information;	Vendor crossreference number;	Order point;
		Lead time;
Safety stock item number;	Lot size;	Class;
	Description code;	Item weight;
Vendor number;	Alternate vendor number;	Tax class;
Out of stock code;		Price code;
Purchase unit of measure;	Stock unit of measure;	Description;
Price break information for up to x breaks.	Suggested retail price;	

42. Maintain a customer masterfile with, as a minimum, the following information:

Number;	Name;	Address;
Ship to address for up to x locations;	Phone number;	Credit limit;
	Year account opened;	Credit rating;
Credit rating date;	Salesman number;	Servicing branch code;
	Date of last sale;	
Tax information for multiple jurisdictions.		

43. Maintain a vendor masterfile with, as a minimum, the following information:

Vendor number;	Vendor name;	Vendor address;
Telephone number;	Vendor minimum quantities.	

44. Maintain an inventory warehouse master-file with, as a minimum, the following information:

Item number;	Warehouse number;	Bin location;
Reorder point;	Safety stock level;	Suggested order quantity;
Date of last purchase order;	Lead time;	
	Last cost;	Average unit;
Total quantity on order;	Quantity on hand;	Quantity on back order;
	Period to date outs;	
Today's out receipts for period;	Year to date direct sale;	Year to date stock sale;
This month direct sale;	Last month stock sales;	On hand at last receipt;
Buyer code;	Cash discount code;	Quantity of last purchase order;
Quantity of last receipt.	Lead times;	

Reports

1. Daily transaction listing for all inventory activity.
2. Physical inventory work sheet for cycle counts.
3. Reorder recommendation report specifying reorder point, EOQ quantity on hand and on order, average usage, and lead times.
4. Back-order report listing all items for which requests for issue have been suspended, including item number, storage location, and required quantity.

5. Inactive inventory report summarizing items for which there has not been any activity for a user-defined (variable) period, including issues, sales, or transfers.
6. Physical inventory differences report with quantities and rupees for book figures, physical counts, and the difference.
7. ABC analysis, including current ABC from the calculated ABC, ABC quantity, ABC rupees, cumulative rupees and percentage of total value.
8. Cycle inventory report with quantities, standard cost, and extended rupees amounts for both book and cycle count, together with actual differences compared to user-defined tolerance limits.
9. Inventory masterfile listing, including inventory number, account name, Rupees amounts for beginning balance, receipts, issues, adjustments, net change, and ending balance.
10. Inventory stock status report with part number, inventory account, quantity on hand, rupees amount of quantity on hand, requirement quantity, on order quantity, allocated quantity, secondary quantity, description, and unit of measure.
11. Inventory revaluation report comparing new standard costs to old standard costs for each account and the change both in rupees and percentage.
12. Weekly or monthly transaction register listing transactions and stock movements.
13. Inventory report listing the number of months of quantities on hand for all parts within each inventory account.
14. On-line inquiry and display for individual transactions including status and level information.
15. Challan or packing list for filling orders.
16. Inventory cross-reference listing based on user-defined criteria.
17. Warehouse transfer report of stock movement between warehouses.
18. Inventory return report.

Transport Management (Module)

For some distribution companies, the use of common carriers solves delivery issue. For others, a fleet of company-operated trucks presents further challenges. The primary objective of the route scheduling system is to enable the fleet to be used in the most efficient manner.

Features

1. Load salesman orders.
2. Process breakage information (truck and warehouse).
3. Process customer information, including data relative to chain-store operations.
4. Extensive edit and validation testing.
5. Rejection only of transactions containing errors.
6. Automatic interface with the inventory control system.
7. Automatic interface with the accounts receivable system.
8. Perform route reconciliation for both pre-sell and driver-sell methods.
9. Produce invoice registers.
10. Accommodate a 13-period fiscal year.
11. Calculate salesman commissions for both pre-sell and driver-sell method.
12. Accommodate up to x chain-store locations.
13. Accommodate upto x days of history.
14. Permit entering transactions for other than the customer's assigned salesman.
15. Accommodate up to x days of future orders.
16. Accommodate sales promotions.
17. Accommodate up to x customer type.
18. Maintain up to x state requirements regarding prohibited transactions.
19. Accommodate up to x customers with x customers active at any time.
20. Process multiple warehouses and multiple companies both with unique inventories.
21. Accommodate x number of active orders at any time.

22. Process prior period adjustments.
23. Allow posting to other subsystems (inventory control and accounts receivable).
24. Transaction editing and notification for :

Poor credit risks	Non-existent salesman
Insufficient inventory	Non-existent customer

25. Perform all editing prior to file updates.
26. Maintaining breakage information and statistics.
27. Maintain a route scheduling masterfile with, as a minimum, the following information:

Customer number;	Customer name;	Route number;
Salesman number;	Normal ordering requirements;	Product/commodity type.

28. Maintain a route scheduling transaction file with, as a minimum, the following information:

Customer number;	Location;	Amount;
Delivery frequency;	Ordering information;	Source code;
Date;		Schedule para.

29. Maintain a load statistics file with, as a minimum, the following information:

Truck number/ID;	Truck type;	Availability;
Size;	Commodity capability;	Usage history;
Driver;		Expected receipts.
Loading characteristics;		

Reports

1. Pre-printed invoices (for use in presell activities).
2. Truck load sheets.
3. Route scheduling work sheet indicating vehicle assignments, territory, distance, customers, driver, load, inventory, return.
4. Pre-printed order forms (for use in driver-sell activities).
5. Sales analysis.
6. Marketing and statistical reports.
7. Customer order list (for use in pre-sell activities).
8. Ticket headers and/or gummed labels (for driver-sell activities).

9. Route reconciliation report (to help eliminate shrinkage).
10. Where applicable, a gratis report.
11. Where applicable, a case promotion report.
12. Inventory requirements report (by supplier, product).
13. Daily sales report (by route, salesman).
14. Sales (by route, by product, by day).
15. Sales to chains (weekly and/or monthly, by chain-store location).
16. Sales to other distributors (by invoice).
17. Truck breakage report.
18. Warehouse breakage report.
19. Receipts and other adjustments to inventory.
20. Return control turnaround documents.

Integrating Controls

This section deals with accounting controls. An understanding of where and when controls are needed, as well as control objectives, will help to decide the extent of controls necessary in your environment.

Understanding Where and When Controls Are Needed

The flow of transaction through the system is the key to understanding where and when controls are needed. In this regard, controls are needed whenever:

- Assets are exchanged (e.g., shipment of goods or delivery of services in exchange for a receivable).
- Liabilities are incurred (e.g., liability arising from receipt of raw materials or services rendered).
- Accounting information is transferred or summarized.

To illustrate these concepts, let us follow the flow of transactions for shipments in a computerised environment. In Fig. 7.2, the transport transaction commences in the warehouse when the customer's order is filled. The goods are forwarded to the transporter for delivery to the customer. After the goods are shipped, the information on the challan is the key entered into the despatch department terminal and transmitted to the computer. Using the transmitted information and the price masterfile, the computer prepares the sales invoice and post the sales information to a sales transaction file.

Each week, the accumulated sales and cash receipts transactions are used to update the accounts receivable file, prepare the sales and cash receipts registers, produce and accounts receivable aging, and post the totals to the general ledger account.

Using the flow of transactions concept, let's review the points at which controls are needed:

Let us explore the reasons and controls that are needed at each and every one of these points:

Table 7.4

Points	Examples of What Can Go Wrong	Result
1. Transportation	*Errors:* Challans not in agreement with goods shipped	Incorrect billings or Unbilled shipments
	Irregularities: Additional goods shipped	Unbilled shipment
2. Transmittal of shipping information to EDP	*Errors:* Information not entered or incorrectly entered.	Incorrect billings or unbilled shipments
	Irregularities: Challan information changed	Same
3. Price changes entered	*Errors and irregularities:* some not entered, some entered in error, wrong file updated.	Incorrect billing
4. Preparation of sales invoice	*Errors:* Wrong transaction file used; invoicing program not run	Incorrect billing, Unbilled shipments
	Irregularities: price file altered; unauthorised program changes	Incorrect or unbilled shipments
5. Update weekly sales transaction file.	*Errors:* Wrong file updated; information lost	Erroneously recorded or unrecorded transaction
	Irregularities: Unauthorised program changes	Same as above

6. Update accounts receivable	*Errors:* Wrong file used; wrong account updated	Customers account updated twice or not updated atall
	Irregularities: Unauthorised program changes	Customer accounts not updated or updated incorrectly
7. Print invoice register	*Errors:* wrong file used, erroneous programming changes	Invalid transactions recorded twice and invalid transactions not recorded Aging incorrect
8. Update general ledger	*Errors:* Wrong file used ledger account	Wrong Journal updated
	Irregularities: Account balance modified	General ledger not updated

EIGHT

In How Many Ways Can I Get My Money?

METHODS, CREDIT SERVICES AND OTHER MODES

Having agreed terms with the buyer, the next step should be to determine the manner of payment. A credit manager is not only to know the alternative modes of receiving payment but also should be aware of the pros and cons of all payment methods.

Common Methods and Services Available

1. By cheque/demand draft
2. Through bank (by sending the documents to consignees banker)
3. Bills of exchange/*hundi*/bill market scheme
4. Letters of credit
5. IDBI/ICICI bill discounting for capital purchase
6. Instalment facilities and hire purchase schemes
7. Lease payment
8. Factoring
9. Credit Card
10. Collection agency in India
11. Contra account
12. Consignment sale
13. Electronic data interchange and credit control
14. Lock box or cash management product
15. Franchising
16. Bank Channel Financing Schemes

In collecting, the right philosophies make you a winner.

—Leonard Sklar

1. By Cheque or Demand Draft

Post-dated cheques should not be considered as settlement on the date it is received but on the date it has to be deposited and realised. As per Section-6 of Negotiable Instrument Act, a cheque is a bill of exchange drawn upon a specified banker and payable on demand. It must be clearly understood that although, as per act, issuing a cheque without adequate funds is a criminal offence, issuing of other bills of exchange like hundi, bill market scheme are not.

Litigation with regard to dishonour of cheques is explained in the Chapter on Legal Path.

2. Documents through Bank

The goods are sent to consignee on 'self' basis, and then invoice and other documents are sent to customer's bank.

This is one of the most secured ways of getting payment. The consignee copy of the LR/RR/Airway Bill on 'self' basis along with Bills and other relevant documents are sent to customer's banker. The banker collects the money before handing over the documents to the customer. The important part of this transaction is the transport receipt (LR/RR/AWB). It should be booked on self basis, i.e. the ownership of the goods will remain with the seller. The seller should ask for road permit whenever required from the customer and then book the goods through bank approved transporter. It is very important to send goods through a bank-approved transporter because these carriers are reputed and do not hand over the goods to their friendly clients without authorised/endorsed consignee copy of LR/RR/AWB. Hence a customer is expected to pay first to his banker, get the documents and then clear the goods. The banker makes a demand draft and send it to the seller. It may be the surest way of getting your payment but not necessarily fastest. A customer after receiving the intimation of the consignment keeps on following up with the transporter. Only when the goods have arrived, he will go to his bank and clear the documents. Collection is actually made between 15–45 days and depends on how good and fast the transporter is.

In case of government department it is slightly different. They wait for bank to intimate them and only then will they process the bill and make the payment. The credit manager should follow up with the bank, requesting them to send the intimation to the respective government departments without delay.

Form 8.1

Sample Documents through Bank

Name of the Bank:
M/S State Bank Of India
Haldia Refinery Campus Branch
P.O. Haldia Oil Refinery
Dist: Midnapur - 721 606

Our Reference:
Inv #: Hyd/Lmps/388
Dtd: 07/08/99

Sub: Bill for Collection.

Order No. HB/981065/02/ PLPJ-62 (SPC) DTD. 27/05/99 for supply of following materials:

Sr. No.	Item Name	Qty.
1.	Intrinsically safe GP300 (146-174 MHz) 16 CH. 1-5w, with DTMF keypad with std. accessories. Item Code: 4228010025	30 nos.
2.	GP Antenna for Base Station GM300. Item Code: 4228010105.	06 nos.
3.	RG 8U Co-axial cable with all necessary end connectors. (30 Mtrs each) Item Code: 4228010935.	06 nos.
4.	Spare 1200 MAH, intrinsically safe NI-CD battery for GP300 I/S. radio. (HNN 8133B) Item Code: 4228011125.	05 nos.

Dear Sir,

With reference to the above, we enclose herewith the following documents.

1. Demand Draft for Rs 9,44,597.00
2. Invoice No. HYD/LMPS/388 dtd 07/08/99 for Rs 9,44,597.00 in triplicate and claimed 100% - i.e. Rs 944,597.00
3. Delivery challan in duplicate No. HYD/LMPS/388 Dtd. 07/08/99.
4. Packing list No. LMPS/388.
5. Goods outward and inspection report No. LMPS/388.
6. Warranty certificate.
7. Customer purchase order copy.
8. Central sales tax certificate in duplicate.
9. Transporter Docket # 2679761 Dtd. 07/08/99. (M/s. Patel Roadways Limited consignee copy.)

Please deliver the above documents to

Chief Finance Manager
M/S Indian Oil Corp. Ltd.
Haldia Refinery
P.O. Haldia Oil Refinery - 721 606
Dist: Midnapur (WB)
against payment of Rs 9,44,597.00

Your charges may be debited to our account and can be deducted from our claimed amount.

Thanking You,

Yours sincerely,
for Arya Ltd.

V. Rao

(Manager - Commercial)

Encl: As above.

INV NO.: HYD/LMPS/388 Date: 07/08/99

DEMAND DRAFT

Rs. 9,44,597.00
On demand please pay to M/s State Bank Of India,
Haldia Oil Refinery Campus Branch,
P.O. Haldia Oil Refinery-721606.
(Branch Code # 7090)

or order the sum of Rupees nine lacs forty four thousand five hundred ninety seven only being 100% of our Invoice # HYD/LMPS/388 dtd. 07/08/99 on account of goods supplied by us through M/s Patel Roadways Ltd, vide their docket # 2679761 Dtd 07/08/99.

To,
Chief Finance Manager
M/s. Indian Oil Corporation Ltd
Haldia Oil Refinery
Dist. Midnapur
West Bengal

for,
Arya Ltd
Manorama, 1-10-98/30
Mayuri Marg, Begumpet
Hyderabad - 500 016
Ph # 040 - 7760765
Fax # 040 - 7760765

V. Rao
Manager - Commercial

Encl: As above.

3. Bills of Exchange/Hundi/Bill Market Scheme

A bill of exchange is an unconditional promise to pay the amount stated on a given date. It has to be accepted for payment by the debtor and is payable to the creditor. Bills are normally drawn by the creditor although they are accepted by the debtor and then passed to the creditor who signs as drawer.

As per Sec. 5 of Negotiable Instrument Act, there are three parties to a bill: Drawer or the maker of the bill, Drawee or the person who has accepted to pay and the Payee who will receive the money. Payee or the holder of the bill will present the bill to drawee and get it accepted by obtaining his signature on it. After drawee signs the bill, he becomes the acceptor.

However it is a common practice to get the bill accepted by drawee's banker i.e. the bank will pay in case drawee does not.

Form 8.2

Specimen of a *Hundi*

Hundi No. 15 Dt: 25/3/93

On acceptance of this Hundi, please pay to Harikishore Singh Electricals or their banker, Bank of Thane, on 9/11/93 a sum of Rs.4,38,344.20 (Rupees four lacs thirty eight thousand three hundred forty four and paise twenty only) being the value of the material supplied to M/s New India Electricals, as per the Challans and invoices stated below:

Invoice No.	Date	Amount
HK/I/00301	31/1/93	2,00,000.00
HK/I/00302	27/2/93	1,50,000.00
HK/I/00303	27/2/93	88,344.20
		4,38,344.20

LR NO. G-35218 dated 16/5/93 of Goa Transport Company.

For New India Electricals, For Harikishore Singh Electricals,

Sd/-	Sd/-	Sd/-	Sd/-
Authorised Attorney	Authorised Attorney	Manager	Accountant

To: New India Electricals
Station Line
Kandivli, Bombay

Co-accepted by the Bank

The benefits of co-accepted *Hundi* are:

(a) A co-accepted bill is better than a promise to send a cheque.
(b) A co-accepted bill is normally presented for payment at the customer's bank. In case the customer does not have sufficient funds then his banker will pay.
(c) A supplier can sue on a dishonoured bill, no other evidence of debts being required.
(d) A co-accepted bill is usually discounted with a bank before its maturity.
(e) A customer in cash-flow trouble may agree to clear the bill say in four instalments. The supplier who holds four co-accepted bills can get them discounted at a time irrespective of their maturity dates.

Hundis are the Indian version of the common bills of exchange.

It is a common practice to raise the *hundi* and get it approved only after the goods are delivered. Thus the relation between the seller and the buyer should be good. It has been found in many cases that the buyer after receiving the goods starts giving excuses like 'you may take your money after 30 days and save the *hundi* cost' or 'we do not have facilities with our banker to accept *hundies*', thus avoiding to pay at a certain future date.

Compared to receiving payment by hundi, it will be far safer to deal with customer (whose payment is suspect) against letter of credit. Dispatch is made only after a letter of credit is received from customer's banker, whereas, in case of hundi the necessary documents are raised and accepted by the buyer only after goods are despatched.

When bills are discounted it is most important to keep their value on record against the customer's credit limit. However, if a customer's bill is always co-accepted by his banker then credit limit can be overlooked.

Bill marketing scheme: The bill marketing scheme is governed by the Reserve Bank of India. This scheme encourages increasing use of bill of exchange as an instrument of credit, and buyers and suppliers are now able to plan their finance bills more realistically. Also, this instrument helps the short term borrower to release his money by discounting the bill of exchange at much lower rate than that of cash credit or overdrawing facilities allowed by the bank.

If your customer is already enjoying the credit, you may ask him to draw the bills of exchange for the period of credit allowed to him. As per rule, the period of bill of exchange cannot be more than 120 days. Your bankers will be able to guide you more effectively of this scheme. A sample format of the bill of exchange to be rediscounted in the Reserve Bank of India under the bill marketing scheme is shown below:

Form 8.3

To
Name and address of buyer
....
....
....

No. ....
Place ....
Date ....

At .... days after date/sight (inclusive of days of grace) pay to us or to our order at .... the sum of rupees .... inclusive of interest at ....

....
Signature of the seller

Note: This bill of exchange has been drawn in connection with the sale of....................(specify the description of goods sold)................covered by ....(number and date of document) like railway receipt, lorry receipt, invoice no., etc.

We accept this .... day of 1994 .... to honour the bill on maturity.

....
Signature of the buyer

---

4. Letter of Credit (L/C)

L/Cs are becoming more and more popular in India for internal trade too. This is the most reliable mode of getting your payment in time, especially where the goods are made to customer's specifications. Production work may not start till the L/C arrives, and the pre-shipment risk can thus be avoided. Where non-standard goods are involved and the buyer is unknown, it is always advisable to quote CIF or delivered terms, payment to be made by L/C.

A L/C is an undertaking by the buyer's bank to pay an agreed sum of money to the seller under certain precisely defined conditions. This has clear benefits to both parties. The seller is now certain of payment from a bank, provided he complies with the credit in every respect. The buyer knows that payment will be made on his behalf if the price, despatch dates, parts of loading and unloading, condition and description of the goods are exactly as ordered.

The confirming or advising bank acts strictly as an agent of the issuing bank and it has no responsibility beyond checking the documents. The bank can only be held liable if it fails to detect a discrepancy or lack of conformity in the documents. The basic principle is that banks deal in documents, not in goods.

Payment under L/C may be 'at sight', i.e. on presentation of specified documents or at a fixed future date (eg. 60 days, 180 days, etc.). For a buyer to agree to L/C terms, he must first arrange that his bank will issue a credit. This will only be possible if the buyer has adequate facilities with his bank. Refusal by a buyer to open a credit may be interpreted as an indication of strained resources and requests for less secure terms should be examined cautiously.

In letters of credit normally:

- The supplier is known as the *beneficiary*
- The buyer who asks the bank to issue the credit is the *applicant, orderer* or *accountee*.
- The bank that opens an LC is the opening or issuing bank
- The bank in the supplier's country that advises the credit to the beneficiary and checks its authenticity is the advising bank.

- If any credit or clause is changed, it is done through a document named amendment, and it costs money for every amendment requested after opening of an LC
- The generally adopted set of rules for credits is known as the Uniform Customs and Practice (UCP) for letters of credit
- When an exporter/seller takes the required document into the bank, he is *presenting* them.
- If the documents are in order, the credit becomes *drawn*.
- In a letter of credit where payment is to be made after a deferred period, correct (or credit-confirmed) documents are *taken up*.
- Documents that are not in order are referred to as *discrepant*. Letters of credit are issued in a variety of ways. They come by post from the issuing bank to advising bank by telex, etc. Sometime they are sent to the seller in a sealed envelope with a request to submit them to the advising bank.

The three common types of L/C are:

(a) *Revocable credits:* Very rarely used, since they offer no protection. Once established they can be amended or cancelled either by the buyer or by the issuing bank.
(b) *Irrevocable credits:* Once opened an irrevocable credit cannot be modified without the consent of both buyer and seller.
(c) *Revolving credit:* is used when a specific quantity of goods are required to be shipped at definite intervals, say every fortnight or month.

Issuing and working of documentary credit:

The Buyer	*The Seller*
The Issuing Bank	*The Advising Bank*

1. The process of issuing a letter of credit should start with the buyer's and seller's contract.
2. To avoid any mistake (cost of amendment) the seller will send a pro forma invoice indicating the specification of the goods, the payment terms, the delivery terms, his

banker's name and address. The seller will also mention whether the payment is at "sight of document" or on a "deferred basis".

3. The buyer must enjoy LC credit facilities, or he may have to keep 100% margin money. He will apply for a letter of credit for an amount, attach the pro forma invoice received from the seller.
4. The LC also mentions the validity period – this is likely to be 15/30 days more than the delivery period. Within this period the seller is expected to submit the prescribed documents – such as invoice, transporter's receipt, inspection notes, etc.
5. The seller will present the documents to his own banker (advising bank) who in turn will check and forward the same to issuing bank (buyer's bank).
6. If issuing bank (buyer's bank) finds the documents in order, their payment will be sent (by TT or telegraphic transfer) to the advising bank and the advising bank will credit the same in the seller's account.

Checklist for Letters of Credit

1. *Preparing information on which customer opens Letter of Credit.*
   (a) Allow sufficient time for possible production delays, e.g. request L/C to be valid one month beyond scheduled delivery date.
   (b) Ensure all particulars are complete and accurate.
   (c) State whether part-shipment and trans-shipment must be permitted.
   (d) For FOB contracts ask that the payment be made against presentation of freight forwarder's receipt.
   (e) If your goods are specially made to customer specification, ask for the L/C to be opened and in your possession before you start manufacturing.
2. *On receipt of L/C, check*
   (a) Is the L/C irrevocable? It must be.
   (b) Is the L/C confirmed by a Indian bank? It should be.

(c) Is your name and address spelt correctly?

(d) Is the name of your customer spelt correctly?

(e) Do validity, expiration and shipping dates give sufficient time to get documents together in time to assure payments, special attention to the juxtaposition of these dates and shipping and airline schedules.

(f) Is the L/C amount enough to cover your quotation? *Also check the following*

- (i) Cost of goods plus profit.
- (ii) Inland transport or airport, including wharfage and handling charges.
- (iii) Ocean/airline transportation charges.
- (iv) Forwarding fees.
- (v) Insurance costs.
- (vi) Miscellaneous charges.

(g) Is description of goods correct? If you decide not to ask for amendment, then the customer's description of the goods must appear on all documents as well as your description.

(h) Is quantity of goods correct?

(i) If required, is partial shipment permitted?

(j) Is shipment permitted/required at a given rate or amount? If so, can you confirm?

(k) Is shipment permitted from any place in India or only from one named place?

(l) Does destination (port of discharge) you quoted, or you and buyer agreed on, agree with L/C?

(m) Are guarantees of any sort required by buyer?

(n) Can properly executed documents as given below be obtained to conform with L/C in the language of the buyer if required?

- (i) Bill of lading
- (ii) Airway bill
- (iii) Parcel post receipt
- (iv) Invoices—commercial, preferential, consular, legalised

- (v) Packing list
- (vi) Insurance policy certificate
- (vii) Certificate of inspection
- (viii) Certificate of quality
- (ix) Is any specified agency required to issue or authenticate any of these documents?

(o) Can you comply with cover of insurance risks required by the L/C? Does credit require policy or certificate?

(p) Compare the conditions of the contract of sale with the L/C.

(q) Where is payment to be made?

If, after having examined the L/C against this checklist and having compared the sales contract with the credit, you find need for amendment or clarification of the credit, contact your customer requesting necessary clarification or amendment, bearing in mind the chance of amendments being received on time to honour shipping and validity dates.

5. IDBI/ICICI Bill Discounting and Rediscounting

If you are selling machinery then your customer may offer the bill of exchange for rediscounting. It may be drawn either by the customer or by yourselves on the customer or customer's banker. Without discussing in great details, we would recommend that one should go through the rediscounting scheme of IDBI and ICICI by obtaining the copy from the institution itself. The procedure laid down is very easy to follow and act upon. A customer will prepare all the documents and comply with the formalities of ICICI/IDBI, and forward all documents to credit manager's department, who then gets it rediscounted from his own banker's (ICICI/IDBI section).

6. Instalment Facilities and Hire-Purchase Schemes

In hire-purchase, a consumer is a hirer of the goods. Until the full price is paid by him, the ownership of the goods will be retained by the seller. If the buyer fails to pay even one instalment, the product is taken back by the seller without any consideration for the sum already paid.

Instalment facility terms are much better than hire-purchase scheme. Instalment sale involves outright sale of the product through the transfer of both ownership and possession from the very beginning when the first instalment is paid. It is a conditional sale i.e. in case of failure to pay the instalment the ownership of the goods reverts back to the seller. Unlike hire purchase, the seller does not appropriate the amount already paid by the buyer in the form of some instalments.

Payment by instalment, hire-purchase, open credit, credit card or monthly open credit are various forms of consumer credit or retail credit. We are trying to discuss those which have become very popular during recent times. Today luxuries like car, refrigerator, electronic music system, etc. can be easily purchased through these various consumer credit schemes.

Consumer credit and business credit differ in the degree of individual exposure and the qualifications required for approval of credit. As a general rule, consumer credit tends to treat all customers alike. Decisions are more often based on gross income and the debtor's monthly payments rather than net worth. Practically anyone who has a certain monthly income can obtain consumer credit, provided his existing debts are not over-whelming.

The modalities of hire-purchase: Hire-purchase is a mode of selling goods as well as financing the price of the goods. In a hire-purchase transaction, the goods are let on hire, the purchase price is to be paid in instalments, and the hirer has an option to purchase the goods by paying all the instalments.

An hire-purchase agreement should stipulate the following:

1. Payments is to be made in instalments over a specified period.
2. The possession is delivered to the purchaser at the time of entering into the contract.
3. The ownership of the goods passes to the purchaser on payment of the last instalment.
4. Each instalment is treated as hire (rental) charges so that if default is made in payment of any one instalment, the seller becomes entitled to take away the goods.
5. The hirer/buyer is free to return the goods without being required to pay any further instalments falling due after the return.

6. In case hirer returns the goods then he will not get back the instalment amount already paid towards hiring charges. The intending buyer is known as the hirer so long as the option to purchase is not exercised.
7. The hire-purchase price of the goods.
8. The date of commencement of the agreement.
9. The number of instalments, the amount of each instalment, due date, the person to whom and the place where, each of the instalments is to be paid.
10. The price at which the goods may be purchased by the hirer for cash.
11. The description of the goods.
12. If any part of the price is to be paid as deposit, down payment or other initial payments and the balance on instalments. In certain contracts, the buyer pays an amount in advance as earnest deposit or as a security for the due performance of his part of the contract. Though the amount of earnest money is adjustable towards the price of the goods, it differs from the price in the sense that while payments towards the prices is recoverable, earnest money is liable to be forfeited if the buyer fails to perform his part of the contract.
13. The owner undertakes a warranty that the hirer shall have and enjoy quiet possession of the goods. That the goods are free from any charge or encumbrance in favour of a third party, at the time the ownership in the goods is to pass.
14. The rights of the hirer to purchase the goods at any time during the continuance of the agreement with rebate (to be calculated in a prescribed manner) giving 14-days notice.
15. To terminate the agreement any time before the final hire purchase instalment falls due. He has to give a 14-days notice, pay the instalments already due before returning the goods. As prescribed, the hirer will have to pay difference in price if he decides to terminate before total instalments paid is not equal to one-half of the hire-purchase price.
16. The hirer is obliged to comply with the agreement, to take care of the goods, not to make unauthorised use of

the goods, to keep owner informed about the location of the goods.

17. The owner has the right to enter premises of the hirer and seize the goods, unless there is a contract to the contrary. However, where the agreement has been terminated by the hirer, the owner cannot seize the goods without the permission of the court.
18. Indemnity clause, Stamp duty, etc.

Some hire-purchase terms

Hirer means the person who obtains (or has obtained) possession of the goods from the owner, under a hire-purchase agreement.

Owner means the person (or a finance company) who lets or delivers possession of the goods to a hirer under a hire-purchase agreement.

Hire means the sum payable periodically by the hirer under a hire-purchase agreement.

Hire-purchase price is the total sum payable by the hirer in order to complete the purchase of, or the acquisition of ownership of goods under hire-purchase agreement, including any sum payable by way of a deposit, down payment or other initial payment, but does not include any sum payable as a penalty or as compensation or damages for a breach of the agreement.

Dealer means the seller of goods to the owner and deliver the goods of hirer's choice to the hirer on instruction from the owner.

A tripartite hire-purchase agreement is arranged with the following modalities:

1. The dealer contacts a finance company to finance hire-purchase deals submitted by him. For this purpose, they enter into a contract drawing out the terms, warranties that the dealer gives with each transaction, etc.
2. The customer selects the goods and expresses the desire to acquire them on hire-purchase (that the customer wants to become a hirer).
3. The dealer arranges for him the full set of documents to be completed to make a hire-purchase agreement. The documents are generally printed by the finance company.

4. The customer then makes the cashdown payment on completing the proposal form. The down payment is generally retained by the dealer as a payment on account of the price to be paid to him by the finance company.
5. The dealer then sends the documents to the finance company requesting them to purchase the goods and accept the hire-purchase transactions.
6. The finance company, if it decides to accept the transactions, signs the agreement and sends a copy to the hirer (customer) along with the instructions as to the payment of the instalments. The finance company also notifies the same to the dealer and asks him to deliver the goods, if he has not already done so..
7. The dealer delivers the goods to the hirer (customer) against acknowledgement and the ownership of goods passes on to the finance company i.e. the finance company becomes the owner of the goods being given to the customer (hirer) on hire.
8. The hirer makes payment of the hire instalment periodically as decided (usually it monthly). In fact, the owner (finance company) insists on all the instalment to be paid by post-dated cheques to be handed over to owner in advance before the seller delivers the goods. This has become a common practice today. The owner to safeguard the post-dated cheques, that they are encashed on due dates, also takes an undertaking from the hirer as follows:

   'In respect of the hire-purchase agreement, we are giving the following post-dated cheques. We authorise you to present these cheques in the bank on due dates of the instalments and we hereby undertake to honour the cheques on presentation. We hereby undertake not to intimate the bankers to stop the payment of the cheques delivered to you. We hereby undertake not to close the bank account without your permission in writing under the terms of the hire-purchase agreement. We hereby undertake that we shall never give you any notice requesting you not to present the cheques given hereunder on due dates. We are aware that on the faith of this undertakings, you have agreed to provide the said Hire-Purchase Finance.'

Credit managers are advised that such an undertaking should be taken if in case they are accepting any post-dated cheques for any reason. Such an undertaking is very common in Lease-purchase Agreement also.

In case of hire-purchase, even the guarantor (if involved) are asked to sign this undertaking.

Advantages of hire-purchase

(a) More new customers are attracted 'through the door on the floor'.
(b) Sales can be made to those customers who cannot immediately pay cash, and impulse buying is encouraged.
(c) The small-scale and medium-scale manufacturers find a great facility in the system. They can install the required machinery and machine tools without having to find the total sum of the capital required for the purpose all at once. In India the National Small Industries Corporation is helping the small industrialist in this manner.
(d) Customers are more likely to consider buying better quality, higher-priced merchandise.
(e) Special credit terms can be arranged to assist in the promotion of any 'slow moving item' or during the period of poor trade.
(f) Bulk buying can be encouraged.

Drawbacks of hire-purchase

(a) People may be tempted by instalment plans to buy things they cannot afford.
(b) It makes the article dealt in costlier. The hire-purchase price includes the interest on unpaid balances, the cost of collection of instalments and the losses owing to default on the part of the customers, besides normal price of the article.
(c) The finance company or the owner, especially in India, runs a very heavy risk of the hirer not paying at all, or not paying on time. In many cases, he has to proceed with legal action against many defaulters, which takes a very long time to conclude. Although the owner has the right to reclaim the articles for which the instalments are not paid, the recovered goods can fetch little because they are after all second-hand goods.

In case if the goods are not easily marketable the owner (finance company) should take a back-to-back guarantee from the dealer that if in case there is a default, and the owner has to reclaim back the article, then such article will be purchased back by the dealer at a depreciated price. This way the owner will at least not have to carry dead stock.

Form 8.4

Specimen Used in One of the Companies for Sale under Hire-purchase Scheme

To: ____

(Name and address of the company granting credit)

Application For Hire Purchase/Credit Sale Account

Goods required____________________________________

Cash price

Terms proposed deposit Rs.__________Weekly/Monthly repayments Rs____________

Surname____________________________Forename________________

(Block Letters)

Address____

(continued)

	How long	Phone
State	1. Owner	3.Tenant-unfurnished
Whether	2. Tenant-furnished	4.Suv-tenant/lodger
	(Delete those not applicable)	

Previous address ____________________________________

____

(If you are not the householder a guarantor may be necessary)

Landlord's name and address

____

(if applicable) ____________________________________

Employers________________________Type of Business________________

(We do not contact employers for references)

Name, address and occupation

of Guarantor____________________________________

(If under 18 or not a householder)____________________________

References: bankers and branch____________________________

Do you wish to pay by banker's order__________________________

Other companies by whom credit facilities have been granted:

Name and address 1____________________________________

2____________________________________

(For office use only)

Hire-purchase account		Credit sale account	Agreement sent:
Cash price	HP price	Cash price	Bank ref.
	Half	Deposit	Trade ref.
Deposit		Rs	(1)
Rs	Third	Service fee	(2)
Service Fee	Commence	Balance Rs	Other
Balance Rs	Rebate	Deposit receipt No.	inquiries

Form 8.5

Specimen of Guarantee

To____

of____

I, the undersigned______________________________________

in consideration of your opening a budget account with a limit of ________ Rs.______________dated______________in the name of __________ hereby undertake to guarantee the due performance and observance of all the terms and conditions on the part of the buyer agreed to be performed and observed and to comply with these terms and conditions upon the failure of the buyer to do so and to pay all the expenses you may be put to in enforcing the said account, and I agree that no relaxation or indulgence on your part in respect of the said terms and conditions shall prejudice your rights under this guarantee.

Signature of guarantor

Signature of witness

Witness' name in full

Address of witness

Date

7. Leasing

It is possible for a buyer to lease many goods, especially capital goods. The lease may be arranged locally with the aid of any leasing company. The manufacturer sells to the leasing company and receives 100% payment on delivery or after installation (as per the condition in the order) at the user's premises. This way, the user is enabled to obtain equipment it could not afford to buy (or which it chooses not to buy because of a high obsolence risk), and repay the amount to the leasing company in instalment as rent. After all the instalments are paid, the leasing company may offer to sell the goods (transfer ownership of goods) for a meager value to the user, until then the ownership lies with the leasing company.

It is certainly a simple transaction but, none the less, it is prudent to see that negotiation for the lease are set in hand reasonably in advance of a payment date so that the three parties, that is to say the supplier, the user and the leasing company (who will become the owner), can each make their own essential arrangements. When the lease agreement is set up, and assuming that both the supplier and the user have complied with the sales contract, the credit manager's burden disappears—his contribution was to steer a worthwhile customer with a cash-flow problem towards an acceptable financial solution.

A lease is a means of financing the use of the asset, and under a lease the title remains with the lessor (leasing company pays for the goods) but a lessee (user) has the full use of the asset during the period of the lease. Furthermore, it is fundamental to leasing, as described here, that the lessee has the use of the equipment of his choice. Leasing can therefore, be defined as: 'A contract between a lessor and a lessee for hire of a specific asset selected from the manufacturer or vendor of such an asset by the lessee. The lessor retains ownership of the asset. The lessee has possession and the use of the asset for an agreed period on payment of specified rentals.

Within the broad definition there are two sub-divisions – the finance lease (also known as full pay-out lease) and an operating lease.

A *finance* lease is a contract involving payment over a certain period of specified sums which in total liquidate the lessor's capital outlay and provides him with profit. The agreed period will be dependent on two principal factors – the lessor's estimate of the useful life of the asset and the lessee's requirements.

An *operating* lease is a different arrangement wherein the asset is not wholly amortized during the opening period of the lease and the lessor is relying on a renewal of the agreement at the end of the opening period, leasing the same equipment to a second lessee, or selling the equipment at or above an estimated residual value. Operating leases are found, for example, with computers, where it is normal practice for the agreement to include a maintenance contract which will be performed by the lessor or his agent. Because of the rather specialised nature of the operating leases they are not further discussed in this chapter.

For a credit manager, the basic definition of the lease is 'use without ownership'. A credit manager is expected to know the leasing arrangement between his customer (user) and the leasing company. He should ask his customer (prospect) to collect a letter from the leasing company confirming the leasing arrangement, and that the leasing company has agreed to finance the value of the good which his customer is about to buy. This is done by the manufacturer or vendor initially sending a pro-forma invoice to the leasing company, where the name of the consignee (user or customer) is mentioned, the good is described, and also the value is mentioned. In return , the leasing company will acknowledge the same.

The credit manager's company, i.e. the manufacturer or the vendor, will then sale the goods to the leasing company and consign or deliver the goods to his customer and obtain an acknowledgement that the goods are delivered and accepted by the customer. The invoice is raised accordingly, i.e. sold to and delivered to.

The leasing company will then receive the invoice and the goods receipts duly acknowledged by the user and a copy of the same from seller also to match the same. After the leasing company is satisfied that the documents are okay, it will make the payment to the manufacturer or vendor.

The credit manager should note that, we have come across many such incidents, where the order is already placed, and the seller is about to deliver the goods without verifying with the leasing company. The negotiation between the user and the leasing company has actually started only after the goods are delivered. Payment term such as "on delivery" should confirm that it is the buyer who will make the payment and within a defined time.

Conditions that generally apply to a leasing agreement are:

1. The lessee enjoys the unfettered use of the equipment so long as the terms of the agreement.
2. The lessee is responsible for the maintenance of the equipment in good working order and for its insurance.
3. Sub-letting is usually prohibited.
4. The lessee undertakes not to move the plant from the site without the lessor's permission.

5. The lessor will have the right of repossession if there is a significant breach of agreement.
6. The lessee is required at the outset to confirm that he has chosen and accepted the equipment. The lessor will not, and cannot, give a warranty as to fitness, but will, as far as he is able, pass on the supplier's warranties to the lessee. In many cases it is advisable for the lessee to obtain the supplier's agreement that the lessee will receive the benefit of the supplier's warranties.
7. The lessee is generally required to settle rental payments (which normally attract sales tax) by way of a standing order on the lessee's bank or by giving post-dated cheques for the total number of instalments (post-dated cheques towards rental period). In majority of the transactions, rentals are fixed (equal monthly instalment) from the outset though for some large transactions adjustments may be made to reflect the changing cost of money during the lease period.
8. If in case the rentals (instalments) are collected by means of post-dated cheques, the user will also have to sign an undertaking to lessor, as in form 8.5.

   'In respect of the lease agreement, we are giving the following post-dated cheques to enable you to present the same on due dates of rentals/instalments falling due. We authorise you to present these cheques in the bank on due dates of the instalments and we hereby undertake to honour the cheques on presentation. We hereby undertake not to intimate the bankers to stop the payment of the cheques delivered to you. We hereby undertake not to close the bank account without your permission in writing under the terms of the lease agreement. We hereby undertake that we shall never give you any notice requesting you to not present the cheques given hereunder on due dates. We are aware that on the faith of these undertakings, you agree to provide the said lease finance.'

   Credit managers are advised that such an undertaking should be taken if in case they are accepting any post-dated cheques for any reason. Such an undertaking is very common in hire-purchase Agreement also. In case of hire-purchase, even the guarantor should sign this undertaking.

Form 8.6

Sample Copy of the Undertaking for Post-dated Cheque/s Issued

Hirer/Purchaser–Name..
(The Drawer)

In respect of The Loan/Hire-Purchase/Lease/Security Deposit/Purchase Order No........................../Invoice No.................. Dated.............. we have issued the following cheques to enable you (payees' name) to present them for realisation on their due dates.

- The drawer hereby confirms that he has accepted the goods and for total cost of the goods he has issued the necessary number of post-dated cheques to the owner/authorised representatives covering all the gross instalments dues/dues as per the terms of the agreement/purchase order, and each such post-dated cheque carries the due date of such gross instalments.
- The drawer hereby unconditionally and irrevocably states that he shall not, at any point of time, question the validity period of such post-dated cheques, or raise any claim that such cheques are valid only for a period of six months from the date of issuance of the cheques and further affirms that he shall ensure the availability of adequate funds in the account of which such cheques have been drawn on the respective due dates.
- The drawer irrevocably instructs/authorises the payee to deposit the said post-dated cheques on the dates stated on the respective cheques and the drawer hereby undertakes to honour the cheques on presentation, and to ignore any communication from the drawer requesting the payee not to deposit the cheques on the date stated on the cheque.
- The drawer hereby undertakes not to intimate the bankers to stop the payment of the cheques delivered to payee.
- The drawer hereby undertakes not to close the bank account without prior permission in writing under the terms of the agreement.
- The drawer hereby undertakes that he shall never give payee any notice requesting payee not to present the cheques given hereunder on due dates.
- The drawer is aware that on the faith of these undertakings, the payee has agreed to provide the said loan/hire-purchase/lease finance/goods to drawer.
- The drawer submits that in the event of any default in honouring the cheques, the payee is at liberty to take action against drawer for the dishonour of cheques under Section 138 of the Negotiable Instruments Act.

Cheque No.	Date Drawn on (Name of the Bank)	Amount Rs
1.	....	....
2.	....	....
3.	....	....

For: ______________________ (Drawer)

Authorised Signatory

Advantages of lease:

1. The user needs not invest the capital in full as a one-time payment.
2. Leasing sanctions are fast.
3. At some point of time during the course of the agreement, if the user does not need the equipment, he can terminate the agreement and ask the lessor to take away the equipment..
4. The interest part of instalment payments is fully chargeable as expense for the purpose of taxation.

Disadvantages of lease could be:

1. User pays higher interest.
2. Lease equipment does not increase user's asset-based value.
3. User normally does not enjoy depreciation allowance till the ownership is transferred to him.
4. User is likely to be penalised if in case the user decides to terminate the agreement and return the equipment. Moreover, the user will not be able to recover the rental already paid.
5. User cannot move leased equipment to another location without written permission from lessor.

A credit manager is expected to understand all these aspects of leasing, to enable him to perform effectively.

8. Factoring

Factoring is a financial service provided, especially in India, by banks and private firms to help traders, manufacturers and service providers to manage their receivables. Unlike in developed countries, for various legal hassles, it is still not very popular in India.

Factors or Factoring Service Provider (FSP) undertake collection/accounting and management of debts of their clients. A factor may either lend against accounts receivable or by purchasing invoices. He will take responsibility of collecting debts. The factoring services may be offered with or without recourse.

In India, since we are still very far from adopting a credit management culture most of the accounts of a firm remains 'open account'. As a result the risk factor against each account does not get evaluated. Thus we take a lot of effort to realise the sale proceeds. It is a known fact that many units die only because they could not collect their money from debtors in time. For small and big scale industry introduction of factoring services will, therefore, prove very beneficial as it will free the industry from hassles of collecting receivables.

Also there is another situation, when your company's banker might feel that the company's financial and business position will not support an increase in the bank's lending commitment. At that point, especially if you are confident that the need to accelerate cash flow, factoring the company's receivable through an established firm or bank (factoring service provider) could be the answer to getting a faster turnaround of your receivable amount.

If not in the start, at some point in your discussion with the factor's representative, he or she will ask for a list of your accounts and copies of recent receivables aging reports. The factor (FSP) will review your experience with the accounts and, from that evaluation, will delete accounts that are unacceptable. If your discussions with the factor lean toward a relationship where accounts are factored on a recourse basis (you guarantee that you will pay if in case his customer does not pay), then the factor will accept more borderline accounts and advance a higher percentage of each invoice total.

To put very simply, a factoring company will advance to you upto 80% of the value of your sales invoices. This means that instead of having to wait until your customer pays up you will receive, virtually immediately, some of the cash. There are number of variations in the basic theme and, not surprisingly, there is a price to pay for it.

The cost of Factoring will be computed in two parts. Finance charges and Service fees.

Finance charges are computed on the basis of the factor's *prime rate plus basis*, on the prepayment made. As you will be charged for what you use, factoring can be a cheap source of funds.

The *service fee* is levied for the work involved in maintaining your sales ledger and collecting the debts due on the invoices. It will be calculated as a percentage of the gross value of the invoice factored, based on (a) the gross sales volume, (b) the number of customers, (c) the number of invoices and credit notes, and (d) work involved in collections.

The service fee will range from 2% to 5% of the gross value of the invoices. The cost of any special service provided will be charged separately.

Three parties are involved in factoring:

1. Factor or Factoring Service Provider (FSP) who advances the client (say upto 80%).
2. Client or seller who discounts his customers' sales invoices with a FSP and receives advance.
3. Customer or buyer of goods from client (seller), who makes the payment against the invoice to a factor on client's advice.

The procedure:

Step 1. The customer chooses a factor (FSP) and completes registration formalities.

Step 2. Seller (client) receives an order from a customer (buyer) for supply of goods or services.

Step 3. Depending upon customer's reputation and payment terms of the order the seller and the FSP fixes customer limit. Up to what customer's invoice amount the factor is prepared to fund.

Step 4. Seller delivers goods and invoice to customer. The seller also encloses a notice requesting the customer to pay the amount to factor (FSP).

Step 5. Seller sends a copy of the invoice to the factor.

Step 6. Factor verifies whether a notice has been sent by the seller to the buyer and then makes prepayment say 80% (or limit fixed, whichever is less) to seller (client).

Step 7. The factor also maintains a sales ledger on behalf of client for a fee.

Step 8. Factor sends periodically statements to customer.

Step 9. Factor follows up with customer, if in case the payment is overdue. It is pre-decided whether the seller or the buyer will bear the interest for late payment.

Step 10. Factor receives payment from the customer.

Step 11. Factor makes balance payment to seller after deducting his fees toward pre- funding, plus service charges towards administration of sales ledger, debt collection etc.

A factor also extends advisory services. Since they are always in possession of various clients' credit information, being expert and experienced in financial dealings they are in a position to give the right guidance.

In India, State Bank of India, Canara Bank and private firms like Wipro are into factoring business. Paint, chemical wholesellers, printing, machinery, electronics industry etc. known to the authors, are taking advantages of factoring services. One of the notes being advertised by SBI factors is:

EDI Factoring and GEDIS Network

We have installed EDI Factoring Network of 'Factors Chain International' Amsterdam, and GEDIS network of VSNL Mumbai, linking corporate office with branches. These networks are able to carry Electronic Data Interchange. Clients and their customers willing to join EDI Factoring Network may contact corporate office for lease details on terminal. We can supply on approval from Factors Chain International, Amsterdam.

Clients and customers who are already using GEDIS Network of VSNL will find our factoring services extremely useful and efficient. Both these networks will contribute to speed in collections to the advantage of the clients. Also, e-mailing of your statements to debtors, available on e-mail addresses will be possible."

Source: SBI Factors and Commercial Services Pvt. Limited.

There are three popular services offered by factor: (a) Invoice discounting (b) Recourse factoring (c) Non-recourse factoring.

(a) *Invoice discounting:* This is the simplest (and fastest growing) service offered by the factoring companies. It is also the cheapest. With this system you prepare your own invoices, keep your own sales ledger and do all your own administration. You also collect all your own debts. The factoring company advances you up to 80% of the value of your invoices which provides you with 'instant cash' to keep the business going.

(b) *Recourse factoring:* In this version the factoring company keeps your sales ledger for you and collects all debts. However, you as a client company, will remain responsible for any bad debts. Perhaps for this reason recourse factoring is said to be most popular with company doing business with soundly financed firms or a wide range of customers who purchase small-value goods and services, where each debt is small and if things go sour the loss will not be very damaging.

(c) *Non-recourse factoring:* With this form of factoring the client company is protected against baddebts. The factoring takes on this risk at a price. The factoring company will insist on vetting the clients' customers for credit worthiness and may choose to reject those it considers to be a bad risk. This, in a sense, reduces the value of the non-recourse service since it limits your freedom to trade with all and sundry and still have protection against a bad debt.

You can of course decide to continue with firms which the factoring company has rejected, but you will be taking a big risk. You are being warned that the company is likely to delay payments or even may go bust. You should be very careful to do business with such risky parties. Without stability, cash flow forecasting becomes cash-guessing—a situation fraught with dangers and anxieties.

Benefits of factoring:

Direct financial benefits: Factoring offers you highly flexible mode of cash generation against receivables. Once a line of credit is established, availability of cash is directly geared to sales. As your sales increase, so does the availability of cash.

Indirect benefits:

(a) The improvement in cash-flow means that optimum stock levels can be maintained. It may also be possible to put pressure on your supplier to offer better deals (e.g. discounts) by virtue of your ability to pay promptly.

(b) You can accept larger orders knowing that you will have the money to cope with them.

(c) Since factor will take over your ledger keeping and debt collection work, you are likely to save on those extra employees which you would have otherwise hired.

(d) More management time is available for attending to other aspects of the business. Attention can be paid to sales, purchase, supply chain, etc.

(e) The chances of losing customers as a result of relationships being strained, by repeated nagging for prompt payment is reduced.

(f) The finance of the business is related to its volume of sales activity rather than a bank manager's opinion of your balance sheet.

Limitations of factoring: There are some limitations to factoring, which should be clearly understood before entering into a factoring agreement. In particular a factoring company will not take on invoices that are already overdue. Factoring is unlikely to be a way to save a business which is already in serious trouble.

9. Credit Cards

They are issued by a number of banks and organizations. By means of these cards, a trader supplies goods to a customer who produces the card, uses this card in an imprinting machine hired from the card company, strikes the bill and subject to checks that the signature on the account compare with that on the card and that the card is valid, completes the sale. The trader is then able to obtain immediate cash payment from the company issuing the card, such payment being subject to a discount covered in the agreement between the trader and the credit card company. This discount may vary on such things as volume of turnover and risk factors.

The customer pays a modest fee each year in certain cases to join the credit card scheme and receives a monthly account of all the charges that have been debited to his account from whatever trades he has dealt with. The account must be paid within a certain time otherwise it attracts interest rate. The advantage from the trader's point of view is that he needs no special finance to assist in his credit business and obtains cash payment on the transaction within a short time. The disadvantages are that the discounting, hiring and stationery cost may be in excess of those costs that he would incur, should he finance the credit trade himself and in this connection, the prevailing bank rate is very important factor. Another disadvantage is that the customers are not tied to his shop as they are with a continuous revolving or budget credit scheme; but against this the advantage is that the trader has potentially many more customers.

Modalities of credit card:

- This is the most easy way of obtaining revolving credit and since the procedure is easy to understand, it has become very popular way of giving and receiving consumer credit. One of the most common ways in which credit terms are now made available to the customers is by the trader agreeing to accept credit cards.
- The credit card company issues a credit card to customers after verifying one or more of the criteria such as, their monthly income, and bank, trade and or personal references and confirmation of employment. This job

of pre-verification are usually undertaken by many collection agencies as an additional service.

- After verification, the credit card company then sets a credit limit i.e. up to what amount the customers can make purchases from traders. With every purchase the credit limit starts diminishing. The only way the customer can keep the credit limit viable, is by making regular payment in full or instalment to the credit card company on a monthly basis.
- This can be a three party arrangement whereby the trader receives payment from the credit card company whom the customer repays by instalments.
- Usually the trader has to obtain approval from credit card company either by telephone or by an electronic read-out from a magnetic stripe on the card, before supplying goods. Given this approval, the customer is allowed to make purchases up to the limit set by credit card company for each individual card holder.
- The credit card details are imprinted on to the sale document which is then signed by the customer and identification is carried out by comparing the signature on the document with that on the credit card.
- The trader benefits by way of additional business but a charge for this facility is made by the credit card company through an agreed discount, which is deducted from the price shown on the sale document before payment is made to the trader.

A statement is sent to the card holder by the credit card company listing the purchases made in the previous month and the card holder can then pay the balance in full, in which case no credit charge is made. Alternatively, the balance can be paid by instalments in which event a charge for credit calculated at a daily basis/monthly basis, as a percentage of the balance, is added each month.

10. Collection Agency & Fair Debt Collection

Old folk saying "*If you want your money back than you must loan money to people who has money*"......now how long he is going to have money is a question of credit worthiness.

The second saying "*Your money, if you don't ask, you don't get*"........how to ask is matter of training & debate.

The third principle I added in my book "Cash before you Crash" is.... "Don't do business with weak, sick and indifferent customers. Chances are that sooner or later you may occupy the next bed."........now "Weak", "Sick" & "Indifferent" are the words needs to be clearly understood.

The question is, in our day-to-day business we have left all these principles behind and are trying to become the buzz word call "result-oriented". The business has to give result. The executive has to give result. The subordinate has to deliver result. You outsource your collection activity to get result and tell the Collection Agency that their fees is directly related to result they deliver.

Personally, I like this buzz word call "result-oriented". Fact is, in pursuing result we leave behind all principles of decency, ethics, mannerism, resulting in social stigma. The collection agent does not care to keep your reputation, and company's image is at casualty. He is aggressive and hungry for results, otherwise he will not get his fees. Instead why can't these business houses have their own Credit and Collection department with their own trained-staff. This is common in other parts of the world.

The collection agency has only one tool to get result... "*the tool of harassment*" as some term it. Business house does not mind so long as this dirty job is being done by some outsider who is actually hired by them. And few days back, we have too much of talk of people who are dying, because they cannot return the loan and can't bear the burnt of collection agency harassment.

Business houses to get result, wants to lure even the pauper to easy credit and when they can't pay, they leave it to the Collection Agency to reward them with their dirty work.

Money is a weakness, and when you get it so easily very likely many are going to fall for the loan, especially when you don't have to prove your credentials or provide guarantor or collateral in many cases. It is not their fault. Someone lured them. Most of them never approached.

What is the way out? In other countries the Collection Agency is mainly attached to a Legal firm....so that proper method is followed to collect dues and over dues

They have enacted laws called 'Fair Debt Collection Practices" for:

- Business houses on how to select Collection Agency
- Collection Agency - their duties and responsibilities
- The rights of the borrower and how they can stop the Collection Agency harassment.

This does not mean that the loan will go away. In fact the law makes it more strict and compelling to return the loan with interest. For this we need to have more teeth in the law. By teeth I mean that our law should be easier to pursue and the judgment should be easier, cheaper & faster. (We all know what is happening to Cheque bouncing cases). Both the lender and the borrower will have to have respect for the law. Why Indian law cannot have teeth is again a question of debate.

Let's start where all these starts – the selection of a collection agency. A small excerpt from my book "Cash before you Crash" guides one on how to select a Collection agency.

"Selecting a collection agency is not a trival matter. In India many security agencies offering security guards to various organisations, shops and housing society is also offering Collection as an additional product. Now, if security guards will collect money from customers then the very effort made in this book is lost. Then there are collection agencies using high-handed-tactic to recover payments, and various firms in India are fancying them.

A good way to select a good collection agency is by deciding the selection grid, such as:

1. Name of the agency and its reputation.
2. Reputation & experience of the owner.
3. Years in business.
4. Collection fee and its basis.
5. It should be non-contingency basis
6. References.
7. How do they go about making the final demand on the customer.
8. Nationwide coverage.
9. Derogatory Information (if any).

In order to complete the selection grid number of questions. First inquire and gather the following information:

1. Number of years in business
2. Reputation and relevant experience of the owner
3. Collection fee on recoveries
4. Does a agency charge a non-contingency fee?
5. How does the agency send or make a final demand to the customer?
6. Is the agency familiar with commercial laws and other legal ethics?
7. Does the agency have a nation wide coverage or the required coverage?
8. Is the agency reputed or bonded or licensed?
9. What is the procedure they adopt after money is collected and before it is handed over to the company? Is it safe and secured? Will they compensate for cheques lost in transit while in their custody?
10. Does the agency handle legal matters such filing suit against customer after last demand, or file bankruptcy proof of claim forms on behalf of clients.

With the exception of reference information, the answers to these questions will provide the credit manager with all the information he needs. These days many banks also are looking out for Collection agency.

Visits to references who are engaging such agencies are advisable, and ask them the following questions:

1. How long have you been doing business with the collection agency?
2. Have you ever had disputes with the agency regarding balance due?
3. Have any referred accounts ever complained about the agency's collection practices?
4. Have you ever had to take away an account from the agency due to unprofessional conduct or poor handling?
5. How successful is the agency in collecting on referred accounts?
6. Do they only follow up for big amount or do they follow up with each and every referred customer?

7. Does the agency remit collected cheques on a timely basis?
8. Do you know of any derogatory information regarding the agency?
9. Why do you do business with the agency?
10. What is the fee structure with agency? When do you pay his fees?
11. Has the agency provided your firm with nation wide service? If so, were you satisfied with their results?
12. How would you rate the agency's collection style?
13. How would you rate the overall level of service?
14. How would you rate the agency's overall performance?

A report card containing comparison of all the agencies considered must be generated so that you can select the right agency in line with the philosophy of the company".

We also need to decide on duties and responsibilities of a collection agency and the rights of the borrower as against a collection agency.

Some suggestions on the procedure to follow up by Collection Agency can include:

1. The third reminder can be marked to the guarantor, reference, employer, and if required, to the local police station.
2. The personal follow up should be only after informing the local police station in writing and proving their credential. The borrower should talk to only those people who can show a stamped copy of the letter filed with local police station.
3. The collection agency's representative should carry his identity card without fail.
4. Every meeting with the defaulter should end with a report about the discussion that took place with likely date of payment or otherwise any other reason given for delay.
5. The calls can be between 7 am. & evening 8 pm.
6. A borrower can file a complaint with the police station about the number of calls which he feels is harassment, too many visits, the language used, the threats made etc.

7. In many countries have enacted Fair Debt Collection Practices Act and it should not be difficult to enact one for India.

11. Contra Accounts

Where firms are both buying and selling to one another, there should be a written agreement between them that the payment by one to other will be made separately i.e. party A will make his payment for whatever he has purchased from B and likewise B will make his payment for all purchases he has made from A, otherwise such account will run into lot of difficulties for a number of reasons:

(a) Disputed items prevent a clean reconciliation and may even lead to both parties claiming a balance in their favour.
(b) Difference in internal cut off dates and payment dates can easily cause friction.
(c) Unless both companies supply each other every month, there will be arguments about when the balance should be paid.

It is essential that any contra arrangement be set out in writing and signed by both parties. Otherwise sooner or later problems of the kind indicated above will arise. Also if one company becomes insolvent, the right of the others to set off debts will only be admitted by a Court Receiver or Liquidator if there is clear evidence in writing.

12. Consignments Sale

Merchandise is commonly sold on consignment, a method of selling merchandise that involves delivering to an agent, a distributor, or a commission agent who represents the manufacturer. The manufacturer, who is known as the consignor, retains title to the merchandise until the consignee sells the merchandise, at which time the title passes to the buyer. The consignee's obligation to the consignor is to represent the consignor company as prescribed in the contract between the two parties, businesses, or companies, and to pay the consignor company its share of the proceeds from the sale merchandise or products.

The right on the consignment remains with the consignor, the receiver returns the goods that have not been sold. These have to be returned whenever the consignor demands, or on termination of the contract.

13. Electronic Data Interchange and Credit Control

Essentially, EDI is a means of doing business without paper. Instead of typing out an invoice (or producing one by means of a computer) and sending it through the post, the 'invoice' is prepared on, or generated by a computer, and sent down a telephone line to the customer's computer.

The customer's computer can then update the purchase ledger and schedule the invoice for payment. There will be no postal delays, much reduced chance of invoice going on astray, no paper work and no excuse on the lines of 'We have not received your invoice'. Other types of errors which can occur when paper is used, or can be said to have occurred in order to provide an excuse for delaying payment, are virtually eliminated when using EDI.

The computers will match the various transactions used in sales/delivery situation. Invoices, goods received notes and purchase orders can be compared and checked and the whole picture will be available to both supplier and buyer on a computer screen at the touch of a key. In addition, the computer can be programmed to detect any errors such as discount calculations and only permit the data to be transmitted when it is correct.

Therefore EDI is shortly going to become a buzzword among corporate credit professionals. EDI is the electronic transaction of routine business data using formats that are standardized and machine-readable. Among other things, it is looked upon as an electronic tool that will enhance the credit department's ability to accelerate cash-flow, monitor and report credit data, and perform cash forecasting.

EDI will create a number of changes affecting how credit departments conduct their business. Some of these include:

- Electronic invoicing of customers (as opposed to a paper generated invoice)
- Electronic receipt of payments from customers via the automated clearing house, (as opposed to receiving

paper cheques or wire transfers), thereby reducing credit reliance, geographic distance or lock box

- Electronic interchange of credit experience (as opposed to the verbal or written interchange of credit experience), and
- Electronic access to customer's accounts payable systems, which enables the credit practitioner to make an 'electronic collection call' to determine whether or not payment is forthcoming.

It is clear that a company utilizing EDI will be able to generate Rupee savings through enhanced cash flow and reduced costs. So how can a company get started?

The first step will be to get the credit control and finance departments which are often responsible for cash-flow to provide financial support for the company. The EDP department could be tougher, EDP will have to support the various EDI applications the credit department will want to implement.

The credit department will want to focus initially on the two applications within the cash flow timeline that will have the greatest impact—electronic invoicing of customers and electronic receipt of the payments.

Electronic invoicing provides an immediate benefit by cutting down on the assignment of free payment days that results from paper invoicing. These free payment days are created when the invoice date lags behind the actual shipment date. But they are generally eliminated by electronic invoicing, which ensures that the shipment date and the invoice date are the same.

To receive payments electronically, a company's bank must be capable of receiving the payment information (advice) from the customer's bank.

The reason why EDI is firmly established in Europe is because it offers several advantages in cash-flow and costs saving. An immediate reason involves some of the nation's largest firms – Fortune 100 companies. These mega-companies, with their enormous economic clout, are beginning to force their vendors to electronically accept and confirm purchase orders, which impact the order entry/credit release cycle. Presently, the ERP software is already offering the following features:

(a) Your company can specify the criteria to be used for automatic credit checks and ensure that these credit checks are performed automatically at sensitive moments in the sales and distribution cycle.

(b) Internal electronic mail can be set up to automatically inform credit controllers if any critical situation should develop.

(c) If a credit staff needs to review a customer's position, the historical data is readily available.

(d) A credit policy in line with your company can be set-up. You can monitor customer's credit line in a centralised or de-centralised manner. You can monitor a single customer or a defined or nominated group of customers. The credit monitoring policy for each group could be different from the other.

(e) Credit data for each customer will be assembled at each credit control area to which the customer might be assigned, e.g. you can maintain the following fields in a particular credit control area and montior for each customer:
   (i) Credit limit
   (ii) Risk category
   (iii) Customer credit group
   (iv) Credit staff group
   (v) Date of next review
   (vi) Text in explanation of the policy
   (vii) Blocked status control information
   (viii) External credit data

Any change in these fields can be done by only a nominated authorised person.

Other features that can be monitored are:

(i) The total loans represented by all the credit amounts that have been approved over all the credit control areas.

(ii) The amount of the highest credit amount so far assigned to a single credit control area.

(iii) The total credit limit set for all credit control areas combined.

(iv) The maximum limit for any individual credit control.

Automated credit control can be arranged to take place at certain logical moments from order receipt to delivery creation and goods issue. In between all the following stages you can arrange to block any documents with a particular credit status check:

(i) Creating material reservations
(ii) Creating purchase requisitions
(iii) Creating production orders/planned orders
(iv) Creating delivery due indices
(v) Printing order confirmations
(vi) Creating deliveries

The credit status can also block the following shipping functions:

(i) Picking advice
(ii) Packing advice
(iii) Posting goods issue
(iv) Printing delivery notes

You can define document value classes according to the total value on the document, to allow specific credit staff members to process documents in value classes within their range of responsibility. Any document of higher value will be referred automatically to a credit controller.

Credit controller's decision can be communicated to all concerned by ready access to online credit, financial, and sales information systems.

As you can see that ERP software which works on the principle of Electronic Data Interchange is able to take over all those credit activities and more which are otherwise difficult and time consuming if performed by human beings. Credit management with the help of computers shall result in significant cash flow dividends.

14. Lockbox or Cash Management Product (CMP)

Lockbox or CMP is a cash management service provided by banks. A company's nominated courier picks up the cheques from various places of India (it can even extend to places outside India) and hands over to the nearest nominated branch of nominated bank. The bank's remote branch on receiving customer remittances, processes the remittances for cheque presentation and clearing. On receiving the clearance of the cheque, the remote branch then sends message to cash management cell (possibly situated in the city where the company's corporate office is located) informing about the status of the fund. The cash management cell then informs the company about its fund position both at remote branches and also at corporate office branch. It is up to the company to inform the bank get the money transferred to corporate office or after keeping a minimum balance in such bank branches and transfer the excess balance on a regular basis.

Unlike transfer through mail or telegraphic transfer which can take anywhere between 5 to 10 days, but in case of CMP it is always by electronic mail. Once the cheques are cleared at the local centre, the information is relayed via faxes, electronic mail or V-sat to the main office almost instantaneously. Refer chapter on EDI, technology plays a very important role in the success of the cash management product or lockbox (the petname for CMP in Europe.

Citi Bank, SBI, Canara Bank and most other banks have dedicated an entire V-sat or Lease lines network to its lockbox or cash management product service.

Opening a single lockbox or a multi-lockbox network can help a company achieve quicker access to funds from customer remittances while freeing up credit personnel to pursue other cash-flow generating activities.

Advantages of Lockbox (CMP) over the alternative:

- Enhance customer collections.
- Accelerate the availablity of funds by reducing customer mail float and check presentation float.
- Obtain earlier notification that customer payments have been received.
- Reduce human error
- Free your collection staff for other collection tasks.

When remittances cheques are sent through courier to office locations, they must be coded for earliest depositing in bank and presentment for cash availability. That's a time consuming process that subjects the company to many potential delays. A lockbox can help the company overcome mail float. A lockbox network with an optimal geographic configuration can reduce and even eliminate unnecessary mail float. Imagine a company whose main office is in Mumbai and its customers in parts of

Assam and Punjab. It takes a long time for a cheque to arrive, then this outstation cheque is deposited for clearance which will take another 15 to 20 days. In other words, having lockbox in Assam and Punjab will certainly reduce the mail float. Secondly, for a small per-item charge, a lockbox bank will assume the task of sorting, coding, and processing customer remittances. A bank can also provide a company with MICR encoding , the first step in a process that allows the company to have remittances automatically put into its accounts receivable system.

It must be mentioned here that a bank lockbox or CMP is not a collection box for paying mobile and pager bills, located in various parts of the cities and being operated either by the company themselves or organised through a collection agency. Of course, while going through this subject, the companies operating collection boxes will get a better and more organised ideas on how to operate these collection boxes more efficiently.

The costs and benefits:

(a) Savings from the lockbox can be quantified based on reductions in mail and cheque presentation float and freed up manpower.

(b) To quantify the mail float savings, the company needs to perform a mail survey of its major customer database.

(c) In process of calculating mail float savings, the credit manager can use data supplied by its mailing departments of main office and branches.

(d) The manpower savings associated with its lockbox or a lockbox network can be derived by calculating the number of visits or travels and its associated expenses that may get curtailed, and the manpower that will be freed for other tasks—and then annualizing the cost of those man-hours.

(e) Before comparing lockbox savings to lockbox operating costs, a credit manager should net out local bank charges, and the interest that they are loosing in the mail float and cash realisation float, and also towards cheque handling and processing.

For a company, lockbox availability will prove crediting of good funds, to cheque deposited at a bank. The funds can be available for business much faster and at a much lower cost.

Lockbox location: The selection of a lockbox location is primarily a function of the geographical distribution of major number of customers. Performing a study of customers and their geographic locations and sales volume will help a company decide where some potential lockbox sites might be.

The next step is to investigate independent survey information about mail times from courier to local bank in those cities. It could be that the courier already has his office there and reliable to collect in and around surrounding town and deposit these cheques immediately to the nominated lockbox/bank.

Therefore, if lockbox sites both look good from geographical and mail-time stand points, the deciding factor will probably be the availability schedules that the company will get at each location.

Selecting a lockbox bank: The following points to be considered while shopping for a lockbox bank:

(a) *Price of lockbox services:* Pricing may be the most critical criteria. When shopping for a lockbox bank, there are number of items that should be compared on each competitive bid. These will include monthly account maintenance charges, per item processing charges, per item photocopying charges, per item micro-encoding charges, per batch charges, daily data transmission charges.

(b) *Availablity schedules for cheques presented:* This is important and denotes the difference in cash-flow for the company and delayed cash-flow.

(c) *Service:* This could be a very critical factor in selecting a lockbox bank. To begin the comparison process, credit manager should request a tour of bank facilities to gauge efficiency. They should ask to meet with CMP/lockbox processing personnel as well as the CMP/lockbox manager—all the while looking to get a feel for the quality of responses they might get to inquiries.

(d) *Operating hours:* Potential lockbox banks should be asked: Is the lockbox open 24 hours a day, seven days a week, or is it open 5 days a week and for eight hours a day? On what holidays does the bank process remittances for next day clearance? Is it possible for the courier to make a late Saturday or Sunday deposit in the bank?

(e) *Mail pickups:* The frequency of mail pickups is critical with respect to the bank's ability to maximize its processing capabilities on any given day. The more mail pickups the greater the amount of incoming remittances that can be processed. While many banks try pickup all 24 hours, whereas there are many banks who have only 5/6 mail pickups or only during 8 working hours. In 24 hour mail pickups, the bank provides for a lockbox situated inside with a slit through the wall, especially for deposits of a particular company. The process of sorting is thus avoided, and the processing for presentation can start immediately.

(f) *Systems equipment and technology:* These should be checked. Is it latest technique that they are using?

(g) *Processing method:* This needs to be understood. Are they using assembly line approach where several people are involved or they are using batch processing where one person and one computer is involved in all the tasks.

(h) *References:* Since most of the banks now have this cash management product, it will be worthwhile to ask for references and visit and interact with them and find out what they feel on every point mentioned above.

Lockbox instructions: Once a company has justified the economics of using a lockbox, and has selected lockbox site or sites and lockbox bank, it must complete the cycle by preparing instructions indicating how the bank should handle the company's lockbox account, including the specifics of how to handle certain contingent events. The instructions will be primarily geared toward meeting the needs of account receivable personnel and the accounting department.

By providing instructions tailored to the company's needs—as opposed to bank standard instructions—the company will ensure that accounts receivable personnel are able to operate in a more efficient manner when executing account receivable system updates and maintenance. Putting the instructions in writing will eliminate any potential misunderstandings related to lockbox/CMP processing.

After selection, a credit manager might want to measure a collection agencys' performance on a per-customer basis, focusing particularly on major accounts.

15. Franchising

To launch a franchising company properly, you need to hire a lawyer, draft a franchise prospectus, and thus cannot be started within no time. On the other hand there are companies who decide to franchise their goods before starting operations. Some of the glaring examples in India, are Bata, Titan Watch, Aptech, BPL, and Mother Care. And today we have many foreign players such as McDonalds, Kentucky, Pizza Hut, Barista, Cafe Coffee Day etc.

Franchising is first and foremost a financing method: It is not a particularly efficient product-distribution system, and most of the profitable franchises are backed by the franchisor to enhance the value of the franchisor's common stock. The first franchise was sold by I.W. Singer, inventor of the sewing machine. A tool distributor in Ohio to whom Singer had granted a territorial dealership in 1886 was selling more sewing machines than Singer could produce. To switch the dealer's payments from after the sale was made to before the sale was made—so Singer could get the cash to produce the product—Singer sold the Ohio dealer a franchise. The dealer gained territorial exclusivity on a very popular product, and Singer gained up-front financing.

Your retail concept, if unique, is replicable in other markets. If your operation manual is complete, thorough and self-explanatory, and if you have an employee who can train someone in implementing the business, then you have something that will generate cash quickly.

If you do not want to franchise your retail business, you can possibly franchise or license parts of it, such as special foods, recipes, trade names.

Franchising also can bring cash in a different way. You might consider the nation's 10,000 locations as potential customers for your product. The franchisee will offer premiums to bring in customers, and you can supply them.

There are basic rules which have to be followed by both sides if such a system is to work.

The franchisor expects from the franchisee:

(a) No competitive trading with other products.
(b) Minimum standard of performance for both—sales and service.

(c) Stocks and lead-time standards as agreed.
(d) Maintenance of premises or equipment to agreed standards.
(e) Prices in accordance with the contract.
(f) Right to purchase franchisee if the franchisee disposes of business.
(g) Financial commitments and information on franchisee's operations.
(h) Display of franchisor's equipment and clear identification with the franchisor.

The franchisee expects from the franchisor:

(a) Passing on of know-how by the franchisor.
(b) Promotional backing for the product or service.
(c) Local promotion for the franchise
(d) Support stocks
(e) Credit
(f) Financial assistance
(g) Managerial and financial advisory services.
(h) Recruitment aid.
(i) Identification with the franchised product
(j) Geographical or industrial exclusivity.

Against this background the franchise agreement is drawn out. A standard agreement format is commonly available in the market.

16. Bank Channel Financing Schemes

Financing Dealer's Network Scheme

Channel financing is, another method of credit financing and getting paid on time. An extension of cash management product specially designed for companies marketing their goods through a dealer's network. Today in supply-chain environment we treat our dealers as partners and this scheme helps both the corporate and its dealer's network in getting finance for larger and more sales. This also provides flexible financing solutions. These customized finance tools and services fuel the growth of companies throughout the entire supply chain, especially for companies marketing their products through a dealer's network.

The nature of facility is usually short-term overdraft, mostly provided by banks and financial institutions. These programmes help the industry's leading companies to adopt and adjust to the changing technology in the marketplace. It creates alternative financing models that support companies' changing strategies and goals. Customers benefit by increased sales, reduced risk, enhanced cash flow and a consistent collection of receivables. Programs range from traditional distribution finance models to transaction management solutions.

Channel finance scheme has built its reputation in part on its industry knowledge and on its intent to learn its customers' businesses from all angles – from cash management to marketing, from product development to risk analysis. Channel Financing uses this information to build market-intelligent financing and servicing solutions that target individual business goals and help companies succeed.

Modalities

1. Parties to the scheme are:
   - A financing or a bank with channel financing product
   - A corporate company who markets its product through dealer network
   - The dealers who are willing to be part of the financing scheme and are ready to abide by the rules of financing process
2. Supply of goods from corporate to dealer
3. Advise to bank/financing institution to make payment for the purchase
4. Payment by bank/financing institution for goods purchased by channel partner.
5. Repayment by dealer to bank/financing institution as per facility term

Channel Finance Benefits to Corporate Organizations:

1. No cost to corporate company
2. Availability of finance to their dealers at lower than current cost

3. Will help in strengthening their relationship with dealers
4. Payment discipline among dealers
5. Efficient management of corporate receivable whilst better cash-flow
6. Indirect credit and collection monitoring. Plus dealer accounts to be evaluated on a periodic basis. A way of disciplining the payment by account to be declared as default if payments are not being made in the account within the stipulated credit period and interest is not serviced
7. Complete information on dealer's sales and their payment habits

Benefits to Dealers or Channel Partners

1. Steady and cheaper source of working capital financing.
2. Helps dealers or channel partners to increase their sales through higher purchasing power
3. Finance facility up to certain limits subject to adhering to documentation and approval procedures
4. Dealers or channel partners may be able to increase profitability by availing of cash discounts from the corporate body.
5. Lower cost of financing
6. Simple paperwork, simple accounting and reconciliation.
7. Online web-based query options
8. Dedicated operational team at bank/financing institutions.
9. Interface with ERP-based users

To know more: Every bank and financial institution has a website to give you complete insights into the channel finance scheme.

Riskwise Payment Terms & Inco Terms

PAYMENT TERMS, CREDIT TERMS, MODE OF PAYMENT		
CASH Or BEFORE DELIVERY	CASH AT THE POINT OF/ON DELIVERY	CREDIT Or AFTER DELIVERY
• Cash, Cheque or DD • Advance (Part) • Payment against Proforma Invoice • Cash On Delivery (COD) • Through Bank (Consignee-Self) • Credit Card		• Hundi • Hundi (co-accepted) • Letter of Credit • Through bank (consignee-customer) • Consignment Sale • Contra Account • Lease payment
• Down payment-say 20% • Hire Purchase – Down payment	* Part payment Say 70% • Installments	* Balance or Final payment – The last 10% • Installment
• Payment against Collateral – Security Deposit, 100% Advance, Bank Guarantee etc.		• Payment against Collaterals– Security Deposit, 100% Advance, Bank Guarantee etc

SUMMARIZING PAYMENT TERMS

Terms of payment consist of:

(a) Payment term or exchange of money

(b) Credit term or period, but certainly after the delivery of goods

(c) Inco terms also known as shipping terms / delivery terms and forms part of pricing.

Bad-Debt Cover

New India Assurance Company has newly introduced cover for bad-debts (business Credit Shield & Credit Insurance). This is subject to conditions and procedures. Customers are first verified by them, before issuing cover.

NINE

First Things First: Tools for the Job

COLLECTION PROGRAMME—PRE-REQUISITES

Truly speaking, collection planning actually starts from the order scrutiny stage. It is absolutely essential that the payment terms in the order are not only within the framework of the company's policy but are also acceptable. The company must be very sure that the payment is receivable. We would like to caution every credit manager that the payment terms mentioned in the order should be correctly interpreted. What we mean is that there may be terms within terms which will surface only at the stage of asking payment and most likely by that time the goods must have already been despatched. Even the L/C may contain some clause which could lead to a dispute and payment may be held up.

One customer included a clause in the L/C that all original documents should be sent to them first before negotiating them through bank. If the credit manager would have accepted this clause, then he would have had to send even the original copy of the lorry receipt. Hence, he requested the customer to amend the L/C, that payment will be made at sight on proof of despatch in original. But the same was not acceptable to the customer, and the credit manager smelt a rat in this deal. The customer then sent an amendment saying photocopies of all documents should be sent to them first to check any discrepancy and once they okayed it, the credit manager will be able to negotiate the same with the bank. This clause formed an integral part of the L/C. The credit manager faxed the copies of bill, challan,

Quality work means to be accurate and on-time.

A statement is a reminder.
Good statements get good results. (Accurate and Timely)
Bad statements get bad results.

inspection note, test certificate, all documents except the lorry receipt. Goods were still not booked for despatch and he asked the customer to confirm by return fax that there is no discrepancy in the documents so as to enable him to despatch their goods and present the lorry receipt along with other copies of documents to the bank. The customer sent him a return fax confirming the accuracy of the documents. The credit manager then negotiated the documents through bank. The point is during this period, the credit manager had enough time to find out about this customer's paying habit. They could have easily held up payment for an indefinite period by mentioning to the bank that there is discrepancy in the documents.

A good collection programme consists of several important steps—keeping a strict vigil on incoming order, maintaining the order status on day-to-day basis, transporting goods as per the instruction of the party, forwarding bills accurately and with proper supporting as per the advice of the customer and by controlling the float.

The pre-requisites can be summarised as follows:

Design Customer friendly system:

- Orders to be checked and then acknowledged.
- Maintaining up-to-date and correct status of each order.
- Order clearance chart for order validation to be filled completely and accurately.
- Points to be considered for checking before forwarding the Invoice to the respective department of the customer.
- A check-list with regard to bill passing procedure in goverment/semi-goverment and big customers is necessary.
- Control of float.
- Cash trap in contract.

Design Customer Friendly System

System	Ask – you can ask the customer and improve it
Sales and order system	- How easy is it for a customer to place an order, how long it will take? - What confirmation does the customer receive; how soon; is it easy to read? - How is the customer kept informed about their order-status; how regularly; do you provide explanation for delays? - How quickly is the order processed; can it be speeded up further? - How flexible is the system; how does it deal with non-standard requests; urgent orders?
Accounts & Invoice systems	- How accurate are the invoices? - How easy it is for the customer to query an invoice? - How easy is it for the customer to pay – in terms of methods of payment? - What credit arrangements are available; how does the customer find out about them – his limits in days and amount; how good is the information?
Delivery systems	- How flexible is the system in meeting customer's needs eg will you deliver when customer want, or only according to fixed schedules; will you give a specific time or 7 x 24? - How do you inform the customer about deliveries: how soon; is it a easy arrangement? - How reliable is the system: do deliveries happen at the time expected: correct goods and quantity; in good condition? - Is there a quality/quantity check before dispatch? - Do you ask for a confirmation from the customer that they have received the consignment in good condition?
Customer complaint system	- Should the complaint be in writing or it can be lodged over the telephone?
After-sales service system	- Can customer contact you easily; whom to contact; what time and how to contact when you are closed? - Can you allocate sales engineer immediately or can you tell them when the sales engineer is likely to visit? - How quickly does the system respond; how long the customer will have to wait for the sales engineer's call or spare parts? - How good is the system follow-up; coordinating sales engineer's visit and availability of spare parts? - How quickly you respond to letters? - How quickly you resolve problems? - Do you follow-up with customer to know that the problem has been taken care off? - Do you take action required with in the organization on the basis of feedback? - How well does the system monitor and analyse complaints; who receives the information; what action are taken?

Orders to be Checked and then Acknowledged

Before quoting or accepting an order make sure that you have conveyed and accepted all the following points, otherwise the order will not be treated as commercially cleared.

Example: A sample checklist of a company with its factory at Mumbai and Pune—

1. Did you understand what customer wants? For what application it will be put to use? Will our equipment work under present load? In short understand a customer's need.
2. Order to be in the name of HO/factory/place of despatch.
3. Back papers are to be attached to the order while forwarding it to HO/factory (from where the goods are to be despatched)
4. Whether description of item is correct.
5. Whether quantity is correct.
   (a) Whether part supply is acceptable or not for large quantity.
   (b) Delivery schedule to be mentioned in the order.
6. Unit price/total price is correct. Discount is applicable and is correct and agreed by you/regions.
7. Whether correct rate of excise duty is mentioned. If exempted, requisite certificate to be enclosed.
8. Whether correct rate of ST/CST is mentioned.
9. Whether ST/CST form is received with order (if applicable).
   Customer's CST No.
10. Is octroi duty is payable? If not, check if octroi exemption certificate (in duplicate) is received with order.
11. Order is to be executed from THANE/PUNE (warehouse or factory) and accordingly mentioned in the order.
12. Security deposit (if any) to be preferably given in the form of bank guarantee. Last preferance should be cash (DD).
13. Is despatch by rail, road or air.
    (a) If by rail, whether destination station is available.
    (b) If by road:

- Whether destination station is available.
- Whether transporter has booking facility in Thane/ Pune.
- Whether road permit is required/received, if not, ask for it.

(c) If by air, clarify who will bear air freight?

14. Prices:

(a) If Ex-Works:

(i) Whether customer has agreed to bear packing/forwarding/ freight and insurance charges. If not, ask customer for his acceptance, unless we have agreed.

(ii) Whether item is to be sent on freight-to-pay or freight-paid basis in which case freight will be claimed in your bill. Ask customer.

(b) If FOR destination:

(i) Door delivery is not to be accepted, particularly when terms of payment are 'through bank'.

(ii) Door delivery can be accepted provided customer agrees to pay for door delivery charges and provided this is not going to create problems in getting your payment.

15. Terms of payment: (order should mention it clearly).

(a) If payment is through bank, whether

(i) name/address of bankers is available. If not, ask customer.

(ii) Their bank charges are to their account.

(b) If payment is against delivery to customer, who will bear delivery charges? If by customer, has he agreed? If not, ask him. Local delivery charges for delivery should be Rs.......

(c) Advance if agreed, should be received with order. Also refer point 18.

16. Inspection clause (If applicable) is mentioned in order with inspection authority's name. Whether shipping release to be obtained?
17. Whether bank guarantee to be given? Bank guarantee format to be forwarded along with order.
18. Delivery period to be counted from the date of receipt of advance (if any).
19. If possible, quotation for industrial division, regional products and products manufactured at HO to be quoted separately.
20. Bill to be sent in our format/their format at which place?
21. Income tax clearance certificate:
    (a) Whenever the PO stipulate that payment will be made only on proof of valid Income Tax clearance certificate, you should provide the same.
    (b) List of spare parts to be quoted separately.
    (c) Order for XXX and YYY products can be the same, but they should be priced separately.
22. List of spare parts to be quoted separately.
23. Order for XXX and YYY products can be the same, but they should be priced separately.

Maintaining Up-to-date and Correct Status of Each Order

If your order is only for one time despatch, then there should be no problem. But suppose it is a staggered order and goods have to be despatched at different times in a different manner and to further complicate the matter, if the goods are to be despatched to various destinations on various dates in specified quantities. In such kind of orders, you may start very well but as more and more despatch takes place, you may get lost. Every time you may have to go back to earlier papers to make yourself up-to-date with the present status of the orders. The best way to maintain status of such complicated order is to have a card index right on the top of the file.

Order status can be maintained as follows (in case the order is processed on the computer, then this should get generated automatically)

(a) Order no. and date
(b) Delivery period extensions/amendment no. and date
(c) Consignee's name and addresses
(d) Quantity schedule
(e) Quantity supplied
(f) Quantity balance
(g) Invoice no./Inspection note no./Place consigned to each supply.
(h) Payment status of each supply.

Filing

Original order and delivery period extension/amendments to be filed at one place.

Note

Filing is a method of arrangement and/or sorting records and documents for its easy availability in case of need. Since the records, papers, and documents of a credit control department cannot be easily handled and effectively preserved without proper arrangement, the importance of filing has gained ground and has become a must. It can be appreciated that if the customer's records and documents are not systematically arranged, it will cause chaos in day-to-day work. It has been noticed in many a case that this aspect does not receive proper attention.

An efficient, simple and comprehensive system of filing and indexing of all correspondence, reports, etc. (both incoming and outgoing) is a necessity. Disorganised and haphazard methods of maintaining paper result in confusion and are inconsistent with the need to maintain efficiency.

A good system of filing will provide for:

1. Classification of papers or documents in such a manner that they can be conveniently located.
2. Holding and preserving them in files and appliances to which access can be had conveniently.
3. Be simple enough, consistent with the requirements of the credit control department.

Correspondence and papers are first grouped and then filed. The grouping or classification may be:

(a) partywise, e.g. correspondent, agent, stockist, customer ; or

(b) subjectwise, e.g. insurance, sales/collection staff and/or a combination of both with sub-division on geographical or other basis.

File may be arranged in alphabetical order, e.g. according to the first alphabet of the title of the file, or numerical order, each title being given a number. Both alphabetical and numerical systems could be combined, if necessary. Some firms adopt different coloured files for identification and all files are invariably housed in filing cabinets located at a proper place.

Order Clearance Chart

Order clearance chart consists of all information needed to execute the order. In fact it is a summary of the full order file wherein all information with regard to despatch of goods, billing, amendment (if any), mode of payment, advance received and the manner in which the documents need to be negotiated are all provided in this chart. The despatch clerk/billing clerk does not have to go through the full file before dispatching the goods or before raising the bill. Hence it is a very important document and should have all correct information. Hence the order processing department should take utmost care and any misinformation may be a disaster.

A sample format used by one electronic company is given in form 9.1

Form 9.1

Sample Order Clearance Chart

Apple Electronics Ltd, A/5-6, Wag Indl. Estate, Bombay.
Order Clearance Chart for   Order No.: 3615/3
Entered on: 25/03/93   Order Date: 25/03/93

Customer information
Attn.: Customer code: C0358
Name: AMC LTD.
C-5, Spring Road,
Bombay 410 049
Order ref no: 55555/NI/L21   Date: 25/03/93
Amendment: Date: / /
Partial delivery
Bank guarantee not required

Delivery extension not required
Region : WEST
Document route : through BOMBAY Office
Payment terms : 100% AGAINST DELIVERY
Claimed % : 100%
Adv. Recd : 0.00 Adv. Adj.: 0.00 Adv. Bal.: 0.00
Paying authority
Bill in the name:
Name: AMC LTD.
C-5, Spring Road,
South Extension Part-1
Bombay 410 049

Charges:
Our bank charges to : Our a/c
Their bank charges to : Party's a/c
Octroi charges to : Our a/c
Freight charges to : Our a/c
Escort charges to : Our a/c
Insurance charges to : Our a/c

Other:
Test certificate : Not applicable
Extra manual : Not applicable
Road permit : Not applicable
Octroi exemption : Not applicable
Bank guarantee : Not applicable
MC note : Not applicable
C.EXCISE DUTY exemption : Not applicable
Inspection : Not applicable (Our Premises/Their Premises)
Shipping Release : Applicable

Products Status

Model No	Rate	Discount	Quantity Ordered	Quantity Supplied	Quantity Pending
TV Spare-5	4750.00	0.00	1	0	1
Refrigerator	1650.00	0.00	2	0	2

Mode of despatch : Road
Exact destination : DELHI
Terms for despatch : F O R
To be consigned to : Direct
CONSIGNEE : Code: C0358
Name: Amc Ltd.
C-5, Spring Road,
South Extension Part-1
Bombay 410 049

Sales Tax: CST
Sales Tax Form Applicable: No Form

Order entered by:

Checked by:

The data should be entered immediately on acceptance of the order.

Points Checked Before Forwarding Invoice

1. Order no./Delivery period extension no./Amendment no. and date/s
2. Contractor/party's name and addresses as per original order.
3. Heads of account to be printed on government bills.
4. Mode of despatch—transport, road permit, octroi, excise exemption (if any), military credit note.
5. Payment terms (part supply or full supply acceptable)
6. Inspection note (government billing) to be checked before supply—description, quantity, serial nos. of the units, signature and departmental seal.
7. In case DP/amendment/s extension is still not received, then provisional DP extension must be received before supply.
8. Bank guarantee/security deposit whether submitted. (if required)
9. In railway receipts, there is a comment made by the booking officer "said to contain" which means that the goods have been booked without verifying actually what is inside. Such railway receipts are treated as unqualified for releasing payment by a few government department, especially defence department. Such payments are released only after goods are received, verified and acknowledged by the consignee.
10. Number of bill copies/gate pass required and addresses at which to be forwarded.
11. Sales tax, warranty/guarantee and insurance certificate to be given.
12. With a few government departments it is a practice to get the order file cleared by their paying authority. This file is cleared after indemnity bond, affidavit for excise duty duly 'notarised', latest annual turnover certificate, income tax clearance certificate, sales tax and CS tax registration certificate, excise rate confirmation certificate from excise department and copy of the profit and loss account and balance sheet are submitted.

Any lapse will surely delay the settlement. Further, invoicing time to be kept at the minimum. Every invoice must be posted within 24 hours of despatch or on acknowledgement of goods by the customer.

Note:

The abbreviation "E and OE" (Errors and Omissions Excepted) is usually printed at the left hand side of the foot of the invoice. The seller, by this expresson, reserves the right to correct the errors or ommissions, if any. If there is any error, the seller sends a fresh invoice to the buyer with a request for cancelling the original invoice. The buyer, if any error is detected, also returns the invoice for the necessary corrections. If any error is detected, than such corrections are carried out by raising necessary "Debit Note" or "Credit Note" as the case may be, by one of the parties.

A Check-list with Regard to Bill Passing Procedure

This not only helps the staff to thoroughly prepare himself for the follow-up but he will be able to forecast the exact time of collection if he knows how much time is consumed at each stage.

Form 9.2

ONGC - Checklist

Following formalities involved to realize ONGC payment:

1. All materials must be inspected prior to despatch
2. Documentation to be done in three sets as under (if documents through bank):

One set	Two set	Three set
(For bank)	FAO (Respective business group	SPO (Receipts)
Original L/R	Copy of L/R	Copy of all documents
Printed bill	Inspection note—Original	
Copy of inspection note	Printed bill—Two	
Copy of guarantee certificate,	Guarantee certificate	
ED gatepass, (if applicable).	Copy of ED gatepass	

(There are four different business groups as far as ONGC is concerned. So, FAO of respective business group will handle documents and payments)

3. Depending upon payment terms with 95% or 98% or 100% bill (Demand Draft) should be made and to be submitted to bank with required documents as mentioned above with copy to FAO and SPO (R) with respective documents as mentioned above.
4. On receipt of required documents and intimation from bank (LSC) FAO will make payment voucher and pass the same for payment.
5. Voucher will go to cash section with bank intimation (LSC). (LSC means Local Short Credit)
6. Cash section will prepare cheque for bank and retire documents from bank. Bank will send D/D to supplier after deducting bank charges.
7. Terms like overdue interest for not making payment for 15 days or 18 days must be avoided because if ONGC cannot retire documents in time such a term will create problem. Supplier has to give letter to bank for waiver of interest clauses etc. Supplier should be very clear to mention the bank charges on supplier's account.
8. Cash section will forward documents collected from bank to SPO (Receipt) who will arrange for collection of material as per order terms.
9. On receipt of material SPO (R) will make GRV (Goods Receipt Voucher) and send the same to FAO for making balance payment.
10. Supplier has to submit another bill for 5% value or 2% value to FAO, who will again pass this bill for payment and send the same to cash section for making cheque in favour of supplier.
11. This cheque from ONGC will be posted by RPAD only. They do not give hand delivery of cheque even to local supplier.

Form 9.3

Defence Bill—Checklist

A. Following documents are required to be prepared by despatch department:
   1. Delivery challans — 4 copies
   2. Excise gatepass — 1 copy
   3. Packing note — 1 copy
   4. R.R. or G.C. note — 1 copy
   5. Inspection report — 5 copies

B. Following documents to be prepared at our end:
   1. Covering letter
   2. Contractors bill (95%) in triplicate
   3. Contractors supplementary bill (5%) in triplicate

4. Contractors supplementary bill for freight in triplicate.
5. Insurance certificate (First two copies to be sent)
6. Declaration certificate (3+1)
7. Sales tax certificate (6+1)
8. Authority letter (1+2)
9. Excise certificate. (1+2)
10. Warranty certificate — Despatched to Ordinance Factory Tiruchirapally (1+2)
11. Customer's original purchase order to be returned when the supply is completed or where there was more than one supply, while submitting the last bill.

Form 9.4

DGS and D Order Check List Before Despatch

1. To check the delivery due date. If required, please get required delivery period (DP) extension before supplying the material.
2. Bank guarantee valid or not? (If given.)
3. Delivery for destination or door delivery.
4. Freight—To pay or paid basis.
5. Transportation—Railway or road
6. Road permit required or not.
7. Bank guarantee acceptance letter received or not?
8. Packing marks on packing if any.
9. Consignee address, nearest railway station, quantity to be supplied.
10. Excise duty and sales tax applicable.
11. Clear railway receipt required.
12. Documents required alongwith supply as per order.
13. Description in inspection note should be as per order, description of material, quantity sr. no. of unit, inspection note date (on or before supply date) signature of inspection authority and seal. If it is to be given by hand delivery, provisional certificate is required on inspection note no. 1.
14. Octroi exemption certificate to be checked for exemption of octroi defence supply—military credit note required or not.
15. Whether type approval required (before supply).
16. Payment terms and documentation required for submission of bills to paying authority.

Inflation erodes the value of money. Predict it; prepare for it.

Debtors cost time and money. When they cost more time and money than the value of the debt, they are not worth having.

—J. L. Spencer, "Getting Paid"

17. Head of A/cs. to be checked. Where bill amounts are debitable. If it is not mentioned then please write to D.G.S. and D.
18. Sales tax concession form applicable or not.
19. Excise duty is exempted or not.
20. Any amendment against purchase order to be checked carefully. Quantity changes, specification changes, delivery period changes, consignee changes, rate changes, destination changes, head of accounts changes, tax and duties changes and payment and inspection authority changes etc.
21. Liquidate damage clauses whether acceptable or not?
22. Material despatched by road, the proof of delivery being the provisional certificate from the consignee on copy no.1 of inspection.
23. General conditions to be checked before supplying the material.
24. Execution of order that the instruction are followed properly.
25. Proprietary Items certificate demanded or not.

Form 9.5

BARC

1. Consignee and place of delivery.
2. Delivery due date and terms.
3. Description of material.
4. Commissioning charges, applicable, if any.
5. Inspection authority.
6. Shipping release note should be as per order and quantity. Obtaining assistant purchase officer's signature and seal on shipping release note before supplying the material.
7. Any declaration certificate required alongwith documents.
8. Obtaining signature on delivery challan with central stores stamps.
9. Taxes and duties applicable at the time of despatch If required, please take delivery period extension and duty amendment before delivery.
10. Octroi exemption certificate obtaining before despatch.

Form 9.6

Railway Bill Checklist

1. Consignees address and nearest railway station, mode of despatch.
2. Payment terms and using bill forms as per order i.e. stock item, capital item, etc.
3. Inspection authority.
4. Inspection note: Description, Sr. nos. of units, quantity should be as per order and Inspector's signature and seal on it.
5. Clear railway receipt to be obtained.
6. If it is a local delivery, then to obtain provisional certificate from consignee on inspection note copy no. 1.
7. Bills to be routed through consignee or directly to paying authority.
8. Security deposit clause is acceptable. Whether to pay cash or submit bank guarantee.
9. Additional certificate/undertaking required for payment.
10. Any documentation required along with bills.

Original Equipment Manufacturers and Endusers

With regard to OEM customers, there is specific request from them to forward the bill and it's supporting in a particular manner, then such check-list should be maintained by the billing department.

Control of Float

Lastly, controlling the float is another aspect of pre-requisites, a must do on a day-to-day basis. The term float is used to refer to the periods that affect cash as it moves through the different stages of the collection process.

The credit manager must monitor timely receipt and effective use of information on the status of the firm's cash receipt, disbursements, and balances. It requires complete and timely reporting on the varying aspects of the system to allow up-to-date monitoring of cash requirements. It also permits the firm to make timely and efficient use of the fund.

We will examine several stages from the time goods are shipped, till the time money is received and realised in our bank account.

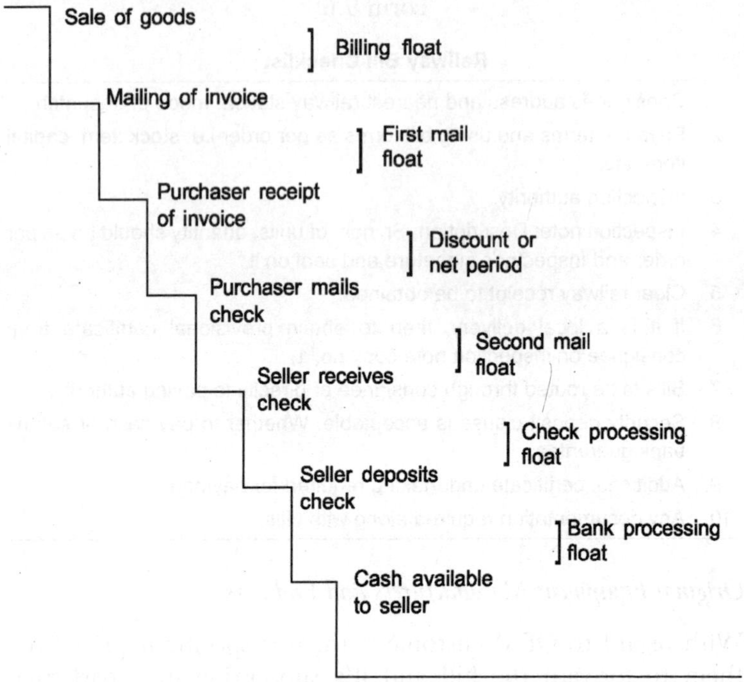

Fig. 9.1 Different Floats

1. *Billing float:* The time between the sale and the mailing of the invoice is the billing float. If there is delay in preparing and mailing the bill, payment will be delayed.
2. *Mail float:* This is the time when a cheque is being processed by the post office, messenger service, or other means of delivery. One must request the customer to send the cheque by courier services or to the nearest office of the seller.
3. *Cheque processing float:* This is the time required for the seller to sort, record, and deposit the cheque after it has arrived in the company's mailroom. On receipt of a cheque it must be sent to accounts department to be deposited immediately.
4. *Bank processing float:* This is the time from the deposit of the cheque to the crediting of funds to the seller's account. Outstation cheques take a long time to realise. They may be deposited at the place of the clearing

branch if you have a bank account in that place. One may even request his bank to purchase the cheque at a nominal cost. There should be constant follow-up with the bank for all cheques still not cleared.

CASE STUDY

About APSEB: From Order to Payment

Secunderabad Branch Manager writes the following letter to Head Office/factory at Mumbai—the precautions to be taken while executing an order, so as to enable his branch to collect money from Andhra Pradesh Electricity Board without any delay:

We have bagged various orders from APSEB last year and as this was the first time we are dealing with APSEB, we had various problems and hurdles before we could receive the payment.

To ensure a faster release of payment, the following points regarding the various steps and documents required are to be kept in mind.

1. *Security Deposit Acceptance Letter:* Orders are released from APSEB and supplier should pay a security deposit @1.1/2 and obtain a letter towards receipt and acceptance.
2. *Test Certificates Acceptance Letter:* Before despatch of material, HO should send the Test Certificates and the same should be submitted to party in TRIPLICATE. A letter towards submission of test certificates and their acceptance for despatch of material should be obtained.
3. *Delivery Date Extension:* Validity of delivery date should be verified, which is normally three months from date of order and if the deliver date is expired, a letter towards extension of delivery date should be obtained.
4. *Delivery Challan:* The material should be delivered to party and signatures on the delivery challan to be obtained.
5. *Bank Guarantee Acceptance Letter:* Bank guarantee should be submitted for the correct time period, on correct value of stamp paper in the format acceptable to APSEB. Generally APSEB requires guarantee for a period of six months over the guarantee period, i.e. 18 months from the date of supply on stamp paper value mentioned in the order.

6. *Hundi:* A Hundi has to be typed as per the format. (This is as good as a cheque once stamped by the Pay and Accts, APSEB Vidyut Soudha)
7. *Invoice*
8. *Excise Gate Pass*
9. *Sales Tax Certificate*

The bills supported with all the above documents have to be forwarded to the Executive Engineer concerned.

Delay-1

{A delay can occur here which cannot be governed by us but should be minimised.}

Executive Engineer will pass the bills along with a Loa (Letter of Acceptance) to the Pay and Accounts Officer—Vidyut Soudha, Hyderabad.

Pay and Accounts Officer will verify all the documents and give us the *hundi* duly passed after deducting any liquidated damage charges etc.

Delay-2

{Depending on the funds position, the *hundis* will be released. Sometimes it takes at least 1.5 month to pass the *hundi*}

This *hundi* has to be submitted to State Bank of Hyderabad—Gunfoundry Branch {Bankers of APSEB}. APSEB sends a list of Letter of Accounts passed for payment. Once the bankers receive this list and our *hundi* is presented a DD will be sent to us.

Delay-3

{APSEB may not send the list to the bankers even after release of *hundis* to parties.}

In the procedure earlier mentioned if there is a delay in any of the points, it finally affects the receipt of payment. We now request HO to kindly take care of the following when dealing with APSEB:

1. Send the Test Certificate three weeks before despatch so that a waival for inspection can be obtained along with the appropriate delivery date extension.
2. Send Bank Guarantee in the correct format, values and period immediately after despatch of material.

TEN

The Game Plan

PLANNING, ORGANISING AND CONTROLLING THE COLLECTION ACTIVITIES

Well, nothing is really sold until it is paid for; and credit trading often means that selling is not complete for many months or even years after the goods or services have been supplied. Many of the bad debts that have to be written off each year are incurred simply by the failure on the part of the creditor to provide a system and a routine for collection of money. Many customers may become defaulters without criminal intent because the creditor fails to apply elementary principles to the collection of money due. The successful recovery of nearly all money due largely depends upon routines properly and regularly applied.

Anyway, we will have to live with the present attitude of the customers and plan our collection in such a manner that it meets more than our monthly working capital requirements. Some companies go to the extent of collecting their money before due dates by offering some kind of incentives and luring its customers to pay before due dates.

TARGET SETTING AND COLLECTION PLANNING

Effective collections do not just happen. They are the result of planning. The targets should be realistic. Different companies follow different policies for setting targets. Let us take a look at three different styles of setting targets:

AGE ANALYSIS OF DEBTORS
FOR CONTROL

K.V.A & T. LIMITED — SALES LEDGER — PRINTED ON : 04/4/94

AGED ANALYSIS OF DEBTORS

AS AT 31/3/94 — PAGE 1

CODE CUSTOMER	BALANCE	UP TO 30 DAYS	OVER 30 DAYS	OVER 60 DAYS	OVER 90 DAYS	UNASSIGNED PAYMENT		TURNOVER LIMIT	CREDIT LAST ACT.	Terms of payment
1001 LDS LTD. TAMBE ESTATE SION BOMBAY-33	21614.18	11500.00	0.00	6114.00	4000.19	0.00	10000.00	10000.00	28.2.93	Through .Bank
2001 C.D.F. & CO. TRADING EST., COLABA, BOMBAY	1040.49	0.00	0.00	0.00	1040.49	287.50	-250.00	2000.00	30.3.93	30 days credit
3001 JAY & JOY LTD., VEER BAZAR, CALCUTTA.	1098.83	0.00	0.00	1098.83	0.00	0.00	500.00	1000.00	31.1.93	60 days credit Hundi
4001 R & D (I) LTD., R & D HOUSE, R & D ROAD, ASSAM	14225.00	14225.00	0.00	0.00	0.00	0.00	21500.00	15000.00	23.2.93	L/c at sight
Totals	37978.50	25725.00	0.00	7212.83	5040.67	287.50	31750.00			
percentage				67.7%	0.00%	19.00%	13.30%			

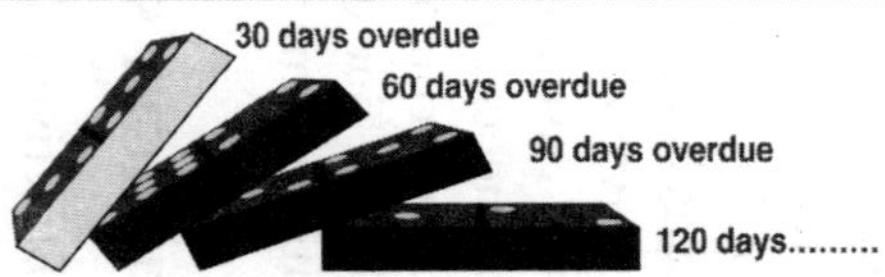

1. On the Basis of Maximum Amount Collectidle

Before setting a target, a credit manager must know its company's budget (receivable investment) or what the business can bear or how much (in amount and in days) debtors the business has planning to finance.

One of the engineering companies draws its yearly budget in the following manner:

Table 10.1: Credit Budget

Receivable Investment	Jan	Feb	March	April	May	June
Receivables (debtors)	75000	62500	71900	86350	100700	85250
Receivables (Annual maintenance)	0	0	0	0	0	0
Credit sales	50000	60000	55000	65000	45000	45000
New AMC	0	0	0	0	0	0
Total receivables	125000	122500	126900	151350	145700	130250
Collections (Sales)	62000	50000	40000	50000	60000	50000
Collections (AMC)	0	0	0	0	0	0
Gross receivables	63000	72500	86900	101350	85700	80250
Less: bad debt (1% of Sale)	500	600	550	650	450	450
Net receivables	62500	71900	86350	100700	85250	79800
Average age (days)	30	36	47	46	57	53

Having known the maximum amount the business really can bear, setting targets becomes a very easy job. The credit manager may set the target as 30 or 36 and so on days of the sales, i.e. in January the debtors should not exceed a figure equals to its 30 days of sale for that month and anything above this figure is collectible.

2. To Express a Target in Cash Terms

At the end of December, a cash target has to be issued which will produce a debtor level of 70 days at the end of January. Total debtors of Rs 50,00,000, December sales Rs 24,00,000 and November sales Rs 20,00,000. The cash target is calculated as shown in table 10.2.

Table 10.2: Used to Measure the Performance of Credit Control Department

Stage I

	Target 70 days
Less number of calendar days in January	(31)
Less number of calendar days in December	(31)
Balance	8 days
= 27% of November calendar days	

Stage II

	Rs.
Cash required is therefore the total debtors at the end of December	5,000,000
LESS (a) All December sales	2,400,000
(b) 27% of November sales	540,000

Therefore the amount required is Rs 20,60,000

3. Target Based on Average Sale Per Day

At the end of November 30, '92, the figures for sales are as in table 10.3

Table 10.3

	North	East	West	South	Total
Sales from Apr. to Oct.92	35909888	9509805	43262237	26551725	115233655
Nov.92	7144537	1600666	6853675	5303663	20902541
Sales for 244 days	43054425	11110471	50115912	31855388	136136196
Average sales per day	176453	45535	205393	130555	557935

Company target : 75 days or Rs 41845142
Here the company's policy decision is to finance debtors not more than 75 days of its average sale.

SETTING TARGET BASED ON MINIMUM AND MAXIMUM AMOUNT COLLECTABLE

The business has to decide the minimum amount that should be collected before month end to meet its working capital requirement.

The credit manager himself works out his own target in a manner that will help him to collect (if possible) all the due & overdue amounts:

All overdue from last month	Rs
Add dues of last month	Rs
Add accountts that will be due during the month	Rs
Plus advances that has to be collected alongwith order	Rs
Total target for the month	Rs

A credit manager must get involved from the stage an order is scrutinised and entered into the computer or cardex until the goods are despatched and bills are raised and posted in the debtors ledger.

A credit manager who is made in-charge for order processing, billing and after- sales-service department will be able to function more effectively. He can be designated as commercial or sales administration manager. Of course, this may not be a viable solution for all companies, but these department heads if they meet very often, shall help in controlling the debtors effectively —by attending to their complaints. They may also come to know the vices of some customers, from one another.

THE PARETO PRINCIPLE, ORGANISING COLLECTION —THE 80/20 RULE

Preparation to Achieve Target and Control of the Operation

If you refer to table 10.1 collection planning flowchart, you will have an idea how a collection programme is planned. The first step is categorizing the total number of debtors into A B C to set priorities. The advantage here is that since the company is expected to work within minimum target (working capital requirements) and maximum target (i.e. the debtors to be brought down to a certain number of days of average sales) a plan should be able to help to cover up maximum parties within a month.

The *second point* to decide is how many customers are to be taken up for follow-up in the first week, in the second week and so on. This will have to be decided keeping in mind the working capital requirement/commitments, the amount of money needed on a weekly basis.

The *third point* of course is avoidable resources. If the sales staff are made responsible for collection then all they will need is back-up support of all information before visiting a customer. If in case the collection staff are employed then there should be a geographical allocation of areas to each one with respect to number of customers to be followed up in that area. This however does not include those customers who will be followed by means of telephones and letters or whose documents are negotiated through bank.

The traditional method of follow-up is to start at 'A', and hoping to reach 'Z' before the month is finished. Even where the number of accounts is small or there are sufficient people to ensure 100% coverage, this is a very inefficient system. It could be that when more amount was needed by the business in the first part of the month, amount collected was very small and the commitments had to be postponed to the later part of the month. Due to this the purchasing of raw material got delayed and the whole production for the month suffered.

The Pareto Principle

Most companies will find that the pattern of their sales ledger follows to a greater or lesser degree the Pareto Principle. This says that 20% of customers account for 80% of business, sales, debtors.

Basing our planning on the pareto principle helps immensely to achieve our objective:

(a) To collect sufficient cash to meet the target for the period
(b) To cover up maximum or all due/overdue accounts.
(c) To reduce overdues to a minimum, with particular reference to high risk accounts.

A statement and its summary can be drawn out as in table 10.4 (based on Pareto Principle):

Table 10.4: Electronics Ltd.—ABC Analysis of Outstanding as on 31-01-00

Part-I Southern Region

Code	Customer Name	Dr Bal	Cr Bal	Advance	Planning (Above 75000)	For (25,001 to 75000)	Follow-up (Below 25000)
A306	Abc & Co Ltd		38423.00				
I454	Bbc & Co Ltd		21229.00				
A577	Ala Limited			6592.00			
B462	Bal Ltd			12569.00			
S051	Shritools Ltd	1810.88					1810.88
M289	Mehrs Pvt.ltd.	13619.00					13619.00
C235	....	....					....
D936	Delta Service.	25020.00				25020.00	
D823	....	....				....	
I561	Isro Systems	72384.00				72384.00	
D190	DGS & D.	75085.00			75085.00		
D961	Dept Of Tele	802662.00			802662.00		
M077	Microtek Ltd.	....			....		
I010	I.Telephone	1916933.32			1916933.32		

Part-II Summary of all the Regions

Code Customer Name	Dr Bal	Cr Bal	Advance	Planning (Above 75000)	For (25,001 to 75000)	Follow-up (Below 25000)
Southern Region—Summary						
Total O/S	21353570.01	176580.76	1132656.50	17064967.04	2850209.13	1438393.84
% of Total O/S 100%				779.92%	13.35%	66.74%
No. of customers 339				63	69	207
Western Region—Summary						
Total O/S	336138080.33	2342119.70	2370668.78	31872844.77	2537300.11	1727935.45
% of Total O/S 100%				88.20%	7.02%	4.78%
No. of customers 377				60	58	259
Eastern Region—Summary						
Total O/S	66110469.94	999092.75	-	33881684.70	1400151.28	828633.96
% of Total O/S 100%				92.22%	66.60%	11.18%
No. of customers 160				17	34	109
Northern Region—Summary						
Total O/S	227181940.92	544792.43	1434896.42	22391863.47	2988045.45	1802032.00
% of Total O/S 100%				82.38%	10.99 %	6.63 %
No of customers 362				47	70	245
Grand Total Summary						
Total	990784061.20	3162585.64	4938221.70	75211359.98	9775705.97	5796995.25
% of Total O/S 100%				82.85%	10.77%	6.38%
No. of customers 1238				187	231	820

In the statement each customer's net balance due has been categorized into A,B & C. In case of southern region following up with 63 customers will help to collect an amount of Rs 170.64 lakh which is 79.92 % of the total debtors.

In the same manner the next part which is regionwise summary says that if the company follows up 187 customers across the country it will be able to collect 82.85%, i.e. Rs 75211360 of the debt. But then a credit manager is expected to cover up all the due/overdue accounts within a period of 25 days to achieve his objectives.

Regional credit controllers must plan and control their operation in the following manner. The planning flowchart in fig 10.1 is self explanatory.

Age Analysis

Next, the most important statement a credit manager is expected to refer to is the age-analysis statement which informs about all those accounts falling due during the month i.e. on due datewise age analysis.

The most effective method that has helped to monitor control overdue debtors on a monthly basis is by asking the branch/regional/zonal heads to comment on old debtors, why the payments are not forthcoming, what is the dispute and how this can be resolved, whether they need any support from head office or factory. A very important part is that they must plan to collect these amounts on a time schedule. They must predict when the problem can be resolved and after that when the payment can be collected.

Table 10.5: Collection Planning – Flowchart

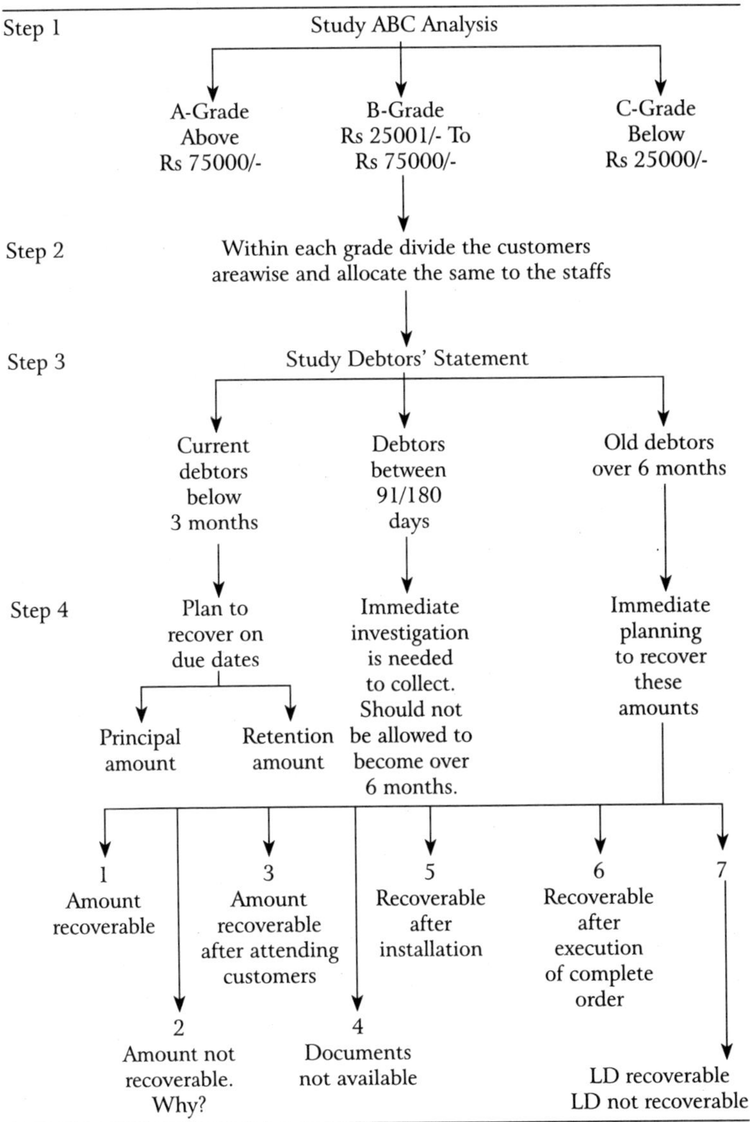

- A-grade customers should be followed up personally.
- For B-grade customers, letters should be sent first. These customers should be followed up personally after A-grade customers are covered up.
- C-grade customers are to be followed up by means of letters, telegrams and telephones.

These comments are generally asked in the age-wise analysis statement, against each bill, on a monthly basis in the following manner:

- Order completion/government procedures/pending
- For documentation/manual/approval
- Bill cancellation pending
- Delivery period extensions/regularisations
- Pending for legal action
- Pending installation/commission
- LD/clauses/demurrage/disc etc. to be adjusted
- Repairs/damages/replacement, etc.
- Expired bank guarantee
- Complaints to be attended by service deptt./production deptt.
- Bill supportings not proper

Apart from these comments, a branch/sales office is also expected to point out the accounting errors or adjustments not carried out where accounting is centralized, say Head Office. For example

Against Bills, a Branch Office Has to Point Out

- Discrepancy in bill calculation.
- Bill cancellation not carried out.
- Bill revised amount to be adjusted.
- Bill posted wrongly, pertains to M/s. _____ A/c code or record no. _____
- Payment received by cash receipt voucher no. _____ or directly or through bank. Check at head office.
- Adjustment of advance of Rs. _____ is required.

Table 10.5 is a sample bill analysis

Against Payment, It Has to Point Out

- Wrongly adjusted amount against bill no. to be correctly adjusted against bill no. _____
- Wrongly credited pertains to M/s. _____ A/c code _____
- Amount pertains to bill no. _____ dt. _____
- Cheque received, subsequently dishonored

- Amount required in lieu of 'C' form
- Amount received in lieu of sales tax difference
- Wrongly appearing should be adjusted with bill no. _____ party code no. _____
- Bill revised amount to be written off
- Octroi charges/service charges/bank interest recovered

Against Advance, a Branch Office Has to Point Out

- Wrongly appearing pertains to A/c. code _____
- To be adjusted with bill no. _______

The credit manager should bring to the notice of the respective departments because of whose delayed action, the payments are held up. He must see that actions are initiated immediately and the debtors are liquidated forthwith.

The advantage of a computer system over a manual ledger is evident in this situation, as a simple program can identify or tabulate the large balances.

Depending on the size of the ledger, the number of staff and the degree of sophistication required, other priorities in the collection routine can also be set. However, it is a normal and good practice for the credit manager and any supervisor or section head to assume personal responsibility for as many 'special' or problem accounts as can be managed, leaving the others to be followed up by other staff members. Many companies make it a practice to collect money by a set of collection clerks. Such practice does not always help. Of course, it depends on the kind of business (Trading or Manufacturing).

In case of trading business, collecting through errand boys could be an appropriate method. A reputed business house, may be able to collect with the help of few collection clerk.

But then with engineering/high-tech product, where greater degree of technical aspects are involved in making of a product, functions from sale to collection must be handled by the sales personnel themselves. Another advantage of sales personnel collecting money is that they come to know the difficult accounts and understand their mistakes in negotiating payment terms and will take more care while negotiating future business so that the money can be collected with more ease.

There is always a big difference between the results of someone doing his best and someone striving to achieve a target. Every person engaged in collection work must be allocated a target to measure their performance. Individual target may be grouped together to give sectional targets which in turn will comprise the department target - branch target - regional target.

Rules for Collection

A company is expected to set up the following rules for collection.

1. When are accounts due to be payable?
2. How soon after the due date shall the first reminder be sent out?
3. How soon after the due date shall the credit privileges on a past-due account be suspended until the account is brought to terms?
4. How many steps shall there be in the standard follow-up and how much time shall elapse between the several steps.
5. Which of the available tools and methods shall be used in the various stages of the follow-up?
6. When shall past-due accounts be turned over to a solicitor/collection agency?

Rules for Follow-up

1. Is an ABC analysis done on overdue accounts?
2. Do you have a systematic procedure for follow-up on slow accounts?
3. Is there a standard sequence of follow-up letters?
4. Is the tone of these letters progressively stronger?
5. Do you use the telephone to contact delinquent accounts?
6. Is your telephone technique effective?
   (at right time, talk to right person & with correct detail)
7. Do you have a late-payment penalty?
8. Do you put delinquent accounts on COD basis?
9. List of provision for bad/doubtful debts.

Plan for Overdue Collection

For Old debtors an Aggresive Action Plan should be decided and it can be planned in the following manner:

Stage I : Identify the problems both in terms of value, number and age.

Stage II : 1. Break it down into controllable limits.
  (a) Reconciliation and adjustment of unadjusted credit and advance.
  (b) Recoverable on________
2. Recoverable after factory provides________
3. Recoverable after after-sales-service/Installation ________
4. Recoverable after extension is fetched for ________ from ________
5. Not recoverable—Why? Please justify.
6. Likely expenses to be incurred (if any)

Stage III : Action plan—draw up guidelines on the use of different techniques such as department to be visited, persons to be contacted, phone calls, reminders, etc.

Stage IV : Monitor results on a weekly basis, giving more importance for a reduction of debtors over 1 year.

Stage V : Accounts which cannot be collected because of sale & service queries must be highlighted and brought to the notice of the appropriate managers every fortnight until action is taken. Copy should be provided to credit control deptt. for follow-up.

Plan During Cash-Flow Drive

Likewise, an aggressive collection drive should be undertaken as and when the company faces cash-flow problem. It can be planned in the following manner :

Define the Problem

Say you have identified your problem as cash-flow slow down. Accounts receivables (A/R) now average 110 days as opposed to 75 days maximum, a 35 days increase.

Study the Problem

It could be because of:

(a) Drastic growth of large receivables—customer with balance overdue amount ranging from Rs.1 lakhs and over.

(b) For e.g. - From August to now

(c) Is it all over the country or there is geographical difference?

(d) 65% of the customers running 115+ days. However, the small accounts pay in time or before time by availing discounts, no single order is on credit.

(e) Have we changed our credit policy?

(f) Some large accounts pay slowly. Could this be due to less personal contacts with them?

Therefore, the possible causes which may be concluded from the above observation are:

(g) Lenient credit policies must be reviewed.

(h) Company is a victim of cash management people—then what corrective steps are needed?

(i) Lenient collection effort must be reviewed immediately.

(j) What is our position as compared to industry—study must be undertaken. Is it the same? What are they doing to improve the situation?

In the true sense, a problem well defined is almost solved. As you define a problem, one possible solution often surfaces. However, it may not be correct to jump to a conclusion. Lot of time is wasted applying hasty conclusions that would be better spent in carefully defining a problem.

Setting Objectives

Your objectives may be to speed up collection of large institutional orders, to stop providing free (almost free) financing to these accounts, and to improve cash-flow. We need to get the biggest accounts to remain (or become) most profitable, cut financing costs, and reduce bank loans. Once the objectives are laid down in writing, it will provide a sense of direction, provide feedback whether or not you are doing the right thing. This can be achieved only after the objectives are spelt out in detail and monitored closely.

They can be described as follows:

(a) Improve collections: Reduce A/R age to say 75 days.
(b) Refer last year's margins or improve over last year's.
(c) Reduce dependence on short term bank financing within next 100 days.
(d) Maintain good relations with bulk customers.
(e) Stop financing the slow-paying large accounts.
(f) Improve collection efforts.
(g) Restrict credit to fast-pay accounts.
(h) Ask for advance, say 40 per cent down, with orders.
(i) Increase discounts.
(j) Charge interest on late payment.
(k) Sell more aggressively & make money on bulk selling.

Putting Your Objectives to Practice

A combination of two or more objectives put to practice will surely put the company's cash flow in right momentum. However, the credit manager should evaluate the effectiveness of every objective from time to time.

While planning the collection of old and new accounts, it is advisable for each staff to fill up 'Debtor follow-up action required' list to keep an up-to-date account of follow up with each customer.

The list may be as follows:

Table 10.6: Debtor Follow-up Action Required List (Staffwise)

Region ______________ Branch ________________ Week No. ______________

Date Due	Payment promised	Customer	Inv No.	Inv. Value	Date	Person Contacted	Payment Promised	Comments

* To be prepared and monitored weekly.
* On the basis of this, debtor follow-up recor d for each customer to be prepared if they do not pay on due date.

When you are following up for collection just remember — crying baby always gets milk. Principle of consisterncy.

The above format in table 10.6 is especially for the credit manager. As regards subordinate staff, they will maintain customerwise card that is discussed in table 10.7.

Table 10.7: Debtor Follow-up Record

Customer name:		Invoice no:	Inv-date:	
Address:		Invoice value:	Due-date:	
Salesman:		Branch:	Region:	
Date of contact	Type of contact	Person contacted & position	Payment promised	Comments

* To be maintained customerwise.

There should be a full time office staff to update each customer's card.

CASE STUDY

A company facing overdue situation, puts an aggressive collection plan into practice.

This case study pertains to a telecom industry and a chemical and paint industry—almost with similar problems and similar results.

- The sundry debtors are very much on the higher side of 160 days of sale. It needs to work within 60 days of your average debtors. To start with, bring down your average *overdue debtors* from 120+ days to "0" days, within a period of three months, it can be considered as good to ease off the cash flow.
- While the finance deptt. is doing everything in its scope in procuring of funds, since the overdue debtors are 120+ days of current year sale , the company has started facing cash-flow problems especially in repayment of loan instalment and payment of interest.
- Further, the pressure on cash-flow will become very much evident by the amount of sundry creditors the

firm will be carrying. No sooner it happens, the firm's reputation and goodwill in the market will start affecting if commitments are not met within reasonable time.

Since company's sales have failed to achieve the required growth (due to slow-down in cash-flow) under the circumstances, the following steps are decided to enhance cash-flow:

Plan 1

- The company is heavily dependent on its dealer's network. Revamp the dealer's network to boost sales.
- Play a balancing act between purchase, production planning, stock level to be maintained, need of the effective physical distribution, and distribution channels, i.e. in this case the dealers' off-take. In short practice supply chain management for optimisation of stock and other expenses.
- Take aside all debtors above 90 days, form a committee at corporate level, form collection team/s at branch level, have an aggressive collection plan in place to wipe out old debtors.

Please note, it is not too late to start acting upon, but then any more delay in taking the right steps the cash flow problem will make things very difficult to manage.

Plan 2

A step by step plan to collect the old debtors is worked out on the following lines:

Step I

Take aside all debtors above 90 days.
Find out whether we are still dealing with them? Why?

Step II

Let's get rid of the wrong attitudes towards old debtors:

1. *The customer is always right:* Rubbish! Many companies go bust because they believe so strongly that the customer must not be upset, they neglect to obtain their essential

lifeblood. The customer is always important, but often wrong—especially if he does not pay his debts on time.

2. *We are doing our best:* Sorry, but it is proved time and again that collection productivity is raised higher than people thought possible by the use of targets, controls, visual aids and staff motivation.

Other points to note:

3. A sale is not complete until the cash is in our bank.
4. Profits are reduced more by slow payers than by bad debts.
5. The sooner we ask, the sooner we are paid.
6. Customers respect suppliers with professional approach.
7. We believe in first class service to customers and we expcct first class payment in return.
8. We can't pay suppliers or salaries with sales – we need cash.
9. A credit sales is a loan of our resources to a customer.
10. There is no liquidity without profit, but profit is not liquidity.
11. Profit is an idea and CASH is a fact.

Step III

Form a committee at the corporate level to be chaired by finance and sales head. Other members of the committee comprise senior staff from sales, administration, purchase, distribution, R and D, accounts and stores. They may be responsible for one or more of the old debt/s.

Step IV

At branch level, form collection team comprising the following characteristics:

- Somebody good in negotiation.
- Somebody good in documentation.
- Somebody good in following up shamelessly.
- Somebody good in ground support.
- Somebody good in talking over telephone. Ladies are preferred.

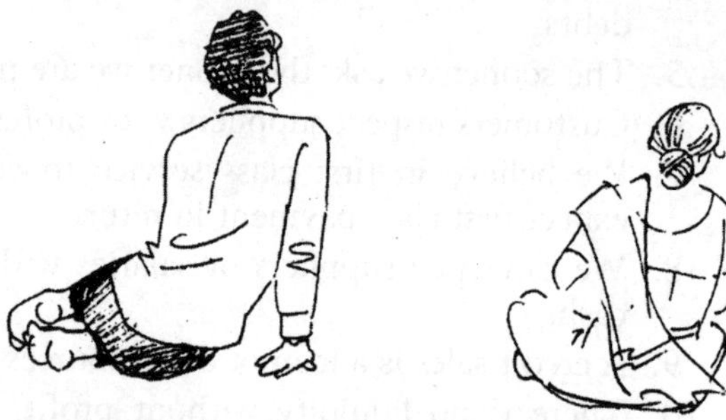

A company with a long overdue collection period is probably selling to marginal credit customers and/or not working hard enough to collect past-due balances.

—Joseph T. Straub

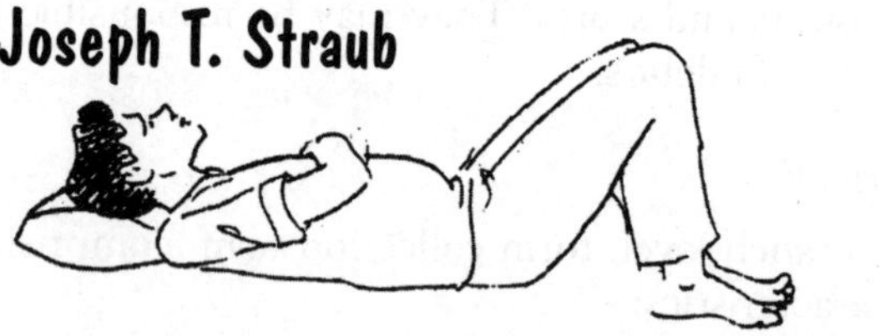

- Somebody good in writing letters.
- Somebody good in supervising ledger accounts, reconciliation.

Most of the team members will be sales staff themselves.

Step V

Decide an incentive scheme, e.g.

A 1% discount on old debt if cleared by certain date. It should be made known to the party that this is one-time incentive with a date deadline.

Step VI

1. Do abc analysis on old debtors on the basis of amount.
2. Study age of the old debtors. The oldest debt to be followed first.
3. Identify the problems both in terms of value, number and age.
4. Break down the overdue debtors into controllable limits.
   (a) Reconciliation and adjustment of unadjusted credit and advance.
   (b) Fix recoverable date.
   (c) Recoverable after factory provides _______
   (d) Recoverable after after-sales-service / Installation _______
   (e) Recoverable after completing balance supply remaining, against order.
   (f) Recoverable after extension is fetched for _______ from _______
   (g) Not recoverable – Why? Please justify.
   (h) Likely expenses to be incurred.

Step VII

Action plan—draw up guidelines on the use of different techniques such as department to be visited, persons to contacted, phone calls, reminders etc.

Step VIII

Monitor results on a weekly basis, giving more importance for a reduction of debtors over 1 year.

Step IX

Accounts which cannot be collected because of sale & service queries must be highlighted and brought to the notice of the appropriate managers every fortnight until action is taken. Copy should be provided to credit control department for follow-up.

The total debtors came down drastically to 90 days (including overdue) of sale within a period three months. The overdue debtors came down to 25 days from 120+ days.

This collection drive also set a correct attitude towards collection, not only in the management hierarchy but also throughout the company. Most of the department's staff having taken part in the collection drive in team, narrated the complete experience to their fellow-department-staff. This made every staff very conscious of mistakes, which they should not repeat.

An eye on the current debtors during overdue follow-up.

(a) For current sale not to become old, decide to tell the dealers that if the money is paid along with order, then deduct say 2% discount and send the cheque/draft (in case of outstation dealer) along with the order.

(b) Those dealers who will make 12 consecutive payments before due date will be entitled to a further one-half per cent (as reward) of total sale for 12 months.

(c) Decide a collection target for each branch every month on current sale. The target may be decided as a percentage of the total debtors or due or over due debtors. Branches which achieve their target say by 20th of the month can be rewarded say 1% of the debt collected. Likewise, if they achieve by 25th, incentive can be 0.75%, or if the target amount is collected by 31st of the month it can be 0.50%.

The branch manager shall decide on a rationale on how to distribute the reward money to each and every staff in the branch including peons and other administrative staff. This will bring about the total collective approach towards collection.

1. Work towards the future and a constructive approach.
2. When telephoning, control the conversation. Use the other persons' name and ask questions to keep the conversation in the right track.
3. Recognise complaints, acknowledge them and deal with them before continuing with the debt collecting process.
4. Start your debt collection process before it is due. Gently, remind the customer and help him to make provision for payment on due date.
5. Make an effort that your company makes a policy to pay an incentive for achieving Collection Target. We already said, that in a company any one can make collection difficult and anyone and everyone is a part of your collection drive. If you have achieved your target than make sure everyone is entitled to collection incentive. We have tried in many companies, the result were unbelievable. These companies do not discuss collection as a problem anymore.

Statement Of Account

Is A Reminder

Balance Forward Statement

Ford Cars Limited,
J.B. Road, Bombay-400025

Statement of Account for the Month of February 1993

To: Date: 28-2-93
AKG & Company
Bombay

Date	Type	Description	Ref.	Debit	Credit	Balance	Remark / Explanation
		Brought forward		0.00			
23/12/92	1Adj	Opening Balance	A679	1098.83		1098.83	
21/01/93	Inv	R'vate Vintage Car	84001	575.00		1673.83	
31/01/93	Pay	Cheque	84001		575.00	1098.83	

Current	30 days	60 days	90 days
0.00	0.00	1098.83	0.00

Amount due: 1098.83

A Monthly Statement Sent to Customer every month serves as REMINDER

A GOOD statement gives GOOD RESULT

A BAD statement gives BAD RESULT

ELEVEN

The Rights of the Supplier

Consumers have rights.

As consumers, we want these rights.

In respect of suppliers, however,
we normally talk only of responsibilities.

Suppliers have right too.

One reason collection suffers is
that those of us concerned with collection
are not conscious of our rights as suppliers,
or we tend to forget them.

Let us spell out some of those rights.
And before we go for collection
let us remind ourselves of these rights.
Also, let us make doubly sure
we have discharged our responsibilities.
Let us operate from a position of strength.

1. We have the right to negotiate
   the terms of credit
   and once that is done
   we have the right to insist
   on the terms being kept.

2. We have the right to take every step
   to see that the terms are kept;
   we have the right to protect
   our rights as a supplier.

"Profit is just an idea, whereas cash is fact."

3. We have the right to make it known that
we are entering into a contract
of exchanging goods/services
and money.

4. We have the right to make it known
that credit given is for a specific period
and by that period payment should be made
and if not made it is a breach of contract.

5. We have the right to execute the terms of credit
for example penal interest
and that is automatically binding.

6. We have the right to insist on payment by due date
and if payment is not forthcoming
and the date of payment is not renegotiated
we can take such action as we deem fit
to protect our future interest
eg. withhold further supplies

7. We have the right to take recourse
to the arms of the law
for any breach of contract.

8. We have the right to protect our interest
of like-placed people
and organise joint action
against the defaulting party.

9. We have the right to negotiate with relevant parties
for the recovery of the dues.

10. We have the right to get the money dues to us
using means ranging from polite to the punitive.

11. In commercial transactions, the rights
refer to the impersonal side of business.

12. The way the rights are exercised
refers to the personal side of business.

13. We will exercise the rights
using judgement, propriety and utmost courtesy,
and without prejudice to business goodwill.

N.H. Atthreya

TWELVE

The Art of Collection— I Collect the Money but Keep the Customers

"Train customer to pay you on time."

COLLECTION FOLLOW-UP

Dear Mr Doe,

Here is a good story they tell of Uncle Joe Cannon.

One member, making the first speech in the House, found its members listless under his oratory. After adjournment, he sought our Mr Cannon and asked him what he thought of the speech.

"Well may be what you said was all right," replied Uncle Joe, "but it seemed to me that you did not make the most of your opportunities."

"My opportunities?"

"Yes. You had several chances to sit down before you did."

Lest we be accused of making too long a speech about the $50 you owe us, we will make just one remark, and then sit down to wait for your answer.

Please send us a *check*.

Now, we're sitting.

Sincerely yours,

L.E. Frailey – "Handbook of Business Letters". Check = Cheque

---

Make sure you celebrate achievement of collection target . . . you can never believe what momentum it can create on your cash-flow.

Assume that you have given 30 days credit and I tell start reminding before 30 days if you want to collect your money on time. Many of you will ask me "How can we ask for our money before 30 days?"

Customer-oriented follow-up is the answer

Make sure everything is to the customer's satisfaction. You are glad that the customer has provided you an opportunity to serve him. You want him to be happy and the customer should come back and do more and more business with you. The following steps are recommended:

1. Deliver, don't just promise; make sure every clause of the contract is delivered and now your goal is to make sure that the customer got what he ordered for and you have to collect your money on time, if possible before time.
2. Understand that the collection activities start as soon as the order is received.
3. Keeping the customer informed of the status of the order
4. Informing customers that the goods are ready for dispatch
5. Informing customers that the goods have been dispatched, and about the mode of transport
6. Finding out whether the goods are received
7. Finding out whether the goods are received in good condition and correct quantity
8. Finding out whether the customer needs any help in using the goods. Assure him that whenever he needs you, he just has to call.
9. Remember, all activities before the due date of payment are reminders and after the due date they can be termed as follow-up.
10. If you want to collect your money on time, you will have to be different. The customer must feel that you care; that you are always there when the customer needs you. The purchase officer is not your customer, but whoever is going to use your product. Make sure that the end-user of your product is satisfied.

11. While doing customer-oriented follow-up you have been making sure that the customer has received not only the goods but also your bill/excise-gate-pass, and all the transaction papers, in order. Ensure that it has reached the bill-passing department, and that the store has sent the store receipt. This way you are helping your customer make the payment. *You* will have to make it easy for your customer to make your payment.
12. Settle any rejection or short-supply settle debit/credit note problems.
13. Collect your money first or collect your money fast. Each collection is a reward of your company's hard work. On collection, profit is actually realized and has a direct impact on your cash-flow.

There are three methods of follow up, the techniques of which will be examined in detail later in this chapter. These are:

(a) By personally visiting the customer.
(b) By telephoning the customer.
(c) By writing letters, telegrams, fax, e-mail etc. to the customers.

Personal Follow-up

A supplier has a right to receive his money from his customer for the goods/services supplied/rendered by him. However, in these days of stiff competition, money is reluctantly paid by the people, various tactics are necessary to recover money. The speed at which one recovers the money depends upon the approach one adopts.

Once you raise a bill, have a will to collect, with skill, and if necessary with 'kill' instinct.

A-grade customers should be followed up personally. They are the company's asset and the source for generating daily funds, contributing 70–80% towards annual working capital requirements. However, a decision has to be taken whether the collection staff, sales staff or the credit manager or any other manager should do the follow-up. This purpose will be decided under one of the two headings.

1. Large companies/government or semi-government where the problems are primarily administrative.
2. Companies whose solvency is doubtful or who persistently pay late.

Major Companies

As far as the first category is concerned, the collection follow-up is usually done by staff. In case of second category, the credit manager or any other manager should make the visit. The second category customers are deliquent customers and it is very essential that a very close watch is kept on those accounts. The collection staff or sales staff whose main job is to visit major customers should keep the following two purposes in mind.

(a) He is expected to establish the best possible personal relationships with key personnel, in order to ensure preferential treatment both in the processing of invoices and the release of payment.In India, collecting money from semi-goverment / government department is a very time consuming procedure. The bill passes through a number of official stages before money is ultimately received. Hence a thorough knowledge of the complete bill-passing procedure and knowing the actual user or using department to certify 'satisfactory receipt' will help in collecting the money fast.

(b) He is also expected to identify queries that will reduce or delay payment and to assist in their clearance.

To be successful in this objective, a collection staff should be friendly and sociable and equally at ease with the purchase supervisor, the account personnel or the top finance personnel. He requires considerable tact and diplomacy to move between accounts & purchasing departments, helping to lift his company's queries out of the log-jam in the buying office & bringing the cheque to the top of the pile. Apart from these requirements, he needs endless patience and determination, the ability to realize when a fresh approach is needed and to recognize when a particular contact is proving valueless. If all his ability fails, then it is desirable for the credit manager to step in and make the next visit along with the collection staff.

The many faces of a customer build relationship with all.

Relationship goes miles.
Making, Keeping and fulfilling commitment continuously is a relationship-building measure.

Deliquent Customers

In case of second category emphasis is not to battle with the administrative problem but to find an answer to questions like when will the account be paid and what are the risks of continuing to supply. Although time may not permit many visits, it is absolutely essential for the credit manager to make at least one visit so as to not to lose touch with these kind of deliquent customers.

The following procedure is recommended.

(a) Make an appointment at the highest level appropriate to the size of the customer. This can range from the proprietor of a small firm through the finance director of a medium-sized concern to the chief accountant of a large company. Very often it is helpful to make arrangements through your sales manager, in which case the buyer may be the first contact. He can prove a useful ally against his own financial people.

(b) Prepare the facts thoroughly before going. A clear summary of the history of the account is essential to demonstrate the justice of your case. Details of all orders on hand plus an estimate of future business will be useful. Finally a review should be made of the latest available status information.

(c) On arriving at the premises, make it a point to see as much as possible of the factory & offices to gain an impression of the level of the activity, the amount of stock or finished goods and the general appearance of the firm. If a tour round is offered after talks have finished, always accept and never hesitate to ask questions—even though they may reveal your ignorance.

(d) The actual approach when discussions begin will depend on the precise reason for the call. If it is simply to obtain immediate payment, having already decided that no more business will be accepted, there is little to do beyond being polite but insistent, give the impression you are prepared to wait all day but make it clear that the next step will be to instruct the solicitors. Never refer to legal action unless you are ready to proceed accordingly and without delay.

(e) No visit is complete without a report. The credit manager should insist on a report within seven days of his visit. The report formats have been discussed in the last part of the chapter on *The Game Plan*.

TIPS FOR SALES REP

Money collection requires very careful customer handling. Here are few tried out practices.

Very often sales rep have to collect due and overdue account. This is not the most pleasing part of the sales-rep's role, yet best carried out by them as they enjoy the best relationship with the customer.

Overdue accounts are a sensitive area for both the seller and the buyer. The business relationship may be at risk if the approach to collecting the money is not carried out professionally. This vital part of customer communication can be enhanced by observing some important points:

(a) *Mention credit and payment terms at the time of order*. If sales rep take the time to explain credit policy when taking the order it eliminates a lot of unnecessary dialogue between the two accounts departments. Many salesrep vague when it comes to payment: they say, 'We will send you an invoice', without following it up with. "Our payment terms are strictly 45 days: is that acceptable to you, Mr Patel?" If a commitment is made to the sales rep by the customer, the experience is usually that few problems arise.

(b) *Dealing with a customer who constantly ignores credit terms*. When a sales representative is trying to collect money from a customer, that is not the time to give him a lecture over his abuse of the credit system. There are two issues to be considered: one is collecting the money and the other is educating the customer regarding future payments. Each of these issues should be addressed in isolation. Collect the money when you can and in what-ever diplomatic way you see fit. When it comes to asking the customer to pay within the credit terms, do it when the money is not due and you may get a more sympathetic hearing.

(c) *Must know all the facts of the case.* Some customers are notorious for querying invoices. Ensure that all queries have been addressed prior to your telephone call or visit.

(d) *Analyse possible reason for non-payment.* Oversight? Notoriously slow? Outstanding query? Change of address?

(e) *Discussion with a person in authority.* Get the name and title of the people who sign the cheques and try to talk to them. Discussion of your business with junior staff members is likely to lead to frustration. If you have no success with them try enlisting the help of the person who gave you the order. In many cases he is unaware of your difficulty and can be most helpful, particularly if you have been a good supplier.

(f) *What to talk to a person in authority.* If the customer is in breach of his commitment to pay within the credit terms, you have every right to enquire as to the reasons for non-payment. It is important to be polite and friendly, while at the same time asserting your commitment to gaining payment. When speaking to the contact, one of these reasons will usually be given:

   (i) *The cheque is already posted.* Ask the date on which the cheque is posted and thank the customer. If the cheque is not received despite this assurance, phone the customer to politely express surprise that payment still has not been received. Apply a little extra pressure.

   (ii) *The cheque is waiting for another signature.* Find out how many signatories are there. Impress on the customer the importance of getting in the cheque. Enquire when the other signatory will be available and arrange to call to collect it.

   (iii) *There is a mistake on this invoice.* If you have done your homework properly, this should not prove to be an insurmountable obstacle. If it is delaying tactic, (and if the mistake is in the calculation) ask the customer to pay the amount that is not in dispute. If a mistake is confirmed immediately, say: 'I can send a credit note to you today, can I arrange for somebody to collect the cheque tomorrow afternoon?'

(iv) *We are facing fund problem at this moment*. Use empathetic expression like: 'We do understand the problem you face in getting the money in these days —we have the same problem ourselves', 'You are normally so prompt with your payments'; or 'We greatly appreciate the business you place with us.' Regardless of the reasons never let a customer away without a firm commitment to pay.

(v) *We have already passed your bill, let me check out the status of your cheque, and I'll phone you back*. The customer is in the driving seat if he takes the initiative in making the vital call. Tell him there is a lot pressure on your telephone line and he may not get through. Suggest that you will phone him instead.

(vi) *Getting excuse after excuse*. If a customer owes money you have every right to exert whatever diplomatic pressure is necessary. Some people are past masters at making themselves 'unavailable' and they require a more aggressively imaginative approach. Some of the following suggestions may be required only in a very severe circumstances. Remember, if you cannot make contact with the signatory who is making it difficult for you, you can't get your money. In these circumstances you may consider any of the following ideas, which have achieved success for others.

- Send the customer a telex, fax or e-mail, stressing how difficult it has been to contact him.
- If needed, phone the customer at home. (Many credit card companies are doing this.)
- Visit his house.
- Write letters to his residential address.
- Make sure to bump into him and act as if it has happened 'by chance' first thing in the morning as he comes into his office.
- Phone his secretary and leave a massage for him to contact you. The only details you give are your first name and an unlisted phone number, stressing that it is 'very urgent'. In using any of these techniques, expect an angry response

from the customers, although sometimes he or she can become polite when embarrassed. Note that, these tactices should be used only when all else have failed.

(viii) *Always thank the customer*. Regardless of the outcome of your discussions, always thank the customer for his time. Courtesy costs nothing, yet achieves so much. Invest in the cost of a telephone call to thank a customer for prompt payment. Tremendous good will be gained by such an inexpensive exercise.

TELEPHONE FOLLOW-UP

Talk at the right time with the right person and with correct detail. In India in many proprietary companies, one gets payment only if they ask the proprietor. Any attempt down the level will not help. In such cases, the credit manager should call up. In some cases the credit manager may call up a senior official, if his subordinate finds it difficult to pursue the matter.

The advantage of the telephone over a letter is that of personal contact. A letter can be ignored but a phone call has to be dealt with. The best possible use should therefore be made of this technique. The human voice is capable of immense variation and the effect produced on the listener depends very much on the tone and the attitude of the caller. The objective is to achieve co-operation, to persuade someone to do something he might otherwise defer or not do at all. The caller must be crisp and businesslike, yet ready to pick up a hint of humour or give a sympathetic ear.

There is a good deal of skill in telephone follow-up. When using the telephone to request payment, make quite sure first of all that you are speaking personally to your debtor before you announce your own identity or the identity of your company. Premature announcement of your identity may well incline the delinquent not to be available.

As you write, so you should speak. Make clear the reason for the telephone call, the urgency of the situation (if more calls have already been made). The first call should be when the goods are sent – trying to find that they reached safely, the second call should be after two to three days to find out that the goods received correct in quality and quantity, the third may be a polite reminder before the account is due. Be cautious. Don't give the impression that debts are being chased before they are due. If queries are mentioned, it may be worth trying to settle them over phone but more usually this is not feasible.

Most common responses over the telephone are:

(a) Which order number are you referring to?
(b) Are you sure the invoice was sent to this branch?
(c) I am sure we paid you last week.
(d) You sent us a credit note which cleared our account.
(e) Can you give me the invoice number?

Always strive for a firm promise of both date and amount. With experience one will be able to judge whether such promises are genuine. In case the payments do not arrive at the promised date, wait for a day or two for postal delays and follow up again. If there is short payment, then the reason should be found out over telephone, asking for a firm date of settlement for the balance amount.

The following suggestions are recommended for following up collection over telephone.

Checklist of things to know before writing or telephoning:

A1. Customer's order number and date.
A2. Name of the person and his department placing the order (if known).
A3. Goods ordered—quantity, type.
A4. Delivery instructions.
A5. Date of delivery, place of delivery.
A6. Despatch note and goods received note-numbers and dates.
A7. Invoice number, amount and date.
A8. To whom the invoice was addressed or sent. The date on which they have acknowledged receipt of the invoice.

Next

B1. Have a list of telephone numbers ready before calling.
B2. Have the customer's account on your desk.
B3. Have paper, pencils and calendar ready for use.

Form 12.1

Example of customers to be followed up over telephone

Telephone no.	Person to contact	Steps	Customers	Total due	Below 6 month	Over 6 month	Promised on	Received on	Remarks	Query passed to	Date
		1ST									
		w	M/s A & Co Ltd								
		e	M/s B & Co Ltd								
		e	M/s C & Co Ltd								
		k									
		2ND	M/s B & Co Ltd								
		w	M/s xxx & Co Ltd								
		e	M/s yyy & Co Ltd								
		e	M/s zzz & Co Ltd								
		k	M/s kkk & Co Ltd								
			M/s rrr & Co Ltd								
			M/s C & Co Ltd.								
		3RD	M/s sss & Co Ltd								
		w	M/s ttt & Co Ltd								
		e	M/s mmm & Co Ltd								
		e	M/s kkk & Co Ltd								
		k	M/s rrr & Co Ltd								

If payment differed then the call is resheduled as discussed with the customers.

B4. Make sure of the name of the person, his designation you are going to talk to. In other words, have a list of definite number of persons to call and call at definite times.

B5. Make sure of exactly what you are going to say before you call.

B6. In case of a dispute, know the latest status exactly and be ready for all possible objections.

B7. Rehearse your approach for at least two minutes before you make your call.

B8. After calling, get the right man over the telephone, identify yourself and your purpose for calling. Use short, simple calls, express your key message in a way it could be understood very easily. While doing so try to visualize your customer in mind.

B9. Try to close the call with an assurance from your customer of a definite date of payment.

Others

C1. Have a list of definite number of calls to make each day.

C2. All calls should be made at the most appropriate time.

C3. Make an analysis of calls after the session is over.

C4. Update customer's follow-up cards accordingly.

C5. Schedule your next calls with these customers if needed.

C6. Try to assess the attitude of the customer over the telephone and decide whether personal visit or writing a letter will be essential to confirm the talk over telephone. This will also depend on number of calls made so far to a particular customer.

With experience one will be able to see words within words, the sign of trouble or potential trouble can be identified. The credit manager must decide how much responsibility is to be given to the phone collectors in pursuing these customers. Lack of time will certainly mean that some at least will have to be passed to the supervisor or manager to deal with but where possible, collectors should be encouraged to follow through.

Don't shy away from discussing money—because cash is survival and cash-flow is growth.

Ten Commandments for Professional Telephone Collection

1. *Be Prepared*: Plan your call carefully, supporting the dialogue with all relevant paperwork.
2. *Be Persistent*: Regardless of what the debtor says, return to asking for payment in full.
3. *Be Prompt*: Ring your debtor at the start of his working day to add urgency to your requirement.
4. *Be Urgent*: Make the debtor feel that he must pay today. Unless you make the debtor feel this urgency, he won't think today is any different from any other day.
5. *Be Courteous*: Build goodwill for your firm, enhance the image already built up. If your debtor feels comfortable about paying, it will make the call atmosphere more relaxed.
6. *Be Tactful*: Remember to acknowledge comments, and always be polite, however the debtor behaves.
7. *Be Business Like*: Keep bringing the debtor back to the point—payment in full.
8. *Be Co-operative*: Show the debtor that you have a sincere desire to help him work out his problems in a way that will be satisfactory to your office and to him.
9. *Be Repetitive*: Keep mentioning the sum required.
10. *Remember*: That your cash-chasing call is not only the end of one sales chain but start of another.

Source: Telephone collection techniques, Pauline Malindine, Australia.

DEBT COLLECTION LETTERS

Writing a letter is an art. One may gather the habit of reading a lot of books on correspondence. But all these won't take him very far because ultimately the credit manager will have to write letters under circumstances quite different from books. However, he can copy the language of a good letter from books. We have been through various textbooks on correspondence, and come across many good ones. Many points like purpose, number, content, design and further action, should be considered before drafting a good letter.

Collection letters for all purpose should have two-fold aims.

(a) to persuade the customer to settle his account, and
(b) to retain his custom and good will.

Hence is the need to write with tact and restraint since it is easy to offend. Besides, it may be that the writer himself is at fault, as where a payment received has not been recorded, or the goods sent or the service given is not satisfactory. A customer whose account is only slightly overdue would understandably be offended to receive a personal letter reminding him of this.

L.E. Frailey writes, 'The matters discussed in a credit or collection letter are often irritating and controversial, and no amount of diplomacy or understanding on the part of the writer can make them otherwise. Sometimes, the credit man is poised like a boy on a fence between two pastures, with a bull on either side. No matter which way he jumps, he may be in trouble. If he is too relaxed in approving credit or collecting a bill, the company may end up with a sour account and the treasurer then puts him through the wringer. If he rejects a doubtful applicant for credit, or insists on the payment of a bill, a customer may be lost and the sales manager accuses him of lack of cooperation. Even the average customer looks suspiciously on his best efforts, and is ready to fly off the handle on the slightest provocation. No business correspondent requires a larger bump of diplomacy, or a greater knowledge of human nature, than does the credit man.

'The writer of a credit or collection letter is not expected to ask for orders, although some of the letters do mention, but he is expected to sell goodwill—to make the news in his letter as painless as possible. In other words, he should be order-minded as well as money minded—not to the extent of being too lenient and always remembering the value of a customer.'

Some Letter-writing Tips

Here are some general suggestions that will assist you in writing the follow-up letters.

1. Use short, simple, uncomplicated words.
2. Use the present tense as much as possible.
3. Use words that create a mental image.

4. Use words that the listener does not have to translate.
5. Use words that appeal to the senses and basic needs.
6. Don't use too general, too complicated, technical words.
7. Don't overuse or abuse certain words.
8. Don't overdo I—Me—My.
9. Don't use words with ambiguous meanings.
10. Don't use slang, colloquialisms or foreign words.

The preliminary steps in debt collection letters, can be as follows:

1. First end-of-month statement of account. To be sent within 5/10 days after due date. To be signed by accounts officer.
2. Printed letter enclosing statement of account.To be sent within 15-18 days after first letter. To be signed by accounts officer.
3. Printed letter. To be sent within 14 days after second letter by registered AD. To be signed by the accounts officer.
4. Letter typed to a senior official under 'Confidential' cover. To be sent within 10 days after last letter by registered AD and signed by department head.
5. Typed letter as mentioned in point 4, giving one more opportunity to pay by fixing a reasonable deadline. To be sent within 10 days after last letter by registered AD and signed by department head.
6. Final letter stating that you have been reasonable and will be compelled to have recourse to law, reluctantly if the money is not paid within 3-4 days or an explanation atleast. To be sent within 10 days after last letter by registered AD and signed by department head.

The first two reminders usually take the form of end-of-month statements of account with a printed forwarding letter. The second letter should be marked with such comments like 'Second Reminder' or 'Account Overdue—please remit' or 'Immediate attention is requested', etc.

Specimen Letters

(Where customer enjoys a credit term and thus all documents, goods, etc. have been sent directly.)

1st step: Send a statement of account pointing out the total amount due.

2nd step: Printed letter enclosing statement of accounts.

Date ....

Dear Sir(s),

Ref: Account No........
....

According to our records the above account, dated .... has not been settled. The enclosed statement shows the amount owed to be Rs. ....

We look forward to an early settlement and to receiving your next order.

Thanking you,

Yours faithfully,

P. S: Statement enclosed

3rd step: First typed letter. (separate for new & old customer)

a. To an Old Customer

Dear Sir, Date ....

Ref:

As you are usually very prompt in settling your accounts, we wonder whether there is any special reason why we have not received payment of the above accounts, already a month overdue.

We think you may not have received the statement of account we sent you on ....and showing the balance of Rs........ as then owing. We enclose a copy and hope it may have your early attention.

Thanking you,

Yours faithfully,

b. To a New Customer........

Dear Sir, Date ....

Ref: ....

We regret having to remind you that we have not received payment of the balance amount of Rs. ...... due on our statement for December ..., sent to you on January 2.

We enclose a copy and would remind you that we quoted unusually low prices on the understanding of an early settlement. It is assumed that non-payment is due to an oversight and we now ask you to be good enough to send us your cheque within the next few days.

Yours faithfully,

4th step: Letter typed to a senior official under 'Confidential' cover.

Dear Sir, Date ....

Ref:

On .... we wrote reminding you that on January 2, balance of Rs........ outstanding and due for payment by January 31 ....

As settlement of this account is now more than a month overdue, we must ask you either to send us your remittance within the next few days, or at least to offer an explanation of the delay in payment.

Yours faithfully,

5th step: Typed letter as mentioned in point 4 giving one more opportunity to pay by fixing a reasonable deadline.

Dear Sir, Date ....

Ref:

We do not appear to have received any reply to our two previous requests of July 5 and 16 for payment of the sum of Rs....... still owing on your account.

It is with the utmost regret that we have now reached the stage when we must press for immediate payment. We have no wish to be unreasonable, but failing payment by August 7.

I am afraid you will leave us no choice but to place the matter in other hands, but we sincerely hope that this will not be necessary.

Yours faithfully,

.... OR .....

I am sure you will agree that we have shown you every consideration and now, failing any reply to our earlier requests for payment, I am afraid we shall have no choice but to take other steps to recover the amount due.

We are most anxious to avoid doing anything from which your credit and reputation might suffer and even at this late stage are prepared to give you a further opportunity to put matters right. We therefore propose to give you until the end of this month to clear your account.

Yours faithfully,

6th & Final step: Letter stating that you have been reasonable and will be compelled to have recourse to law, reluctantly if the money is not paid within 3-4 days, or an explanation at least.

Date ....

Dear Sir,

Ref:

We are surprised and very much regret that we have received no reply to the further letter we sent you on .... regarding the long overdue payment of Rs....... on your account.

Our relation in the past have always been good. Even so, we cannot allow the amount to remain unpaid indefinitely, and as we have received no replies to any of our several requests for payment, we are now reluctantly compelled to have recourse to law, unless the amount due is paid or a satisfactory explanation received by the end of this month.

Yours faithfully,

... OR ...

Dear Sir,

We are disappointed not to have received any word from you in answer to our letter of .... concerning non-payment of the balance amount of Rs........ outstanding on our December statement.

As our business relations in the past has always been pleasant and friendly we are now making one final request for payment in the hope that it will not be necessary to turn the matter over to a solicitor. This we should find very distasteful. We have therefore decided to defer this step for seven days to give you the opportunity either to pay or at least to send us an explanation.

Yours faithfully,

... OR ...

Dear Sir, Date ....

Ref:

We are quite unable to understand why we have received no reply to our letter of ...., the third, we have sent you requesting payment of the balance of Rs........ still owing on your account with us.

We feel that we have shown reasonable patience and treated you with every consideration, but the time has now come when we must regretfully take steps to recover payment at law, and the matter will now be placed in the hands of our solicitors.

Yours faithfully,

Where Documents are Negotiated through Bank

The whole activity of recovering payments through customers' bankers is controlled in the following manner:

After bills are forwarded to the customer's bankers, a copy of the forwarding letter should be filed in a box file named 'pending-payment through bank'.

The letters may be filed date-wise in case of payment at sight or on due date-wise, where credit period is allowed.

Everyday on receipt of payment the forwarding letters against which payments have come, should be removed from 'pending-payments through banks' file to 'payment recovered' file.

Thus only those documents against which payments are yet to come will remain in the 'Pending – payment through bank' file.

Ref No: AKS/CC/BANKREM1 Date ....

REMINDER I

Dear Sirs,

Sub: Retirement of documents from bank

Ref: 1) Your order no. ....dt...........
2) Our bill forwarding letter No. PVC:EL:INV:
dt. ....addressed to bank, under copy to your office.
3) Our invoice no. ....dt.........for Rs.............

Vide our letter no. ....dt.............. you were requested to clear the above mentioned documents from your bank within 15 days because the goods might get damaged at Transporter's/Railways godown due to mishandling.

We very much regret to inform you that till date you have not retired the documents from the bank and would, therefore, request you to please act immediately.

We hope you will reciprocate our best intention of supplying quality product to our customers by clearing the goods fast.

Please, therefore, clear the documents immediately on receipt of this letter.

Thanking you and assuring you of our best attention at all times.

Yours faithfully,
for Electron Ltd

A.K. Sodhi
Collection Officer—Credit Control Deptt.

P.S. If you have already retired the documents, please ignore this letter.

By Regd AD/Courier
REMINDER II

Our ref. no. AKS/CC/BANKREM2 Date ....
Dear Sirs,

Ref: Your P.O. no. .... dt.........
Sub: Our invoice no. .... dt...........
for Rs. ....
....

Despite our letter no. .... dt .... and subsequent reminder letter no. .... dt .... we regret to inform you that the above documents still remain uncleared from the bank. We would, therefore, submit ourselves as follows:

1. You will appreciate that we cannot keep the goods for an indefinite period without your communicating to us the reason for non-clearance as there is every possibility of the same getting damaged at Transporter's/Railway's godown due to mishandling. Also our transit insurance does not cover goods beyond 15 days.
2. In case the goods are damaged and needs to be repaired by us, we will surely consider the length of time you have taken to clear the above documents and may pass on the charges to your account.
3. Any demurrage/penalty will be to your account. We, therefore, once again request you to look into the matter and retire the documents from the bank immediately on receipt of this letter.

Thanking you,

Yours faithfully,
for Electron Ltd

A.K. Sodhi
Collection Officer—Credit Control Deptt.

P.S. If you have already retired the documents, please ignore this letter.

By Regd AD/Courier
REMINDER III

Ref No: AKS/CC/BANKREM3 Date ....

Dear Sirs,

Ref : Your P.O. no. .... dt............
Sub : Our invoice no. .... dt...........
for Rs. ....
....

In spite of our letter no. .... dated .... followed by our two reminders dated .... and .... (copies enclosed) and telegram, we regret to point out that the above documents have still not been retired from the bank.

We are now constrained to inform you the following:

1. We should not be held responsible for damages to goods due to mishandling at Transporter's/Railways godown.
2. Any repair/maintenance is required to be done to the unit, the cost of the same will have to be borne by you as our transit insurance does not cover the same for such a long period.
3. In case you do not retire the documents within 15 days from the date of receipt of this letter, we will have no other choice but to call back the documents and clear the goods at your cost and consequences. We will treat your order as canceled and advance, if any, will be adjusted against the expenses incurred by us.

We hope you will not allow such an unpleasant situation to arise and take necessary steps to retire the documents from the bank forthwith.

Thanking you,

Yours faithfully,
for Electron Ltd

R. K. Saha
Manager—Credit Control Deptt.

P.S. If you have already retired the documents, please ignore this letter.

Where documents are sent directly to the Dealers/Agents. Here the following can be used.

Ref: AKS/CC/DIREM1 Date..................

REMINDER I

Dear Sir/s,

Ref : Your P.O. no. .... dt. ....
Sub : Settlement of our invoice no./s............
for Rs. ....
....

We would like to bring to your kind notice that the goods against the above mentioned purchase order was despatched on................and you were informed vide our letter no. ....dt.................

As per our records, till date we have not received your payment in settlement of the said invoice/s.

We are not sure whether it has slipped your attention or the payment has been held up on purpose—if so, then please let us know the reason for the same.

We sincerely hope that you will expedite our payment on receipt of this letter or inform us the reason for the delay in payment.

Thanking you and assuring you of our best attention at all times.

Yours faithfully,
for Electron Ltd

A.K. Sodhi
Collection Officer—Credit Control Deptt.

Encl : Statement of account/copy of the earlier letter.

Ref No: AKS/CC/DIREM2 Date...............

REMINDER II

Dear Sir/s,

Ref : Your P.O. no. .... dt. ....
Sub : Settlement of our invoice no./s............
for Rs. ....
....

We do not appear to have received any reply to our request of.................. for settlement of the amount due on us against our above mentioned invoice/s.

It is with utmost regret that we have now reached the stage where we must press for immediate payment. We have no wish to be unreasonable, but you will appreciate that at the time of accepting your order we did not resort to any advance payment.

Further, we have taken a policy decision to consider the length of time taken to settle each bill before extending any kind of services.

We look forward to receiving your cheque/DD by return post.

Thanking you,

Yours faithfully,
for Electron Ltd

A.K. Sodhi
Collection Officer—Credit Control Deptt.

Encl: Copy of our earlier letters/copy of the statement

Ref: AKS/CC/DIREM3 Date...............

Reminder III

Dear Sirs,

Ref : Your P.O. no. .... dt. ....

Sub : Settlement of our invoice no./s............
for Rs. ....
....

We are both surprised and disappointed not to have heard from you in answer to our two letters of.....................and referred bills. This failure either to clear your account or even to offer an explanation is all the more disappointing because of our past satisfactory dealings over many years. As things are, you cannot blame us if we say we cannot allow matters to rest here and we are afraid that unless we hear from you within ten days, we shall have to consider seriously the further steps we ought to take to obtain payment. We hope you will not pave way for us to take such an extreme step, which in all probability we would like to avoid, in consideration of our past harmonious dealings.

Thanking you,

Yours faithfully,
for Electron Ltd

R.K. Shah
Manager—Credit Control Deptt.

Encl: Statement of account/copies of our earlier letters

Reminder to various Department/ Customers for balance payments

Ref:AKS/CC/BALREM1/ Date.................

REMINDER I

Dear Sirs,

Sub: Payment of balance amount

We would like to bring to your kind notice that payment terms in respect of our bills mentioned below were as follows:

While we have received the first part of the payment, we are yet to receive the balance amount, as per details given below.

Bill No.	Date	Bill Amt. Received	Less. Amt.	Bal. Amt.

We would request you to kindly send the above balance payment/s immediately.

However, if you have already made the payment/s, we would request you to please furnish us the cheque details.

Your immediate action will be highly appreciated.

Thanking you and assuring you of our best attention at all times.

Yours faithfully,
for Electron Ltd

A.K. Sodhi
Collection Officer—Credit Control Deptt.

Ref.................. Date...................

Dear sirs,

Sub : Payment of balance amount

We refer to our earlier letter no. .... dated................wherein we have brought to your notice that balance payment/s against the following bill/s remained unpaid.

Bill No.	Date	Total Amt. Received	Less: Amt.	Bal. Amt.

A considerable time has passed since then and during this period we have neither received our payment nor you have explained the reason for withholding the said amount.

We hope you will appreciate that after complying with all the conditions of your order, you should also reciprocate by sending the balance payments forthwith. Kindly post your cheque today.

Thanking you and assuring you of our best attention at all times.

Yours faithfully,
for Electron Ltd

A.K. Sodhi
Collection Officer—Credit Control Deptt.

For more discussion on collection letters, refer Chapter 16.

Collection—Telegram/Telex/Fax/E-mail

Ten Collection Telegrams / Telexes That Work

Western Union reports that its extensive tests show the following ten telegram messages to be highly effective in pulling in collections for overdue accounts.

1. Please advise if cheque covering your account now due has been mailed.

2. You have apparently overlooked your (monthly) payment. May we have your cheque promptly please.
3. Today is last day you can take advantage of cash discount.
4. Only immediate compliance of my letter (date) will save your credit.
5. Urge you wire your intentions on your account immediately to protect your future credit rating.
6. Must withhold shipment of order received today until past account settled. Wire remittance immediately to ensure prompt delivery.
7. Urgent we receive payment this week. We value your friendship too much to be compelled to resort to legal action.
8. Imperative remittance on your account sent immediately to avoid action by our lawyers.
9. Wire full payment by (date) or it will leave us no choice but to proceed immediately.
10. Payment tomorrow imperative to prevent repossession of items charged your account of (date).

A telex message addressed personally to the right person can be very effective, partly because it is a rather unusual method of follow-up and partly because it always carries a sense of urgency. Hence it should be best reserved for special occasions, say after second reminder or before sending a legal notice. It should not be used regularly as it could be a cause of annoyance with customers.

Other Aids

Stickers

Very few companies put a self adhesive sticker with words like 'Payment Overdue—please pay' or 'This is our First Reminder' requesting their customers for payment. Very rarely used. It could be a very temporary measure for follow-ups as they are cheap enough to run a few months' trial. Stickers like 'Urgent' or 'Immediate Action Requested' will surely be able to invite attention.

Gimmicks

Beware of gimmicks. They sometime work but a busy trader is trying to deal with a volume of accounts persistently, and gimmicks cannot be counted as successful measure. Little coloured labels 'Have you forgotten us' and the like are rarely good collection procedures.

Stopping Supplies

It is a crude way of getting your payment but certainly not the end of business with the customer. The primary duty of the credit manager is to protect the company's investment which may occasionally necessitate suspending delivery to minimize a possible bad debt and more frequently to extract payment from a doubtful customer.

There are occasions when a customer pleads for continuation of deliveries on the ground that the product is essential to the life of the company. Whether this is true or not, the credit manager must be alert not to increase the size of the risk.

Stopping supplies should be a last resort, invoked only when it is apparent that no real effort is being made to put matters right.

Non-payment because of dissatisfaction should never result in a stoppage, unless the customer is being totally unreasonable, e.g. withholding Rs 10,000 when only Rs.500 are in dispute.

Customers who do not pay as a deliberate policy should be cut off as soon as the condition is recognized. If the fear is of losing business, then the cost for delay should be built into cost price. A list should be maintained of such customers and if any order is received from any of these customers, they should be considered for pro-forma terms.

Any blacklist prepared should be in close liaison with Sales & After Service department.

Legal action is also a means of collection of payment. This is dealt separately in a later chapter.

Suspension of account has to be continuous and must cover all eventualities. Too much time should not be spent on one individual defaulter, if in the process a number of small defaulters remain unchecked. A large number of small bad debts may well amount to more than one large item which has taken too much

Collection follow-up Slogans :-
Please
Don't Make Us Get Tough
WE'RE TRYING TO BE BRAVE!
But We Really Need the Wampum!
We Feel TERRIBLE!
HAVING TO REMIND YOU!
GO AHEAD and SHOOT US...
A CHECK
we just noticed...
You're A Little Delinquent
it would be AWFUL ROUGH
Without good customers like you.
IF YOU'RE NOT GETTING GOOD RESULTS
Why don't you try our line
WE'VE LOOKED EVERYWHERE FOR YOUR CHECK
Could it still be in your checkbook?
Please PAY US SO
I CAN PAY THEM AND THEY CAN PAY HIM AND HE CAN PAY YOU
PAST DUE!
This account has no doubt escaped your notice. Will you please send us a remittance by return mail
2ND REQUEST!
We have to again remind you of this overdue account.
Please remit in full by return mail.
FINAL NOTICE!
If this account is not settled by it will be placed in the hands of our attorney for collection
and Please let us be Paid Next Amen
Pssst! If you pay us we won't tell anybody else.
Thank You
Your Business is Appreciated and We Hope to Serve You Again
I'll bet you just overlooked this
WE'RE IN A PINCH
WE NEED YOUR CHECK PLEASE!
PLEASE SETTLE this small account at once and avoid us the expense of sending another statement

of a supervisor's or managers time. Properly controlled collection of accounts should not be difficult and if successfully operated, it can even be made enjoyable.

PAYING CHARACTERISTICS

Collection can be regarded as a challenge between the debtor and the collector. If the creditor is determined to see that his profits are preserved, the debtor pays and pays promptly. Before conclusion, it will be very interesting to note Sidney Carter's analysis of customer paying characteristics. In his *Handbook of Modern Retailing*, published by the Rice-Stix Merchants Service Bureau, Sidney Carter supplies an useful analysis of customer paying characteristics.

In all, he lists twenty different types of buyers—any one of which might be visualized by the credit correspondent while handling a particular case.

1. Pays promptly and prides himself on it.
2. Takes all the time possible because he has other uses for his money.
3. Buys the limit on credit, then pays cash — sometimes to other merchants.
4. Easy going — needs to be reminded a number of times.
5. Hates to let the money go or likes to keep it in the bank as long as possible.
6. Sickness or other unusual circumstances prevent prompt payment.
7. Will pay to keep from losing his credit standing.
8. Will pay only when convinced he must have to avoid trouble.
9. Unfortunate or indulgent. He wishes to do the right things but cannot control his family's buying.
10. Withholds payment because he has a grudge against the store.
11. Thinks because he gives the store virtually all of his business, he is entitled to take more time to pay.
12. Never did intend to pay. This buyer does not succeed so well in getting credit established because of the organization of the modern credit structure.

13. Lives in the future, post-dates checks, thus buying on "cash credit".
14. Reckless.
15. Installment contracts use up a large portion of his income, making it difficult for him to pay on due date.
16. Poor financier. Honest enough but simply cannot get his affairs untangled. Always more or less in "hot water".
17. Lives beyond his means. Will pay in time but will take all the time he can get.
18. Has old debts which interfere with prompt payment of current obligations.
19. Out of town. Has plenty of money and cannot believe there are any people or institutions who need money to run their businesses. Goes to Europe for six months and leaves the caretaker to file the bills away.
20. Carelessness or oversight. Not systematic. Forgetful, interested in other things, does not keep records.

ART OF COLLECTION

1. Set monthly collection target.
2. Take account of Pareto principle, the 80:20 rule for collection planning. Concentrate first on 'larger debt' and on 'old and larger debt'.
3. Use an aged-debtors list, but exercise discretion as to how to use it. Ask for justification on overdue accounts. Extend support and solve the problems so that these accounts are settled within a decided time.

   If old debts are too high than you must form a separate task force to see that old debts are collected within a time frame.
4. Preparation is needed whatever type of action you are taking – personal visit, letter or telephone call.
5. Conclude discussion with a summary of what has been agreed during personal visit.
6. Make your letters (and telephone calls) humane. Avoid Shakespearean expressions and accounting jargon. Use a friendly tone and make it as easy as you can for your customer to do what you want him to do.

7. Work towards the future and a constructive approach.
8. When telephoning, control the conversation. Use the other persons' name and ask questions to keep the conversation in the right track.
9. Recognise complaints, acknowledge them and deal with them before continuing with the debt collecting process.
10. Start your debt collection process before it is due. Gently, remind the customer and help him to make provision for payment on due date.
11. Make an effort that your company makes a policy to pay an incentive for achieving Collection Target. We already said, that in a company any one can make collection difficult and anyone and everyone is a part of your collection drive. If you have achieved your target than make sure everyone is entitled to collection incentive. We have tried in many companies, the results were unbelievable. These companies do not discuss collection as a problem anymore.

HANDLING DEALERS MANAGEMENT AND CREDIT CONTROL

Alliances or Partnering with Channel Member

A Dealer buys your product to sell it as-it-is and makes money on your investment. Therefore, this marketing channel has to be fully administered.

A Dealer today is treated as a strategic business partner, alliance, network, and a customer who makes money on our investment. *Marketing Channels can be viewed as sets of interdependent organizations involved in the process of making a product or service available for consumption or use.*

Modern concept of dealership is:

Make it easy for me; I'll make it easy for you.
Let's get together.
Let's partner.
Let's co-venture the business.
Let's share.

Let's become a strength.
Let's serve together
Let's create more value for our customers.
Let's reach out.
Let's find out new business opportunities.
Let's create more sales and grow together.
Let's prosper.

"What can we do together, so that both of us can improve our business, whistle enhancement of profit and cash flow?" This is a question to be asked very often in the course of the alliances in action.

A dealer is a kind of customer who buys and then sells the goods in an as-it-is condition, and in the process he makes a margin called profit. His investment could be very negligible as compared to the manufacturer of the goods.

The manufacturer, the end-user, the reseller and the government departments are our customers. Out of these four types of customers, one of them is a dealer (or reseller/channel). The readers are expected to know to design, develop and maintain effective relationships with and among channel members by using both strategic and managerial frames of reference in order to achieve sustainable competitive advantage. The readers must also concentrate upon the way in which marketing channels can provide customer service – both for the end-user they serve and the organizations they work for.

Dealers want to receive goods and service in time. But, when it comes to payment, most of them dillydally. Thus, one of the pressing problems of many organizations is the collection problem, especially from their channel partners. Money that is due does not come in time, and occasionally, not at-all, thus landing the company in embarrassing and stressful situations. Creditors pester, deliveries suffer, production suffers and the opportunities are lost.

The ideal approach is to select the right channel partners. Next, prevent collection problems by tackling them in time. The worst is to hope that time will take care of things. The tragic thing about channel problems is that the more severe the problem, the less energy the people have to solve the problem. They succumb to a sense of helplessness and hopelessness.

Individual consumers and corporate/organizational buyers are aware that literally thousands of goods and services are available through a very large number of diverse channel outlets. What they might not be aware of is the fact that the channel structure, or the set of institutions, agencies and establishments through which the product must move to get to them can be amazingly complex. Usually, combinations of institutions specializing in manufacturing, wholesaling, retailing and many other areas join forces in marketing channel arrangements to make possible the delivery of goods to final customers.

This book will deal with overdue receivables, preventive action, and with focus on managing dealers and related credit and collection problems. While every aspect has been dealt with in detail in the relevant chapters, here we shall summarize dealers' credit control.

DEALER/RESELLER AND CREDIT CONTROL

I. Dealer Selection

1. Selection criteria

Can he demonstrate:

- Consumer demand (or projected demand, if it is a new product)
- Projected gross margin
- Expected volume
- Merchandise suitability
- Maintaining prices and terms
- Service level offered
- Reputation
- Is he suitable for your quality of the brand
- Promotional assistance
- Credit assistance he is asking for – the amount and period
- The security deposit he is willing to keep
- Vendor's distribution policy (national, regional or local, selective or intensive)

2. *Dealer's Credit-worthiness*

- Ability to pay on time – bank/trade reference
- His payment habit – market reputation
- Is he paying other creditors on time?
- Did you approach him or he approached you?
- Sales reps report on his market standing
- His bill passing procedure
- How many signatories are there?
- Balance sheet analysis for deep study, if it is a big order

II. Point of Approval – Activities

To study management practices a DEALER adopts:

- Order processing
- Inventory control
- Inventory planning and forecasting
- Distribution and physical
- Distribution requirements planning
- Material requirements planning
- Purchasing
- Transportation analysis
- Traffic routing and scheduling
- Warehousing management
- Stock locations
- Labour utilization and analysis

This will give a fair idea of his abilities.

So far, we have been trying to find his Character, Capital and Capacity. In today's environment there are three more 'Cs' – Competition, Cost and Cash Flow. Checklist to check on three 'Cs' can be:

Competitive Prompts for Dealers/Consumers

- Are they competitive with respect to price?
- What are the terms of competition?
- Is service a factor?
- How important is quality in the marketplace?

- What is the nature of competition?
- Can they survive in case of a major price war?
- In case of consumer being manufacturer, study manufacturing technology being used – old/new/ getting obsolete, etc.

Cost Prompts for Dealers/Consumers

- Are they doing more with less?
- Have costs been reduced or increased?
- Are there any cost reduction programmes in place?
- Were any customer service control measurements utilised?
- How well contained are the costs?

Cash Flow Prompts for Dealers/Consumers

- Can cash flow sources support the business?
- What is the quality of earnings?
- How strong is the borrowing wherewithal?
- Are there any hidden costs associated with cash flow?
- What are the industry standard for earnings and cash flow?

III. Credit Approval

- Application form
- Credit limit is usually set for new and existing dealers based on dealer's estimated level of monthly purchases
- Bank and trade reference
- Next, we have to find out whether we are covered for the amount – SD and collateral are enough.
- If not, we need to set and appropriate payment terms.
- Make each dealer aware of his credit limits.
- Vetting of new orders by credit control norms
- Even though you have approved his credit, part advance is still a preferable proposition

IV. Post-Sale Credit and Collection

Collection follow-up

- Start collection drive before the due payment date.
- Send statement of accounts on time.
- Make the exact date of payment known.
- Ensure sales staff understands payment terms.
- Make a phone call or write letter immediately after the goods are despatched.
- Call again few days after to find that he is satisfied with the goods.
- Solve debit note/credit note problems, replacement problems immediately.
- Attend to complaints immediately.
- Make call before due dates and remind him how much amount is falling due and when. Help him to make a provision in his cash flow to pay you.

CERTAIN DISCIPLINE

- Never allow the dealer to break his credit limits.
- Never allow a dealer to break his payment terms.
- Monitor dealer's accounts on a regular basis andc study his payment habits.
- Deposit cheques immediately.
- In case cheques bounce, act immediately.
- There is nothing wrong with dumping – it gives a chance to your channel members to make extra profit/money. By now they already know that you are going to dump and they have already worked out a plan for earliest liquidation.
- Start some points system for paying on time or before due dates. Reward him quarterly – converting the points into incentives.
- Encourage advances with prompt payment discount.
- Never have contra accounts. Pay separately for each transaction.
- Those dealers purposely delaying payment should be warned. You are not his banker.

- If he does not improve, ask for advance with order.
- Send pro forma invoice to pay before despatch.
- A dealer having fund problem and has started delaying payment needs to be studied closely. If required, work out a payment plan.
- Side-by-side try and appoint another dealer so that your sale in that area does not suffer.
- In some cases you may have to decide when to STOP supplying.
- Modern trend is to decide and get rid of unwanted dealers.

A few more points:

- Develop 'Wow' attitude for every collection made by your sales rep/other staff members.
- Set monthly collection target and if achieved celebrate collection.
- Like a score board, put a board mentioning the day's collection and cumulative collection for the month.
- Chase big debt before small ones – Pareto principle
- In case of goods lost or damaged during transit, file Insurance claim immediately and follow-up for settlement.

V. Danger Signals

Look out for potential trouble and payment held-up

- The dealer insists he is buying on extended terms or he is entitled to a discount.
- The dealer says that he is unable to pay.
- The dealer offers to pay part now and part next month.
- The dealer offers or sends an 'on account' payment.
- Payment is made later and later each month.
- Promises are persistently broken.
- The volume of unresolved queries is having a serious effect on payments.
- Contra claims are made.

Readers are requested to refer to chapter 8 'Methods of payment – Channel Financing'.

Handling a Project and Credit-Collection Management

Project management became a major approach to managing business and government undertakings in the 1990s. Although we have been carrying out projects for years, it is only recently that project management has become a recognized management discipline.

Project management is a management approach concerned with getting a job done on time, within budget, and according to specifications. Infinite resources are not available to apply to projects. A project manager has to operate under the triple constraints of time, budget and specifications. Work is usually carried out by cross functional team. When they finish, they return to some other assignments. Therefore, it is imperative to make a fault-free planning starting right from planning, executing, controlling and collecting your payment. Apart from time there is a huge constraint on your cash-flow if payment is not collected on time. Readers are requested to read the earlier chapters and then make an attempt to understand this summarized version on project and credit collection management.

Definition of 'project':

'Managing a movement from one state to another'

'The product/service comes into existence at the end of execution.'

In a project nothing fails like success.

—Richard Pascale

Harson, a project consultant, defined project management as 'the achievement of a project's objectives through people, and involves the organising, planning and control of the resources assigned to project, together with the development of constructive human relation with all those involved, both in-company and with the other companies involved.'

Main Characteristics

The principal characteristics and implications of a project are:

1. It is an undertaking which has defined objectives, often including time, financial and technical performance goals.

2. It has defined starting and ending points.
3. It uses a wide variety of resources and skills and involves cost and time.
4. It involves the co-ordination across organisational boundaries of groups and organisational units.
5. It is an instrument of change and is unique.

Project Stages

1. Select your project
2. Set up and contract
3. Plan what to do
4. Implement
5. Monitor and report
6. Complete and review
7. Manage multi-projects

Understand the difference between an everyday task and a project task:

Issue	Every task	Project
Undertaking:	Familiar	Unfamiliar
Staff:	Known	Temporary
Team roles:	Established	Uncertain
Relationships:	Cooperation	Negotiable
Authority:	Clear position	Little/indirect
Information source:	Routine	New/uncertain
Attitude to change:	Desirable	Essential
Momentum:	Maintained by system	Threatened by system
Time-scales	Extended/long-term	Ring-fenced/finite
Coordination:	Hierarchical	Network/matrix

Primary information needed to execute the project

1. **Time:** How much time? How urgent is the project? What will happen if status quo is maintained?
2. **Cost:** How much money do you need? How much will be saved by changing the procedure?
3. **Quality:** To what standard must the outcome be measured?
4. **Quantity:** How many? What will happen if quality is sacrificed for quantity?

Prepare Checklists: All four categories must be balanced against each other.

Control Element	What is likely To go wrong?	How and when will I know?	What will I do about it?
Quality			
Cost			
Time			
Quantity			

Filling Tenders/Quotes – Pre-requisites

1. Cash traps in contract (also refer to follow-up and relationship management)
2. Set quality and quantity objectives: ideas, problems and issues to resolve.
3. Plan and schedule time and cost: feasibility of objective, specify outcome and plan everything you can.
4. Implement plan: action; delivery of the outcome specified
5. Evaluate results of the project: take 'delivery' of project, correct any defects and learn lessons for next time. (What went well, what didn't go well and what would you change?)

Project is teamwork. The norms of forming a team are:

Team building will depend on participation of all kinds, feedback on the assessment of output, and a sense of fun and excitement.

—Francis Kinsman

Theory has it that any group (work based or otherwise) will follow the four stages of development:

1. **Forming:** The group first gets together with its common aim.
2. **Storming:** A short while after the group forms, aims and objectives are questioned and the group experiences conflict from within.

3. **Norming:** Because of the conflict, policy and procedures are drawn up and agreed upon by the consensus of the group.
4. **Performing:** The group adheres to the policy and procedures and works effectively towards its aim.

Project Team Building

Excellent team effort is solidly integrated around well-defined projects. Team members are selected so that they work together as a team and bring a proper balance of skills and knowledge such that every member's contribution is individual and valued. Leadership is recognized in terms of both social and task parameters. Responsibility for the timely and complete delivery of the project lies with the team members, but they are not physically or psychologically separated from their peers and the team becomes neither exclusive nor incestuous. Commitment to the success of projects is at a constant high level.

Average: The effective use of project teams is diluted by the commingling of status and seniority needs with skill, knowledge, and psychological traits indicative of effective membership. People are generally committed, but the politics of the situation put some restraint on the ability of the team to exploit the full potential of each member. Some project groups work well, others experience severe problems of group dynamics which can only be resolved by external intervention.

Unacceptable: Individual drafted into multifunctional workgroups tend to join as representatives of the operation from which they come. Hidden agendas and parochial concerns dominate the interactions and little real work is done. Seniority and status rather than skill or knowledge defines who does what and outcomes are unacceptably variable.

MORALE: THE RIPPLE EFFECT

Use MORALE to encourage and motivate staff going through change:

Myself : Your concentration
Open : Communicate
Remember : Every detail – what they want from you

Attention : Personal attention
Listen : Never refuse attention
Esteem : Flatter with honesty

Determining the Right Agenda

- Who does your solution need to perform for?
- What results and benefits should the solution produce?
- What costs or penalties do you want to avoid?
- What limitation and restrictions apply?
- What do you want to happen?
- What do you not want to happen?

SWOT Analysis

Strengths /Weaknesses	Opportunities /Threats
• People/management expertise • Facilities/building and equipment • Technology • Marketing/sales development skills • Reputation/image • Financial resources	• Political/social/economic changes • Competition, locally or even nationally • Market size and trends • Profitability of market • Needs that your products fulfil • Likelihood of these needs changing

Project Control Instruments

- Gantt chart
- PERT Chart
- Cash Flow statement

Activities after Order Is Received

1. Checking the order.
2. Checklist for site preparation and readiness. Any delay needs to be recorded and communicated by letter/ minutes to avoid LDs.
3. Maintaining status of the order
4. Order clearance checklist before goods are despatched to site/s
5. Checklist for billing.
6. Understand customer's bill passing procedure.

Follow-up and Relationship Management with:

You must understand the many faces of the customer and develop relationship with each one of them.

1. DECIDER: Authorises and initiates project and agrees the terms of reference.
2. RECOMMENDER: Wants change and needs to be convinced it is an integral part of the business. Projects always have friends and enemies. Ensure this person is on your side!
3. USER: Benificiary; implements and influences Recommender.
4. GATEKEEPER: Experts who are listened to by Decider and secretaries/personal assistants who can limit or extend access to Decider/Recommender.
5. STAKEHOLDERS: Can be outside the project entirely (e.g. legal, moral and ethical third parties).

FOLLOW-UP

1. Understand milestones. Keep a tab over Gantt chart/ PERT chart and cash-flow statement, so that the invoices are raised and forwarded at the right time.
2. Invoices to be forwarded to the specified department with correct supporting
3. Personal/letter/telephone follow-up
4. Complete installations, commissioning, training, manual etc. on time
5. Follow up for taking over certificates
6. Follow up for sales tax concession forms
7. Follow up for return of bank guarantee
8. Follow for reducing or waiving liquidated damages. This is possible if you have maintained a proper paper work and can prove that the delays were caused by customer, such as coming late for inspection, delayed payment, etc.

Project management is a management approach concerned with getting the job done – on time, within budget, and according to specifications. The primary focus should be on result for the customer and yours. Only focused follow-up on time will give you better collection and cash-flow.

THIRTEEN

The Art of Collection— The Difficult Ones

SOME BASIC PRINCIPLES

One good way to solve a problem
is to prevent a problem.

This is especially true
of a collection problem.
It is true that
it is much more 'fun'
to solve a collection problem,
spending large chunks of energy and ingenuity.

Only, the cost of the 'fun'
can be high—it can be so high
that survival of the corporation
can itself become a problem.

Those who have enjoyed this fun—
even a couple of times—
would prefer the preventive approach.

This explains
why in this book
we have devoted more pages
for a system of credit management.

Collection problems largely emerge
because they are allowed to become so.
They do not become problems overnight.

"The one training I arrange for ALL my men is collecting."

They become problems
because of acts of commission and omission
on the part of one person or another
in our organization.

Overemphasis on gross volume sales
and absence of focus on nett
Absence of policies,
non-observance of policies,
absence of systems/procedures,
selective non-observance of systems,
absence of focus and vigil,
presence but in fits and starts basis,
a blaming culture:
these constitute some of the reasons
for chronic collection problems.

At the same time
despite our best intentions and efforts,
there can be problems
of undue delays in payment.

1. Act Early

If payment is due on 31st of a month and you don't get it, act on that day and from that day.

2. Renegotiate

Customers can have bad times temporarily. On a case by case basis, extend credit but insist on payment by the deferred date.

3. Help Him Indirectly

If the customer needs help in raising finance and the like, do help him. You are actually helping yourself.

4. Explore a Barter

If he has goods of some kind which you can use or which you can dispose of, take it as an adjustment and relieve him of his liability.

5. Consider 'Political' Ploys

Unofficial approaches at times help. They may do the trick. Only they will have their cost and consequences. When we seek help of the devil, it will extract its price. We have to decide which price is more.

6. Initiate Court Action

If the customer is not amenable to adjustments and alternatives, consider a court action. Courts may move slowly in our country but they move.

7. Write Off

If you don't have the stomach for strong measures because of the many costs involved, write off and be done with it. So that you can get the 'benefit' of write off, observe meticulously all that the authorities want you to observe to claim that 'benefit'.

8. Learn a Lesson

Whatever you do, draw a lesson from the experience and put it to work by a proper system.

Who is a Customer? *One Who Pays on Time*

To continue with the main theme of this book "Do you calculate how much INTEREST PER DAY your company is loosing on OVERDUE DEBTORS? i.e. on bad customers, on bad business, on bad quality-sales. First they eat away your profit. Then they start eating into your investment. In this era of water thin margin, how many sales transactions you must have made just to earn little profit. And if this is being eaten away by slow payers, you got to do something about it. *Every member of your staff works to satisfy a customer. Their reward is in that payment and when that doesn't come, it dampens everyone's hard work.*

It is my firm belief that especially when a firm is growing, your banker is very happy. It will come forward with more loan facilities. When a company is growing, many controls go out of hand. One-way temptation to grow is to sell like hell. But, the fact is, if a company is doing business with customers who have no respect for commercial contract, than your banker makes a lot of money (by way of interest) and your customers are prospering at your cost.

Today what we need is quality sales. The customer should pay and pay on time. Sometime you may have to take bold decisions. Train him. If he does not improve—fire him. Such customers comprises 2% of your total customers. However, if the over-due customers are more than 2% than you are not selecting your customer properly. If your selection procedure is good than you are not working hard enough to collect your money. When dealing with difficult customers just remember—*Turnover is vanity, Profit is sanity and Cash is fact.*

For the last two decades in the worldwide manufacturing industry markets, capacity has continued to exceed demand, with the result that customers have become much more selective in placing their business, and only the most efficient organizations survived. Indian customers are quite rightly becoming more demanding in terms of value of money, performance of the equipment purchased, and its reliability in service. It is against this background that a business has commitments to provide state-of-art products, at prices that customers are prepared to pay, and that give good service.

Having purchased your products, a permanent relation has to be developed with the customer, and to do so, one of the key ingredient is attending to their complaints promptly (if any).

Today, customer satisfaction should be our motto at every stage of working. Customer satisfaction can only be met by executing their orders in toto in all respects. This calls for serious discussion with the potential customers regarding technical and commercial aspects of their requirements. Qualified technical staff should be in a position to guide customers for the right specification of the products. In a nutshell, you should be able to see the customer's requirements from the customer's point of view. It will be worthwhile, before we discuss the concept of complaint, that the credit manager understands the following:

What is a Sale?

A sale is exchange of goods, merchandise or service for money.

What is an Order?

An order is an agreement to supply goods, merchandise or service and shall mean the order with attachments, supplements and amendment issued by the buyer to the supplier and suppliers' acceptance thereof. Only such conditions as are mentioned in the order shall be valid.

I always give your firm big orders.
Execute my orders — don't insist on payment on time.
Its time to decide who is a good customer and who, a bad customer!
I always pay you on time.
Make sure I get full attention on my orders.

Supplier shall acknowledge the receipt of the order in its entirety without exception. The acknowledgement should bear the order number and date. The terms and conditions of the order and buyer's acceptance of it will constitute entire agreement between the supplier and the buyer.

When is a Sale Complete?

To a Supplier: A sale is complete only when the money is collected in full.
To a Buyer: A purchase is complete not only when the goods are received but also the supplier has adhered to all the conditions and complied with the formalities laid down in the order.

What is a Customer?

- A customer is the most important person ever to contact us – in person, by a mail or by telephone, to have purchased our goods with aspiration.
- A customer is not dependent on us – we are dependent on him.
- A customer is not an interruption of our work – he is the purpose of it.
- We are not doing the customer a favour by serving him – he is doing us a favour by allowing us to fulfil that function.
- Customers are not cold statistics, they are human beings with feelings and emotions like our own.
- A customer is not someone with whom to match wits. Nobody ever won an argument with a customer.
- Customers are people who bring their wants, needs and aspiration. It is our job to cater for them, profiting the customer and our company.

Customer's Expectations

Next, it is important for a credit manager to understand what is a *customer* and his *expectation from your company* before he buys, then at the point of buying, and then again what he expects after buying a merchandise. Customer service programmes of many companies evolve around customer's aspirations. These are:

Pre-transaction Elements

1. Written statement of policy.
2. Statements to reach the hands of customer.
3. Infrastructure—organisational structure.
4. System flexibility
5. Very high standard of technical services.

Point-of-transaction Elements

1. Stock-out level
2. Ability to back order.
3. Elements of order cycle
4. Timeliness
5. Trans-shipment
6. System accuracy
7. Order convenience
8. Product substitution

Post-sales-transaction Elements

1. Installations, warranty, alterations, repairs, parts
2. Product tracking
3. Customer claims, complaints
4. Product packaging
5. Temporary replacement of product during repairs

COMPLAINTS

Corrective action must be taken as needed to reduce the variance between actual performance and the set standard. It is an established fact that the choice of product depends on Quality, Price, Delivery and Service. It is against this background a credit manager should deal with complaints.

Having accepted the order, it will be the prime duty of the company to execute the same without giving any chance for grievance.

What one should bear in mind is that the satisfaction of one customer is as good as an advertisement in the newspaper.

We would like to highlight the various reasons that we had come across due to which our payments got delayed.

(a) Goods have been supplied without receiving amendments such as delivery date, price difference, excise duty difference, etc.
(b) Indefinite delay in executing the order
(c) Part supply
(d) Non-delivery due to delay in transportation
(e) Wrong goods supplied
(f) Goods being rejected
(g) Quantity
(h) Damaged goods
(i) Frequent late delivery
(j) Various charges
(k) Bad service
(l) Cancellation of order due to late execution
(m) Manuals not being given along with goods
(n) Test certificate not being given in time
(o) Complaints concerning quality

A credit manager must ponder over the reasons/complaints because of which their customers don't pay in time or delay payments indefinitely. Every month a statement should be taken out, categorized into the following groups and the same brought to the notice of the management.

1. Inefficiency in office procedure in executing the order
2. Customer's dissatisfaction due to various reasons discussed above.
3. Delays due to customer's office procedure in passing your bill.
4. Some customers have a habit of delaying payments purposely.
5. Financial crisis faced by customers.

Inefficiency and Dissatisfaction

The first two points can be taken care of, provided the customer oriented operation concept is strengthened, while the other points need to be tackled by the field staff by developing a permanent kind of relation with the customers. The field staff should also keep abreast of each customer's payment habit and use their best judgment in order to receive the money in time.

Inefficiency in an office could be of various kinds. It is only our customers who point out our inefficiency and these complaints should be treated as profit, not pain, because many complaints are genuine.

Dealing with Complaints

Our Attitude

(a) We must naturally want to know whenever customers have cause to complain. We would rather receive complaints than have the customers abandon us and take their trade elsewhere.
(b) A complaint will provide us the opportunity to explain, to put things right and preserve customer goodwill.
(c) A complaint may suggest ways in which our product or service could be improved.

Rules to Be Followed

(a) It is certainly a sound practice to assume that the customer may be right.
(b) If you cannot deal with the complaint promptly, acknowledge it at once. Explain that you are looking into it, and will send a detailed reply later.
(c) If the complaint is unreasonable, point out the fact politely, and in an agreeable manner.
(d) If you are to blame, admit it and put matters right immediately.
(e) We should not try to excuse ourselves by blaming any of our staff. We are, after all, responsible for what they do.
(f) Whether you allow the complaint or not, thank the customer for telling us about it.

Office Procedure

Delays due to customer's office bill passing procedure or any other excuses can be also of various kinds. 'We are short of staff',

'The staff who is handling your file is on leave', 'We have not received your invoice', 'We are short of funds', 'The signatory is out of town' are common excuses. Sometimes the real reason is not known until persistent probing from a supplier unearths a fault in the system no one had noticed.

It is always worth asking how the invoice approval procedure works. If there is time, meet the persons responsible in the stores, the bill passing clerk and the supervisor who is responsible for moving invoices onto the approval for payment list.

Deliberate Policy

There are a few companies which set out to take as much out of the creditors as they can get away with. They buy time giving so many excuses.

(a) If you give us a discount we would pay you more quicker.
(b) All our cheques have to go to Head Office for counter signature.
(c) The goods are not yet approved by our quality control as it does not meet the samples we have sent you.
(d) Your case is being reinvestigated as the price is found on the higher side.
(e) Our computer is down—cheques cannot be issued.
(f) Educate him on terms of payment.
(g) Train him to pay on time or otherwise you will be compelled to change his terms.
(h) Show him how much you are loosing (in interest alone) doing business with him.
(i) Persistent follow-up (don't give up). They know sooner or later you will stop chasing them.
(j) Make sure you get your payment and ....
(k) Decide, next time whether you would like to do business with him.

The credit manager must be able to see through all these attempts to hide the fact that his company is being used to provide free working capital. Such customers may claim that they are getting 90 days credit. If investigated, it will transpire that they are not getting 90 days but taking away 90 days.

Absolute refusal to accept such treatment is the correct attitude but it must sometimes be tempered by the commercial circumstances. The market strength of a customer can result in his being able to dictate terms, especially if orders are scarce and the factory is operating at less than full capacity. The credit manager will only tolerate this after close discussion with sales management & he should always try to put a time limit on the arrangement.

Customers who purposely delay, become delay masters in due course for three reasons:

1. He delays because you allow him. If you don't ask you don't get. You have not reminded him for your payment before due date. You felt, payment come without asking. You did not make it clear that how serious you are with your payment terms. They will pay only after you remind them.
2. The second type needs coaxing. This type of customer follows the principle of collecting early and delaying all payments – they believe, such practice is sound financial management. It is his policy that until few reminders have been made he will not pay. May be, he will start processing the bill only after three or four reminders, thinking that you are doing a great favour. This type needs a strict face-to-face talking. You should discuss with him with facts and figures i.e. how much you have lost doing business with him (interest lost on overdue period, plus cost of number of calls and visits, plus waste of time and effort). If they improve they are your customer.
3. He starts to delay because he believes that suppliers should be patient when it comes to asking money. He runs his business at others costs, especially suppliers. Even if he accepts 30 days credit, but, makes it a policy not to pay, except under extreme endurance. He will have innumerable reasons to delay (actually not pay) your payment. He thinks it is his birthright to delay (actually not pay). He may even guide you to take legal action against him. (because he is impressed that law is on his side). Surprisingly, you find such customers enough in number and very much prospering. If you don't supply, someone else will.

You, will have to decide whether you have started your business for making profit or your customers to make profit at your costs. First, persistently follow-up, don't give-up. They know that sooner or later you will give-up following-up. Whoever gives up first will be the looser. Sometime no-business is better than doing bad-business and may have to take hard decision. Get rid of such customers or change their payment term to cash.

Financial Crisis

Customers who are facing financial or fund problems, or victims of unexpected misfortune are very few. Such cases demand sympathetic consideration. Dealing severely or taking legal action will result in waste of money and time.

A better way of dealing with such cases is by working out a solution to be mutually agreed upon by both sides. Without embarassing the customer, the credit manager should be able to work out the solution by getting replies to his following questions:

(a) Why did we not receive our payment?
(b) How can he pay? or How can we help him in settling our dues?
(c) When will he be in a position to settle our dues? Can we wait that long?
(d) Does an instalment facility work? How many instalments he is asking for? Can we wait that long?
(e) Is he in a position to keep his proposed promises?
(f) Whether he should be allowed to buy goods while settling the old dues?

The credit manager's solution will be based on the amount of money involved, past experience with the customer, whether the solution is practically workable and what will be its effect on company's cash flow.

Contra Accounts

Another fairly common problem is that of contra accounts. If the customer is also supplying goods, it is only natural that he will not pay sooner than he receives payment. The most satisfactory

Confrontation is best handled with calmness, reasoning, justification and not by anger or ego.

Form No. 13.1

Sales Follow-up Report

Branch: ____________________ Serial No. ____________

Customer's Name: ____________ Division: ____________

____________ Account No.: ____________

Inv. No.	Date	Amount	Inv. No.	Date	Amount

Date of follow-up:

Person contacted: Designation:

Report:

Whether goods/equipment supplied to Customer's satisfaction?

Whether there is any shortage?

Whether instalation is complete?

Whether paperwork in order?

Any other complaints?

Staff's signature ____________ Customer's Signature ____________

Date ____________ Date ____________

* To be sent along with despatch of goods/ posted.

* To be reported by the customer within 15 days.

arrangement is either for both parties to exchange cheques at month-end (assuming similar payment terms) or for one side to pay the net difference. Matter should not be complicated by involving supplies made to sister concern or to any other company in the group.

Sometimes to catch up with sales target, goods are sent before schedule. Also sometimes the delivery is delayed for months and suddenly the customer is bombarded with 2-3 schedules all together. The fact is that the customer may not have provided for such deliveries. Hence improving control over despatch area and deferring the payment by a reasonable time can be the only solution.

After-sales Follow-up

After-sales follow-up should be intensified in order to instill confidence in the minds of our customers about the quality of our products and the services that we render them. This will be a source of trustworthiness for them and the same would help us in collecting our payments without much delay.

A sales staff should visit the customer whenever required immediately after the material has been delivered. In case of any complaints, the same may be reported. This format is being used by one engineering company.

A Customer Service Cell is needed to receive the various complaints of customers and give a feedback to the respective departments. The concept of 'aftersales follow-up' will help in identifying the problems and taking corrective action in time, before payment is due.

Substandard Quality

This point is being discussed to emphasize the importance of Quality Control. If this is not considered seriously, the credit manager may face a major hurdle in settling disputes and collecting payment. Poor quality will have a very bad impact on the total business.

The fact that poor quality costs money must be obvious to everyone. Yet, many an industry has been slow to take up quality assurance as a discipline.

With the emergence of many foreign competitors, there is need that every business in India should gear up to have a system for reporting the 'unquality' costs in the organisation so that there is a yardstick against which to test the likely profitability of proposed improvements. Unquality costs are due to things like complaints, rework, scraps, trouble shooting and warranty. These costs need to be uncovered as fully as possible.

For a business, quality should mean

- Meeting the customer's reasonable needs and expectations (quality and output)
- Running the internal working of the business as efficiently as possible (quality of operation)

Money and effort spent on reducing such figures are likely to provide a better return on investment and in a shorter time.

For better returns a quality improvement programme should be undertaken on the following lines:

1. To develop and maintain the quality system;
2. To negotiate with customer's quality representatives;
3. To negotiate with departments within the firm to ensure that quality problems are resolved;
4. To carry out audits of internal and supplier's quality system;
5. Continuing improvements;
6. Searching/Developing tools for improving skills and departmental working.

Every step needs to be spelt out in detail depending upon the nature of the business and its products.

Complaints Management

Talking about quality, we may be going out of the credit management preview, but if you want your money to be collected on time, then the quality aspects should be on the top of the agenda. A credit manager may find the quality of the firm's product a stumbling block that needs to be crossed again and again if money has to be collected. If low quality product is produced, then every credit could be delinquent. However, if only a batch or a particular model is defective, then it is the duty of a credit manager to make an issue of it to his management.

Despite our best efforts, there are always going to be situations in which a customer becomes unhappy. What a business does when these occasions occur, and how much the organization learns from the experience can have a sizable effect on the organizations' future health and vitality. A business can view complaints as opportunities, it can continously update the complaint process, and it can use the complaint information to target the improvement efforts. This means that an organization can often benefit from making a unhappy customer happy. Although many companies have not learned this lesson very well, many companies have become very good at complaint management. From such examples we have derived several principles to use in guiding the organization's response to a complaint. These are:

- Communication links from frontline staff to every one in the organization, through information system, so that an immediate reply can be given to the customer with regard to the problem—who will look into the problem, and how much time it will take to convey the outcome of their findings.

- A sense of urgency is to be advocated. This means that someone from the company is immediately on the customer's side, working to bring about a successful resolution to the complaint. This is not same as immediate resolution of the problem. Some problems will take a long time to solve. However, someone in the company should always represent the complaining customer's interest.
- A key to complaint management is delegation of authority to the frontline staff. Taking a problem up through channels would simply be too slow. For this reason, and because of speed of resolution is important, authority to settle complaints is best handled at the front line.
- Responsiveness means that the customer is told as soon as possible, how soon the complaint can be resolved. If it cannot be resolved quickly, the company must communicate the fact, and indicate exactly what is being done to address the problem. In fact, several of the principles we have discussed so far go hand in hand with responsiveness. For example, the better the communication links and databases the faster the response in many instances. Likewise, an empowered frontline tends to have the authority to resolve problems quickly. In general, two things must be done to ensure that the customer considers the company to be responsive, regardless of whether the problem can be solved immediately or not. The company must (1) respond immediately to all communications by the customer, preferably by phone, and (2) inform the customer of what is being done to solve the problem and how long it is likely to take.
- Finally, do not further inconvenience the customer. Whenever the organization has made a mistake, it is the organization's sole responsibility to make things right.

LIQUIDATED DAMAGE (LD)

We have already discussed that LD is an amount deducted by the buyer for delivering goods after stipulated time. Liquidated damage is an undesirable precedent. Looking to the high volume of amount involved in LD charges, a credit manager must look for some alternative in order to avoid this liability. On the other hand, late delivery does not meet the approval of the customer. If it is an indent order, the period of each stage should be forecasted as accurately as possible. The following points may be considered:

- The period required for design & approval.
- The period required for developing proto and approval.
- The period required to manufacture the product of desired quantity.

In case any of the above referred to steps gets prolonged due to unforeseen circumstances, an appropriate letter is to be written to the ordering authority justifying the reason for the delay. This delay could be from both the sides or from any one side. Therefore, when the goods have been ultimately delivered and if any LD charges have been deducted, all this correspondence will help us to lodge a protest note against imposition of penalty and thereby we may be able to get at least the amount reduced if not waived.

Thus the quotation should be very specific about the period each stage is going to take. Moreover, such period should be planned very carefully. Further, it may so happen that the design may have been completed at the stipulated time but the buyer may have taken a longer time to approve it or the buyer may decide to change the original design. Likewise, during the development, delay has taken place or for that matter due to change in original plan the production of such product called for rescheduling. Such matters should be recorded and also are to be brought to the notice of the buyer at every stage. This way a case is built up and one will be in a better position to prove that the LD deduction is not justified.

Many government departments have a procedure of writing to their various users to inform whether any loss was suffered due to delay in supply. If not, they refund the LD penalty amount. One must, of course, apply for such refund after the complete order has been executed.

Before we conclude, we would like to caution the credit manager to look out for some warning signs of delayed payments:

1. The customer insists he is buying on extended terms or is entitled to a discount.

2. The customer says he is unable to pay—No funds.
3. The customer offers to pay part now and part next month.
4. The customer offers to or sends an on account payment.
5. Payment is made later and later each month.
6. Promises are persistently broken.
7. The volume of unsolved queries are having a serious effect on payments.
8. Contra claims are made.
9. Goods delivered after delivery period.
10. Bill copies are not received or respective departments have not received the bill copies.
11. Goods sent on verbal orders.
12. Cheque signatory is out of town.
13. Goods received in damaged condition or short received.
14. Part of the consignment is rejected.
15. Bank guaranttee not given to the customer towards advance or performance.
16. Test certificate and or inspection certificate not enclosed.
17. Wordings in order/amendment & inspection note differ.
18. Advance not adjusted in the bill.
19. Order price and bill price differ.
20. Excise duty or sales tax not charged correctly.

Key Points

Recognise that debt collecting is often a matter of negotiating and requires the use of negotiating techniques. Try hard to:

- Avoid an adversarial situation.
- Work to 'both-win' situation.
- Be prepared to make concessions – especially those which cost you little or nothing but may be very valuable to the other person.
- Don't underestimate your 'power.'
- Keep the other person's viewpoint continually in mind.
- Avoid quick deals.
- Avoid harassment – it's illegal.

Make use of meetings. They can be a good opportunity to collect some money.

FOURTEEN

The Art of Collection—The Legal Path

No matter what type of business one is involved in, a time will come when the normal approach to a customer to settle his account gets exhausted and one has to look elsewhere for its collection.

Generally it is best to exhaust all internal collection options before turning to outside help. Of course, the key is in knowing when internal efforts are no longer likely to bear fruit. It may be time to take a customer's account very seriously when:

- The customer repeatedly breaks payment commitments.
- Stops paying down its account for 60–90 days or more.
- No longer returns telephone calls and avoids meeting or
- Is paying off other suppliers but shows no intention of paying your money.
- In case when the owner has suddenly closed his business or the owner is missing. In this case the seller without wasting any time should file a Nominal Case (NC) at the buyer's jurisdiction police station. This NC proof will be needed to be produced in the court of law where you are fighting your case.

Whether a debt can be classified as bad at that stage must depend on the particular circumstances of the case, but it would be prudent to make provision for it subsequently as 'doubtful', once its collection has to be placed in the advocate's hand. Once an account has reached this stage, there are only two more courses open to the creditor, either to place the matter in the

Your repertoirs for getting debtors to pay you should now be as large and creative as the excuses many debtors invent so they can hang onto your money as long as possible.

Leonard Sklar

Because our creditors don't payus

Because we don't have cash

Because we have other urgent commitments

Because we generally don't pay in time

Because you have not done the full job

Because we have not received your bill

Because we just can't pay!

Because your honour is at stake

Because we've urgent commitments

Because I'll lose my job

Because my boss says: Without cash don't come

hands of the senior officer or the director/managing director to take up the matter at that level of debtor's firm and if that also fails, to employ an advocate.

It is essential to choose one's advocate carefully. It is advisable in these days of specialisation to select one who is a specialist in this type of work. There are a few firms now that wish to involve themselves exclusively in collection work but then if your file is in order and if all the steps are taken to build up a case, then any advocate will be able to pursue your case.

Before going legal, important points to ponder with:

1. **Does the customer have the money?** If they don't, very likely you may not get your money even after judgment is in your favour. The judge takes a very sympathetic view against those who accept their liabilities but want time to pay. The payment may be in small installments. You should be prepared to accept.
2. **Will the customer evade his responsibility?** Impossible, but do not underestimate the defaulters, they are expert in legal matters. They can come out unexpected points in the court and keep prolonging the trial.

   Your customer (defendant) may have the following options:
   - Pay the amount claimed;
   - Do nothing;
   - Admit all the claim and ask for time to pay;
   - Defend the claim;
   - Defend part of the claim, admit part of the claim and pay the admitted part;
   - Defend part of the claim, admit part of the claim and pay the admitted part and ask for time to pay the admitted part;
   - File a counterclaim in conjunction with all but the first two of the above.

   This does not happen to some customers who are rogues. Some may be facing real personal tragedies. If your paper work is in order to prove your point and a good advocate, expert is such matters should be able to pursue the matter efficiently and effectively.

3. **What are the chances of winning?** Do you have the correct identification of the defendant/s. Many times it is found the premises in which they run their business is on rental basis, and fine morning they have closed down their business. It is therefore very important that you must know with whom you are doing business and they can be summoned to court. If your paper work can prove each point of dispute, if you can prove you have delivered what was promised and can prove the same, you should not hesitate in taking legal action.
4. **Are you prepared for the cost?** Court fees, Advocate fees, legal and other costs need to be considered before you file your case. Big amount of dispute should be pursued immediately.
5. **Are you sure what terms govern the contract?** Sellers often misunderstand the legal position. They do not try to understand "What is a delivery?, Where is the jurisdiction?". The Seller often rely on fine prints on the backside of their own paper work. That may not hold good always. The buyer has also printed many terms and conditions on the back of his paper work. The advocate will have to advise you on this.
6. **Is Arbitration possible?** It is in the agreement. If not – what is the way out? Will the other party agree to such a settlement. In case of technical matters arbitration helps much better. Because it is handled by some expert, mutually agreed upon. More over a arbitration is fast, continuous, cost effective, without publicity and the judgment is fast. If it not agreed in the original agreement try to negotiate on the pretext that both sides will benefit.

A customer that is having problems paying your invoices is probably also having problems paying other suppliers too. Therefore, your legal action may well put you into competition with these other suppliers and early decisive action may give you the advantage of getting judgment faster.

Fair Chance: A final warning letter informing the customer/ defaulter informing him that if the over due amount is not paid by certain dates (prescribed by law) then Seller will have no choice to proceed against him in the court of claiming the principal-amount, interest-till-date for the period the amount is over due and the advocate/legal cost. The idea is to claim the maximum possible amount.

Small scale industries can claim the interest amount (for the period of delay) even from all Government departments at Compound rate of interest.

Once you have selected a Advocate/solicitor who should represent you, then allow the solicitor do his job. They are after all the experts. This is cost effective approach and most likely to achieve the maximum payment in the minimum time.

Advocates are not allowed to charge percentage of what they recover and will normally charge a fee based on the amount of work done, whether the debt is recovered or not. The basis of the charge is for negotiation between the creditor and the advocate.

In India, we are not inclined to go to court because it is a time consuming as well as a costly process or because we are not famaliar with legal steps. Let us assure you that a credit manager may be a student of commerce but he will be able to pursue all legal cases. Under section 138 of The negotiable instrument act 1988, summary suits (civil procedure code Rule No. 2) of 1908 and even winding up petitions u/section 433/439 of Company's act can be handled very successfully. In our experience, a case of dishonoured cheque may take maximum 3-4 months to settle. A summary suit/winding up petition can take about a year, because deferred payment terms could be granted to the debtor by the court. This became possible because the cases were prepared very carefully keeping the following background in mind.

A number of points need checking before legal proceedings are started:

1. The law of limitation allows three years to recover a debt (three years from the date of sale or three years from the date of liabilities accepted but disputed for various reasons) & if the debt is outstanding for a longer period, it means the debt becomes bad. A claim should be filed in the court for the recovery of debt not later than 3 years.
2. Is it certain that the debt is not disputed? Check thoroughly with the sales office that there are no unanswered queries on price, delivery, etc.

3. Is the name and trading style of the customer verified? The importance of careful checking when a account is first opened now becomes apparent.
4. Is it reasonably certain that the customer has sufficient assets to pay the debt? This is generally more difficult to establish with a sole trader or partnership than with a limited company, but personal assets are available to creditors in the former cases. One will have to approach the company Registrar Office to avail of the above information with regard to a limited company.

When an advocate has been instructed, prior to initiating any proceedings, he will wish to make a formal application to the debtor for payment. It is only in exceptional circumstances that he will dispense with a letter before action: first because there is usually a fair chance that the debtor will respond in some way to a letter and secondly by not doing so an advocate may be putting a debtor to unnecessary costs.

The advocate, in order to be able to act quickly and effectively, will require certain information from the creditor. He will need to know the exact name and address of the debtor and precise details of the account he is being asked to collect. Clearly, the debtor will take advantage of any error or omission in order to prevaricate and so delay payment. Much valuable time will be lost if the creditor gives his advocate incorrect information and in particular it is important to identify the debtor accurately.

Proceedings can be commenced in either Lower Court or a High Court. The choice between Lower Court & High Court will be partly dictated by the amount and nature of debt.

The detailed procedure of legal action is beyond the scope of this book. Our advice is that the credit manager should be familiar with various stages and alternative courses of legal action. It is advisable to consult a lawyer as and when the problem arises. This way he will be also educating himself.

DISHONOUR OF CHEQUES

'Cheque Victims' Grievances Forum', Mumbai, invited all those who are affected by cheque bouncing to join hands and put forward their suggestions for changes in the system that the cheque once issued should not bounce and if this is not respected then the court procedure should help them to recover their money immediately. They published a glaring study which revealed that almost 40,000 cases of cheques bouncing are pending in various courts of Mumbai. Within nine years from the date of making cheque bouncing a criminal offence, such a huge backlog has been created. Every year 12,000 to 15,000 cases are added to this backlog, but only about 2,000 cases are disposed of. Even out of these, 99 per cent cases are settled because the victims of cheque bouncing become frustrated and settle the matter by taking whatever the defaulter is ready to pay. Only 20 to 25 cases are decided through a court judgement. Thus, instead of being a deterrent, this has encouraged unscrupulous elements to default.

The best of intentions of the law has been defeated by ineffective implementation. The situation needs to be remedied immediately. It has to be brought to the notice of the government and the administrator of Justice that people has started loosing faith in our legal system. The machinery of Justice will crumble under such a heavy backlog.

The financial services companies offering credit through hire purchase, leasing are most affected. And for the dealings between industries, cheque bouncing has become an instrument to cheat. The bouncing cheque criminal case under section 138 applies to those cheques which have bounced due to no funds in issuer's account. In other words, a case against issuer cannot be filed where the issuer has enough balance which covers up the cheque amount, but after issuing he can advise the bank not to honour the cheque on presentation, on the pretext of having dispute.

Various judgements have been published from time to time and the key points of these are:

- A cheque is valid for six months and it should be presented to clearing bank during the course of its validity period. Effective from April 1, 2012 the validity of banker's cheque, drafts, pay order will have to be presented within 3 months of the date of issue. So next time you receive a cheque or draft make sure it is presented quickly, so as to reach the clearing bank within 3 months. (source Times of India dated 6th November, 2011, pg 1 & pg 13)
- If the drawer has not filled in the date, the holder of the cheque can fill in such a date and for all legal purposes this becomes the date of issue or drawal.

- Post-dated cheques are those which carry a future date, at times several months down the line. Such cheques can be presented to the banker for encashment only after this date.
- The reason for cheque bouncing can be of many folds—the drawer may have closed his account with the particular bank. He might have expired. He may be facing a liquidity crunch.
- Supreme Court: Can't hold director liable without making firm party. Source: *Hindustan Times* 7 May, 2012.

Now section 138 to 142 of the Negotiable Instrument Laws (Amendment) Act, have been inserted on April 1, 1989 to provide speedy and effective remedies. Under this section the errant drawer can be imprisoned for a term upto a year, or a fine which could be twice the amount of the cheque or with both. So, firstly you must keep your paper work pucca and secondly, comply with the date formalities of sending notices within 15 days of dishonour, and thereafter if the drawer does not pay, file a case within next 30 days.

- If postdated cheque is issued to you by a corporate entity (which includes a firm or an association of persons), section 141 provides that every person who was in charge of and responsible to the company for the conduct of its business and the concerned company can both be proceeded against and penalised. Except the Nominated and Sleeping Directors.
  1. Further Judgment: However, the judgment has been fine-tuned with a new judgment in August, 2005 – the complainant must know who is the responsible director and staff in customer's company for cheque dishonour, and the complaint/court case should be filed against these people and against every director.
  2. Further Judgment: "Date: 12th March, 2007 – Economic Times Reported Cheque Bouncing: Only the person in-charge is guilty. (add in the further change to judgement 12.........)......In the case of Western India Industries.

     The Bench comprising Justice Arijit Pasayat and Justice L.S. Panta said "The provision (Section 141 of the Negotiable Instrument Act) clearly shows that so far as the companies are concerned if any offence is committed by it then every person who is Director or employee is not liable. Only such would be held liable if at the time when offence is committed he was in-charge and was responsible for the conduct of the company."

The court dismissed the appeal which had sought proceedings against the director and employees of a company that issued cheques but on being presented got dishounoured.

3. Further Judgment: (Source: Times of India dated 3rd December, 2011). All directors and partners of a company is responsible for its day-to-day functioning would have to face trial if the cheques issued by the firm bounces, the Bombay High Court said. Dismissing a petition filed by two former directors of Kautons Retail India urging the court to quash proceedings against them for around for around 60 bounced cheques amounting to 1.2 crore, Justice M. L. Tahaliyani said that no interference. The disputed facts could be decided at the time of trial. The accused "can demonstrate before the trial court that the offence, if any, was committed without their knowledge and they have exercised due diligence to prevent the commission of the offence", the judge said.

- If the company is under winding up process, if cheques are issued during this time and these cheques bounce then the directors can be punished, they cannot escape their penal consequences.
- The new code makes it clear that complaint must be a corporeal person who is capable of being physically present in court. Even if a complaint is made in the name of an incorporeal person, it is necessary that a natural person represents such juristic person in the court and is that natural person who is looked upon to be the complainant in the case. In other words, when the complainant is a body corporate, it is de jure complainant, and it must necessarily associate a human being as de facto complainant to represent the former in court proceedings.

- The complainant need not be the original person who filed the case, but it could be another person representing the complainant's firm. During the course of the proceeding, the original complainant named by the company to represent the case may have left. The Supreme Court suggested, as a pragmatic proposition, that no Magistrate shall insist that the particular person, whose statement was taken on oath at the first instance, alone can continue to represent the company till the end of the proceedings.
- Some high courts have held that a cheque could be presented for encashment on any number of occasions within the period of its validity but there could be only one cause of action, that is for the last dishonour. The third set of high court judgements hold that only the first dishonour, and not the subsequent ones, would invite prosecution. Now therefore the question arises—when does the cause of action arise?

  The Supreme Court has now identified the point where the cause of action arises in the dishonouring of cheques. It is the point when there is failure to make the payment within 15 days from the date of receipt of notice. Since there is a definite point of time, such an occasion can arise only once. Therefore, the frequent visits of the debtor and his assurance should not confuse the creditor regarding his legal rights.
- In Modi Cements vs K K Nandi, the Supreme Court held that even if the drawer stops payment after issuing the cheque and informs the payee, the offence under Section 138 would be committed.
- The Supreme Court in number of cases pinned down the defaulters who tried to escape their liabilities dishonestly by issuing a stop payment instructions to their bankers knowing fully well that the cheques issued by them would be dishonoured due to insufficient funds in their bank account.
- If the drawer has not filled in the date, the holder of the cheque can fill in such a date and for all legal purposes this becomes the date of issue or drawal.

- Post-dated cheques are those which carry a future date, at times several months down the line. Such cheques can be presented to the banker for encashment only after this date.
- The reason for cheque bouncing can be many fold—the drawer may have closed his account with the particular bank. He might have expired. He may be facing a liquidity crunch.
- The guarantor is liable to pay.
- The Karnataka and Mumbai court awarded penalty, jail term, also legal expenses and interest costs in cheque bouncing cases.
- If a notice or summons is sent with correct address by registered AD, the notice will be taken as served.
- It is not easy to avail of any shelter behind the verdict that stop instruction was made known to the payee, before the cheque was presented. The defaulters have to prove beyond doubt that there were sufficient funds in the bank account at the time the cheque was presented. It has to be shown that the cheque was dishonoured mainly because of stop payment instructions.
- Many unscrupulous drawers take shelter behind this verdict. The best safeguard would be to ensure that whenever post-dated cheques are accepted, an undertaking is taken from the drawer of the cheque as follows:

The Undertaking

- The drawer hereby confirms that he has accepted the goods and for total cost of the goods he has issued the necessary number of post-dated cheques to the Owner/Authorised representatives covering all the gross instalments dues/dues as per the terms of the agreement/ purchase order, and each such post-dated cheque carries the due date of such gross instalments.
- The drawer hereby unconditionally and irrevocably covenants that he shall not at any point of time question the validity period of such post-dated cheques or raise any claim that such cheques are valid only for a period of six months from the date of issuance of the cheques

and further affirms that he shall ensure the availability of adequate funds in the account of which such cheques have been drawn on the respective due dates.

- The drawer irrevocably instructs/authorises the payee to deposit the said post-dated cheques on the dates stated on the respective cheques and the drawer hereby undertakes to honour the cheques on presentation, and to ignore any communication from the drawer requesting the payee not to deposit the cheques on the date stated on the cheque.
- The drawer hereby undertakes not to intimate the bankers to stop the payment of the cheques delivered to payee.
- The drawer hereby undertakes not to close the bank account without prior permission in writing under the terms of the agreement.
- The drawer hereby undertakes that he shall never give payee any notice requesting payee not to present the cheques given hereunder on due dates.
- The drawer is aware that on the faith of these undertakings, the payee has agreed to provide the said loan/hire-purchase/ lease finance/goods to drawer.
- The drawer submits that in the event of any default in honouring the cheques, the payee is at liberty to take action against drawer for the dishonour of cheques under Section 138 of the Negotiable Instruments Act.

Rules for Taking Legal Action—Dishonour of Cheques

In case a cheque is dishonoured, the credit manager should take the following steps, as prescribed by the law.

Step I: This letter representing notice of demand should be sent within 15 days from the date of receipt of dishonour memo. In the new amendment the 15 days is changed to 30 days. Two specimens are mentioned below:

Specimen 1 of notice of demand for dishonour of cheque/s to be sent within 30 days of cheque dishonour.

Ref: Date:

To

(By registered A.D.)

Dear Sirs,

Sub: Dishonour of cheques—Notice under Section
138 of Amended Negotiable Instruments Act.

We regret to inform you that your cheque/s detailed below was/were dishonoured by the bank.

Cheque Nos.	Date	Amount	Drawn on (Name of Bank)
________	______	______	______________
________	______	______	______________
________	______	______	______________
________	______	______	______________

We hereby give notice to you under Section 138 of Amended Negotiable Instruments Act—demanding payment within 15 days from the date of receipt of this letter.

If we do not receive your DD for Rs. ____________in lieu of dishonoured cheque/s within 15 days, we will hand over the matter to our legal counsel to prosecute you according to law, demanding amount due interest and legal expenses from you.

Yours faithfully,
For ALBC CO. LTD

Credit Controller

Specimen 2 of notice of demand for dishonour of cheque/s to be sent within 30 days of cheque dishonour VP/CC/V-100A

12th May, 1999

To
M/s. V.K. & T. LIMITED
VKT House, Plot No. 283/289,
Patil Indl. Estate, Bombay.

Dear Sir,

Sub : Dishonour of cheque—Notice under section
138 of Amended Negotiable Instruments Act.

We regret to inform you that your cheque detailed below was dishonoured by the bank.

Cheque Nos.	Date	Amount	Drawn on (Name of Bank)
______	______	______	______
______	______	______	______
______	______	______	______
______	______	______	______

We hereby give notice to you under Section 138 of Amended Negotiable Instruments Act—demanding payment within 15 days from the date of receipt of this letter.

If we do not receive your DD for Rs............ in lieu of dishonoured cheque within 15 days, you are liable to be prosecuted under the above mentioned section under which you are liable to be punished with imprisonment for a term which may extend to one year or with fine, which may extend to twice the amount of the cheque or with both.

Under the circumstances, we hereby call upon you to make the payment of Rs........... within a period of 15 days from thedate of receipt of this notice, failing which, we shall hand over the matter to our legal counsel to take necessary action against you in the competent Court of Law, and in that event, you shall be liable for all the costs and consequences resulting there from.

Thanking you,

Yours faithfully,

for V.P. & CO. LIMITED

Credit Controller

Step II: We must wait for payment for 15 days from the date of receipt of such letter by the customer as evident from the acknowledgment card received.

Step III: If the party still does not pay within this period, then within one month from the 15th day, we must file complaint under section 138 of the Negotiable Instrument Act.

NEW AMENDMENT U/S 138 OF NEGOTIABLE INSTRUMENT ACT

- The case has to be decided within 6 months.
- New rule is that the notice period is increased to 30 days from 15 days.

LEGAL ACTION

Make sure you have a watertight case before proceeding; being right is not enough, you have to be able to prove that you are right.

—J. L. Spencer in his book "Getting Paid"

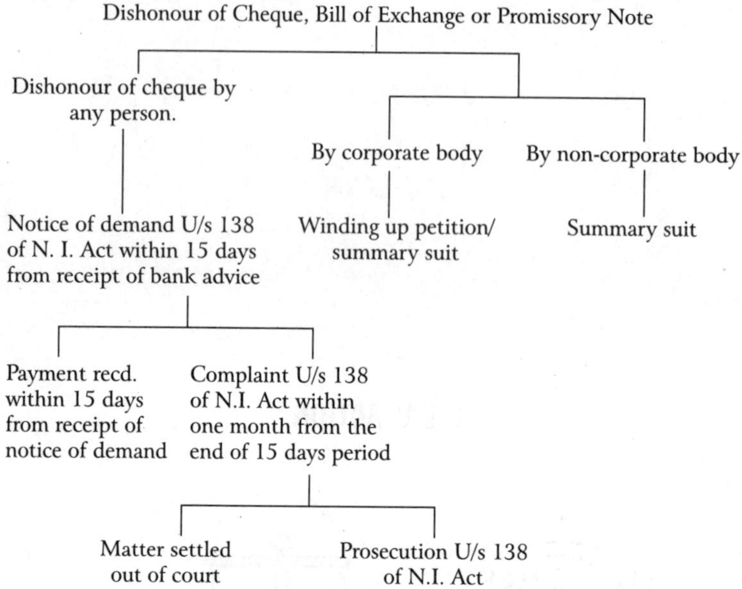

Fig 14.1 Practical Legal Remedies

- Other than penalty, the imprisonment increased from one year to two years.

SUMMARY SUITS

The object underlying the summary procedure is to prevent unreasonable obstruction by a defendant who has no defence. The order is confined to suits of negotiable instruments bill or note and is confined to superior courts. The order provides for a summary procedure in respect of certain suits. The essence of Summary Suits is that the defendant is not, as in ordinary suit, entitled as of right to defend the suit. He must apply for leave to defend within ten days from the date of the service of the summons upon him and such leave will be granted only if the affidavit filed by the defendant discloses such facts as will make it incumbent upon plaintiff to prove consideration or deposit a sum to be decided by the court may deem sufficient for granting leave to the defendant to appear and defend the suit.

Suit under the Penal Code

There are many transactions which result in civil as well as criminal liabilities. Cheating, misappropriation & theft are undoubtedly the transactions of this type.

While a civil proceeding is on with a customer, one can also file a criminal case against the same customer under Indian Penal Code as per Sec. 415/420 for dishonesty/concealment of facts and for this the punishment could be imprisonment extending to one year or with fine or with both.

WINDING UP PETITION (against limited companies)

If a firm cannot pay its debtors then it has no right to continue its trade but to wind up. Under section 433/439 of company's act, one can file suit in the High Court against any of its debtors. When all other attempts have failed, we found this step to be most effective.

Before proceeding one must make sure of having undertaken all the precautionary measures discussed in the first part of the chapter. Next send a demand notice giving 21 days time to settle else you will file winding up petition against it.

Specimen of Notice

NOTICE UNDER SECTION 434 OF THE COMPANIES ACT I OF 1956.

Dear Sir,

Under instructions from my Clients M/s. Eastern Steel Works having office at A-75, Road No.21, Thomas Indl. Estate, Kurla I have to address you as follows:

Pursuant to the negotiations and quotations given by you to my Clients vide your letter bearing Ref. No. 86/W/SS/001 dated May 13, 1998 my Clients placed with you their Purchase Order for the supply of 10 Nos. of Soft Start Units at the price and on the terms and conditions set out in my Clients' letter dated May 15, 1998 addressed to you. Alongwith the said Purchase Order, my Clients paid to you the sum of Rs. 99,000 by Cheque No.330002 drawn on Bank of Bangal, Kurla Branch, Kurla towards advance which amount has been duly encashed by you. Subsequently the said Purchase Order was canceled as the sample Soft Starter despatched by you was not found suitable and was therefore returned to you which was duly accepted by you and you agreed to refund the amount of Rs.99,000 to my Clients. By your letter No. O/86/W/P/003 dtd. Sept. 26, 1999 addressed to my Clients, you informed my Clients that you were making arrangements for the refund of the amount of Rs.99,000/- to my Clients.

You have till this day not refunded the said amount of Rs.99,000/- to my Clients despite repeated demands having been made upon you by my Clients. You are bound and liable to pay to my Clients the said amount of Rs. 99,000/- along with interest at the rate of 18 per cent per annum thereon from May 15, 1998 till the date of actual payment and my Clients are entitled to recover the same from you.

In the circumstances above stated, I am now instructed by my Clients or to me as their Advocate the sum of Rs. 99,000/- along with interest at the rate of 18 per cent per annum thereon from May 15, till the date of actual payment within 21 days from the date of receipt of this statutory notice by you failing which my Clients will be constrained to initiate recovery proceedings against you including proceedings for winding up or liquidation of your company which will be entirely at your risks as to the costs and consequences thereof.

Please treat this as a statutory notice under Section 434 of the Companies Act I of 1956.

Yours faithfully,

Rajiv Kamat

Copy to : Eastern Steel Works

If this attempt fails then one can go to court. The court hears the petition—and any opposition to it—and decides whether to issue a winding up order. Actually the first stage is for admission of petition and the second stage is to issue notice/s to the other party/parties and then the hearing takes place. Several creditors may join in the petition. If a winding up order is made, the Official Receiver takes up charge of all the assets as provisional liquidator. His initial duty is to assess the financial condition of the company including the causes of failure and make recommendations about further enquiries. Having prepared a statement to this effect, the Official Receiver then must call a first meeting of the creditors. This meeting decides whether to appoint an outside liquidator in place of Official Receiver and whether to appoint a Committee of Inspection. The liquidator's task is to realise the assets of the company and distribute them in accordance with the following order of precedence.

1. Secured creditors—excluding holders of floating charges
2. Liquidation costs
3. Preferential claims (principally rates, taxes, National Insurance & a limited amount of wages & salaries)
4. Holders of floating charges.
5. Unsecured creditors
6. Shareholders

It is important to note that compulsory winding up can be initiated in other cases also. Under Section 433/439 of the Companies Act 1948, a creditor who owed at least Rs 500/- can make statutory demand for payment—called serving 21 day notice—since if payment is not paid or disputed within three weeks a winding-up petition can be issued. This method thus bypasses the lengthy procedure of action through the court from the issue of a writ to the obtaining of a judgement. This is recommended in case of large companies who persistently neglect to pay suppliers. While their ability to pay is rarely in question, often only the threat of a winding up petition will extract money.

ENFORCEMENT PROCEDURES

There are a number of ways in which judgement may be enforced, depending on the circumstances. Before any execution costs are incurred, however, the creditor should try to find out whether there are any assets. Obtaining judgment is of no value if the debtor is insolvent.

1. *Seizure of goods by the bailiff or sheriffs' officer (High Court)*: This is usually more effective against companies or partnerships where items of value can be found in any office, e.g. typewriters, copying machine and furniture, as compared to a private house in which the wife of the debtor can claim to own all the furniture. In both situations there is the danger that goods are under a hire

purchase agreement. Nonetheless, the threat of seizure often brings results.

2. *Attachment of earnings*: This is generally unsuccessful, depending in the first instance on the court deciding how much protected earnings should be and, secondly, on the debtor's employer co-operating fully. Since debtors are not normally in stable employment, the problems of tracing them and enforcing fresh attachment orders are immense. This remedy is only available against individuals in employment.
3. *Garnishee order*: If the creditors can establish that a third party owes money to the debtor, application can be made for a garnishee order which requires the third party to pay the amount direct to the creditor. The most common method is to garnish a debtor's bank account.
4. *Charging orders*: A rarely used method, giving the creditor a charge on land, property or stocks and shares owned by the debtor.
5. *Bankruptcy*: The threat of bankruptcy can be very effective, providing the creditor is sure that sufficient assets are available and he is confident the debtor will prefer to pay rather than go out of business. However, if the business is near collapse, there is little advantage in giving the final push since all creditors will be treated equally by the Official Receiver.

It is more skillful to find ways of extracting payment without causing bankruptcy. The procedure in case of bankruptcy is as follows:

(a) A bankruptcy notice is issued by the court and served on the debtor personally.

(b) Unless paid or disputed within ten days, it becomes an act of bankruptcy

(c) The creditor (alone or jointly with others) presents a bankruptcy petition (must be within three months of the act of bankruptcy).

(d) The court hears the petition and if satisfied issues a receiving order.

(e) The affairs of the debtor then come under the control of the official receiver, whose function is to distribute any asset among all creditors in accordance with the following order of precedence.

1. Secured creditors
2. Bankruptcy costs
3. Preferential claim, principally rates, taxes, national insurance & a limited amount of wages & salaries.
4. Unsecured creditors
5. Deferred creditors
6. The bankrupt

Note: A detailed description of all the court procedures has been deliberately avoided in the book. Should refer to the relevant law and consult an attorney for legal action, if in case all other attempts have failed.

SUING AN OVERSEAS DEBTOR

Suing a customer in foreign country—very likely a country with a different legal system—can be tricky. While drafting a contract, take a precaution on which the business will be based. Ensure that dispute (if any) can be settled in a court of your choice, in your jurisdiction and a form of law which you prefer.

This can be ensured by this clause in the contract: Any dispute arising out of this contract will be governed by Indian law and referred to the High Court of Justice of India.

The existence of such a clause will enable you to issue a writ in an Indian Court and to seek leave to serve it in another jurisdiction.

This will ensure that the dispute will be dealt with in accordance with Indian Law. In addition, you will avoid the danger of loosing your case as a result of bribery of court officials, judges or witnesses—a widespread practice in some parts of the world.

Please note, the wording of the appropriate clause in your contract is a job for a lawyer (even if the resulting wording appears to be very simple), as the whole question of jurisdiction is a complex one.

Lastly, obtaining a judgement against a foreign individual or a corporation is by no means the end of the story. The greatest difficulty then is enforcing a judgement when you have it.

It is always advisable to get a export credit insurance from Export Credit Guarantee Corporation India Limited—a company wholly owned by the Government of India. It functions under the administrative control of the Ministry of Commerce and is managed by a Board of Directors representing Government, Banking, Insurance, Trade, Industry etc.

(Do not Forget to thank the Customer)

Dear Mr. Doe

Your account with us is now paid up-to-date. If, in the course of transactions, we have left some doubts in your mind as to the policy we have maintained, please be assured that our deepest concern has been to strengthen our business relationship.

The personal touch is too often overlooked in the handling of large volumes of correspondence: therefore, if we have not thanked you for your co-operation, let us do so now.

We will look forward to the opportunity of serving you once again.

Cordially,

L.E. Frailey—"Handbook of Business Letters"

FIFTEEN

The Perceptions and the Facts

MANAGEMENT INFORMATION SYSTEM AND CREDIT CONTROL

The MIS in credit control department should help in controlling day to day activities, taking corrective action in time, to forecast the future course of events, and of course measure the performance of the credit control department on a monthly basis. Do not create too many reports just to score points, only those reports which will help your company to achieve the above.

A few reports have been already discussed in the earlier chapters. In every company, few reports like customers' ledger, agewise analysis (on bill datewise or credit due datewise) are very common. Few companies find the information quite substantial to control their activities. However, with the emergence of so many 100 crores companies credit management is becoming more and more important. To add to this these companies would like to control their activities on a product divisional level, regional/branch or zonal level, thus making the reporting in credit control more and more complex.

MIS in credit control department should be able to highlight the following features:

- It should be on a monthly basis. Depending on the urgency and importance, it could be more frequent—daily or on a weekly.
- It should contain statistics which are very easy to understand.
- Highlight three basic measurements—debtor's level, cash and dues.

- Objectives achieved so far by comparing the same with the budget.
- Highlight trend, whether it is improving or deteriorating.
- Highlight problems , cases of dispute for which payments are held up.
- How strict is the company's credit policy.
- Serious bad debts, justifying the reasons.

We have come across many such reports being used by various companies to effectively control their daily, weekly, monthly and yearly functions. Some of them which we found useful are discussed in this chapter.

The daily information consists of the total amount collected on date and the cumulative figure upto that date of the month. They may be broken up into division's collection, zonal collection salesmen's collection etc.

Monthly Reporting

The monthly information will consist of a summarised result for the whole month just over. One such monthly report is Form 15.1:

Form 15.1

Sample Monthly Report

From : Credit Controller
Head Office

To : All Regional/Branch
Managers

October 9, 1999

Sub : Debtors'position as on September 30, 99 and collection target for the month of October 2003.

The amount collected by each region last month as against the target set for them is as follows:

	North	East	West	South	Total
Target	6800000	2800000	10000000	7000000	26600000
Collected**	3863487	1238482	9401855	4588582	19092406
	2936513	1561518	598145	2411418	7507594

** Collection includes advance amount

Excepting Western Region, other Heads of Regions are requested to explain us the reason for such a poor collection in spite of sizable debtors at their disposal. We expect their replies to reach us within a week's time.

Further, no progress can be seen in the debtors over six months which goes to prove that hardly any effort is being made eventoday to collect or wipe out over six months debtors. Of course I understand that considerable amount of debtors are held up for various reasons for which certain formalities are to be complied with by our production departments. Apart from this, no other debtors should be pending in over six months slot except for deduction towards liquidated damages and genuine disputes. We find whatever collections are being made are only from the current sales and that also the figure is very much below our expectation.

We must realise that with each month passing, the debtors over six months are becoming very difficult to collect and the company is losing revenue because of lack of determined efforts from regions. We sincerely hope that the concerned region will make all out efforts to wipe out old debtors.

At the end of September 30, 2003, the figures for sales are as follows:

	North	East	West	South	Total
Sales from Apr. to Aug. 03	21654403	8165986	27866091	17533902	75220382
Sept. 03	7664764	851423	11372836	5161730	25050753
Sales for 183 days	29319167	9017409	39238927	22695632	100271135
Average sales per day	160214	49275	214420	124020	547930

Sundry debtors as on September 30, 2003 are as under:

Region	Less than 6 months	In days	More than 6 months	In days	Total	In days	Advance
North	11509282	72	10781903	67	22291185	139	854461
East	1387067	28	1732068	35	3119135	63	221335
West	9975807	47	6294829	29	16270636	76	2213977
South	8407228	68	3920083	32	12327311	100	1720244
Total	31279384		22728883		54008267		5010017
Debtors in days :		58		41		99	

** Debtors' figure excludes sister concerns

Company target : 75 days or Rs 41094750 (i.e. the regions are requested to work within 75 days of their average sale per day).

It is evident that the debtors' position more or less remained stable. In the last month debtors in days was 97 and in this month it is 99. North & West have recovered considerable amount from over six months debtor. However, South and West figures show upwardly by 4 days and 2 days respectively which proves that we are still not able to prevent our debtors from becoming over six months.

I am sure you will agree with me that 6 months is a time enough to take care of all the complaints, disputes etc. and also to recover the amount.

Having allowed the debtors to grow, I sincerely request every region to collect and achieve their current month collection target on a war-footing. With sales being high in the month of September 03, it should not be difficult for any of you to achieve current month's target which is given below.

Region	Target for Oct'03 (In Lakhs)
North	120
East	20
West	100
South	80
	320

While setting target shortfalls upto last month has been considered.

Please organise your collection in a manner that you should achieve the target figure and any failure of which should be justified by addressing a letter to our Managing Director. With regard to very old debt, I once again request you to make your all out efforts to collect the same. If needed, you may fix up expense budget to collect the same.

Regards,

Two other reports that are drawn on a monthly basis to assist the cash flow management are age-analysis billdate-wise and due date-wise i.e. the amount already due and the amount that are going to be due during the current month—a target CM is expected to collect. These we have discussed in earlier chapter.

Form 15.2

Age Analysis

i. Bill datewise:

	Total	Region 1	Region 2	Region 3	Region 4
1 to 30 days					
31 to 60 days					
61 to 90 days					
91 to 180 days					
181 to 360 days					
Over 1 Year					
Total					

ii. Due datewise:

	This month	Last month	2 months prior	3 months prior	4 months prior	5 months prior
Not yet due						
1 Month overdue						
2 Month overdue						
3 Month overdue						
4 Month overdue						
Extended terms						
Total gross debtors						
Doubtful debt provision						
Total net debtors						
Contingent liability—any court case						

If the monthly report shows a trend (improving or deteriorating) the credit manager should explain why. The next report (Table 15.1) studies the debtors' movement (trend) at regional level, they are summary of branches under them. This report describes the movements of debtors for last six months. Each month is further broken up into below and over six month debt.

Table 15.1: Debtor's Movement—Summary

Month	Regions	Opening debtors balance	Add sales	Less colle--ction	Add/less adjust--ments	Closing debtors balance C/Fd	Breakup Below 6 months (In Lakhs)	Above 6months
Mar.92	North	21001570	12067935	4303240	-1423433	27342832	153.20	120.22
	East	5310416	3046343	1291206	-721936	6343617	43.29	20.14
	West	18234530	10549111	8667467	271674	20387848	150.61	53.26
	South	11967626	14256932	4472061	-296808	21455689	170.11	44.44
		56514142	39920321	18733974	-2170503	75529986	517.40	237.89
				In Days		140	96	44
Apl.92	North	27342832	1371013	6387641	-1397135	20929069	91.13	118.15
	East	6343617	1030149	2252047	133044	5254763	34.02	18.51
	West	20387848	2865563	8391573	-1169991	13691847	86.74	50.16
	South	21455689	3002449	9066625	1020079	16411592	128.24	35.87
		75529986	8269174	26097886	-1414003	56287271	340.15	222.72
				In Days		203	123	80
May 92	North	20929069	4212906	2683808	-665536	21792631	106.86	111.05
	East	5254763	932671	1614700	-128543	4444191	25.86	18.58
	West	13691847	4409969	6761374	2425306	13765748	88.29	49.36
	South	16411592	1720111	4677733	291803	13745773	102.95	34.50
		56287271	11275657	15737615	1923030	53748343	323.97	213.50
				In Days		167	101	66
Jun 92	North	21792631	7318614	6162858	549579	23497966	129.32	105.65
	East	4444191	2604866	921532	-1837227	4290298	21.07	21.83
	West	13765748	8351168	7148036	2102909	17071789	121.21	49.50
	South	13745773	6100573	4970101	-541123	14335122	109.73	33.61
		53748343	24375221	19202527	274138	59195175	381.34	210.60
				In Days		118	74	44
Jul 92	North	23497966	2885187	7964852	-651960	17766341	69.07	108.59
	East	4290298	2475407	1212488	-121851	5431336	35.21	19.09
	West	17071789	5729699	7464543	770025	16106970	108.36	52.70
	South	14335122	4189709	2981778	-127282	15415771	126.04	28.11
		59195175	15280002	19623661	-131068	54720418	338.69	208.50
				In Days		113	70	43
Aug.92	North	17766341	5866683	4814224	-25332	18793468	80.80	107.12
	East	5431336	1122893	2104347	-784137	3665745	19.25	17.39
	West	16106970	6509692	7766450	-954811	13895401	79.82	59.12
	South	15415771	2521060	6626510	167416	11477737	83.01	31.75
		54720418	16020328	21311531	-1596864	47832351	262.91	215.41
				In Days		97	53	44

Almost on the same line, the report (Table 14.1) mentions about the target set and target achieved by each region during last six month.

Table 15.2: Target Fixed & Target Achieved
June 99 to Nov 99

Month	REGION	Sale for the nonth In Rs	Opening debtors In Rs	Target fixed In Rs	Target A % over debtor	Target achieved In Rs	% over target	Collection as a % over debtors
Jun 99	N	7318614.00	23497966.00	10600000.00	45%	6162858.00	58.14%	26%
Jul 99	O	2885187.00	17766341.00	12500000.00	70%	7964852.00	63.72%	45%
Aug.99	R	5866683.00	18793468.00	8000000.00	43%	4814224.00	60.18%	26%
Sep.99	T	7664764.00	18793468.00	6800000.00	36%	3863487.00	56.82%	21%
Oct.99	H	6590721.00	22291185.00	8500000.00	38%	6457151.00	75.97%	29%
Nov.99		7144537.00	21934594.00	8000000.00	36%	7193110.00	89.91%	33%
		37470506.00	123077022.00	54400000.00	44.80%	36455682.00	67.01%	29.83%
Jun 99	E	2604866.00	4290298.00	2100000.00	49%	921532.00	43.88%	21%
Jul 99	A	2475407.00	5431336.00	3500000.00	64%	1212488.00	34.64%	22%
Aug.99	S	1122893.00	3665745.00	3000000.00	82%	2104347.00	70.14%	57%
Sep.99	T	851423.00	3665745.00	2800000.00	76%	1238482.00	44.23%	34%
Oct.99		492396.00	3119135.00	1500000.00	48%	518129.00	34.54%	17%
Nov.99		1600666.00	3160476.00	1500000.00	47%	1259788.00	83.99%	40%
		9147651.00	23332735.00	14400000.00	61.19%	7254766.00	50.38%	31.91%
Jun 99	W	8351168.00	17071789.00	6800000.00	40%	7148036.00	105.12%	42%
Jul 99	E	5729699.00	16106970.00	8000000.00	50%	7464543.00	93.31%	46%
Aug.99	S	6509692.00	13895401.00	8000000.00	58%	7766450.00	97.08%	56%
Sep.99	T	11372836.00	13895401.00	8000000.00	72%	9401855.00	94.02%	68%
Oct.99		4023310.00	16270636.00	7000000.00	43%	5892609.00	84.18%	36%
Nov.99		6853675.00	13907609.00	7000000.00	50%	5205302.00	74.36%	37%
		42840380.00	91147806.00	46800000.00	52.07%	42878795.00	91.62%	47.57%
Jun 99	S	6100573.00	14335122.00	6500000.00	45%	4970101.00	76.46%	35%
Jul 99	O	4189709.00	15415771.00	8000000.00	52%	2981778.00	37.27%	19%
Aug.99	U	2521060.00	11477737.00	8000000.00	70%	6626510.00	82.83%	58%
Sep.99	T	5161730.00	11477737.00	7000000.00	61%	4588582.00	65.55%	40%
Oct.99	H	3856093.00	12327311.00	6500000.00	53%	3810529.00	58.62%	31%
Nov.99		5303663.00	12445564.00	6500000.00	52%	5859117.00	90.14%	47%

Table 15.3 is an information on number of bills (in amount) pending in the respective months (for last six month). This statement helps in verifying whether current debtors are in control.

Table 15.3: Sale Made During Last Six Months & Bills Pending for Collection Region

		Nov.91	Dec.91	Jan.92	Feb.92	Mar.92	Apl.92	Total
North	Sale made	3183665	2164006	7835246	5823177	12067935	1371013	32445042
	Bills pending For collection As on 30/04/92	543003	780001	1000863	1000008	4505233	1284125	9113233

East	Sale made	821373	863523	1739770	1207977	3046343	1030149	8709135
	Bills pending For collection As on 30/04/92	323094	313159	139731	792964	942928	921095	3402971
West	Sale made	5581747	4012468	5879875	7493162	10549111	2865563	36381926
	Bills pending For collection As on 30/04/92	135538	279481	25733	1074725	4380553	2778840	8674870
South	Sale made	4595170	4242991	4790467	4171680	14256932	3002449	35059689
	Bills pending For collection As On30/04/92	84584	408872	768826	1635729	7304309	2621711	12824031
	Total sale	14181955	11282988	20245358	18695996	39920321	8269174	112595792
	Total bills Pending for collection	1086219	1781513	1935153	4473426	17133023	7605771	34015105
	% On sales	7.65%	15.78%	9.55%	23.92%	42.91%	91.97%	30.20%

Statements showing effect of interest on profit for failure to collect in time (i.e. within 75 days as per the policy of the company) is presented in Table 15.4

Table 15.4: Effect on Profit for Failure to Collect (on due date): An Example

	Third Quarter		Fourth Quarter	
	Dec.91	Ideal Month	Mar.92	Ideal Month
-Sales	119225695	119225695	198087370	198087370
-Debtors	50282875	32793179	75529986	40462493
-Credit days	115	75	140	75
-Net profit (Say 20%)	23845139	23845139	39617474	39617474
-Cost of credit (Bank int @ 24%)	9050918	5902772	18127197	9710998
- Final net profit	14794222	17942367	21490277	29906476
- Increase in profit (If our debtors could have been brought down to 75 days)		3148145		8416198

LOAN FROM BANK AGAINST ACCOUNTS RECEIVABLE

The receivables also help in raising finance. In the Table 15.5 the budget is based on the sales forecast and credit period being offered by the company. This statement is also helpful to forecast the cash flow and the information serves as the base when the company would like to avail temporary finance from bank.

A bank extends credit facility only on debtors below six months as the same are considered to be secured. However, in exceptional cases the bank may consider extending credit facilities on over six month debtors. If we are able to prove that they are good or atleast a part of it is good.

Loans against pledge of accounts receivable are made by commercial banks, usually between 70% to 90% value of the quality debtors. While doing so, the lending bank takes the following precautions:

Table 15.5: Budget (Receivable Investment)

	Jan	Feb	March	April	May	June
Receivables (Debtors)	75000	62500	71900	86350	100700	85250
Receivables (Annual maintenance)	0	0	0	0	0	0
Credit Sales	50000	60000	55000	65000	45000	45000
New AMC	0	0	0	0	0	0
Total Receivables	125000	122500	126900	151350	145700	130250
Collections (Sales)	62000	50000	40000	50000	60000	50000
Collections (AMC)	0	0	0	0	0	0
Gross Receivables	63000	72500	86900	101350	85700	80250
Less: Bad Debt (1%) of	500	600	550	650	450	450
Net Receivables	62500	71900	86350	100700	85250	79800
Average Age (days)	30	36	47	46	57	53

- They reserve the right to select the account that will be acceptable to them as security.
- Accounts typically are accepted with recourse, i.e. the borrower agrees to replace those accounts that are not paid in time with acceptable accounts or to reduce the amount of loan accordingly.
- The lender advances only certain percentage of the face value of the accounts pledged, say 75% to keep a good margin to cover his risk.
- Loan agreements provide that the borrower must submit in support adequate evidence about the validity of the accounts and has to authorise the lender to inspect the borrowers' book on demand.

Aid to Cash-flow

Projecting a cash-flow involves the usual conflict between detail and overload. You want to make sure the sales forecast, recast in the cash-flow, is accurate, but you don't want to get bogged down in too much fine tuning. One way to strike a balance is to keep track of the average age of receivables, except for start-ups, which require guess work to a large extent, this comes from the balance sheet and P. & L.

$$\frac{\text{Net sales average}}{\text{Trade receivables}} = \text{Number of receivables turns year}$$

$$\frac{365}{\text{Receivables turn}} = \text{Average age of receivables.}$$

Thus if sales were Rs 7,00,000, and receivables averaged Rs 40,000 there would be 17.5 turns, for an average of 21 days. In other words, non-cash sales turn to cash, on average 21 days later:

700/40 = 17.5 (turns)
365/17.5 = 21 (days)

Figuring timing on sales

1. Annual sales Rs ____________
2. Average receivables Rs ____________
3. Total credit sales (average receivables) 12 times = Rs ____________
4. Receivables turn(annual sales)/(average receivables) = ____________time
5. Average age of receivables 365/(Receivable turn) = ____________days
6. Percentage of credit sale/(Total credit sale/(annual sales) = ____________%
7. Percent of cash sales 100% minus (percentage of credit sales) = ____________%

As an example of how to use this form, here is how the figures we will use in the cash flow budgeting example are derived.

1.	Annual sales		Rs 700,000.00
2.	Average receivables		Rs 40,000.00
3.	Total credit sales (average receivables) times 12	=	Rs 480,000.00
4.	Receivables turn (annual sales)/(average receivables)	=	17.5 times
5.	Average age of receivables 365/(receivable turn)	=	21 days
6.	Percentage of credit sales(Total credit sales)/(Annual sales)	=	69%
7.	Percentage of cash sales 100% minus (Percentage of credit sales)	=	31%

Credit and collection patterns tend to be stable. Since you'll be tracking receivables anyway, you may find that you already have a good grasp of the age and importance of your receivables. Following the above example, one third of each months' forecasted sales will come in as cash in the month booked, the remainder in the following month. While the average age is 21 days, we would suggest a little slack.. Receivables have a nasty habit of growing old and want to be conservative. Say for example, March sales in the previous year were Rs 28,000, of which two-thirds turned to cash in April. The cash-flow statement is drawn after these points are considered. If sales timing is not figured properly then cash flow statement will be wrong.

STATEMENT ON HELD-UP/DISPUTED PAYMENTS

Lastly, the credit control department or the branch/regional/ zonal heads are expected to make a summary of all those payments held-up for various reasons. For eg. here is a statement summarised by an Electronic company.

Categorization of Accounts Receivables
Payment Held-up as on 31/01/99

Annex. No	Category	Pending Amount (In Lacs)
Annex.1	Order completion/Govt. procedures/pending	Rs. 15.24
Annex.2	For documentation/manual/approval	Rs. 23.87
Annex.3	Bill cancellation pending	Rs. 04.03

Annex.4	Delivery period extensions/eegularisations	Rs. 42.38
Annex.5	Pending for legal action	Rs. 00.54
Annex.6	Pending installation/commiss.	Rs. 00.24
Annex.7	L.D. clauses/demurrage/disc etc. to be adjusted	Rs. 06.86
Annex.8	Repairs/damages/replacement etc. Rs. 05.30	
Annex.9	Expire of bank guarantee	Rs. 01.22
Annex.10	Complaints to be attended by service dept./production dept.	Rs. 01.01
Annex.11	Bill supportings not proper	Rs. 00.59

** This statement should be drawn every month.

The credit manager should bring these to the notice of the respective departments for whom the payments are held-up. He must see that the actions are initiated immediately and the debtors are liquidated forthwith.

MEASURING PERFORMANCE OF CREDIT CONTROL DEPARTMENT

Most companies will find the following ratios useful:

1. Debtors expressed as number of days of sales (DSO) as against what is the DSO you have decided to work with or how much day sales you have decided to finance.
2. Debtors to be broken up into 'due' and 'overdue'. The overdue percentage of total debtors is increasing or decreasing. The overdue debtors should be collected and wiped out.
3. Aged analysis within total overdues. The older the dues the more difficult it is to collect them. May be, you may have to make provision to write-off older debts.
4. The total amount of disputed overdues and the number of customer accounts involved. May be the customer is right in disputing, and your total debts are projecting a misnomer picture.
5. Debtors as a percentage of sales. Does your company accept to finance so many debtor or does the total debt need to be brought down immediately.
6. Cash collected for a period as a percentage of total cash collectable for that period or cash collection targeted as against cash collected. If collection is not in line with your budget, the firm's growth is likely to be affected.

7. Bad debts and provisions for doubtful debts, as percentage of sales. To expand the business the company is likely to take more risk by allowing more credit. In the process the marketing department may be tempted to sell to those delinquent customers without referring it to credit investigation. In many companies, a provision is made in the budget that a certain percentage of the sale can be accepted as doubtful or bad-debt. If the actual amount of provision and bad-debt write-off is more than what is budgeted, a detailed investigation may be needed.

These ratios have been discussed in various parts of this book. Such ratios will give some depth to the measurement of debtors, and comparisons with budget, previous month and relevant items of last year indicate areas for improvement. Action plans and staff targets can be based on such formats.

CREDIT CONTROL DEPARTMENT AS A PROFIT CENTRE

In India there are two schools of thought, one that the credit control department is essentially a collection department especially old and difficult one because to collect from current debtors is salesmen's responsibility. The credit manager need not do any credit investigation or decide on credit or payment terms – it is left to the sales manager and his boys.

In the second school of thought, attended by very few, they believe that credit is a start of a relationship with the prospect and thus a credit control department may be made responsible for credit investigation, setting each customer's credit limits and deciding on their payment terms. This will make credit department responsible for almost all the companys' cash flow. If this is the case, then a profit center concept can be worked out.

Credit managers with this profit centre mentality are more likely to engage in a conscious effort to recover bad-debt write-offs. They might also set budgets for travel and boarding expenses by forecasting out-of-state trips. It is in a position to formalize game plan, get it approved by top management, and put it to action. The result will be a credit department functioning as a profit center that can quantify its contributions to the firms' net profitability.

The credit department adds to cash flow through reductions in accounts receivable. It negatively impacts or detracts from cash flow when it allows days sales outstanding to rise or when bad-debt write-offs occur. Each of these credit yardsticks, as well as others, can be quantified into revenues and costs generating a credit department profit and loss statement.

Income or Revenue Sources

- Monthly, Days Sales Outstanding (DSO) reductions below budget quantified at cost of funds.
- Interest income from assessing finance charges for late payments.
- Incremental profitability from selling to high-risk customers.
- Bad-debt recoveries.
- 'Credit saves' refers to a successful attempt at reducing or zeroing out a high-risk customer's balance prior to the customer's bankruptcy. At-risk cash flow that is collected as opposed to being lost as a bad debt.

Credit Costs

- Credit department salaries.
- Hardware and software expense.
- Bad-debt write-offs.
- Monthly DSO increases above budget.
- Subscription and other expenses
- Travel and boarding expenses incurred in visiting customers and attending seminars.

An example of ABC and company Limited, credit departments' P and L analysis as on 31.03.99

Revenue Sources

Monthly DSO reduction quantified	Rs. 364200.00
Interest income	31500.00
Incremental profitability	2553327.00
Bad-debt recoveries	12354.00
Credit saves	238299.00
Total Revenue Sources	31,99,680.00

Less :
Credit Costs

Credit departments salaries	Rs. 379500.00
Hardware and software costs	66000.00
Bad-debt write-offs	49809.00
Monthly DSO increases quantified	69330.00
Subscription and other expenses	10500.00
Travel and boarding expenses	29151.00
Total credit costs	6,04,290.00
Credit department net profitability	25,95,390.00
Credit revenue/Cost coverage ratio	5.30

Cost of Slow Payments, Extended Terms & Incremental Contribution

Part 1

Customer	YTD sales	% slow payments	# of days slow	Cost of slow payments	# of days extended terms	Cost of extended terms	Funds cost	Variable cost %	Variable costs	Incremental contribution
ABC	1,00,000	55%	14	Rs 181.81	15	Rs 354.17	8.5%	45%	Rs 45,000	Rs 54465
XYZ	50,000	0%	0	Rs 0.00	0	Rs 0.00	8.5%	45%	Rs 22500	Rs 27500

If you work on the basis of above formulas the answers will be:
1. Cost of slow payments : (((1,00,000*55%) * 8.5%) / 360) * 14 = Rs 181.81
2. Cost of extended terms : ((1,00,000 * 8.5%) / 360) * 15 = Rs. 354.17
3. Incremental Contribution : 1,00,000 – ((1,00,000 * 45%) + 181.81 + 354.17) = Rs 54,464.02

Part 2

Step 1 – Cost of slow payments

Variables

A = Year-to-date Sales
B = Percentage of Slow Sales
C = Cost of Funds
D = Number of days slow
E = Cost of slow payments

Formula

$$[\{(A*B)*C\} / 360]*D = E$$

Step 2 – Cost of extended terms

Variables

F = Year-to-date sales
G = Costs of funds
H = Number of days extended terms
I = Cost of extended terms

Formula

[(F*G) / 360] * H = I

Step 3 – Incremental contribution

Variables

J = Year-to-date sales
K = Variable cost per cent on sales
L = Cost of slow payments
M = Cost of extended terms
N = Incremental contribution

Formula

J – [(J*K) + L + M] = N -

Source: Facts, figures and format provided by a credit manager during flight from Los Angeles to Dallas.

The credit manager in India is likely to be more successful and achieve greater recognition, if he can devise formal credit and cash flow strategies for operating.

Accounts Receivable Statistics for Comparison with Industry Standard

Most credit managers develop accounts receivable statistics in order to judge the condition of their firms' accounts as of certain dates. They evaluate the condition of accounts against historical trends for the company, industry and economy.

The following statistics are helpful in describing the condition of outstanding accounts in reports:

1. Days Sales Outstanding

This measure indicates, as of a specific date, the accounts receivable balance in terms of the number of days sales. If, for example, normal credit terms are 30 days and there are 40 days sales outstanding, the company has not been collecting the outstanding balances within the 30 day credit period. The formula for the calculation is as follows:

$$\text{Days sales outstanding} = \frac{\text{Trade accounts receivable balance}}{\text{Average daily credit sales}}$$

The average daily credit sales should be for the period in which the accounts receivable balance arose.

2. Accounts Receivable Turnover

This statistic measures the frequency with which the accounts receivable are collected. Since the calculation reflects a period of a time, an average accounts receivable figure is used. The formula for the calculation is as follows:

$$\text{Turnover} = \frac{\text{Total credit sales}}{\text{Average accounts receivable}}$$

If, for example, total credit sales are Rs. 4 million, and the average accounts receivable is Rs 1 million, then the turnover of receivables is 4. As the turnover rate increases, the probability of collection decreases.

3. Average Collection Period

Average collection period represents the average time period required to collect the balance on credit sales. The formula for the calculation is as follows:

$$\text{Average collection period} = \frac{\text{Average trade receivable} \times 365 \text{ days}}{\text{Credit sales}}$$

If, for example, the rate of average trade receivables to total credit sales is 10%, then the average collection period is 36.5 days.

SIXTEEN

The Long Arm of the Law: Audits

ACCOUNTS RECEIVABLES AND STATUTORY REQUIREMENTS

On first consideration it may seem strange to bring the subject of auditing within the purview of the credit control. However, since a credit manager's operation and records will be periodically reviewed, sometimes continuously by the internal and external (or statutory) auditors, he should be aware of the audit objectives and the various technique applied to verify the same.

It may not be correct to say that the internal and external audits are identical in purpose and only differ in personnel. Originally, the work carried out by the two kinds of auditors was much the same. However, the statutory audit is made on behalf of the shareholders and its reports are addressed to them. The external auditor is not bound to comment on whether the business is being run efficiently, while this consideration is becoming more and more important to the internal auditor, because his services are supposed to contribute to the overall efficiency of the business.

This chapter also books into all those statutory requirements a credit manager needs to be familiar with. On a day-to-day basis he has to face the internal auditor, the external (statutory) auditor and it is imperative that he understands the formalities needed to be complied with regard to Companies Act and Income Tax Act.

Although there is very little difference between programs set by them, we have listed them separately. A detailed audit programme is intentionally avoided.

INTERNAL AUDIT

The main goal of an internal audit is to enable the credit department to maximize its corporate role of protecting the company's investment in accounts receivable while generating the required levels of cash flow on a consistent basis.

The management should audit the credit department on an annual basis.

On a broad level, the audit should cover:

- Policy and philosophy of the company and credit department
- Procedures
- Controls
- Annual credit review process both for new and existing customers.
- New customer credit investigations
- Collections
- Credit reporting and scope of forecasting
- Collection agency activity
- Credit department performance measurement
- The credit department budget

The objective of the audit is to review all areas of the credit function to ensure that the department is operating as effectively as possible.

Once the audit has performed, management along with credit department can create an action plan to eliminate problem areas.

Internal Audit for Sales and Trade Receivables

Internal Auditing Techniques generally used corresponding to Auditing Objectives of Account Receivables and Sales can be summarised as below:

Objectives	Method
(a) Verification of receivable balances.	Written confirmations, vouching and comparison. (specimen letter printed later)
(b) Determining net realisable value on the balance sheet date.	Scanning, written confirmations, oral inquiry, and vouching.
(c) Classification of receivables on the balance sheet.	Written confirmation, comparison, oral inquiry and scanning.
(d) Determining any pledged or discounted portions. verification.	Written confirmation, vouching, scanning, oral inquiry and
(e) Determining existence of ownership and value. inquiry and scanning.	Written confirmation, vouching, physical inspection, oral
(f) Reasonableness of sales total.	Comparison.
(g) Internal control procedures evaluation of effectiveness.	Receivables—oral inquiry; Sales - vouching, verification, oral inquiry, comparison, accounts analyses, and scanning.

The Internal Auditor analyses the debtors by breaking up each customer's account in the following manner:

Analysis of total debtors' accounts

1. Customer's name
2. Opening balance
3. Credit sales
4. Expenses (Freight etc.)
5. Bills dishonoured.
6. Cash or bank payment.
7. Cash or bank received.
8. Discount allowed
9. Bills received.
10. Sales returns
11. Allowances
12. Bad debts
13. Closing balance

Further, an Internal Auditor is also expected to appraise the management on operating improvements (if needed) with regard to sales accounting system of the company. The activities generally evaluated are:

(a) Delays in receipt of despatch advices (challan)
(b) Invoicing time
(c) Banking arrangement

(d) Transfer of funds to head office
(e) Dishonour of cheques
(f) Suspension of despatches
(g) Credit control vis-a-vis outstandings
(h) Packed stocks reconciliation
(i) Claim on carriers/insurance
(j) Recovery of sales tax concessional forms, bank guarantee and earnest money or security deposit

EXTERNAL (STATUTORY) AUDIT

Audit Objectives for Sales and Trade Measurables

The audit objectives are to establish that all the sales during the period under audit have been accounted for and that the amounts appearing in the books and accounts as result of these sales transactions can be relied upon, including the balances in the account of customers.

Audit Steps (interim visit)	Applied Yes	Applied No	Comments
1. Analyse company's accounting procedures for sales invoicing and trade receivables.			
2. Review sales accounts and schedule monthly sales and explain fluctuations.			
3. Select deliveries to customers (despatch notes) for checking with:			
(a) Sales order for correct quantities, prices terms and conditions.			
(b) Approved price list or approved discount schedule for unit prices and discount.			
(c) Invoice for all details. Trace invoice to customer ledger and note invoicing delay.			
(d) Check calculations, extensions on invoices.			
(e) Trace collection for invoice and check supporting voucher.			

Additional blocktest should be applied if any weaknesses are revealed.

4. Trace sales invoices through sales register/ledger to sales accounts in general ledger (credit for sales, debit for trade receivables).
5. Check for selected products the discharge from inventory records by adding up items sold in a week as per daily delivery notes/ sales invoices.
6. Check number sequence of delivery notes/sales invoices.
7. Select credit notes and check with
   (a) Price list and invoice for price corrections
   (b) Receiving slip, inventory records and invoice for goods returned
   (c) Approval
   d) Trace with customer ledger and sales ledger
8. Agree listing of customer accounts to general ledger at interim sample date.
9. Audit Steps (Final Visit):
   Obtain direct confirmation of selected trade receivables. (specimen letter provided later)
10. Review listings of debtors for balance to be classified as creditors or inter-company balances.
11. Agree listing of customer accounts to general ledger at year end.
12. Analyse listing of customer accounts, list old items, review major balances, inquire into provision for balances considered doubtful of recovery and check additions.
13. Proper authorisation for discounts allowed, any charges waived or concessions offered.
14. Review credit notes issued after year end and inquire into credits outstanding and list all items relating to old year. Establish the status of returned goods.
15. Review listing of bad debts to be written off and conclude on the adequacy of the

provision. Write-off must be authorised by Board of Directors or appropriate delegated authority (by applying any of the test mentioned below)

1. Whether the amount is regularly settled & the advantage of each discount taken by the debtor. In such a case, the debt is good.
2. Whether the debt is outstanding beyond the period of credit allowed. If so, it may mean that the debt is doubtful.
3. Whether the payments are on account & the balance tends to increase. If it is so, it means that the party is financially weak.
4. Whether an old balance is being carried forward & the new goods are supplied for cash. If so, it may mean that the debt is doubtful.
   It is also possible that the old balance may be due to a dispute. The possibility of the old balance having been paid and the cash misappropiated should be considered in such cases.
5. Whether cheques or bills received against a debit balance have often been dishonoured. If it has been the case it shows the party is not financially sound and that the debt may be doubtful or may prove bad some day.
6. Whether any note regarding non-payment, like "account stopped", in liquidators hands', 'in bankruptsy', 'in liquidation', or 'disappeared & address unknown', etc. is made on the ledger account. If so, he should thoroughly scrutinise the case to find out whether the debt is doubtful or bad.
7. The law of limitation allows three years to recover a debt, and if the debt is outstanding for a longer period, it means the debt is bad.
8. If the payments are irregular, the debt may be good and may prove to be bad some day.

16. Conclude on the overall audit satisfaction for sales and trade receivables.

Specimen letter for obtaining confirmation from client.

To Date : April 18, 2000
K.V.T. & A. Limited,
KVT House,
Mumbai-Agra Road,
Mumbai - 400 002

Dear Sir,

Sub: Confirmation of balance

In connection with the audit of our accounts by M/s. S.L. Dota & Co., Chartered Accountants, 29, 4th Floor, Lalbagh, Mumbai-003 we like to state that your account with us shows Debit/Credit balance of Rs.____________ as on 31-03-2000.

If the amount shown is in agreement with your books, please sign in the place provided below and return this letter directly to our Auditors with a copy to us. Your immediate compliance to this request will be highly appreciated.

In case, no reply is received within 15 days from the date of issue of this letter, it will be assumed that the balance shown in this letter is correct.

Thanking you,
Yours faithfully,
for ACBC & Co. Limited

(T.D.S. Desai)
General Manager – Finance
CC : Our Auditor
We confirm that the above stated amount is correct as on 31-03-00.

Signature of the Party

Auditor's Name & Address

Note: The form is being sent in triplicate. One copy duly signed to be sent to the auditors and the other to this office and one copy to be retained by you.

The list should be prepared in a columnar form to find out 'good', 'doubtful' and 'bad' debts. The experience of previous years should also be taken into consideration to find out whether adequate reserves have been created.

INCOME TAX & ACCOUNTS RECEIVABLES (DEBTORS)

As per the Income Tax Act the loss on account of bad debt can be claimed as deductible expenses in the year the amount is written off & not in the year the amount is provided for.

Valuation:

- Accounts receivables should be valued at their face values less an allowance for bad and doubtful debt as appropriate.
- While valuing debtors account, confirmation of all debtors should be obtained as far as possible.
- Each & every account should be examined with regard to discount allowed, sales returns, material rejected by customer etc to ascertain correct value of accounts receivable.

WRITING OFF BAD DEBTS

The credit manager will be required to give an account of his bad debts, and a journal for this purpose should be kept with indication as to the reasons for writing off. Once more, different methods may be agreed with the firm's accountants for so doing, but finally a figure will be arrived at on completion of the financial year, when all debts so written off, and retained in a bad ledger for that purpose, can be transferred to the private journal. Normally the bad debts will be given as a percentage of turnover, and this will vary with the type of business done and provision made when assessing mark up.

Provision for Bad and Doubtful Debts

A further requirement will be a bad-debt reserve provision. If the subsidiary card index file is kept, it will be simple to abstract and list balances at the stage at which they may be labelled doubtful.

The credit manager should scan this list and using his experience of the accounts involved should make an appraisal of those for which bad-debt provision should be made.

Accounts receivables (debtors) are often considered to include some accounts which are not likely to be realised in full or in part. Accordingly, at the time of preparing the final accounts, to ascertain fair profits for an accounting year, it is necessary that adequate provision is made for such accounts, as may be difficult to realise in full.

1. The provision is made after a careful classification and analysis of outstanding accounts receivables as to their realisability.
2. Sometimes, provision is made as percentage to total credit sales or to total amount of accounts receivables outstanding as on the date of preparing profit and loss account and balance sheet.
3. As and when any specific debtors accounts are determined to be worth less and collection attempts abandoned, they are written off.
4. The amount of provision for bad and doubtful debts is charged against profit in profit and loss account while it should appear under the current liabilities and provisions, on liabilities side of the balance sheet. However, in company balance sheet such provision is deducted from the assets side, from sundry debtors. The amount of 'Provision" charged to profits is calculated as follows:

   'Provision' = Total provision required – (Existing provision in the opening balance sheet – bad debts written off).
5. In order to maintain effective control, every write-off of the balance of a customer's account should have managerial approval.
6. However, sometimes, bad debts are recorded only in respect of accounts specifically indentified or appraised as not realisable and no advance provision is made for anticipation of accounts proving worthless.
7. In the balance sheet 'sundry debtors' appears under 'current assets' as per requirement of Schedule VI of Companies Act.

In Schedule (forming part of balance sheet)

Considered goods:	
Sundry debtors:	
Over six months	Unsecured
Other debts	Secured
considered doubtful:	
Over six months	Unsecured
Others	Secured
Less: Provision for doubtful debts	

Collection of Accounts Receivables Previously Written Off

Sometimes a customer's account previously written off is subsequently realised. In such a case the realisation is treated as income for that year.

Points to Note

1. Debts due by directors or other officers of the company or private companies or firms respectively in which any director is a director or a member or a partner should be stated separately.
2. Debts due by other companies under the same management shall be disclosed with the name of the companies.
3. The maximum amount due by the directors or other officers of the company at any time during the year should be shown by way of note.
4. Provision for doubtful debts, shown as deduction, shall not exceed the amount of debts considered doubtful and any surplus of such provision, already created, should be shown under 'Reserves and surplus' under a separate sub-head 'Reserve for doubtful or bad debts."
5. The amounts to be shown under sundry debtor shall include the amounts due in respect of goods sold or services rendered or in respect of other contractual obligations but shall not include the amounts which are in the nature of loans and advances.

SEVENTEEN

Service Industry: . . .Selling the Invisible

Concern Selling: Making the product behind the idea
Concept Selling: Selling the idea behind the product

SERVICE MARKETING

"Identifying and satisfying the needs and wants of consumers by providing a market offering to fulfill those needs and wants through exchange processes, profitably."

Services are provided to certain quality standards, they are frequently offered with guarantees and many service organizations have developed high-levels of brand name awareness (hertz, McDonald, Holiday Inns for example).

Special Characteristics of Services

Intangibility: **Pure services cannot be seen or touched**. They are ephemeral performances that can be experienced only as they are delivered.
Inseparability: The success of the goods manufacturers is vitally dependent on the oil services they provide. The goods which a manufacturer often produced in a location far away from the customer, however, service production often requires the presence of the customer—and of the other customers.
Variability/Hecterogeneity: **Services can vary greatly**. Different frontline personnel have different abilities. Services are performances and often involving the cooperation and skill of the several individual, and are unlikely to be same every time.

The habits of sharpening the saw regularly means having a balanced systematic programme for self-renewal in the four areas of our lives; physical, mental, emotional, social, and spiritual. Without this discipline, the body becomes weak, the mind mechanical, the emotions raw and the spirit insensitive and the person selfish.

—Stephen R. Covey
"The 7 Habits of Highly Effective People"

Collecting money is everybody's business.

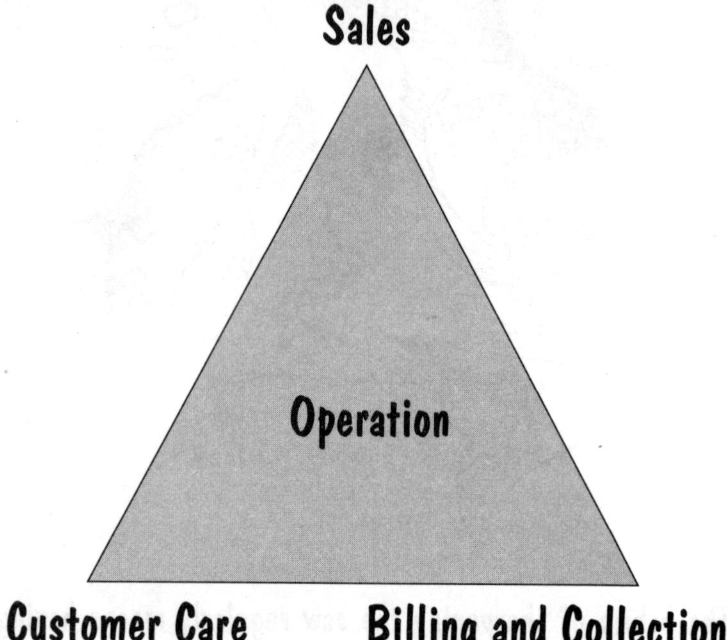

If these departments don't coordinate with each other, you will have too many bad accounts, many defaulters and large overdue.

Even the same person will give less or more focused services different times.

Perishability: Services cannot be maintained as inventory, since they are performed at real time.

Change in service is permanent: Even if you're on the right track, you'll get run over if you just sit there. —*Will Rogers*

Other Features:

- Sensitivity to time
- Difficult to measuring and controlling quality
- Difficult to experiment
- Unlike product, a buyer never sees what he is going to actually receive.
- You cannot return a service. The whole business is on trust. Service selling is people-sensitive. Therefore in service marketing—people are marketed.
- Customization of offering
- Personalization of Buyer-Provider relationship

Services: Both Productivity and Quality are of Key Importance

Service quality is measured on:

1. *Technical quality:* The overall efficiency with which a business/bank handles its customer accounts in terms of prompt statements, rates of interest offered and so on.
2. *Functional quality:* The way the service is actually delivered; this includes personal courtesy, the service environment in terms of comfort and decor and the customer's own role. (In case of long queues, if guidance is provided to make filling of form simpler?)
3. *Ease to use*
4. *Scope for cost reduction*

Clients or Consumers Evaluate Service in Two Ways

1. Experience
2. Credence—qualification and credentials

What is Credit in a Service Industry?

You part with service and wait for your payment. Incase of non-payment you will not be able to recover your service back.

However, if there is collaterals, or title on the goods you may be able to salvage some damage.

Unique Features—Customer Base
Mass Production and Mass Distribution
The Number of New and Repeat-Customers

Difference in Credit Policy
For Manufacturing Industries

- Liberal Credit—Strict Collection or
- Strict Credit—Liberal Collection or Payment Terms

For Service Industries

- Strict Credit—Strict Collection

CONSUMER AND COMMERCIAL CREDIT

Some methods of relieving the financial problems in the various stages of production and distribution are essential to the effectiveness of a mass distribution economy. If businesses depended exclusively on bank loans and their own capital, they would not be able to marshal the financial capacity they do with commercial credit.

The widespread use of commercial credit and much of its importance as a form of business finance stemmed from the nation's economic developments. As the nation grew, so did distances between the manufacturers and their customers. With the development of transportation and communication systems, population and businesses spread over vast geographic areas. Parallel to these developments, mass production and mass distribution methods assumed their place in the economy. Retailers also increased in number, and large-scale production became necessary to meet the wants of the growing population. As a result, trade was transacted on a more impersonal basis and over greater distances. Speed of commercial transactions became essential as competitive forces intensified. To achieve effective production and distribution systems in this changed economy, businesses needed some method of financing goods as they moved through production and marketing phases.

This phase of credit is defined as the medium of exchange that an individual consumer or a corporate is offered by a seller of goods or services or by a lender of money in order to obtain these goods / items and repay at some future time. The extent to which consumers use credit, varies. While some individuals buy only a bare minimum on credit, others start using credit early and remain in a state of indebtedness through out their life. Credit allowed to individuals or end users are commonly known as Consumer credit, whereas credit allowed to business houses or any other organisation is called Business credit. Both are to be handled differently.

THE VARIOUS FORMS OF CONSUMER CREDIT

- Retail or revolving credit—Common in the credit card business.
- Instalment credit or hire-purchase—Purchase of television, fridge, electronics music system, washing machine, etc.
- Open charge credit—Mostly allowed by shop or departmental stores to buy during the month and pay in full in the first week of the subsequent month or within 30 days.
- Service credit—Mostly allowed by consultants, lawyers, doctors, electricity, telephone & cellular, paging, radio trunking, and courier service companies .
- Real estate or housing finance to individual, to corporate and construction companies, etc.

Consumer credit principles successfully serving both vendors and customers are based on type of goods or services, initial down-payment, the total balance amount and schedules of payments, instalments terms (generally the unpaid amount should not be more than the resale value of the goods), collateral, finance or interest charges. Also repossession procedure (in case of default or dishonouring of cheque/s) and rebate for pre-payment are also decided.

For example:

(a)	Total price	565.00
(b)	Less: Down payment	56.50
	Balance to finance	508.50
(c)	Plus: Interest charges	61.02
	Total loan / obligation	Rs 569.52

In God we trust

Everybody else . . . on CASH BASIS!

Interest charges are calculated for the period of loan requested by the customer. Thereafter, the period and the number of instalments are decided. After a proper understanding, the agreement is drawn out.

A FEW DEFINITIONS

The Consumer

The consumer is the final *consumer* of goods or services. The term *consumer* is interpreted by most to mean the final consumer, who is not necessarily the customer. Take the example of mother or father who is buying breakfast cereals. The chances are that they are intermediate customers, acting as an agent on behalf of the eventual consumers (their family) and, in order to market cereals effectively, it is clearly necessary to understand what the end-consumer wants, as well as what the parents want.

It is always necessary to be aware of the needs of eventual consumers down the buying chain. Another example will be the purchasing officer buying on behalf of his organisation, the eventual consumers can be production head, the R&D head etc.

The Product

The product plays an important role in marketing management. A bad product is unlikely to be compensated for by good management. A product (or service) is the total experience of the customer or consumer when dealing with an organisation.

COMMERCIAL CREDIT

As the raw materials are processed or converted into semi-processed goods, they are sold to manufacturers of finished goods who may offer credit in exchange. This is known as commercial credit because the manufacturers are acquiring goods for further fabrication or for the operation of their businesses. (Other forms of credit, in whole or in part, help the manufacturers pay workers, meet overheads, and cover other manufacturing costs.) As the goods are manufactured into finished product, they are sold to wholesalers or industrial houses. This transfer is again accomplished by commercial credit – wholesalers offer their credit to the manufacturers in exchange for the goods. Finally, retailers offer their credit to obtain an inventory of finished goods. Commercial credit transactions take place each time goods change ownership until they are purchased by the final consumer.

Commercial credit, then, is used by all kinds of business enterprises to finance the acquisition of goods or services. The transactions may be very informal: one business orders goods or services and another delivers. Evidence of the transaction is an account receivable in the sellers' accounting record. The buyers' evidence of the transaction is an account payable in its accounting records. Few businesses are free from frequent credits and debits to these assets and liability accounts. Furthermore, although there is no precise data to support the point, the vast majority of all goods and services flowing through the production and marketing processes are financed this way.

At times (in a credit crunch period) some of the largest and best rated companies slow down payments to smaller and weaker creditors, thus forcing the smaller companies to carry them. This is a very common practice in India. In fact to take away credit from smaller companies is considered as prudent cash-flow management.

CUSTOMER CREDIT

What Credit Does for Consumers

Individual consumers basically use credit for mainly three reasons:

1. *To raise standard of living*. Most homes and costly items are purchased through credit and paid for over a long period. A number of commodities with high unit value are now common in today's life styles.
2. *Convenience* is a vital reason why consumer credit has become so generally accepted.
3. *Pressure of necessity*. Necessity is a third reason why many consumers use credit. Some circumstances—marriage, birth, death, sickness, and similar events—demand a large immediate outlay. Not having sufficient reserves for the occasion, individuals secure a loan or use their credit for goods or services.

What Credit Does for Retailers and Service Business

1. It enables them to sell more goods or services by allowing customers to purchase on credit.
2. It permits them to purchase goods on credit.
3. Cash loans from commercial banks or other financial institutions enable them to meet the expenses and expand their operations.

What Credit Does for Financial Institutions

They all fill the vital need of providing cash to consumers and businesses. This may involve long or short term borrowing or something in between. It may involve buying accounts receivable and notes payable, thus providing needed capital to various types of businesses. Financial institutions are credit institutions. They accept their customers' credit so customers can use the cash received to buy goods and services and to carry on their own personal and business transactions. Interest income from credit transactions is the leading source of revenue to financial institutions.

Competition in Consumer Credit

Today, competitors' policies influence other vendors' decision. Credit is one of the most important services retailers provide their customers. Retailers without credit services are in weakened competitive position. For example, durable goods are commonly purchased on credit. Indian consumers expect this arrangement, and the chances are that they will buy high-unit-valued items from those firms that can satisfy this requirement.

Credit Policy

A company should take a policy decision on the credit period and payment terms that it is going to allow. This decision should evolve from the factors like:

(a) What the competitors are offering.
(b) Financial resources or power of the seller.
(c) The volume of orders expected. Its effect on sales and profits.

(d) Rate of stock turnover.
(e) The nature of product being sold or character of the goods.
(f) The class of customer and the nature of credit risk.
(g) Government policies in acquiring the raw material.
(h) Location of the customer and transportation facilities.
(i) Expected returns on investment.

The credit period and the terms of payment together should be able to generate the required cash flow, the volume of sales, the projected profitability and yet keep the risk of each transaction at minimum.

Policy should be also very clear on treatment to old debt and write-offs. Close checks should be maintained on the bad and doubtful debts and an index maintained showing the performance of the debtors in terms of debts with relation to average daily sales. A safe measure is assessing whether the potential customer is financially sound and will pay in time. Thus a company must conduct a risk analysis and categorize its customer and set credit limits appropriately.

Activities of Consumer Credit Department

The controller or person responsible for marketing, in cooperation with the credit manager, often has the responsibility for coordinating the objectives of credit operations with the overall objectives of the firm. If a firm wants to adopt a more lenient credit policy in an effort to stimulate sales, the controller, in cooperation with the credit manager, has to translate this policy change into a new program of decision making in the credit department. Of course, the actual operating head of the credit section is the credit manager.

The activities may be divided into:

(a) *Promoting*: Credit promotion for finance company is a need and it is usually assigned to one or more people.
(b) *Interviewing*: Interviewing personnel, gather data about credit applicants and help determine whether to accept the credit.
(c) *Authorising*: The authorisation people have responsibility for certain phases of identification and authorisation.

(d) *Collecting*: Those involved in collection keep slow accounts on a paying basis or stop granting credit to bad risks.

Basic Functions of the Consumer Credit Manager

Regardless of the type of business and the type of organization under which the consumer credit department operates, consumer credit managers must perform certain basic functions to accomplish its duties. These usually include the following:

1. To assess the credit standing of both existing and new customers.
2. To select the appropriate payment terms which will determine:
   - Maximising of sales and profits.
   - Minimising of bad-debt losses.
   - Utilising of invested funds efficiently.
3. Cooperating with other internal departments.
4. To control the debtors' ledger.
5. To collect from debtors at an agreed time, ensuring that trade will continue with these customers.
6. Dealing through investigation agencies and with external collection agencies.
7. Emphasizing public relations and the retention of customer goodwill.
8. To monitor and collect bank guarantees / earnest money deposit or security deposit with various government departments.
9. To raise and follow-up for settlement of marine insurance claims.

Basic Responsibilities of Collection Managers

Collection managers, working at times under the direction of the credit managers, have the following responsibilities:

1. To aid the working capital position of the firm by securing collection of receivables as quickly as possible and at minimum cost.
2. To reduce bad-debt losses. This involves deciding when an account should be considered a loss. It generally is

recommended that any amount that six month past the credit period should be considered bad and may have to be written-off.

This does not mean that collection efforts should stop at this time – accounts written-off as bad-debt can still be recovered.

3. To aid the sales effort. An individual free of overdue debt is much more likely to make purchases at the firm than a customer with a guilty conscience over an overdue bill. Such customers make future purchases at the competing firms.
4. To ease pressure between customer and firm by straightening out any misunderstanding that stands in the way of the payment. In fact, here the collection manager doubles as a public relations person.
5. To help make policy decisions concerning credit and collections. For example, what policy should be established concerning slow accounts, paid-up slow accounts seeking new credit?
6. To select collection agencies or liasion with legal firms' to collect money from slow or no paying accounts.

Along with these are also included those duties elaborated in the basic functions of the consumer credit manager.

The Staff

They need to tune into the firms' strategy for recovery management. The staff need to be trained to keep organisation goals and feel their key result area is achieving target (timely and accurately) is very important for the profit of the organisation.

If the credit authority is different from collection staff, they should be in close contact. Paying habit and need for a change of credit amount is needed or not can only be decided if they exchange hotline communications.

The customer service should also play a crucial role in taking care of the customer and whether he has any complaint. The attitude should be of facilitator of credit and not favour towards customers. They should be also able to differentiate whether a customer's complaint is genuine or it's an excuse to postpone payment. Whether a customer needs any help in payment, and can they work out a mutually accepted arrangement.

Terms of Sale

In each such credit transaction, the seller and buyer must understand the conditions for payment, generally known as the terms of sale, credit terms, or payment terms. It is sound business practice to quote terms of sale on all invoices covering the shipment and all instruments associated with the sale contract. If specific terms of sale are not quoted, the buyer can legally presume that any terms customary in that line of trade are applicable. The buyers' obligation to meet the terms of sale arises when the seller delivers the goods or services or meets other specified conditions of sale. The terms of sale applicable in consumer credit transactions are peculiar to this type of credit.

Selection of the appropriate payment term is also a vital step in establishing the supplier/customer relationship because this together with the credit limit decision will determine not only the resulting rate of cash-flow but also the volume of sales permissible.

Setting Credit Limits or Credit Lines

The credit limit is the maximum amount allowed for a specific period. This amount serves as a guideline to account performance. *This is also called a credit line*. It fixes the maximum risk believed to be acceptable and the limit needed to accommodate the sale volume.

Credit personnel will have to use the term credit limits to refer to maximum limits and the maximum amount of credit the consumer is permitted to charge. A better term might be guide or line, since the limits are not absolutes but merely guides in the handling of an account. They can be changed freely, should circumstances warrant it. Regardless of what they are to be called, limits are useful in the operation of the credit system.

At certain times, the account may be completely reviewed. Using credit limits, credit managers free themselves of the responsibility of making day-to-day decisions. They exercise their judgement at the opening of the account, and if their judgement is sound, it will continue to govern. Limits also help the credit department to handle the slow paying accounts.

A company should release money or credit card only after proper documentation is completed.

Credit Checks

The basic credit qualities that need to be investigated is payment record of existing customers and for potential customers one need to investigate his or her income, employment, residence, marital status, age, reserve assets (if any) and collateral. Credit verification can be categorised into:

(a) Residence verification through document proof and visit.
(b) Employment verification for the self-employed or businessmen.
(c) Employment verification for those who are employed (drawing salary).
(d) Verifying customer contact by visiting his office
(e) The repayment capacity of the borrower is determined. To arrive at the comfortable repayment capacity (in equated monthly instalments) of the borrower, his income, age, qualifications, number of dependents, spouses' income, assets liabilities, job stability and continuity, saving history, insurance policy, etc. are taken into consideration.

Appropriate forms have been designed by some of the reputed consumer financing companies in India and they are in line with what is being followed in other parts of the world especially in USA and UK.

These forms are divided into four parts:

(i) The basic questions dealing with the purpose of loan.
(ii) The visit, the actual conversation in detail, the needed information gathered from the applicant.
(iii) The visit to the guarantor's residence and obtaining the necessary information.
(iv) Lastly, the fourth part deals with the observation made by the credit investigator during his visits, inside the house as well as by talking to the neighbour or relatives etc. This is very important, as this should give the required confidence and help to the credit investigator in recommending or rejecting the case.

Credit investigator must keep in mind that references, informants, and credit reporting agencies do not create credit information. Credit information is created only by consumers, who are constantly creating information about themselves through their conduct and activities. Such information becomes credit information when it can be used to predict a credit applicant's future behavior. It is important credit information when, if known, it would influence a credit decision.

When making a credit investigation, the credit executive should do so in a manner designed to collect facts rather than opinions. Questions should be phrased to induce informants to reply factually rather than with loosely stated opinions or judgements. Informants should be asked questions that they are likely to know the answer for. Asking informants questions about things they are not likely to know is an invitation to reply with opinion rather than fact and is also a temptation not to reply at all.

Grading a customer, setting up the credit limit and credit period is generally done after evaluating the following points (and there is a wide scope in improving each question or the number of questions to fit nature of business and the type and amount of loan being discussed).

Pre-credit Sanction Stage

(a) Find out whether the customer is credit worthy
(b) Check out very carefully his bank, trade and or personal references.
(c) What is the customer's credit rating with the bank ?
(d) Does the customer have a loan ?
(e) Is the loan secured? What kind of security?
(f) When is the loan due?
(g) Is the customer an individual or a corporate?
(h) *In case of an individual:* Is he in a confirmed job?
    (i) Is he ready to pledge collateral, or is their anybody who will stand guarantee for the loan or credit?
    (ii) Check out the bonafides of the guarantors, their permanent residence address.
(i) *In case of a corporate:* Check what is the corporate structure?
    (i) Who are the principals of the company?
    (ii) What is the business experience of the principals?

(iii) How long has the company been in this business?
(iv) Who else gives them credit?
(v) What are the company's total assets?
(vi) What are the projected revenues?
(vii) What has been the track record in recent years? You may need to analyse the firm's balance sheet.
(viii) Can it provide adequate security?

Housing Loans

One way to buy a house is to pay cash. But the typical Indian family is not in a position to do this, and thus must arrange to finance its house purchase. Most families can afford only the minimum i.e. the down payment and are forced to secure the remainder of the purchase price by mortgage from lending institutions. The larger the down payment, the smaller the total interest payment over the term of the mortgage. Buyers, however, do not use all their savings for the down payment, thus helping themselves to their reserves to fall back on if extraordinary expenses arise or income falls in future.

In case of housing loan, the practice is to have minimum prescribed down payment and first mortgage of the house / property (for which the loan is being provided) by depositing its title deed or any other collateral to cover the cost of property/ loan. In case, the property is in the construction stage, additional security may be required, just in case the construction does not complete at all.

For additional security, the borrower is asked to provide solvent guarantors who will agree to repay the balance loan amount if in case of default by the borrower. However, lately, housing finance companies are not asking for guarantors and this is helping them to attract more customers seeking housing loan. The housing finance companies make sure that the title of the property (which is going to be financed and mortgaged) is clear, registered, marketable, and free from litigation / encumbrance.

Collection System

Promptness and regularity of payment must be built into the system for the following reasons:

(a) A lax collection policy often indicates incompetent management. This can affect the purchasers' attitude towards the products the firm sells.

(b) Experience shows that there is a definite correlation between the length of time debts are unpaid and the volume of resulting bad-debt losses.

(c) Slow collection tends to result in the loss of future sales because slow-paying customers are reluctant to buy from firms they already owe money to. Of course, creditors may show an even stronger reluctance to sell such customers.

(d) Failures to enforce collection encourages imprudent purchasers. Thus foolhardy buyers may plunge headlong into unwise buying, knowing that a firm will permit an excessively long time to pass before it takes drastic legal action, if it ever does so.

Collection Planning

Two most important statements to control the complete collection activity will be:

1. Due datewise age analysis statement
2. Collection planning and follow-up on the basis of Pareto's Principle.

Example: A sundry debtor's list with due datewise age analysis.

Customer	Current	30 days +	60 days +	90 days +	etc.
AAA	120.00	250.04	50.00	100.00	
BBB	625.00	1000.00	3900.60	0.00	
CCC	293.00	700.20	500.40	990.00	
DDD	1000.00	2020.15	0.00	0.00	
EEE	388.20	405.10	26.77	0.00	
FFF	0.00	200.00	40.00	56.65	

1. *Due datewise and customerwise age analysis of each bill.* This will help credit manager to understand the number of customers, the number of invoices and the total amount which is due or overdue and needs a different strategy to follow-up. Other important features of this statement are that it helps a creditor to become pro-active and do his collection planning, the credit manger or the collection

department will much in advance know how to tackle the following points:

- Know who is due for payment and which accounts are overdue.
- Know who needs a collection call.
- Systematically follow-up with every customer who needs attention.
- Keep track of customer promises.
- Review and record the status of each outstanding invoice during a collection call.
- Know what is said on the past collection calls.
- Know when to withhold credit to a customer.
- Instantly replace a lost invoice / statement. Today we have more options for encouraging speedy payment. You can always fax the invoices to avoid mail delays. And wherever possible receive the payments into your bank account from the customer via electronic funds transfer.
- Decide how frequently to follow-up with each customer.
- Instantly access the details of an invoice to answer any questions.

2. *Collection planning* for achieving utmost collection within a decided period can be done by means of proper planning. One such planning is based on Pareto's Principle stated by Vilfredo Pareto, can be applied to debt collecting as it can to a wide range of business activities.

Commonly known as the 80:20 rule. The 80:20 rule, when applied to debt collection, implies that since most of the problems will be caused by only a small percentage of customers, if valuable time and effort should be concentrated on this small percentage, it will be costly. Although focused attention should be given to these low-value large number of customers but a company will also follow-up with the other customers so that cash target is achieved, sourcing the cash flow of the firm.

If you analyse your experience, it will show that if follow-ups are primarily aimed at the few, *plus* special attention to the large-value invoices the cost of doing so will be kept low but with much better result.

Therefore, many companies have decided to adopt Pareto's Principle for their collection planning and follow-up.

They *categorised* each invoice into *A, B, C* or even *D* type. For example:

Step 1: A firm decided to treat all invoices above Rs 1,00,000 as A-type. All invoices value ranging from Rs 50,000 to Rs 1,00,000 as B-type. Between Rs 30,000 to Rs 50,000 to be C-type and lastly, all invoices below Rs 20,000 to be treated as D-type.

Step 2: In the A-type all high value invoices were shown and the strategy was to follow them up first and if possible, in person.

Next, in the B-type the invoices with medium value (pre-defined) appeared and the strategy was to follow them up in person immediately after or much along with A-category invoices.

C-type invoices are taken up for follow-up after A and B type are covered. In the meantime they are followed up by sending reminder letters.

In *D-type*, being all low-value invoices, the list could be very long. Our experience says that 80% of the number of customer fall in this category who represents only 20% of the total debts. The cost of collecting such invoices by personally following up can be too high. Therefore, invoices are followed up by means of letters and making telephone calls, and if these attempts fail, then such accounts are handed over to a collection agency for collecting.

Collection Activities

(a) In general, the collection route tends to break down into three chronological stages—Initial agreements, Polite reminders and Aggressive strategies. It is very effective if done in the following manner:
(b) Collection on the debt begins by sending a monthly statement, clearly stating the total amount due and the due date, after which interest be charged for late payment. Maximum amount is collected by this method.
(c) Then the collection on debt begins by contacting the delinquent customer. It usually takes the following form:

(i) Charge interest for delays
(ii) Reminder notices. This should also include copies being marked to guarantors also.
(iii) Pre-printed follow-up notices and letters. Copies being marked to guarantors also
(iv) Telephone calls.
(v) Personalized collection letters, informing that they will have no choice but to hand over the account to a collection agency. Copies being marked to guarantors also.
(vi) An outside collection agency takes over the follow-up.
(vii) In case collection agency fails, legal action is taken. This is mostly against account with big debts. Guarantors to be made party to this case.

(d) Another major collection problem faced by all the companies doing business in credit cards, leasing and hire-purchase, is Bouncing of Cheques, mostly the instalment payment cheques. For a detailed discussion on bouncing of cheques please refer to the chapter on "Legal Action".

Collection Problem with Consumer Credit

Over the years, some firms have developed a classification of debtors similar to the following:

(a) Debtor misunderstood terms.
(b) Disputed amount.
(c) Careless or inefficient customer.
(d) Small amount involved, and customer therefore ignores.
(e) Slow by habit and by nature.
(f) Poor business management.
(g) Temporarily out of funds but good.
(h) Could pay but must be forced.
(i) Terms chiseler.
(j) A fraud

A creditor may classify a past-due debtor into one or more of these categories and, from previous experience with similar customers, follow a pre-determined policy to collect the amount due. Let us discuss them one by one:

(a) *Debtors misunderstood terms.* When this is the true situation, the solution is simple. Clarification of the credit terms and what is expected of the debtor should result in prompt payment. Sometimes a professed misunderstanding of the terms may be merely an excuse. However, misunderstandings do occur, and businesses must take care to handle such cases in a manner that will maintain a maximum amount of goodwill. Sometimes salespeople, in an effort to make sales, assure customers that they can pay "whenever they wish to pay," this lack of co-ordination between sales and credit can make for customer ill-will and may require reselling the customer when the true terms are spelt out.

(b) *Disputed amount.* Disagreement between the seller and the buyer as to the quality and the condition of the goods sold is to be expected from time to time. The buyer may withhold payment until some type of satisfactory agreement can be reached.

(c) *Careless or inefficient customer.* Again, collection from this customer should not be major problem. Pressed with a variety of other problems and cares, this business executive has just overlooked making payment. The debtor may use an inefficient system to keep track of when bills are due or may just be careless or even forgetful. In most cases a simple reminder that the amount is due and immediately payable brings in payment with no loss of customer goodwill.

(d) *Small amount involved, and customer therefore ignores.* People feel that if the indebtedness is small, they may ignore it for the time being, wait until the account becomes larger, and then write just one cheque to cover the entire amount. In such cases the debtor firm is making no attempt to escape payment; it is simply pursuing a delayed action that results in 'future' payments to the creditor. In addition to the nuisance and trouble involved in having to start the collection procedure, there is always the problem that what is small to one firm may not be small to another.

(e) *Slow by habit and by nature.* Some firms and their accounts payable personnel are notoriously slow in making payment. Payment is received only after various type of follow-ups and persuasions are applied. The firm that sells to this types of customer, and knows beforehand that the customer is of this type, should carefully analyse the gross margin on any sale and compare it with the expenses involved in making the sale. Such expenses tend to be high because of the cost of collection process. Even at the risk of loosing a customer, the executive assigned the collection task should adopt a strict policy toward the firm that is slow by habit and nature. Such customers have a poor concept of responsibility and generally are undesirable and unprofitable accounts.

(f) *Poor business management.* Firms falling into this category account for perhaps the largest number of difficulties for the collection manager. Often the staff of these firms are honest and optimistic but they overbuy. Because of poor business management, they find that they cannot meet the terms to which they agreed. The creditor must decide whether there is any hope that such a business manager will learn to conduct buying activities profitably before determining whether to follow a strict or a lenient collection policy. Can the business manager be salvaged and made into a good customer? If the answer is no, the relationship should be terminated quickly.

(g) *Temporarily out of funds but good.* This type of customer is usually delinquent because of condition beyond his or her control, such as illness, business conditions, or other developments. The debtor is not actually attempting to avoid payment, and the delinquency should not be viewed as a reflection on the debtors' integrity, but this should not delay the collection action. An amicable adjustment or extension of the credit period should be made quickly as possible, and the creditor should insist that the terms of new agreement be carried out to the limit of the debtor's ability.

(h) *Could pay but must be forced.* This type of customer is somewhat similar to the customer that is slow by habit and by nature. However, in dealing with this group, more persuasion and even threats must be used to obtain payment. Most of the time unless they are pursued vigorously, payment is unduly delayed or never comes. Credit standing means very little to this customer who has become accustomed to severe collection methods. For this reason, in its dealing with this chronic delinquents the collection department should force the issue immediately and strongly, at the very moment when the accounts become past due. Please remember, less severe action will have little value, and the creditor will get no return for the expense involved.

(i) *Terms chiseler* or one who interprets the cash discount terms always in his favour. A cash discount unlike trade discount is allowed as a reward for paying before or during pre-determined period which is always before due date.

At least two types of chiselers have been observed. One is the type who regularly deducts cash discounts even when making payments after expiration of the cash discount period. Firms vary as to their policies in such situation. Some return the cheque and request full payment, while others retain the cheque and inform the customer as to why he is not entitled to cash discount and therefore he will have to make the balance payment. Whichever procedure is followed, the action taken should be accompanied by a clear, concise statement that credit terms are being violated. How strong and threatening the statement should be, largely depends upon how profitable the customer is to the firm and how much the customers' future business is desired.

Another type of chiseler is the customer who makes only a partial payment, sends a post-dated cheque for the balance with deductions for cash discount, or dates a cheque back so that the date is within the discount period. The chronic offender who operates this way should be told the 'facts of credit' much more emphatically than the first-time offender who simply may have been careless.

(j) *A fraud.* The creditor should show this dishonest debtor no consideration, nor should it make any effort to retain this debtor's goodwill or possible future business. Just as soon as the creditor's firm is convinced that the debtor is dishonest and is engaged in fraudulent actions, the account should be handed over to an attorney, or if possible to a collection agency. Time is the essence in dealing with such offenders, and there is little reason to go through all the steps normally followed in a collection process.

Fraud with the intention to churn-over: The consumer business is plagued by these types of customers. Customers first enjoy the facilities from one firm, and when their drawing reaches the credit limit, without paying, they conveniently switch over and start availing credit from other firm. This practice is rampant in credit card and cellular phone industries. Timely billing and despatching, collection on due date, immediate follow-up in case of default, timely deactivation of facilities will help such firms to keep their overdues in control. These days collection agencies are entrusted to follow-up such cases.

Follow-up of Debtors

Many firms divide their customers segment-wise, according to the type of business they are in: employees group, employers group, builders group, whole-sellers, dealers, retailers, etc., and the follow-ups are done with each of them after studying each group's peculiarities. In consumer credit business, the number of customers are always very large and a balance has to be found between covering up all the customers within a period of 30 days and achieving the required cash flow or cash collection.

There are three methods of follow-up:

- Personal follow-up.
- Communications (various) or writing letters
- By making telephone calls.

Personal visits may be the best method, but often you will find them time consuming. Your unscheduled visit may be inconvenient for both you and your customer. A visit is a confrontation that requires an immediate response, and your customer may not want to answer right now. A phone call can have some of the same drawbacks. The number of customers for consumer credit is always large and under such circumstances a letter becomes the best mode of follow-up. A collection letter should be used in a manner that it, comprises, if not complete, at least ninety per cent of collection follow-up procedure.

In an organisation, you will never know which one of your employees could be your source of collection—perhaps from the most difficult customers. Anyone in your organisation may know somebody who can help in the customer's office. Time and again this has proved true in many companies.

A letter can be read when there is time to absorb it, often cost less than a phone call, provides a permanent record, can express your personality well, and can communicate your thought exactly as you wish.

Successive letters can be signed by the employees of increasingly higher rank or company officers: first the account receivable supervisor, then the accountant, then on to the collection manager, credit manager, Vice-president, Legal counsel, and company Managing Director. The higher the rank of the signer, the stronger the impact. Therefore a collection process starts with a request for or offer of credit and proceeds as far as necessary, which can include settlement by court action.

Effective Collection Letters

The primary advice is to address your letter to the decision maker. That will result in faster action than by sending the letter to the department involved. It will end up there, but with direct instructions from the responsible person. The recommendations listed here will not fit every situation, but you will find a quick review of them beneficial when you start to write your collection letter.

1. Start collection procedures immediately after the account becomes delinquent.
2. Let your reader know in the first sentence itself that this is a collection letter.
3. Be persistent. Keep at it.
4. Make collection letters brief, but not curt.
5. Avoid stilted language. Be clear. Be specific.
6. Be firm but reasonable.
7. Be kind, helpful and respectful.
8. Be friendly and sympathetic.
9. Always retain your customer's goodwill.
10. Treat your reader as an honest person.
11. Appeal to the individual interests and feelings of your readers. Consider their points of view.
12. Never lower yourself by displaying anger, pity, contempt or malice.

13. Never repeat an appeal made in a previous letter.
14. Provide a flexible collection plan.
15. Provide your debtor with a reason why it is to his advantage to pay promptly.
16. Make each successive letter stronger.
17. State the amount due in each letter.
18. Many collection letters mention interest charges are being added to late payments. This can be properly done only when such interest charge is mentioned in the original purchase contract or invoice.
19. Imply that the debtor will pay.
20. State how payment may be made.
21. Include the original due date.
22. Politely ask for payment – without apologising.

Format of a Collection Letter

1. State or imply that this is a collection letter.
2. Mention data relevant to the situation.
3. What you are asking for.
4. How the reader can be helped. Depending on the type of transaction you can appeal to customer's credit standing, self-interest, fairness, friendship, cooperation, duty, fear, honour, sympathy, loyalty, justice, or pride. If your customer is facing financial problem, you can decide to extend payment terms, facility to pay minimum due now and balance later, change the terms of future sale, etc.
5. Reasons for paying now.
6. Make the request for payment.

Time intervals between letters normally vary from fifteen to thirty days, depending on the kind of goods you are selling. Is it a perishable goods to a department store or is it a refrigerator to an individual? Letters may continue for periods of three months to six months before it is handed over to a collection agency or an attorney.

For many firms collection letters form the complete follow-up procedure and if this fails, the defaulter's accounts are then handed over to external collection agencies.

GUIDELINES

1. Never knowingly break the law, and never test the law without prior legal approval.
2. Always perform at least a cursory review of a financial statement within two days of receiving it.
3. When guarantees or collateral are put into effect, always acknowledge it in writing to the customer.
4. Never hold a customer order without letting the customer know it is on hold.
5. Never accept post-dated cheques without taking an undertaking from the customer that it will be honored on presentation. If the cheque is dishonoured by bank then start the collection procedure by sending notice as laid down in the amended Negotiable Instrument Act, Section 138.
6. Never unknowingly allow any collateral or guarantees to expire.
7. Never delay or forget to deposit a collected cheque. The collection float is too long and it may be too late by the time you realise that the cheque was bad:

   Collection float can be described in the following manner:

Cheque mailed → Cheque received	Mail float
Cheque received → Cheque deposited	Processing float
Cheque deposited → Availability of funds at bank	Availability float
	= Total collection float

8. Never make critical credit decision without the benefit of reviewing all the facts first.
9. Never bad-mouth the competition, another customer, or your company during customer's visit.
10. Never play 'god' with the company's funds concerning write-offs, settlements or when extending credit. It's not funny money.
11. Never extend credit to an unknown new customer without at least performing a minimal credit investigation.

Sir, for the last two months I was trying to get in touch with you, . . . now, can I have my payment ? ? ?
..OOUPS!
TOILET
GENTS

12. Always notify the marketing department when customers are being referred for collection, and in case customer's credit terms being revoked.
13. Never raise credit limits without a minimal credit review.
14. Never provide extended credit terms without legal documents.
15. Never understate or overstate data on credit reports due to perceived management pressure.
16. Never holdout or delay on advising senior management of bad-debts write-offs or bad news due to perceived management pressure.
17. Always document customer visits in writing.
18. Never succumb to marketing pressure if there is an immediate customer viability problem.
19. Never lie on behalf of the company or a customer.
20. Never believe a trade rumor about a customer unless it can be substantiated.
21. Always remember that a balance sheet only represents the financial condition of a firm as of a particular date.
22. Never stop attempting to get financial disclosure from slow paying customers.
23. Never visit a customer without first reviewing the credit file in detail.
24. Never make a promise or commitment to a customer, knowing that the promise will have to be broken.
25. Never make the critical credit mistake twice.
26. Never accept a gift or benefit from a customer nor socialize with one where it might be possible to develop a conflict of interest.
27. Avoid comparing financial ratios across industries.
28. Always remember that credit is a privilege, not a right.

Exceptions to the rules should be made only under justifiable circumstances.

COST OF CREDIT OPERATION

Credit activities incur costs in soliciting new accounts, investigating credit applications, making decisions on whether to accept or reject, preparing and issuing identification cards, preparing and handling monthly statements, receiving payments from customers, tracing and contacting delinquent accounts, investing capital in accounts receivable, and bad-debts. Other costs involve equipment, stationery supplies, space, and utilities. Offsetting these expenses, the business can increase its sales and profits and earn income from interest charges.

Both credit and collection managers to do their job effectively should be aware of cash management product, functions of collection agencies, terms of payments, and the various modes of getting payments. Collection work is trying , and collection managers and their staff need patience, persistence, and resourcefulness. How well credit and collection managers perform their jobs determines the impact that collection activities have on their firms. They always walk on a tightrope, trying to decide just how much effort to make and how much expense to incur in attempting to bring an indebtedness to a satisfactory conclusion.

Controlling Credit and Collection Policies and Monitoring Procedures:

1. All customers, especially new customers should fill out a credit application – before any credit is extended.
2. Subscribe to credit-verification and reporting agency services such as Mirainform, Onicra. Dun & Bradstreet etc.
3. Require customers to sign a statement of contract to avoid misunderstanding.
4. If your customer do not stand by its commitment, inform CIBIL.
5. If it a doubtful case, obtain personal guarantees from the owners of the business as well as from their partners.
6. Assign a due-dates to all the bills, include them with customer shipments, and/or provide electronic transfer procedures.

7. Offer discounts to early payers.
8. Establish an interest penalty for late payment.
9. Appoint a permanent manager to handle collections.
10. Establish an internal review of all your accounts.
11. Monitor new accounts and their payment habit at least for first three month. If they delay warn them. Show that you are a professional.
12. Remind every customer before due-date, starting with most tardy customers.
13. Problem customers should be put on C.O.D. basis.
14. Meet defaulters, find out the reason for default. If it is not your fault in executing order than they must be warned for being late. Late them commit to a firm date.
15. Celebrate collection by appreciating the effort made by collection staff.
16. Collection agencies (if selected) should be put on commission basis.

APPENDIX I

Bank Guarantees—
The Agony from Three Years to Thirty Years

Bank guarantees are one of the facilities extended by the bank. A supplier is allowed to give to his various customers bank guarantees towards advance, security deposit, performance etc. totaling upto a certain sum of maximum amount decided by the bank. Once this limit is utilized the bank will turn down further request for issuing new bank guarantees. As a result new business securing advance payment or any big value order where the customers would like to play safe by securing a bank guarantee from the supplier towards non-performance, may be lost. Apart from these a bank guarantee costs money, i.e. all banks resort to charging commission on each bank guarantee issued and and on those bank guarantee which are expired they prefer to keep margin ranging from 10% and above on the value of the bank guarantee.

Commercial banks' guarantee business, constitutes a significant portion of their non-fund earnings. As a result of the Indian Contract (Amendment) Act, 1996, Section 28, which became a law on January 8, 1997, specifies that unless the original guarantee is received back from the beneficiary—government department—banks would not be able to cancel the bank guarantee till the limitation period of thirty years. And in cases where beneficiary is a private firm, the limitation period is three years.

We all know that the government departments are not in the habit of returning the original guarantee papers to the banks after the purpose is served. Till now, banks use to notify the beneficiary government department and round off the contingent liability. Now, this procedure will not work any more. If the government departments refuse to return inspite of bank sending notices, the bank will have to continue providing for the liability in its balance-sheet for a period of thirty years after which the papers would be considered void.

Banks have issued instructions to their branches to the effect that bank guarantees are not to be reversed unless the original guarantee is returned duly cancelled and consequently the branches have been asked not to return the margin held in such guarantees.

For fresh guarantees to the government, branches have been instructed to obtain 100 per cent margin by way of fixed deposit or cash and that the same should be held until surrender of the original guarantee duly cancelled.

All these, therefore, call for an aggressive plan to collect the expired bank guarantees in time and operate below the limit prescribed by the bank so that the new bank guarantee can be offered for new business.

Further, for a customer, there is not much of a difference between bank guarantee and earnest money deposit. Both act as security against supplier's specific non-performance. The only difference is that earnest money deposit is to be placed in hard cash, bank guarantee is a guarantee given by bank against some specific failure on part of the supplier's side. From the supplier's point of view bank guarantee should be preferable to earnest money deposit as it involves only deposit of a nominal amount with a bank.

We will discuss this subject in three parts:

1. Action to be taken prior to issue of bank guarantees.
2. Controlling/monitoring bank guarantees.
3. Collecting expired bank guarantees from customers for cancellation.

Action to be taken prior to issue of bank guarantees:

1. To check whether bank guarantee is provided in the contract/terms of tender and it is fair to supplier. One party who had been given bank guarantee for securing

advance against its order wanted to extend the validity of bank guarantee. Although the supplier was ready with the equipment, the party wanted to postpone the lifting of the material. In such cases extension should not be given.

2. To provide for bank guarantee in place of earnest money deposit (cash) wherever possible as earnest money deposit involves only nominal deposit.
3. To provide bank guarantees as soon as money is due against submission of such bank guarantees, as per contract.
4. To check the draft of guarantee before the same is submitted to accounts for submission to bank.
5. To ask for bank guarantees well in advance so that sufficient time can be given to bank for issuance of bank guarantee.

Controlling/Monitoring of Bank Guarantees

For controlling bank guarantees, it is necessary to maintain a record of each bank guarantee submitted in the following format:

BG no., Name of party, Party's order no., O/A no., Amount due-date, and Reason for issuing the same (i.e. Security Deposit, performance, etc.), Name of the issuing banks, and lastly the Remarks column to be entered by the person who is responsible for getting back the BG. In case the BG needs to be amended for extension the person should be in position to justify the reason why condition of the order could not be fulfilled in time. Extension of BG to be made only for valid reason and for reasonable periods. Progress status must be maintained.

Periodically critical review has to be made on all BGs and especially outstanding BGs.

This information can be maintained preferably on computer so that every month one can have information regarding bank guarantees maturing during the month.

Collecting Expired Bank Guarantees from Customers

The following five methods of collecting/canceling expired bank guarantees are found effective:

1. To collect the bank guarantee by personally visiting the customer.
2. To enclose a readymade letter along with a request to the customer to sign and send back.
3. To get 'No Complaint' letter from the site engineer and submit the same to customer's bank guarantee department/accounts department.
4. To request the customer to return the bank guarantee in a fortnight time as it has expired.
5. To request the bank to cancel the bank guarantee as customer has not responded to your letter, nor returned the bank guarantee.

Samples of readymade letter to be signed by customer

To,
The Branch Manager
Bank of Bengal
Thane

Dear Sir, Date ....

Ref: B/G No. ________________ dated ____________

Sub: Cancellation of B/G issued against P.O. No.___________
dated ___________ for Rs ___________

We would like to confirm that the above goods against the above mentioned Purchase Order No. has been satisfactorily executed by M/s. A. E. Ltd. and we have no claim.

You may kindly cancel the captioned B/G and oblige.

OR

Since the copy of the B/G is not traceable at our end we request you to kindly cancel the above mentioned B/G.

Thanking you,

Yours faithfully,

(Rubber Stamp of the customer is a must, preferably on customer's letter head)

You may write a letter to your customer on the following lines:

"We are pleased to inform you that B/G submitted to you against our Purchase Order No._________ dated ________ for Rs._________ towards SD/Performance/Advance has expired on___________ & the period to lodge your claim (if any) has also expired on ___________

During this period we did not receive any complaints from you/your site.

OR

During this period the technical queries raised by your site staff have been already attended to their satisfaction.

In view of the above, we request you to return the captioned BG to enable us to surrender the same to our banker.

We look forward to receiving the same within a fortnight.

Thanking you and assuring you of our best services at all times.

Yours sincerely,

C.C.: Branch Manager, Bank of Bengal. Incase the party does not respond to our request, then you must treat this BG as canceled under advice to us.

This is a sequel to the above letter. If the party does not respond to the request, then after waiting for about 15-20 days, one must write and exert pressure on the bank to cancel the BG. Usually the bank will give 15 days notice to the customer.

Sample of letter to the bank for cancellation of BG

To
The Branch Manager,
Bank of Bengal,
Thane Branch

Dear Sir, Date ________

Ref: Expired BG No. ________ Dt ________ for Rs ________favouring M/s _________________________________

This is to certify that the work, in respect of which the captioned guarantee was issued by you, has been duly performed and the concerned department on whose favour the said guarantee was issued, has no claim to make on the basis of the guarantee issued.

In the light of the above, please treat the above guarantee as canceled under advixce to us.

Thanking you,

The credit manager will be successful in collecting all the bank guarantees if the following points are kept in mind:

1. To approach the customer in proper time.
2. To give proper reference by quoting customer order no. in your letter.
3. To attach proof of your performance along with the letter.
4. Ready-made draft letter to be sent from customer's side in case the bank guarantee is not traceable at his end.
5. Different banks practise different procedures for cancellation. However, it will only be slightly different from those mentioned above.

A bank guarantee is a sort of absolute undertaking on the part of the bank under an arrangement with its customer to pay to the creditor whenever the guarantee is invoked by the latter. The bank's obligation to pay arises on demand and not on breach.

APPENDIX II

Handling Goods-In-Transit Insurance Effectively

TRANSIT INSURANCE—THEY WILL SETTLE ONLY IF . . .

Where the sale is on 'C and I' or 'CIF' basis, you are expected to arrange insurance for the total invoice value, (including freight charges). The risk should be covered from the place it is loaded upto final destination. This may come to an end immediately after unloading or up to the end of a declared period after unloading. Since these despatches are of a regular nature, the supplier should take a floating policy or open policy & not specific policies where each consignment has to be separately covered. In the open policy, the advantage is that the information regarding all the despatches are declared at one time usually in the first week of the subsequent month.

With Regard to Rail/Road/Air Transit Insurance, a Credit Manager Must Understand the Following:

1. He is not permitted to make a profit out of an insurance claim.
2. He may take a Basic Inland Transit (Rail/Road) cover or wider 'All Risk' cover. The basic covers risk like goods damaged by fire, lighting breakage of bridges, collision with or by the carrying vehicle, overturning of the carrying vehicle, derailment or accident of the carrying railway wagon/vehicle. In wider cover, all risks of loss or damage are covered.

3. In case there is a change of truck during the voyage, prompt notice should be given to an underwriter otherwise the cover will cease to operate.
4. The cover does not operate in case of willful misconduct of the insured, in case of ordinary leakage or ordinary loss in weight, if the packing is of substandard nature, delay inherent or nature of the subject matter insured, war risks, strike risks and damage caused by terrorists.
5. Strikes, riots and civil commotion risks may be covered on payment of extra premium.
6. Mostly with many goverment departments it is found that they do not open the packing even for months. In such cases an extra premium for extra period with a notice served on the consignee to verify the consignment before the end of the extra period should help.
7. The insured must adhere to the prescribed (declared) packing as agreed at the time of taking the policy.
8. The insured will be compensated in case of total loss where the goods are totally damaged, if approved by the surveyor.
9. The insured may be compensated partially only to the extent of cost of repairing the damage and forwarding the goods to their destination. A surveyor is the best judge to decide such cases.
10. If the loss is due to common peril, the amount of compensation is based on 'General Average' basis.
11. A cargo totally lost or partially lost due to theft, loss during loading/unloading are compensated accordingly. In such cases the insured should demand shortage/damage certificate from the transporter and also lodge his claim under Registered A/D directly on the transporter for the value of the goods short delivered or damage, with a copy to underwriter.
12. If, after opening the packing, the goods are found damaged totally / partially, it could be due to jolt and jerks during transit. The surveyor will be able to decide such cases and the extent of compensation.
13. For totally damaged cargo the surveyor may decide the salvage value of the consignment to be shared by the cargo owner.

14. The consignee must retire the goods immediately or within seven days from the date of arrival of goods. In case the LR/RR is not received the goods still can be cleared on the basis of an 'Indemnity Bond' furnished to the railway/ transporter administration.
15. Where an entire consignment has not arrived by rail even after two months from the date of booking, the consignor and the consignee should write to the railway administration to enable it to trace the consignment. It should be a registered letter addressed to GM, Railway or Chief Commercial Superintendent.
16. In case the entire consignment has not arrived by rail within four months, a 'non delivery' certificate should be demanded from railway administration. In any case such demand should be made by registered A/D letter within six months from the date of R.R.
17. In case of partial delivery, compensation has to be claimed for goods not delivered. The railway will give a 'partial delivery' certificate after inserting a remark to that effect, in the delivery book. A photocopy of this extract from the delivery book, duly endorsed by railway administration is enough to serve as 'non-delivery or partial delivery' certificate.
18. In case a damage is noticed at the time of delivery, open delivery should be demanded. A copy of the open delivery should be retained to submit to the insurer. The value of the loss to be compensated is to be decided by the surveyor. Hence on taking delivery the consignment must be left untouched until surveyed. Such survey should be undertaken at the earliest.
19. Survey fee has to be paid while obtaining the survey report from the surveyor. This fee is refunded by the insurer if the claim is admitted. Hence this should be included in the claim bill raised on the insurer.
20. Documents needed for settlement of a claims are:
    (a) Original insurance policy/certificate/declaration duly endorsed by the assured and the consignees.
    (b) Supplier's invoice and packing list.
    (c) Consignor's/consignee's copy of the lorry receipt/ railway receipt.

(d) Original open delivery/non-delivery/short delivery certificate issued by the carrier, duly signed under their seal, indicating the designation of the person signing the document; if not obtained the reason thereof.

(e) Original insurance survey report together with the receipt for fees paid.

(f) Copy of letter lodging claim on the carrier under registered A/D together with a copy of claim bill.

(g) Postal acknowledgment receipt of your letter lodging claim on the carrier.

(h) Carrier's reply in original to your claim on them.

(i) Copies of further correspondence and original replies from carrier/consignees.

(j) Your claim bill on insurance company will be in triplicate.

(k) In case of claim on rebooked consignment, the reason for re-booking. Lorry receipt to that effect and correspondence exchanged between yourselves and clients, carrier/bank and a pre-despatch inspection report by an independent surveyor or an officer from your office at the place of despatch.

(l) In the event of undelivered package/s being subsequently offered for delivery, an open delivery should be taken and certificate obtained from carrier in case of loss/damage for transmission to you.

(m) Letter of subrogation.

(n) Special power of attorney (if it is railway claims).

(Draft copy of letter of subrogation and letter of attorney will be available with your insurer.)

We are presenting here a series of letters (sample) which may come handy while raising and settling your Rail/Road/Air transit claim. They are presented in order of sequence:

First Letter for Raising the Provisional Claim

BY REGD. A.D.

REF: AKG/INS/SWGR/91. April 3, 1991

Lords Insurance Co. Ltd
Division No. III
1, Shakespeare Sarani,
Calcutta - 700 001.

Dear Sirs,

Sub: Despatch of one GEC Make – 22 KV, Vacuum Circuit Breakers alongwith accessories vide Invoice No. 3473 dtd.29-1-91 and Con.Note No.77033 dated 29-1-91 and Invoice No.3503 dtd. 4-2-91 and Con.Note No.77052 dtd. 4-2-91 from Naini Works to M/s. Group Engineers, Pune.

We enclose herewith a damage report submitted by the consignee with copies of the consignment notes and invoices as mentioned above. We shall let you know the cost of the damages in due course but in the meantime kindly treat this as Provisional Claim for Rs 1,25,000/-.

We shall be pleased if you kindly arrange for a survey of the same. We give herebelow the name and address of the consignee where the material is lying.

Executive Engineer
M.S.E.B.
Akurdi Sub-Station
Pune.

Thanking you,

Yours faithfully,
For The Gelec Co. of India

A.K. Shah
Credit Controller

Encl: As above.

C.C: B.V. Mehta, Asst. Adm. Officer, NIC, Bombay. With a request to allocate a surveyor at the earliest from Bombay itself.

Second Letter to the Transporter or Railway Raising the Claim on Them. It should be sent by registered A.D.

BY REGD. A.D.

REF: AKG/INS/SWGR/91. April 19, 1991.

M/s. National Road Carriers
P-15, New C.I.T. Road
(Terretty Bazar) Ground Floor
Calcutta - 700 070.

Dear Sirs,

Sub: Despatch of 16 Nos. of Switch Gears supplied to Masjid 22 KV Sub-Station vide Inv.Nos.18966,18970,18971 dated 7-3-91 Inv.No.18972 dated 9-3-91 and Inv. No.18214 dated 22-3-91 and Con. Note Nos. 344, 349, 350 dated 7-3-91 and 352 dated 9-3-91 from AEI Works, Calcutta to BEST Undertaking, Bombay.

We enclose herewith a copy of the letter No.CO/STORES-26/PRSS/91 dated 18-3-1991 received from the consignee M/s. BEST Undertaking informing about the damages .. or .. shortages alongwith copies of the consignment notes and invoices as mentioned above. The approximate value of the damages being Rs 1,25,000/-.

It should however be clearly understood that yourselves as the carriers should be held primarily responsible for any damages sustained on the goods in transit on account of rough handling and be liable to bear all costs of repairs/ replacements, as may be necessary. Therefore, please find our claim bill of Rs 1,25,000/- with a request to settle the same immediately.

Yours faithfully,
For The Gelec Co. of India

A.K. Shah
Credit Controller

Encl: As Above.

C.C: B.V. Mehta, Asst. Adm. Officer, LIC, Bombay.

Third Letter is Addressed to the Surveyor Requesting Him to Survey the Damaged/Short Received Consignment

---

Messrs J.D. Engineers
Insurance Surveyor lane
Bombay.

Dear Sir,

Sub: Survey of our damaged goods at MSEB stores, Sangli.

We have been informed by Lords Insurance that they have allocated your office for the above survey. We therefore request your representative to call at our office so as to enable the undersigned to handover all the relevant papers and details.

Your immediate action in this regard will be highly appreciated.

Thanking you,

Yours faithfully,

C.C: Lords Insurance Co. (For information)

Encl. Copy of the insurance policy.
Copy of the complaint received from the consignee.
Copy of the letter from underwriter appointing you as surveyor.

Fourth Letter is for Informing the Consignee that a Surveyor Appointed by the Underwriter will be Shortly Visiting Them

---

REF: AKG/INS/SWGR/91 April 10, 1991.

M/s. Great Engineers
Block-No. -1
Roche Apartment
Pune - 411 009.

Dear Sirs,

Re: Survey in respect of d amages sustained on GEC Make - 22KV VCB despatched Vide our Inv. No. 3473 dated 29-1-91 as per Cons. Note No. 77033 dated 29-1-91 And Inv.No.3503 dated 4-2-91 as per Cons. Note No. 77052 dated 4-2-91.

This is to inform you that M/s. J.D.Engineer (Surveyors) Pvt. Ltd have been appointed by National Insurance Company Ltd. To conduct survey of damaged VCB at your site, Mr. R. K. Pillai, Surveyor from M/s J.D.Engineer (Surveyors) Pvt. Ltd will be visiting your site on thursday, April 11, 1991 to conduct the survey.

You are requested to assist him and extend co-operation.

Thanking you,

Yours faithfully,
For The Gelec Co. of India Ltd.

A.K. Shah
Credit Controller—WR

C.C: Mr. R.K. Jain,
M/s. A.Engineer (Surveyors) Pvt. Ltd, Bahadur Mansion, 2nd Floor, 22, Bombay South Marg, Bombay - 400 021.

Letter for Raising the Final Claim May be as Follows:

BY REGD. A.D.

REF: AKG/INS/SWGR-20/91. May 27, 1991.

Lords Insurance Co. Ltd.
Division No. III
1, Shakespeare Sarani, 6th Floor
Calcutta - 700 071.

Dear Sirs,

Sub: Despatch of one GEC Make- 22 KV, Vacuum Circuit Breakers alongwith Accessories from Naini to M/s.Group Engineers,Pune at Akurdi Sub-Station as per Inv. No. 3473 dated 29-1-91 vide Con.Note No. 77033 dated 29-1-91 and as per Inv. No. 3503 dated 4-2-91 vide Con. Note No.77052 dated 4-2-91.

We enclose herewith the following documents against our final claim:

1. Original Survey Report No.RP/M-5916/91 dated 16-4-1991 and No.RP/M-5917/91 dated 16-4-1991 issued by M/s. J. D. Engineer (Surveyors) Pvt. Ltd., Marine & Automobile Surveyors And Loss Assessors, Rajabahadur Mansion, 2nd Floor, 22, Bombay Samachar Marg, Bombay - 400 023.
2. Surveyor's Original Bill No.RP/M-5916/91 dated 16-4-1991 for Rs 855/- and Bill No.RP/M-5917/91 dated 16-4-1991 for Rs 855/-.
3. Surveyor's Original Receipt No.1434 dated 20-5-91 for Rs.855/- and Receipt No.1435 dated 20-5-91 for Rs.855/-.
4. Copy of Invoice No. 3473 dated 29-1-1991 and Invoice No. 3503 dated 4-2-1991.
5. Copy of Consignment Note No. 77033 dated 29-1-91 and No. 77052 dated 4-2-91.

6. Copy of the letter No.AKG/INS/SWGR/91 dated April 3, 1991 towards claim on Transporter - M/s. Kataria Carriers, H.O.133/198, Transport Nagar, Kanpur - 23. Also enclosed is the A.D. card.
7. Copy of Transit Insurance Declaration of above mentioned claim.
8. Our Final Claim Bill No.INS/SWGR/20/91 dated 27-05-1991 for Rs.26,404.80.
9. Letter of subrogation duly filled and signed.
10. Letter of attorney as per your formalities.

Kindly acknowledge receipt of the same.

We now request you to settle our claim at the earliest.

Thanking you,

Yours faithfully,
For The Gelec Co. of India

A.K. Shah
Credit Controller

Encl: As above.

APPENDIX III

Sales Tax— The Government's Booty

Tax on sale or purchase is a state subject. Each state has enacted its own separate Act. State can levy tax if the transaction is within the territorial jurisdiction of the state and if it is "sale" within the meaning of sale of goods act, 1930.

If the sale in within the same state then local sales tax act is applicable. When for sale the goods move from one state to another state then central sales tax act is applicable.

It is beyond the scope of this book to discuss the different states' sales tax acts, however, few important points on central sales tax are mentioned.

THE CENTRAL SALES TAX ACT, 1956 (A Few Important Points)

1. Liability for Registration

(a) When any single transaction of sale in the course of interstate trade takes place.

(b) Voluntarily, on application, the registration can be obtained by a dealer registered under local Act. The application for registration has to be moved within thirty days of the date on which the liability arises.

2. Tax on Inter-state Sale

(a) In case of declared goods—double of the local state sales tax rate.

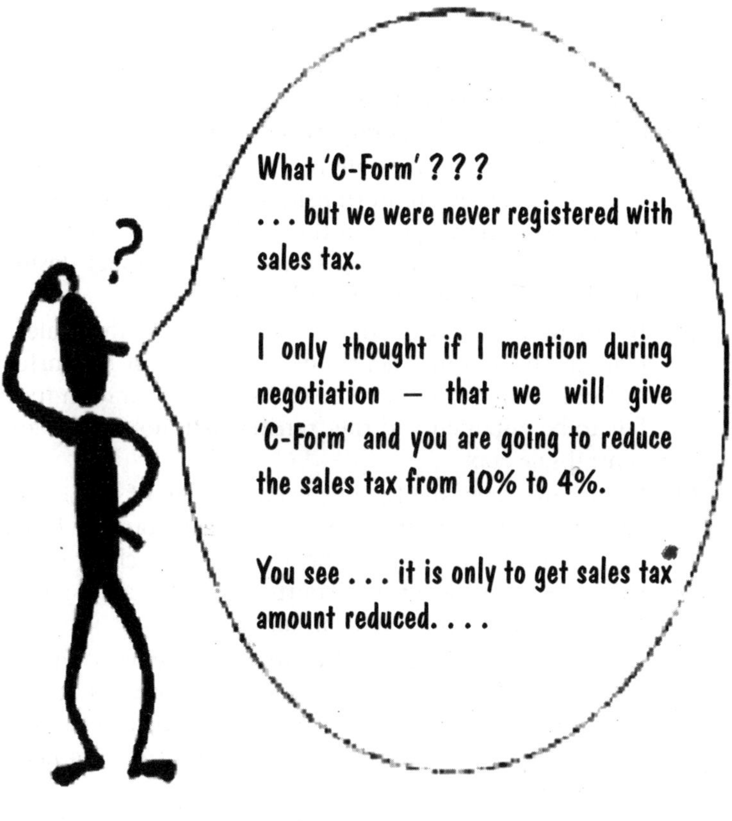

Over SMART CUSTOMER

(b) In case of other goods—10% or the rate of local sales tax. whichever is higher. If local rate is less than 4% then at local rate of sales tax.

In both the cases, if the local sales tax rate is nil, no central sales tax shall be charged.

(c) There is no sales tax on transfer, exchange or sale of goods/documents when the goods are high seas level (out of Indian territory).

3. Declaration Forms

(a) If the purchasing dealer gives to the selling dealer, a declaration form C for use by registered dealers or form D for use by government departments only, tax shall be reduced to 4% or local rate, whichever is lower.

(b) Subsequent inter-state sale by transfer of documents of goods, when they are in transit, are exempted subject to certain conditions given in the Act and the same can be availed by using form E(i). In case the customer desires to sale it to another customer E(ii) is issued.

(c) In case of transfer of goods outside the state to the dealer's place of business in other state known as 'branch transfer' or from agent to principal or vice versa, declaration form F is to be obtained and the transfer shall not attract any central sales tax.

(d) In case of purchase of goods from a dealer of other state with the intention to export the same out of India, declaration form H has to be given to the selling dealer by the purchasing dealer (exporter) and the sale shall not be liable to tax under central sales tax act.

(e) Inter-state sale of goods after receiving delivery thereof being purchased from a dealer of other state, is not fully exempted from central sales tax. A tax at lower rate is charged on such a transaction and form C or form D are used for claiming the lower rate of tax.

(f) One C form or D form can cover more than one bill of one financial year.

4. Transfer of Goods to Own Place of Business in Other State or Sale on Consignment

In view of the letter No. 8/22/90 ST(Vol.III)dtd. 28.9.67 of the Government of India, Ministry of Finance, Dept. of Revenue & Insurance addressed to Finance/Revenue Secretaries of all States and Union Territories, the dealer has the option to discharge the onus to the satisfaction of the sales tax authorities in any other manner other than furnishing form 'F'.

It may so happen that, say, material is despatched from Bombay to a customer in Delhi, but, for some reason customer either refuses or fails to take delivery thereof. In such cases the Delhi branch if registered under CST may take the delivery from the transporter and issue form 'F' to Bombay.

5. Penalties

In the following circumstances, a dealer can be penalized:-

(a) On deliberately furnishing a false declaration or certificate.

(b) On failure to get registered or furnish security.

(c) On false representation while purchasing that the goods purchased are covered by his certificate of registration.

(d) On falsely representing while purchasing that he is a registered dealer.

(e) On failure, without reasonable excuse to use goods purchased for the purposes mentioned in form 'C'.

(f) On holding forms obtained by him not according to the provision of the Act.

(g) On collecting tax in contravention of the provisions of Sec. 9A.

The penalty is six months imprisonment or fine or both. In case of a continuing offense, a daily fine not exceeding Rs. 50/- per day can be imposed. Other penalties for delay in filing of return and/or late payment of tax etc. are governed by the local state sales tax laws.

SALES TAX FORMS FOLLOW-UP LETTERS

First Letter

REF.: ACCTS/ST/

Dear Sirs　　　　Date ....

Sub: Non-receipt of sales tax forms

This has reference to our supply to you vide our bill/s referred below. It is observed that sales tax form has still not been received by us as agreed.

You are requested to verify the same and arrange to send immediately and oblige.

S.No.	Your P.O. No. & Dt.	Bill No.	Date	Amount Rs.
1.				
2.				
3.				
4.				
5.				

Thanking you,

Yours faithfully,
For THE G.A. Co. Ltd.

Second Letter

REF.: ACCTS/ST

Dear Sirs,　　　　Date ....

Sub: Non-receipt of Sales Tax Form.

We refer to our letter no. ________ dated ________ informing you about the non-receipt of form against our bill no. ________ dated ________ and regret to state that the same has still not been received by us.

We had levied the concessional rate of sales tax as it was agreed that you will be submitting the sales tax form which is still awaited by us.

You are once again requested to treat the same as urgent and arrange to send the form immediately without any further delay.

For your ready reference and immediate action, we are enclosing herewith copies of the bills.

Please note that if we do not receive the form in time, then we will be forced to send our debit note towards the additional tax payable in the absence of the form together with applicable interest.

Yours faithfully,

For The G.A. Co. Ltd.

Encl: As above.

Third Letter

REF.: ACCTS/ST

Dear Sirs, Date ________

We refer to our various reminders resting at your end informing about the non-receipt of Sales tax forms against our bills referred below and regret till date, neither we have received the forms nor any correspondence in this regard from you.

S.No.	Invoice No.	Date	Amount Rs.	Your Order No. & Date
1.				
2.				
3.				
4.				
5.				

We are therefore constrained to raise our Debit Note No. ________

dated ________ for Rs. ________ (Rupees ________________) towards the same which is enclosed herewith in duplicate.

Please arrange to send your demand draft for a like amount in our favour immediately.

Thanking you,

Yours faithfully,
For The G.A. Co. Ltd.

Encl: As above.

APPENDIX IV

What is Credit Insurance?

Courtesy: Ahmedabad Management Association
Source: Introduction Leaflets of New India Assurance

Credit insurance provides a business with protection against failure of its customers to pay their debts. Like any form of insurance, credit insurance is purchased to protect a business from a large loss that could impair its performance.

Despite a company's best efforts, large or catastrophic losses occur due to:

- one large long-term buyer unexpectedly failing.
- a significant change in the market (or economy) where a number of buyers become distressed and are unable to meet the obligations in time.
- a sudden shift in the political or economic conditions of a buyer's country (exports)

It is also a risk management tool that can provide concrete solutions for the trade expansion issues you are considering. The Credit Insurance Policy is an insurance product—rather it sets in motion an ongoing process of partnership between you and the insurer. The insurer vets a debtor's creditworthiness and monitors his financial position to identify his possible problems. If a debt goes bad and cannot be collected (or collected only partially), a claim is paid.

Process Overview

1. Payment of premium.
2. Delivery of goods and dispatch of invoices.

3. Prevention of claims through credit risk management, risk monitoring and credit control methods.
4. Payment of bills on or before due date.
5. Indemnification
6. Recovery proceedings

Why Business Credit Shield?

New India's business credit shield is not just another insurance product. It is an investment in a financial service product. Unlike other insurances, it pays for itself and is much more beneficial than self-insurance. It's a risk management tool, which gives you peace of mind to concentrate on your resources and triggers alert signals for impending default. It is a useful tool in achieving financial objectives and improving financial performance. It can also assist in developing more favorable financing arrangements.

- Achieves Financial Objectives
    - Increases cash flow and profitability
    - Protects one of your largest assets i.e. accounts receivable
    - Improves the quality of financial planning
- Better Access to Capital
    - Financiers value the security of insurance cover on receivables and may be prepared to give greater credit on more favourable terms.
- Streamlines Financial Performance
    - Reduces bad debt reserves
    - Minimizes risk
    - Positive effect on growth rate
    - Improves return on assets
    - Reduces days sales outstandings (DSO)
    - Lowers borrowing costs
- Enhances Competitiveness
    - Improves customer relationship
    - Reduces risks of entering new market
- Recovery Service
    - Negotiate/pursue initially to help getting payment

- For amicable settlement preserving good relations
- To recover debts through the courts
- Better recoveries leading to lower premium cost.

Tailor Made Solutions

In a fiercely competitive climate, and with the increasing globalization of trade, credit insurance has gained major importance both as a safeguard against bad debt and as a tool for assisting growth. Each company is different, has different needs and these needs change and develop over time. With a view to providing your business with solutions genuinely geared your specific needs. New India Assurance brings you this Business Credit Shield, backed by a single and made-to-measure contract, regardless of the trade sector in which you operate.

Partners in Your Risk

While you continue grouping and expanding your business to new fields and horizon we provide you the support, cover and advice and relieve you from the trade risk in your debtors. In fact we are partners in your business protecting you and sharing your risk and would like to strengthen this partnership further. And to reassure you on our capabilities and strengths we showcase in about us, the strong foundation on which we are set up and the infrastructure available to service you.

Courtesy —New India Assurance

APPENDIX V

Abbreviations
The Long and the Short

@	=	At
A.a.r.	=	Against all risks
A/c	=	Account
A.C.N.	=	Air Consignment Note
A/D	=	After date; Alternative date
Ad Val	=	Ad Valorem—according to value
A.N.	=	Advice Note
A.P.	=	Additional Premium
A.V.	=	Ad Valorem—average
A.W.B.	=	Air Way bill
B/D	=	Bank Draft
b.d.i.	=	Both days inclusive
B/E	=	Bill of Exchange
Bkg	=	Breakage
B/L	=	Bill of Lading
B/P	=	Bills Payable
B/R	=	Bills Receivable
B/S	=	Bill of Sale
Bulk	=	A whole cargo
C.A.D.	=	Cash Against Documents.
C.B.D.	=	Cash Before Delivery
C.D.	=	Customs Declaration
C and D	=	Collection and Delivery
C and F	=	Cost and Freight

C and I	=	Cost and Insurance
c.f.	=	Cubic Feet
Cge Pd	=	Carriage Paid
Cert. inv.	=	Certifed invoice
Ch. Fwd	=	Charges forward
Ch. ppd	=	Charges pre paid
C/I	=	Certificate of Insurance
C.I.F.	=	Cost Insurance and Freight
C.I.F. and C.	=	Cost, insurance, freight and commission
C.I.F. and C.3.	=	Cost, insurance, freight, commission at 3%
C.I.F. and e.	=	Cost, insurance, freight and exchange
C.I.F. and i	=	Cost, insurance, freight and interest
C/N	=	Credit Note
C.O.	=	Certificate of origin
C.O.D.	=	Cash on delivery
C.P.	=	Charter party
C.P.A.	=	Claims payable abroad.
C.R.	=	Compound risk, Current rate
Cr.	=	Creditor, Credit
Ctge.	=	Cartage
C.W.O.	=	Cash with Order
D/A	=	Documents against acceptance
Dbk	=	Drawback
D/D	=	Demand
D/d	=	Days after date
D/N	=	Debit note
D/O	=	Delivery order
D/P	=	Documents against payment
D/R	=	Deposit receipt
Dr.	=	Debtor, Drawer
D/S	=	Days after sight
D/W	=	Dock warrant. Dead weight
E. and O.E.	=	Errors and ommissions excepted
Exd	=	Examined
Ex Int.	=	Without interest
Ex Mill	=	Buyer pays charges after delivery at mill

Ex Quay	=	Buyer pays charges after delivery at quay
Ex Store	=	Buyer pays charges after delivery at store
Ex Slip	=	Buyer pays charges after delivery at slip
Ex Wharf	=	Buyer pays charges after delivery at wharf
F.a.a.	=	Free of all everage
F.a.M.	=	Free at mill
F.a.q.	=	Fair average quality, Free alongside quay
F.A.S.	=	Free alongside the ship: from this point the buyer is responsible for the costs of loading on board, etc.
F.C.L.	=	Full container load
F/d	=	Free docks
F.O.B.	=	Free on board
F.O.C.	=	Free of charge
F.O.Q.	=	Free on quay
F.O.R.	=	Free on rail
F.O.S.	=	Free on steamer
F.O.T.	=	Free on trucks
F.O.W.	=	Free on wagons
F.p.	=	Fully paid
F.w.d.	=	Fresh water damage
G/A	=	General average
Gr. Wt.	=	Gross weight
Grs. T.	=	Gross tons
H/c	=	Held covered
I/L	=	Import licence
I.L.C.	=	Irrevocable letter of credit: once opened, except under special circumstances, it cannot be cancelled
I.S.S.	=	Indian Standard Specification
Itu	=	Indian thermal unit
L/A	=	Letter of authority
LASH	=	Lighter aboard ship
L/C	=	Letter of credit
L.C.L.	=	Less than container load
Lkge	=	Leakage

L.R	=	Lloyd's register
M/d	=	Months (after) date
Min. Wt.	=	Minimum weight
M.I.P.	=	Marine insurance policy
M.O.	=	Money order
Mos.	=	Months
M.P.	=	Months after payment
M.R	=	Mate's receipt
M.S.	=	Months (after) sight. Motor ship
M.T.	=	Mail transfer
m.v.	=	Motor vessel
N/A	=	No account, Non-acceptance, Not applicable
n/d	=	Not dated
Net wt.	=	Net weight
O.C.	=	Open cover
O/d	=	On demand
O.P.	=	Open policy
O/R	=	Owners risk
P.a.	=	Per annum
per pro	=	By power of authority (per procurationem); On behalf of
P.f.	=	Pro-forma
P/N	=	Promissory note
P.R.	=	Parcel receipt
R/A	=	Refer to acceptor
R/D	=	Refer to drawer: used in banking when a cheque is returned unpaid for lack of funds
Ro-Ro	=	Roll on, Roll.off
R.P.	=	Reply paid; Return of post'; Return premium
S.B.	=	Short bill: payable on demand or sight
S.D.	=	Sea damaged; Sight draft; Short delivery
S.N.	=	Shipping note
S.R.C.C.	=	Strikes, riots, and civil commotions
T.I.R.	=	International road transport
T.L.O.	=	Total loss only
T.M.O.	=	Telegraph money order

T.P.and N.D.	=	Theft, pilferage, and non-delivery
T.Q.	=	Tel quell (rate of exchange; Tale quale (according to sample)
T.T.	=	Telegraphic transfer
U/D	=	Under deck
U/p	=	Under proof (spirit)
U/W	=	Underwriter
W.A.	=	With average
W.B.	=	Waybill
Wd.	=	Warranted
W/M	=	Weight or measurement
W.P.	=	Without prejudice
W.P.A.	=	With particular average
W/R	=	Warehouse receipt
W.R.O.	=	War risks only
W/W	=	Warehouse warrant

Bibliography

Adair, John, *Training for Communication,* Gower Publishing Company, 1981.

Banerjee, Asis and Sampat Mukherjee, *Managerial Economics,* New Central Book Agency, 1985.

Bangs, David H. Jr, *Creating Customers,* Visions Books Pvt. Ltd., 1993.

———, *Managing by the Numbers,* Visions Books Pvt. Ltd., 1993.

Bannerji, *Commercial Correspondence*, A R Sheth and Co., 1973.

Bassett, P.H., *Computerized Accounts,* BPB Publications, 1992.

Bird, Malcolm, *How to Collect the Money you Owed,* Judy Piatkus (Publishers) Ltd., London, 1990.

Bittleston, and Shorter, *The Book of Business Checklists,* Associated Business Press, London, 1981

Brown, J.R. and L.R. Howard, *Principles and Practice of Management Accountancy*, The English Language Book Society and Macdonald and Evans Ltd.

Buckley, Neil, 'Consumers Know What they Want,' *Financial Times,* April 10, 1995.

Chakraborty, S.B., *Guide to Auditing*, Wadwa and Company, 1993.

Chaterjee, Satya S., *An Introduction to Management—Its Principles and Techniques*, The World Press Pvt. Ltd, 1989.

Chowdhary, Anil, B. Roy, 'Cash Flow Management', *Management Technologist*, 1992

Constantin and Flaush, *Discover the Resources in your Marketing Channel,* Business July-1986

Credit Management Handbook, Gower Press, 1976.

Crosby, Philip B., *The Eternally Successful Organization*, McGraw Hill Book Company, 1988.

Cundiff, Still and Govoni, *Sales Management*, Prentice-Hall of India Pvt. Limited, 1993.

Customer Service: How to Achieve Total Customer Satisfaction, Kogan Page, London, 1987

Davar, Rustom S., *Principles of Management*, Progressive Corporation Private Ltd., 1990.

Dellinger, Susan, and Deane, Barara, *Communicating Effectively,* Chilton Book Company, Pennsylvania, USA, 1980.

Doctor R.A., and A.H. Doctor, *Complete Commercial Correspondence*, A R Sheth and Co., 1975.

Frailey, L.E., *Handbook of Business Letter*, Super Book House, 1991.

Fritz, Roger, *The Business Troubleshooter,* Career Press, 1995

Gallinger, George and P. Basil Healy, *Liquidity Analysis and Management,* Addison-Wesley Publishing Company, 1987.

Garg, Vinod Kumar and Bharat Vakharia, *Enterprise Resource Planning Strategy*, Jaico Books, 1999.

Gartside, L., *Model Business Letters*, English Language Book Society, Macdonald and Evans, 1985.

Gopalakrishnan P. and Sunderesan M., *Materials Management*, Prentice-Hall of India Pvt. Ltd., 1992.

Gralla, Preston, *The Complete Idiot's Guide to Online Shopping,* Alpha Books,1999

Gupta, S.L., *Sales and Distribution Management*, Excel Books, 1999.

Gupta, S.N., *Dishonour of Cheques*, Universal Book Traders, 1993.

Gupta, S.P. and V.H.P. Pinto, *Handbook of Insurance Claims,* Consultech Services, 1987.

Hampton, John and Cecilia Wagner, *Working Capital Management*, John Wiley and Sons, 1989.

Hartley, John, *Electronic Data Interchange*, University Press, 1997

High, Cockerell, *Insurance: Teach Yourself Books*, Hodder and Stoughton, 1989.

Horne, Van James C., *Financial Management and Policy*, N.J. Prentice Hall, 1988.

Hume G. and J.E. Bayley, *Manual of Commercial Correspondence*, Wheeler Publishing, 1978.

India Credit Management Data Book, Gower Press.

Ingersoll, Jonathan, *Theory of Financial Decision Making*, Rowman and Littlefield, 1987.

Jones, Graham, *How to do Business on the Internet,* Jaico Books,1999.

Jonquieres, Guy de, 'British Warned of Threat to their Profits", *Financial Times,* June 28, 1993

Kanter, J., *Management Information Systems*, Prentice-Hall of India Pvt. Ltd., 1990.

Kennedy, Gavin, *The Perfect Negotiation,* Rupa and Company, 1999.

Khan, M.Y., *Financial Services*, Tata McGraw-Hill, 1997.

Khanna, K.K., *Physical Distribution Management,* Himalaya Publishing House, 1985.

Kotler, Philip, *Marketing Management*, Prentice-Hall of India Pvt. Ltd., 1992.

Kuchal, S.C., *Financial Management*, Chaitanya Publishing House, 1990.

'Let's get down to Business, Comrade,' *Financial Times,* July 9, 1994, Section II.

Manuals—Computer Applications in Receivables Accounting and Distribution Management, Kalpana Softwares, 1993.

Mavrovitis, Basil P., *Cashflow, Credit and Collection,* Probus Publishing Company, Chicago, Illinois, 1990.

Mayo, Owen G. (ed), *Consumer Credit Control,* Gower Press, 1971.

Menon, K.S., *Purchasing and Inventory Control,* Wheeler Publishing, 1993.

Meyer, Harold E. and Scott A. Sievert, *Complete Credit and Collection Model Letter Book,* Prentice Hall,1990.

Morse, Stephen, *Management Skills in Marketing,* Excel Books, 1993

O'Brien, James A., *Management Information Systems*, Galgoia Publications (P) Ltd., 1991.

O'Reilly, Daragh and Julian J. Gibas, *Building Buyer Relationship,* Macmilan India Ltd, 1998

Palat, Raghu R., *The Credit Report*, Jaico Publishing House,

Parker, R.H., *Understanding Company Financial Statements*, Penguin, 1972.

Powers, Melwin, *Think and Grow Rich,* Wilshire Book Company, California, USA, 1966

Sarkar, N., *Book-Keeping and Accountancy*, Academic Publishers, 1990.

Stern, Louis W., Anne T. Coughlan, *Marketing Channels* (Fifth Edition), Prentice-Hall of India, New Delhi, 1998.

*System Development Methodology: Pocket Summary References,*QGPC Doha-Qatar, 1987

Tavistock, Rojers, *Managers, Personality and Performance,* London, 1963

The Bank Credit Card Business (Second Edition), Macmillan India Ltd., 1999.

The Manual of Modern Credit and Collection Practices: Modern Business Reports, Alexander Hamilton Institute, USA, 1976

Weymes, Pat, *How to Perfect Your Selling Skills,* Wheeler Publishing, 1995.

Will, Mimi and Donette Dake, *Concepts in Information Processing,* Allyn and Bason, Inc., 1990.

Woodruffe, Helen, *Services Marketing*, Macmillan India Ltd, 1998.

In-House Corporate Power-Workshops

1. Costs Reduction Strategy Programme (2 days) for all Department-heads
2. Commercial Negotiation for Sales – selling your higher price & value-added sales (2 days)
3. Commercial Negotiation for Purchase – buying at lowest-overall-price & value-added purchase (2 days each)
4. After-Sales-Service – to retain customers & create more sales (2days)
5. Manage Dealers for Growth (create dealer's loyalty)
6. Write WINNING One-up SALES PROPOSAL – Increase you order booking ratio
7. SALES PRESENTATION that makes more sales
8. PRESENTATION SKILLS that change minds
9. MARKETING – Taking on the competition
10. INCOTERMS 2000 – (Costing in Import & Export)
11. Time Management for Executives
12. Project Management
13. Customer Relationship Management
14. Business Planning – For Growth
15. Making Business MEETING that work
16. CONTRACT Management for Selling & Buying
17. SELLING to & Managing KEY & PROFITABLE ACCOUNTS

Corporate Consultancy

1. Turn Around Process for Loss-Making Companies
2. Strategies for Growing Faster
3. Credit & Collection
4. Cost Reduction Strategies
5. Business Process RE-ENGINEERING
6. Distribution & Sales Administration
7. Improving Company's Image

Afterword

About External Customers

All decent people live beyond their incomes nowadays, and those who aren't respectable live beyond other people's. A few gifted individuals manage to do both.

—Saki

Source: Economic Times, Mumbai

Survival is Not Compulsory

—John Yates

You can choose what you want